THE ONE YEAR® BOOK OF

DISCOVERING JESUS IN THE OLD TESTAMENT

THE ONE YEAR® BOOK OF

Discovering
JESUS
IN THE Old Testament

NANCY GUTHRIE

TYNDALE
MOMENTUM™

The nonfiction imprint of
Tyndale House Publishers, Inc.

Visit Tyndale online at tyndale.com.

Visit Tyndale Momentum online at tyndalemomentum.com.

TYNDALE, Tyndale's quill logo, *Tyndale Momentum*, the Tyndale Momentum logo, and *The One Year* are registered trademarks of Tyndale House Publishers. *One Year* and The One Year logo are trademarks of Tyndale House Publishers.

The One Year Book of Discovering Jesus in the Old Testament

Copyright © 2010 by Nancy Guthrie. All rights reserved.

Cover photograph of door copyright © by Alan Keohane. All rights reserved.

Cover photograph of rock copyright © by Mark Hunt/Getty Images. All rights reserved.

Cover illustration of red brush stroke copyright © Ingram Publishing/Photolibrary. All rights reserved.

Author photograph copyright © 2013 by Jimmy Patterson. All rights reserved.

Designed by Ron Kaufmann

Edited by Stephanie Voiland

Unless otherwise indicated, all Scripture quotations are taken from the *Holy Bible*, New Living Translation, copyright © 1996, 2004, 2007 by Tyndale House Foundation. Used by permission of Tyndale House Publishers, Carol Stream, Illinois 60188. All rights reserved.

Scripture quotations marked NIV are taken from the Holy Bible, *New International Version*,® NIV.® Copyright © 1973, 1978, 1984 by Biblica, Inc.® Used by permission. All rights reserved worldwide.

Scripture quotations marked NIrV are taken from the Holy Bible, *New International Reader's Version*,® NIrV.® Copyright © 1995, 1996, 1998 by Biblica, Inc.® Used by permission. All rights reserved worldwide.

Scripture quotations marked NKJV are taken from the New King James Version,® copyright © 1982 by Thomas Nelson. Used by permission. All rights reserved.

Scripture quotations marked KJV are taken from the *Holy Bible*, King James Version.

Scripture quotations marked ESV are taken from The ESV® Bible (The Holy Bible, English Standard Version®), copyright © 2001 by Crossway, a publishing ministry of Good News Publishers. Used by permission. All rights reserved.

Scripture quotations marked NASB are taken from the New American Standard Bible,® copyright © 1960, 1962, 1963, 1968, 1971, 1972, 1973, 1975, 1977, 1995 by The Lockman Foundation. Used by permission.

For information about special discounts for bulk purchases, please contact Tyndale House Publishers at csresponse@tyndale.com, or call 1-800-323-9400.

ISBN 978-1-4143-3590-2

Printed in the United States of America

26   25   24   23   22
11   10   9   8   7   6

Jesus took them through the writings

of Moses and all the prophets,

explaining from all the Scriptures

the things concerning himself.

LUKE 24:27

INTRODUCTION

I grew up going to Sunday school . . . and vacation Bible school and church camp and training union (which was our Sunday night version of Sunday school). Along the way, I learned my share of Old Testament Bible stories. From the story of Adam and Eve I learned that I should not listen to the devil's lies. From Noah I learned that I should be willing to stand alone against an evil world. From Abraham I learned that I should be willing to sacrifice what is most precious to me. From Jacob I learned that I should expect to experience the consequences of my deceit. From Joseph I learned that I should run from temptation. And it goes on from there.

Most of my life I have read and been taught the Old Testament as a series of life lessons or faith lessons. Its chief characters were held up as heroes to emulate or villains to disdain. I knew that the Old Testament spoke of Christ, but in my mind that was limited to the prophecies about the coming of the Messiah. I did not see that, in fact, all of the Old Testament is preparing us to understand who Christ is and what he came to do. I did not understand that the people in the Old Testament were not true heroes. In fact, the Bible takes care to expose their flagrant flaws. Their imperfections and limitations serve to point to the need for a true hero, a perfect son, a better provider, deliverer, savior, judge, prophet, priest, and king.

What I did not see is that the Old Testament tells a story that only finds its completion in Jesus Christ. I did not see that Jesus is the offspring of the woman who will crush the head of the serpent. Jesus is the ark that protects the faithful remnant from judgment. Jesus is the fulfillment of all the blessings promised to Abraham. He is the greater Isaac, the beloved Son of his Father, offered as a sacrifice, who was not spared from the knife. Jesus is the stairway Jacob saw in his dream on which God comes down to earth. Jesus is the greater Joseph, the One whose suffering put him in place to become Savior to all who come to him for food amid the famine of this world.

And those are just a few highlights from Genesis.

Jesus is the reality to which all of the sacrifices and offerings and festivals point. He is the fulfillment of the Tabernacle and Temple, making his home among us. He is the greater Moses who brings his people out of slavery to sin, the greater Israel who is not disobedient in the wilderness, the greater son of David whose Kingdom will last forever, the greater Solomon who is the Prince of Peace. He is the weeping prophet, the greater Jonah who runs toward sinners rather than away from them, the Bridegroom, the Branch, Isaiah's child who is born.

Though this is not the way I learned to read and understand the Old Testament—and perhaps not the way you have read and understood it up to now—this is clearly the way Jesus read, understood, and taught it, and therefore the way his disciples began to teach it after his departure.

Jesus often said that he fulfilled specific Old Testament passages. At the beginning of his ministry, he went to the synagogue in Nazareth and stood up to read from the Old Testament scroll of Isaiah:

> "The Spirit of the LORD is upon me,
>   for he has anointed me to bring Good News to the poor.
> He has sent me to proclaim that captives will be released,
>   that the blind will see,
> that the oppressed will be set free,
>   and that the time of the LORD's favor has come."
>
> He rolled up the scroll, handed it back to the attendant, and sat down. All eyes in the synagogue looked at him intently. Then he began to speak to them. "The Scripture you've just heard has been fulfilled this very day!" (Luke 4:18-21)

Those who heard Jesus say this were amazed, but ultimately infuriated, because they understood exactly what he was claiming.

Yet according to Jesus, it is not just individual prophecies or passages that point to him. It is the Old Testament Scriptures as a whole. Jesus said to the religious leaders, "You search the Scriptures because you think they give you eternal life. But the Scriptures point to me!" (John 5:39). Jesus was saying that the entirety of the Old Testament—its history, its promises, its people, its laws, its ceremonies, its songs—all of it is all about him.

Perhaps the clearest and most intriguing thing Jesus said about fulfilling the Scriptures came after his resurrection, as he walked along with two of his disciples on the road to Emmaus. They didn't recognize that it was Jesus who was walking with them, and they began telling him how heartbroken they were. They had hoped Jesus was the Messiah, and now, in light of his crucifixion, it seemed their hopes had been dashed.

> Jesus said to them, "You foolish people! You find it so hard to believe all that the prophets wrote in the Scriptures. Wasn't it clearly predicted that the Messiah would have to suffer all these things before entering his glory?" Then Jesus took them through the writings of Moses and all the prophets, explaining from all the Scriptures the things concerning himself. (Luke 24:25-27)

When I read this, I am disappointed that the account stops there. This is a conversation I would have liked to have listened in on in full! How amazing itmust have been to have Jesus himself walk through Genesis, Leviticus, Judges, Psalms, Proverbs, and Isaiah, saying, "This is about me. . . . This is about the work I came to do. . . . This is about the mercy I came to lavish on sinners. . . . This is about the sufficiency of my salvation. . . . This is about my deliverance from slavery to sin. . . . This is about the judgment that was poured out on me at the cross. . . ."

Later Jesus appeared to the rest of the disciples and said, "When I was with you before, I told you that everything written about me in the law of Moses and the prophets and in the Psalms must be fulfilled" (Luke 24:44). Then, once again, he did what he had done before. Luke records: "Then he opened their minds to understand the Scriptures" (24:45).

When we read through the sermons in Acts and through the rest of the New Testament, we realize that those who learned how to read the Old Testament from Jesus went on to present the gospel of Jesus in the same manner he did—not beginning with his birth or his teachings or even his death and resurrection, but beginning with the Old Testament. The New Testament writers teach us how to read and understand the entire Old Testament with gospel eyes.

This is how we will seek to discover Jesus through the pages of this book over the coming year. We're not looking to impose or insert what is not there but to bring to light what is clearly there—though we might have never seen it before. As we move through the books of the Old Testament, we'll see that they anticipate Christ's suffering and glory in their own ways. We'll embrace the story of the acts of God in human history in light of where it leads—to the climactic achievement of Christ.

It is my prayer that you will, along with me, stand back in wonder at the magnificence of God's plan for redemption and at his providence and power to bring about that plan. I hope that, along with me, you'll discover more reasons to trust the whole of Scripture and to love the God of Scripture. I hope your mind will be challenged and your heart will be broken by the beauty of Christ on display through the whole of the Old Testament. And I hope that as we look together at how the Old Testament prepares us for the person and work of Christ, we will move closer to worshiping him according to his marvelous and matchless worth.

Nancy Guthrie

PENTATEUCH

JANUARY 1
BEFORE HE MADE THE WORLD

Usually it makes sense to start at the beginning. But when looking for footprints of the eternal Jesus, we have to start before the beginning—before the "in the beginning" of Genesis 1:1—because the Bible repeatedly speaks of a time before time when God's plan for the world, centered in Jesus Christ, took shape.

What was the plan God was making before time began? Paul tells us in a letter he wrote to Timothy: "God saved us and called us to live a holy life. He did this, not because we deserved it, but because that was his plan from *before the beginning of time*—to show us his grace through Christ Jesus" (2 Timothy 1:9, emphasis added).

Since before time began, God has wanted to show us something—something significant that puts the glory of who he is on display. He has wanted to show us his grace—to shower his forgiveness on people who don't deserve it. Jesus has always been and will always be at the center of that plan.

The sending of Jesus into our world as a man who died for sin was no afterthought to fix what Adam and Eve ruined. Sending Jesus was no plan B but God's glorious plan A from before the beginning! "God chose him as your ransom long before the world began," Peter explained (1 Peter 1:20). Paul put it this way, "Even before he made the world, God loved us and chose us in Christ to be holy and without fault in his eyes. God decided in advance to adopt us into his own family by bringing us to himself through Jesus Christ. This is what he wanted to do, and it gave him great pleasure" (Ephesians 1:4-5).

Before the beginning, God knew that he would make us and that we would reject him. He knew that we would need a Savior and that the only One who could save us would be his own Son. From eternity past, Jesus has been the center of God's plan. And into eternity future, Jesus and his work on the cross will continue to be the center of God's glorious plan.

† *You who loved me before time began, how could I ever question your plans for this world and for my life? Your magnificent plan to display your glory and your loving plan for me began before the beginning, and I am humbled and quieted before such a Sovereign God.*

JANUARY 2
CREATOR

"In the beginning God created" (Genesis 1:1). How did God create? He spoke each aspect of creation into being. Throughout the rest of the Old Testament, we continue to see the power of God's creative word as it comes again and again through the prophets: "This is what the LORD says."

It is no accident that the first words in the Gospel of John are exactly the same as the first words in the book of Genesis. John writes: "*In the beginning the Word already existed. The Word was with God, and the Word was God. He existed in the beginning with God. God created everything through him, and nothing was created except through him*" (John 1:1-3, emphasis added). This sheds light on the mystery of who the "us" was when God said, "Let *us* make human beings in our image, to be like us" (Genesis 1:26, emphasis added). John tells us, "The Word was with God, and the Word was God." John wanted us to understand that Jesus is the agent through whom everything created was called into being. He tells us that Jesus is the *logos*, the outward expression of all God is. So every time we read the phrase "then God said" in the first chapter of Genesis, we know that it is Jesus, the living Word of God, accomplishing God's creative work.

> Christ is the visible image of the invisible God.
> > He existed before anything was created and is supreme over
> > > all creation,
> for through him God created everything
> > in the heavenly realms and on earth.
> He made the things we can see
> > and the things we can't see—
> such as thrones, kingdoms, rulers, and authorities in the unseen world.
> > Everything was created through him and for him.
> > > (Colossians 1:15-16)

If everything was created not only *through* him but also *for* him, that means everything that exists, exists for Jesus. Nothing in the universe was created or exists for its own sake, but rather to make the glory of God more fully known.

✝ *Creator of all there is, I marvel at what you have made, what you have spoken into being. Seeing you as Creator helps me to see what I was made for. I was made for you, and I am yours.*

HIS SPIRIT FILLS THE EMPTINESS

God's story begins with God's Spirit hovering, filling what was empty with his own power and life: "The earth was formless and empty, and darkness covered the deep waters. And the Spirit of God was hovering over the surface of the waters. Then God said, 'Let there be light,' and there was light" (Genesis 1:2-3).

So from the very beginning, and over and over again in Scripture, we see that this is who God is and the nature of what he does: God, through his Spirit, fills up what is empty to accomplish his purposes in the world. God filled Sarah's empty womb. "It was by faith that even Sarah was able to have a child, though she was barren and was too old. She believed that God would keep his promise. And so a whole nation came from this one man who was as good as dead—a nation with so many people that, like the stars in the sky and the sand on the seashore, there is no way to count them" (Hebrews 11:11-12).

The same Spirit who filled the emptiness of earth and the emptiness of Sarah's womb was at work when the angel said to Mary, "The Holy Spirit will come upon you, and the power of the Most High will overshadow you. So the baby to be born to you will be holy, and he will be called the Son of God" (Luke 1:35).

This earth was filled with the light of Christ as he walked upon it, and even as he left this earth, he promised the Spirit would still be at work. "You will receive power when the Holy Spirit comes upon you. And you will be my witnesses, telling people about me everywhere—in Jerusalem, throughout Judea, in Samaria, and to the ends of the earth" (Acts 1:8).

Jesus promised that the Spirit of God would come and fill the emptiness his followers felt at his departure in a way that would comfort them and empower them to impact the world around them (John 14).

✝ *Spirit of God, how I thank you for coming upon me and overshadowing me, making new life where there was deadness, bringing light where there was darkness. I simply cannot create new spiritual life on my own. I need your power to work inside me so that Christ can be born in me.*

JANUARY 4
THE TRUE LIGHT

The world began as one huge mass of unarranged material shrouded by impenetrable night. Then, on the first day of creation, "God said, 'Let there be light,' and there was light. And God saw that the light was good. Then he separated the light from the darkness. God called the light 'day' and the darkness 'night'" (Genesis 1:3-5).

It wasn't until the fourth day of creation that "God made two great lights—the larger one to govern the day, and the smaller one to govern the night" (Genesis 1:16). Before that, there was light in the world, but no sun in the sky.

John identified the source of this light when he began his Gospel with a poetic tribute to this Light. He recognized Jesus as the Light that penetrated the darkness even before the sun was set in the sky:

> In the beginning the Word already existed.
>> The Word was with God,
>> and the Word was God.
> He existed in the beginning with God.
> God created everything through him,
>> and nothing was created except through him.
> The Word gave life to everything that was created,
>> and his life brought light to everyone.
> The light shines in the darkness,
>> and the darkness can never extinguish it. (John 1:1-5)

"The one who is the true light, who gives light to everyone, was coming into the world," John wrote (John 1:9). This Light is no mere reflector of the sun's light but is the source of light, the One who spoke the sun into being.

Jesus later spoke of a time to come when "the sun will be darkened, the moon will give no light" (Matthew 24:29). For those who have rejected the true Light, that will be a day of deep mourning. But for those who have embraced the Light, that day will usher in a new way of living in the Light. Jesus himself will be present among his people, and we will live with him in a city that "has no need of sun or moon, for the glory of God illuminates the city, and the Lamb is its light" (Revelation 21:23).

† *True Light, your radiance penetrates the darkest places in the world I live in and the darkest places in my heart. Shine on me now and into eternity.*

MADE IN HIS IMAGE

The final creative act on day six of creation began with this divine delibera-
tion: "God said, 'Let us make human beings in our image, to be like us'"
(Genesis 1:26).

What does it mean to be made in God's image? We are in God's image in
our ability to think and feel and love, in our ability to understand right from
wrong, and in our ability to make choices. We're like him in that he is Spirit
and we have a spirit. We are patterned after our Maker.

But something terrible happened to that divine image when Adam
and Eve sinned. The image of God in humans became distorted and dam-
aged. So now, although we are still in his image, aspects of that image have
become twisted, and the sinful nature we inherited from Adam and Eve has
been passed from generation to generation. We long for the day when that
marred image of God in us will be restored to its original beauty. Yet God has
planned to do something even greater than restore what his image in us once
was in the Garden. God intends for the original image of God in humankind
to be restored and even superseded by the greater glory of becoming a new
creation in Christ.

Jesus is "the visible image of the invisible God" (Colossians 1:15),
"the exact representation of his being" (Hebrews 1:3, NIV). And "those
God foreknew he also predestined to be *conformed to the likeness* of his Son,
that he might be the firstborn among many brothers" (Romans 8:29, NIV,
emphasis added).

God intends to conform us to the image of Christ—and the completion of this process is still in the future for us, on the day Christ returns and
we are given resurrection bodies. Yet we are, even now, being glorified—our
inner lives and characters are being gradually changed into his likeness by the
sanctifying power of his Holy Spirit. This is not something we do, but something we receive. The righteousness and holiness that are the image of God
in us are created in us, not elicited from us. "We are God's workmanship"
(Ephesians 2:10, NIV).

✝ *I am your child, made in your image, but you have not yet shown me all of
what I will be like when you appear. But I know I will be like you, for on that
day I will see you as you really are.*

JANUARY 6

HE FULFILLS OUR DESTINY

God created humanity with a magnificent destiny in mind:

> God said, "Let us make human beings in our image, to be like us. They will reign over the fish in the sea, the birds in the sky, the livestock, all the wild animals on the earth, and the small animals that scurry along the ground."

> So God created human beings in his own image.
> In the image of God he created them;
> male and female he created them.

> Then God blessed them and said, "Be fruitful and multiply. Fill the earth and govern it. Reign over the fish in the sea, the birds in the sky, and all the animals that scurry along the ground." (Genesis 1:26-28)

Psalm 8 celebrates this magnificent destiny of human beings: "You made them only a little lower than God and crowned them with glory and honor. You gave them charge of everything you made, putting all things under their authority" (8:5-6).

But when we read these verses in Psalm 8, we're struck that they do not line up with the reality we're now living in. God made the world and gave it to us to cultivate and nurture. But this was before sin's ruin entered the world and everything changed. Now nothing is the way it was created to be. Rather than ruling over the earth, we are painfully subject to a cursed creation. Rather than being fruitful, we find ourselves living in futility.

The writer of Hebrews quotes Psalm 8 and confirms the disconnect between our destiny and our reality when he says, "We have not yet seen all things put under their authority." Then he points us toward the answer, the ultimate, perfect man who has fulfilled everything God originally intended for humanity: "What we do see is Jesus" (Hebrews 2:8-9).

We know Psalm 8 is not yet fully true of us. But it is true of Jesus. And through our identification with Christ, our oneness with Christ, we also fulfill the destiny originally designed for us.

† *Fulfiller of humankind's destiny, here I am, living in this in-between time that is marked by tears and pain and death. But as I identify myself with you I can say, "Because I am in Christ, all things will one day be under my authority. I will rule with Christ in glory forever and ever!"*

JANUARY 7

He Was Made Restless so We Can Rest

Genesis offers us a day-by-day account of the creative work of God in making the world, as well as the rest he enjoyed after that work was done.

> God looked over all he had made, and he saw that it was very good! And evening passed and morning came, marking the sixth day. . . . On the seventh day God had finished his work of creation, so he rested from all his work. And God blessed the seventh day and declared it holy, because it was the day when he rested from all his work of creation. (Genesis 1:31; 2:2-3)

God looked over what he had done and saw that it was good, so he could rest. But when we look over the work of our hands, the attitudes of our hearts, the words on our lips, and we realize that they are *not* good, we wonder how we will ever be able to rest.

The writer of Hebrews points the way: "All who have entered into God's rest have rested from their labors, just as God did after creating the world" (Hebrews 4:10). There is only one way we can rest from our labor: by depending on the work of another whose works are infinitely good.

The writer of Hebrews wants us to understand that the reason we can rest is because of the work Jesus has done. When we enter into Christ, we can rest, not because we are good or because what we've done is good, but because Jesus is good. He has given us his own goodness as a gift.

Our rest is made possible because of the restlessness Jesus endured on the cross in our stead and the work he accomplished for our benefit. On the cross, Jesus writhed in agony, struggling for breath. But it was not mere physical agony. Jesus was experiencing the restlessness that is continual for those who persist in rejecting God. It was *our* restlessness he took upon himself, not his own. On the cross, "God made him who had no sin to be sin for us" (2 Corinthians 5:21, NIV). Jesus experienced the infinite restlessness we deserve so that we can enjoy his all-encompassing rest.

† *Jesus, only in you can I find the rest my soul craves. Only through being united to you can I be confident that God looks at my life and says, "It is good." You have accomplished the work that I never could. So I choose to rest in you and your finished work, now and for eternity.*

JANUARY 8

SECOND ADAM

In Romans 5:14 Paul tells us something amazing about the first man, Adam, and about God's purpose in creating him. Paul said that Adam was a pattern or type of One who was to come—Christ. Adam was a real man, and his experiences were real, yet his life was never only about him. Adam was created as a type, or representation, of Christ, the One who was to come. As a type, Adam foreshadowed a greater Man to come.

Why does this matter? It shows us that when Adam sinned, God, though certainly saddened by it, was not surprised. God knew that they would sin, and he had a plan from the very beginning to show his sin-conquering grace through the death of Jesus Christ on behalf of guilty sinners.

Long before Adam sinned in the Garden, God had determined to put his glorious character—his patience and forgiveness and justice and wrath—on display by sending his Son, the second Adam, who would be superior to the first Adam in every way. While the first Adam took something good from us and brought death, the second Adam gives us everything we need to live. "The Scriptures tell us, 'The first man, Adam, became a living person.' But the last Adam—that is, Christ—is a life-giving Spirit" (1 Corinthians 15:45).

From eternity past, God intended that the sin-bringing Adam would serve to point us to the sin-bearing second Adam. "The sin of this one man, Adam, caused death to rule over many. But even greater is God's wonderful grace and his gift of righteousness, for all who receive it will live in triumph over sin and death through this one man, Jesus Christ" (Romans 5:17).

Every one of us lives under an unavoidable eternal reality: either we are connected to Adam and destined to die, or we are connected to Christ and destined to live forever with him.

† *Second Adam who brings forgiveness instead of condemnation and life instead of death, you were there long before we needed you. Your grace in abundance is available to us—grace that is greater than all our sin.*

WITH ME IN PARADISE

Before earthquakes, tornadoes, hurricanes, and human desecration ever began, there was a beautiful place on planet Earth unlike anything our eyes have ever seen. It was indeed a paradise—a garden located in a place called Eden. Adam and Eve lived in this paradise where they lacked nothing and enjoyed everything—including the personal presence of God.

But in the midst of this paradise, Adam and Eve, representing the human race, grabbed hold of something other than God in an attempt to find joy and satisfaction. They opened the door to sin that day, and it came rushing into every aspect of existence, taking away their freedom and unfettered enjoyment of God himself. Into the purity of the paradise God had created, sin brought a poison that penetrated everything. Adam and Eve were sent away from the paradise, banished from the perfection they once enjoyed.

But God, in his mercy, determined that those who are his would not be shut out of paradise forever. He has made a way to enter in. Jesus made it clear to the thief hanging on the cross next to him that he opens paradise to those who turn to him in repentance and faith.

> One of the criminals hanging beside him scoffed, "So you're the Messiah, are you? Prove it by saving yourself—and us, too, while you're at it!"
>
> But the other criminal protested, "Don't you fear God even when you have been sentenced to die? We deserve to die for our crimes, but this man hasn't done anything wrong." Then he said, "Jesus, remember me when you come into your Kingdom."
>
> And Jesus replied, "I assure you, today you will be with me in paradise." (Luke 23:39-43)

Jesus welcomed this thief—and one day he will welcome all those who come to him—into a paradise even more grand than Eden. He is, even now, preparing a paradise for his people to live in—the new heaven and new earth. The paradise of Eden was just a preview of the paradise to come. Jesus will be there, in the center, to welcome us in.

† *Jesus, remember me when you come into your Kingdom. Remember my sorrowful repentance. Remember your great mercy. And welcome me into the paradise of God.*

JANUARY 10
TAKE AND EAT

God planted a garden that was the perfect habitation for Adam and Eve. Everything Adam and Eve could possibly want was there. "The LORD God placed the man in the Garden of Eden to tend and watch over it. But the LORD God warned him, 'You may freely eat the fruit of every tree in the garden—except the tree of the knowledge of good and evil. If you eat its fruit, you are sure to die'" (Genesis 2:15-17).

God generously provided food and welcomed Adam and Eve to his table to eat—with only one prohibition. Then Satan slithered into this picture, offering his own invitation to eat. He urged Eve to eat freely the fruit of the forbidden tree. And tragically she and Adam indulged their appetite for satisfaction apart from God. Suddenly the joy and peace they had known disappeared. New feelings raged in their hearts—horror, wretchedness, insecurity, remorse, shame. They looked at each other and knew that things would never be the same again. The chill of danger and the fear of darkness swept through Eden.

Through Adam and Eve's simple act of taking and eating, humankind lost spiritual life. But it is also through the act of taking and eating that spiritual and eternal life is restored. Jesus said, "I tell you the truth, unless you eat the flesh of the Son of Man and drink his blood, you cannot have eternal life within you" (John 6:53). "Take and eat" is a sign of restored fellowship with God. Just as taking and eating what was prohibited by God led to damnation, so does taking and eating of God's provision of Christ lead to salvation. "As they were eating, Jesus took some bread and blessed it. Then he broke it in pieces and gave it to the disciples, saying, 'Take this and eat it, for this is my body'" (Matthew 26:26).

Was Jesus thinking of his Father's first invitation to take and eat of his goodness in the Garden? Was he thinking about Satan's wicked and twisted invitation to take and eat?

When Jesus invited his followers to take and eat his body, he knew what that invitation would cost. It would require the death of his body. But it would also require the resurrection of his body. As we take and eat of both the death and the resurrection of Christ, we proclaim that we truly have life.

† *Feast of heaven, provided generously by God, I come to your table, and by faith I take and eat your body, your life. I find my nourishment—indeed, my very existence—as I feed upon you.*

11

THE TREE OF THE KNOWLEDGE OF GOOD AND EVIL

Adam and Eve were welcome to enjoy all the goodness in the Garden of Eden to their hearts' content. But God's permission was paired with his prohibition: "You may freely eat the fruit of every tree in the garden—except the tree of the knowledge of good and evil. If you eat its fruit, you are sure to die" (Genesis 2:16-17).

What was this tree of the knowledge of good and evil? To have the knowledge of good and evil means to claim the independent right to decide for oneself what is good and evil (true and false, beautiful and ugly). It was proper for God to have that right, not humans. God knew that it would be utterly devastating for people to cut the cord of dependence from him and claim "the knowledge of good and evil" for themselves. That's why he said, "You must not eat it . . . if you do, you will die" (Genesis 3:3).

But the fruit of this tree looked delicious to Eve, who ate it and then gave some to Adam. And they did indeed attain the knowledge of good and evil, but their new knowledge was from the standpoint of *becoming* evil and *remembering* how good they once were. They traded the freedom of enjoying what is good for slavery to what is evil.

God had told them this would happen, but they didn't believe him. Now they realized that what God had said was true and what Satan had said was a lie. How would Adam and Eve and all those who came after them find a way out of this?

The only way out is by eating the fruit of another tree—the Cross of Christ. On this tree hung the One who restores the knowledge of the good that Adam and Eve lost when they chose evil. No other tree so fully manifests such a vast knowledge of good and evil—the infinite goodness of Christ and the damning evil of those for whom he died. By eating of the fruit of this tree, all those who have descended from Adam and Eve can reclaim the life they lost and restore the relationship of glad dependence and obedience they left behind. "The sin of this one man, Adam, caused death to rule over many. But even greater is God's wonderful grace and his gift of righteousness, for all who receive it will live in triumph over sin and death through this one man, Jesus Christ" (Romans 5:17).

† *I, too, am tempted to seek wisdom apart from your Word, God. I, too, lust after independence from your wise boundaries. But now I take and eat of the fruit of your Cross, and I am sure to live.*

JANUARY 12

BONE OF HIS BONES

God has always had it in his heart not only to create humanity, but also to become human and to relate with us as one of us. In making man in his image, he made him for relationship.

> The LORD God said, "It is not good for the man to be alone. I will make a helper who is just right for him. " . . .
>
> So the LORD God caused the man to fall into a deep sleep. While the man slept, the LORD God took out one of the man's ribs and closed up the opening. Then the LORD God made a woman from the rib, and he brought her to the man.
>
> "At last!" the man exclaimed.
>
> "This one is bone from my bone,
> and flesh from my flesh!
> She will be called 'woman,'
> because she was taken from 'man.'" (Genesis 2:18, 21-23)

At this point, the biblical writer injects some perspective on what God has done: "This explains why a man leaves his father and mother and is joined to his wife, and the two are united into one" (Genesis 2:24).

Much later, another biblical writer points us to what God did in this union to help us to understand not only marriage between a man and a woman but also the mysterious union between Christ and his church: "As the Scriptures say, 'A man leaves his father and mother and is joined to his wife, and the two are united into one.' This is a great mystery, but it is an illustration of the way Christ and the church are one" (Ephesians 5:31-32).

The joy Adam expressed in this being who was drawn from his body is a foreshadowing of the joy Jesus takes in his church, which is his very body. As the woman came from Adam's side while he was in a deep sleep, so the church came from the bleeding, wounded side of Jesus when he was in a three-day deep sleep of death. "The church is his body; it is made full and complete by Christ" (Ephesians 1:23).

The day is coming when Jesus will rejoice over his bride, the church, like Adam did when he shouted, "At last!" Finally Christ's bride will be with him, in his presence forevermore.

† *How is it that I could be united as one with you, Jesus? What a glorious and mysterious work you have done to make me worthy of such infinite oneness!*

JANUARY 13
HE COVERS OUR NAKEDNESS

There was once a day when there was no shame because there was no sin to be ashamed of. "The man and his wife were both naked, but they felt no shame" (Genesis 2:25).

But then came sin, and in came the shame. "She took some of the fruit and ate it. Then she gave some to her husband, who was with her, and he ate it, too. At that moment their eyes were opened, and they suddenly felt shame at their nakedness. So they sewed fig leaves together to cover themselves" (Genesis 3:6-7).

Adam and Eve tried to perpetrate a literal cover-up. The shame of what they had done and who they had become was overwhelming. So they tried to close the gap between what they once had been and what they now were by covering up and presenting themselves in a new way. This was the origin of hypocrisy.

But sin is not a problem we can simply cover up by our own efforts. Neither is it a problem that can be solved by a bunch of leaves—but only by pain and blood. "Without the shedding of blood, there is no forgiveness" (Hebrews 9:22). God met Adam and Eve in mercy, providing robes made of the skins of animals to cover their nakedness. The God who made the world with a word could have made garments of cloth for Adam and Eve, but their clothes were made from the skins of animals. In this way he not only provided what they needed to make their way in a new world marked by sin, but he pointed to the day when he would solve the problem of their sin and shame decisively and permanently. He would do it with the blood of his own Son who, "because of the joy awaiting him . . . endured the cross, disregarding its shame" (Hebrews 12:2).

The clothing of Christ is available to all who come to him for it. But many are blind to their own nakedness and suppress their sense of shame. Jesus said to the church in Laodicea, "You don't realize that you are wretched and miserable and poor and blind and naked. . . . Buy white garments from me so you will not be shamed by your nakedness" (Revelation 3:17-18). His offer extends to all who know the shame of sin and desire to be covered in the clothing of Christ himself.

† *Jesus, I am naked and ashamed, and there is nowhere to hide. I'm weary of my hypocrisy and my attempts to cover up. I need your sacrifice to cover my nakedness. I need your grace to take away my shame.*

TEMPTED IN THE GARDEN

When God placed Adam and Eve in the Garden of Eden, he said, "You may freely eat the fruit of every tree in the garden—except the tree of the knowledge of good and evil. If you eat its fruit, you are sure to die" (Genesis 2:16-17). But soon the serpent came along and questioned what God had said: "Did God really say you must not eat the fruit from any of the trees in the garden? . . . You won't die!" (3:1, 4).

Adam and Eve were put to the test in the Garden by the temptation of Satan. He took God's words and twisted them, causing Adam and Eve to doubt God's goodness and provision. Satan suggested that God was withholding something good from them and tempted them to reach out and grab what would make them like God himself. Sadly, Adam and Eve failed the test.

There was only one way to turn the tide of death brought about by the first Adam's failure when tempted, and that was through the second Adam's faithfulness when tempted. But while Adam faced temptation in the bountiful Garden, where his every need was met, Jesus was "led by the Spirit into the wilderness to be tempted" (Matthew 4:1). While Adam and Eve lacked nothing when approached by Satan, Jesus was in the last stages of starvation.

Whereas Adam and Eve started questioning God's words when they were tempted, Jesus met temptation at every turn by quoting God's sure and certain Word. Whereas Adam and Eve questioned God's provision, Jesus celebrated it. And whereas Adam inherited shame and alienation from life with God in the Garden, Jesus inherited a dominion and Kingdom that is God's own Kingdom.

Later Jesus did, however, also face temptation in a garden. It was not the Garden of Eden, but the garden of Gethsemane. He was tempted to avoid the Cross, tempted to turn away from God's plan and provision for him. But once again Jesus passed the test. Once again he submitted himself to God and entrusted himself to God, saying, "I want your will to be done, not mine" (Matthew 26:39).

† *Tested and proven One, because you have gone through suffering and testing, you are able to help me when I am being tested. And I know that you will not allow me to be tempted beyond what I can stand, but you will show me a way out so I can endure faithfully.*

HE CAME TO DESTROY THE WORKS OF THE DEVIL

On the day when Adam and Eve fell into sin, God made a promise. But this wasn't a promise for good to his people, as are most promises we read in the Bible. This was a promise of death to the serpent, or Satan—the one who had tempted Adam and Eve to sin. "I will cause hostility between you and the woman, and between your offspring and her offspring. He will strike your head, and you will strike his heel" (Genesis 3:15).

Beginning with Eve's first offspring, her son Cain, God's people must have begun to wonder at the birth of every baby if this was the one who would fulfill this unique promise of God to destroy the devil through Eve's offspring.

The promise of the offspring of Eve was fulfilled when Jesus was born to Mary. Jesus was that promised offspring, the One who would finally crush the head of the enemy, Satan. John said this is exactly what Jesus came to do. "The Son of God came to destroy the works of the devil" (1 John 3:8).

But Satan did not go down without a fight. He, too, fulfilled the promise God had made. He struck the heel of the Promised One, using every tool of evil at his disposal to bear down on Jesus. The battle began in earnest when Jesus went away to the wilderness to fast and pray. There Satan attacked Jesus at every possible point of vulnerability—to no avail. The battle continued all the way to the Cross, where Satan thought he had finally won. But the Cross was not the defeat of Jesus; it was the deathblow to Satan. When Jesus gave up his spirit and died on the cross, Satan thought he had killed Jesus. But "in this way [God] disarmed the spiritual rulers and authorities. He shamed them publicly by his victory over them on the cross" (Colossians 2:15).

Satan's power is wielded in the world in the form of death. What gives him that power is sin and the estrangement from God it brings. But on the Cross, Jesus did what was necessary for us to be reconciled with God. The devil thought he was defeating Christ, but in reality Christ was reconciling us to God, defeating the devil, and delivering us out of his clutches. "Only by dying could he break the power of the devil, who had the power of death" (Hebrews 2:14).

† *Death Destroyer, you have defeated the devil and put him in chains. And the day is coming when he will be thrown into the fire and utterly destroyed. You will fulfill your promise to destroy Satan, along with his power to rob, kill, and destroy. Come quickly, Lord Jesus!*

HE WILL CRUSH SATAN

God's curse on the serpent in Genesis 3 does not, at first glance, seem to hold out any hope for humanity. It appears to be a declaration of war. And in fact, it is. "He will strike your head, and you will strike his heel" (Genesis 3:15).

In a sense, the pronouncement of the Curse was a declaration of war— but not a war between God and people. God declared his hostility toward Satan and the reign of sin and death. From this point forward, in Scripture and in history, we see two opposing forces at war in the world: the Kingdom of God and the kingdom of Satan. There is no neutral territory, no area of life that is free from the struggle. Both God and Satan lay claim to all things.

When Jesus came, he described his coming as a significant advancement in this war. "From the time John the Baptist began preaching until now, the Kingdom of Heaven has been forcefully advancing, and violent people are attacking it. For before John came, all the prophets and the law of Moses looked forward to this present time" (Matthew 11:12-13). The most decisive battle came at the Cross, when Jesus disarmed his enemies of the power of death and shamed them publicly with his victory. Death could not hold him.

Though the decisive blow has been laid and the reign of sin and death is sure to be destroyed, we live in a time when the Kingdom of God is hidden to all but those who have faith in Jesus Christ.

Paul's letter to the Romans ends with these words: "The God of peace will soon crush Satan under your feet" (16:20). The battle is still raging between the Kingdom of God and the kingdom of Satan, but there is no question which kingdom will be victorious.

John was given a vision of the day when this war will come to an end, when the glorious Kingdom will be fully consummated. "The devil, who had deceived them, was thrown into the fiery lake of burning sulfur, joining the beast and the false prophet. There they will be tormented day and night forever and ever" (Revelation 20:10). Finally, the chosen offspring will have struck the final blow on the serpent's head, and he will be crushed.

† *Triumphant King, how I long for the day when Satan and his power to deceive and destroy are finally gone for good. But as I live now, in this in-between time, use me to advance your Kingdom in this world. Take over in my own heart and life until they become territory conquered by your love and mercy.*

JANUARY 17
YOU ARE LIFE

In Genesis 3, God pronounced a curse on the serpent, the earth, Adam and Eve, and all their descendants. So we might expect that Adam would slink away under the weight of all of the bad news. But Adam also heard hope in what God said. He heard the promise of an offspring who would reverse the Curse. Adam's first words after hearing the Curse express his faith in what God had promised: "The man—Adam—named his wife Eve, because she would be the mother of all who live" (Genesis 3:20). God said Adam would die, returning to dust; yet Adam immediately named his wife Eve because she would be the mother of all the living. Adam caught the promise buried in the Curse, and by naming his wife "life," he confessed his faith that God would indeed bring the blessing of life out of this curse of death.

Adam had failed the test in the Garden. He had failed to live up to all that God had intended for him. Yet here he teaches us to put our hope in the One who will not fail. Faced with certain death and inevitable suffering, Adam put his hope in the promise of the offspring who would crush the head of the one who led him into sin. The anticipation began for the Son who would come. The woman would experience painful labor to bring him forth, but the confident hope of all those who believed God's promise was that when he came, he would put an end to pain.

Here is the hope for all of us who have inherited this nature of sin from our father, Adam: that we might also learn from him how to stare the curse of death in the face and celebrate the promise that this curse is not God's final word. God's final Word is his Son, Jesus, who said,

> I tell you the truth, those who listen to my message and believe in God who sent me have eternal life. They will never be condemned for their sins, but they have already passed from death into life. And I assure you that the time is coming, indeed it's here now, when the dead will hear my voice—the voice of the Son of God. And those who listen will live. (John 5:24-25)

✝ *Lord, you are life itself, and we believe you are the promised offspring sent to break the curse of death. Because of you, we do not have to live in this sin-cursed world of pain only to die. Instead, we live with the confidence that we have already passed from death to life in you.*

THE TREE OF LIFE

Life was at the center of the Garden of Eden. Eating fruit from the tree of life would result not only in length of life but also in a quality of life that was rich, satisfying, and secure. But when Adam and Eve chose instead to eat from the tree of the knowledge of good and evil, they forfeited their access to the tree of life.

> The LORD God said, "Look, the human beings have become like us, knowing both good and evil. What if they reach out, take fruit from the tree of life, and eat it? Then they will live forever!" So the LORD God banished them from the Garden of Eden, and he sent Adam out to cultivate the ground from which he had been made. After sending them out, the LORD God stationed mighty cherubim to the east of the Garden of Eden. And he placed a flaming sword that flashed back and forth to guard the way to the tree of life. (Genesis 3:22-24)

Adam and Eve were exiled from the Garden. And while the exile was terrible, it was also a grace. Had they eaten from the tree of life in their spiritually dead condition, they would have perpetuated that existence indefinitely. Thus the Garden would have become hell on earth, populated with the undying dead—forever living and forever dead.

Ever since Adam and Eve were banished from his Kingdom, God has been working out his plan to bring his people back in. But how will we get past the flaming sword that guards the way to the tree of life? Christ alone bared his neck to that sword to take the full judgment of God for sin. Christ alone will lead his people into this Promised Land, this paradise, this Eden, and there we will eat of the tree of life and live forever.

John was given a preview of this forever garden and described it for us: "On each side of the river grew a tree of life, bearing twelve crops of fruit, with a fresh crop each month. The leaves were used for medicine to heal the nations" (Revelation 22:2). One day this will be the reality we live in. We'll drink freely from the river of life and eat our fill from the tree of life. We will no longer be banished. We'll be home.

† *Tree of life, it is you who stands tall at the center of the Garden. There you forever bear in your risen body the scars of your suffering. And because I have you, I have life. Because of you, though I, too, deserve to be driven out, I've been welcomed in.*

JANUARY 19

He Gained for Us
More than Adam Lost for Us

Adam lived in the Garden, where God walked with him, provided for him, and infused his life with purpose and satisfaction. When Adam sinned, he lost his perfect intimacy with God and his enjoyment of a perfect world. He became estranged from God and at odds with the wife God had given him. His meaningful work became burdensome toil. His unfettered innocence transformed into a deep sense of shame he tried to hide. Adam not only lost all of this for himself, he lost it for us, too.

That is why the coming of Christ is such good news. By his perfect life and sacrificial death, Christ has restored for us what Adam lost for us. But Christ not only reversed the effects of the Fall, he brought us into a reality far better than even Adam enjoyed. All who have been redeemed by Christ have gained more through the last Adam than we lost through the first Adam.

We hold *a more exalted position*. Before the Fall, Adam lived in an earthly paradise, but we are seated "with him in the heavenly realms because we are united with Christ Jesus" (Ephesians 2:6). We have been given *a nobler nature*. Before the Fall, Adam possessed a natural life, but in Christ, we "share his divine nature" (2 Peter 1:4). We have *a new standing before God*. Before the Fall, Adam was innocent, but Christ goes beyond restoring innocence to giving us his own merit so that we "become righteous through faith in Christ" (Philippians 3:9). We share *a better inheritance*. Before the Fall, Adam was in charge of Eden, but "because we are united with Christ, we have received an inheritance from God" (Ephesians 1:11). We are capable of *a deeper joy*. Before the Fall, Adam could not experience the bliss of pardoned sin and divine mercy. We also enjoy *a closer relationship with God*. Before the Fall, Adam was merely a created being in the image of God, but we are "members of his body" (Ephesians 5:30). Jesus is not ashamed to call us his brothers and sisters (Hebrews 2:11).

Through the redeeming work of the Cross, we as believers have been given far more than Adam ever enjoyed. This is how Adam's sin leads to the exaltation of Christ: "So God can point to us in all future ages as examples of the incredible wealth of his grace and kindness toward us, as shown in all he has done for us who are united with Christ Jesus" (Ephesians 2:7).

† *Gracious Christ, you have gained for me so much more than Adam lost for me. My joy is in knowing that throughout the ages to come, I will still be enjoying new waves of your goodness and grace.*

JANUARY 20
HE WILL LIFT THE
CURSE ON ALL CREATION

As a result of Adam and Eve's sin, God's curse fell not only on humanity, but also on all of creation. "The ground is cursed because of you," God told Adam (Genesis 3:17). The apostle Paul described it this way: "Against its will, all creation was subjected to God's curse. But with eager hope, the creation looks forward to the day when it will join God's children in glorious freedom from death and decay. For we know that all creation has been groaning as in the pains of childbirth right up to the present time" (Romans 8:20-22).

Just as Adam's promised offspring broke the curse on Adam and Eve, he also set in motion the breaking of the curse over creation. The Bible ends with John's vision of the coming day when the Curse will be gone for good: "I saw a new heaven and a new earth, for the old heaven and the old earth had disappeared" (Revelation 21:1).

God's purposes of redemption through Christ have never been limited solely to humanity. His intention has always been to reveal his glory in and through the creation and re-creation of the natural world. He pictured this grand plan in the Old Testament story again and again. It wasn't only Noah and his family in the ark, but also the entire animal kingdom. Abraham and his Israelite descendants were not only promised spiritual renewal but also the fruitful land of Canaan. The prophets, too, spoke of a future in which the full glory of God's Kingdom will exist, describing it in not only spiritual but physical terms—the wolf will lie down with the lamb, the desert will blossom with flowers (Isaiah 11:1-9; 35:1-10; 65:17-25; Ezekiel 36:33-36).

When John wrote that he saw the new heaven and new earth coming down out of heaven from God, he was not describing a literal descent of a second earth from the sky. He was describing the final culmination of the regenerating work of Christ. The heavenly country Abraham longed for (Hebrews 11:16) is not a land somewhere in the sky; someday *this* earth will be a new earth—an earth in which there is no more curse.

† *Great Redeemer, not only have you redeemed my life from the pit, you are redeeming your creation. One day I will live in this glorified creation with you. Then I will no longer have to fear natural disasters or deadly viruses or dangerous animals. You will lift the curse on all your creation.*

THE CURSE BECAME HIS CROWN

In the Garden as God originally created it, there were no thorns. But that changed when Adam and Eve sinned. God said to Adam, "Since you listened to your wife and ate from the tree whose fruit I commanded you not to eat, the ground is cursed because of you. All your life you will struggle to scratch a living from it. It will grow thorns and thistles for you" (Genesis 3:17-18).

From that day on, this instrument of pain intruded into the perfection of the original creation. Every pricked finger, every overgrown field, every ugly thornbush was meant to be a reminder of the frustrating pain of sin. But when Christ came, he transformed the thorn from a reminder of the Curse into a reminder that he has broken the Curse by taking it upon himself.

> Pilate had Jesus flogged with a lead-tipped whip. The soldiers wove a crown of thorns and put it on his head, and they put a purple robe on him. 'Hail! King of the Jews!' they mocked, as they slapped him across the face. John 19:1-3

What better symbol than a crown of thorns to speak to what Jesus was about to accomplish on the cross? "When he was hung on the cross, he took upon himself the curse for our wrongdoing" (Galatians 3:13).

While a crown is usually a symbol of authority and honor, this crown was a tool of humiliation. However, in the sovereign plan of God, this crown of thorns became a symbol of what Jesus accomplished in his humiliation. He wore the thorns we earned by our rebellion when he broke the curse of sin.

Revelation describes a day when we will be in a new garden where "no longer will there be a curse upon anything" (Revelation 22:3). Jesus will be there, wearing a crown—in fact, many crowns—but no longer a crown of thorns. And because he wore the crown of our curse when he went to the Cross, we will be there too. We'll lay our crowns before him, saying, "You are worthy, O Lord our God, to receive glory and honor and power" (Revelation 4:11). The Curse and its thorns will be gone forever, and Jesus will give us the crown of life.

† *Jesus, I should be the one who feels the thorns pressing into my forehead. I should be the one who bears humiliation and scorn. It is my face that should be spit upon, my back that should be beaten. But you have taken it all for me—every sting of the Curse. Instead you give me the honor of being your child, your heir, and you welcome me into your home forever.*

JANUARY 22
BORN OF A WOMAN

Eve took to heart God's promise that her offspring would crush the offspring of the serpent, so that even though childbearing would involve pain, it would also bring hope: "Adam had sexual relations with his wife, Eve, and she became pregnant. When she gave birth to Cain, she said, 'With the LORD's help, I have produced a man!'" (Genesis 4:1).

Eve recognized divine help in conception and hoped that this son would be the offspring spoken of by God. She hoped that Cain—her gift from God—would rise up and crush the serpent, putting an end to the miseries of the Curse.

But it was not to be. God did not accomplish his redemptive plan in Eve's generation. Cain inherited the sinful nature of his parents, making it obvious he was not the promised offspring. And so, with every successive generation, each mother hoped that her son would be the one. Generations came and went—many births and deaths—with still no promised seed. "All these people died still believing what God had promised them. They did not receive what was promised, but they saw it all from a distance and welcomed it" (Hebrews 11:13). The people and even the prophets "wondered what time or situation the Spirit of Christ within them was talking about when he told them in advance about Christ's suffering and his great glory afterward" (1 Peter 1:11).

Finally the time came, the right moment in human history, according to God's providential direction and preparation of peoples and nations. "When the right time came, God sent his Son, born of a woman, subject to the law" (Galatians 4:4). Jesus stepped out of eternity to bind himself in time and history, to enfold his glory into the womb of a woman.

As he began his ministry Jesus announced, "The time promised by God has come at last! . . . The Kingdom of God is near! Repent of your sins and believe the Good News!" (Mark 1:15). Finally, the offspring of the woman had been born. He was the One and this was the time when the miserable curse would be broken. He would be bruised, but through him all sons and daughters of Eve who turn to him in faith will be blessed.

✝ *Lord of time, you are directing history to accomplish your redemptive purposes in the world and in my little life. So I can trust your timing. I can wait for you to fulfill your promises. You will not be slow.*

JANUARY 23
HIS BLOOD
SPEAKS A BETTER WORD

It must have been a startling sight to murderous Cain—the bloodied, lifeless body of his brother, Abel, killed in a resentful rage because God had accepted Abel's offering while rejecting his own. Perhaps Cain thought he had silenced Abel and no one would know of his crime. But a voice went up from the spilled blood into the presence of God.

> The LORD asked Cain, "Where is your brother? Where is Abel?"
>
> "I don't know," Cain responded. "Am I my brother's guardian?"
>
> But the LORD said, "What have you done? Listen! Your brother's blood cries out to me from the ground! Now you are cursed and banished from the ground, which has swallowed your brother's blood." (Genesis 4:9-11)

If the blood of Abel cried out to God from the ground, what did it say? Surely it spoke of Abel's faithfulness. It lamented God's creation destroyed without cause. It appealed to the Judge of all the earth to exact justice. Certainly Abel's blood spoke a curse over the one who had done wrong.

The writer of Hebrews says that the blood of Jesus, shed at the Cross, "speaks a better word than the blood of Abel" (Hebrews 12:24, NIV). While Abel's blood screamed out from the ground for justice against the one who murdered him, the blood of Jesus cries out from the Cross for mercy for all who murdered him. The blood of Jesus speaks a blessing, not a curse, over those who have done wrong. It welcomes rather than banishes.

The blood of Jesus speaks *for* us, not *against* us. The voice of the sprinkled blood of our Mediator, Jesus, says, "I love you. I forgive you. I have purchased you. I will cleanse you. I am protecting you. I will keep you. I will always be with you."

† *Lord, you come to me saying, "What have you done?" And whatever I have done, however black and filthy my sin may be, the voice of your Son's blood cries out to you to bless me rather than curse me. I hear the blood of Jesus saying, "You will be blessed. I have forgiven your sins. I have set my mark on you, and no one can harm you."*

JANUARY 24

HE OPENS THE WAY INTO THE CITY OF GOD

After Cain killed his brother, God banished Cain from the land and sent him out to be a homeless wanderer on the earth. "Cain left the LORD's presence and settled in the land of Nod, east of Eden. . . . Then Cain founded a city, which he named Enoch, after his son" (Genesis 4:16-17). Cain sought to satisfy his need for belonging and significance by building a city—his own world, a mechanism for living successfully on his own terms, separated from God.

But the future of humanity was not limited to the descendants of Cain living in the city of man, apart from God. "Adam had sexual relations with his wife again, and she gave birth to another son. She named him Seth. . . . When Seth grew up, he had a son and named him Enosh. At that time people first began to worship the LORD by name" (Genesis 4:25-26).

Even today there is the city of man—the people of this present age who consider themselves too good for God, too self-sufficient to need him. There is also another group of people, another city. This city wasn't built by people, and it can't be destroyed by people. It's the city of God. And while the city of man is passing away, the city of God will last forever.

Seth's greatest offspring, Jesus, faced temptations regarding the city of man. As Jesus fasted and prayed in the wilderness for forty days, "the devil took him to the peak of a very high mountain and showed him all the kingdoms of the world and their glory. 'I will give it all to you,' he said, 'if you will kneel down and worship me.'"

But Jesus saw the city of man for what it is. "'Get out of here, Satan,' Jesus told him. 'For the Scriptures say, "You must worship the LORD your God and serve only him"'" (Matthew 4:8-10).

Perhaps Jesus could hear the echo of the cry of the angels, "Babylon is fallen—that great city is fallen!" (Revelation 18:2). He knew that day was coming. Perhaps he could smell in his nostrils "the smoke from that city" when it will be utterly destroyed (Revelation 19:3). But certainly he saw in his mind's eye "the holy city, the new Jerusalem, coming down from God out of heaven" (Revelation 21:2).

† *I want to live forever in the city of God with you, Jesus. The city of man is enticing but empty. It makes promises it can't keep. But the city of God satisfies; it keeps its promises. Throw open the gates of your great city to me, Jesus, so I may enter in with everlasting joy.*

THE HOPE OF
EVERY GENERATION

In Genesis 5, we find the genealogy of descendants flowing out of Adam, the first man. "When Adam was 130 years old, he became the father of a son who was just like him—in his very image. He named his son Seth" (Genesis 5:3).

A record of Adam's descendants goes on from there—Adam lived 930 years, and then he died. Seth became the father of Enosh. Seth lived 912 years, and then he died. Enosh became the father of Kenan . . . and so on.

God had created Adam in his image, but that image became corrupted when Adam sinned. Now Adam and each of his descendants after him could do no more than father a son who was like himself—fallen and sinful. With every generation, hopes were raised that this would be the son, the offspring, who would put an end to the Curse that had brought death. But then that son would also die. The genealogy pressed forward, looking ahead for that one. The promise would not be fulfilled until he came.

And then he came. And rather than a record of descendants flowing out of him, his biographers provided a record of his ancestry flowing into him. Luke began by recording that "Jesus was known as the son of Joseph" and worked his way back through the generations of David and Boaz and Judah and Abraham and Shem and Seth—all the way to Adam, ending with "Adam was the son of God" (Luke 3:23-38).

All history had groaned and shuddered in childbirth, waiting for him. Jesus is the descendant that Adam and every son since Adam had yearned for. And when he came, the wait was over. The search ended. It was culminated in Christ. The true goal of all the carefully recorded lineages had arrived. With this Son, the "and then he died" pattern of Adam's descendants would be brought to an end. Jesus turned back the tide of the Curse as he broke the power of death and was raised to everlasting life.

"Everyone died—from the time of Adam to the time of Moses," Paul wrote in Romans 5. "The sin of this one man, Adam, caused death to rule over many. But even greater is God's wonderful grace and his gift of righteousness, for all who receive it will live in triumph over sin and death through this one man, Jesus Christ" (Romans 5:14, 17).

† *Blessed Son of Man, how grateful I am to know that my future is not determined by my human ancestry but by your gracious choice to write my name in the Book of Life before the creation of the world.*

JANUARY 26
HE OVERCOMES THE EVIL IN ME

At the end of Genesis 1, we read, "God looked over all he had made, and he saw that it was very good!" (1:31). But when we come to Genesis 6, things have changed dramatically. "The LORD observed the extent of human wickedness on the earth, and he saw that everything they thought or imagined was consistently and totally evil. So the LORD was sorry he had ever made them and put them on the earth. It broke his heart" (6:5-6).

From "very good" to "totally evil." God looked right into the depths of human souls now corrupted by sin. He read their thoughts, examined their convictions, and followed their reasoning. He traced their imaginations, emotions, and ambitions. And what he saw was not people who were sometimes evil or somewhat evil, but people who were consistently and totally evil.

This is our true character apart from God's grace. Our sins are not episodic events scattered on the surface of our lives; our sins tell us the dark truth about ourselves. We are not nice people making bad choices; we are evil people proving the thoroughness of our evil.

How will we who are completely evil ever make it back into the good graces of God? We know God can't tolerate evil, so does that mean we are doomed to destruction for the evil that permeates our hearts and lives?

God has made a way back. He has made available a cleansing. It comes fully and only through the person and work of his Son, Jesus:

> Once we, too, were foolish and disobedient. We were misled and became slaves to many lusts and pleasures. Our lives were full of evil and envy, and we hated each other.
>
> But—"When God our Savior revealed his kindness and love, he saved us, not because of the righteous things we had done, but because of his mercy. He washed away our sins, giving us a new birth and new life through the Holy Spirit. He generously poured out the Spirit upon us through Jesus Christ our Savior. Because of his grace he declared us righteous and gave us confidence that we will inherit eternal life." (Titus 3:3-7)

† *Once I was far away from you, God. I was your enemy, separated from you by my evil thoughts and actions. But now you have reconciled me to yourself through the death of Christ. Now I am holy and blameless as I stand before you, without a trace of evil. Only you are good enough and powerful enough to overcome the evil in my heart, and I love you for it!*

JANUARY 27

SAVED BY GRACE

The world had gone wrong. "The LORD observed the extent of human wickedness on the earth, and he saw that everything they thought or imagined was consistently and totally evil" (Genesis 6:5). However, there's a "but" in this bleak picture. "But Noah found favor with the LORD" (6:8). In other words, though Noah was wicked, God gave him the gift of his grace so that Noah could become "a righteous man, the only blameless person living on earth at the time, [who] walked in close fellowship with God" (6:9).

We might think that Noah found favor in the eyes of the Lord because he was righteous and blameless. But it's the other way around. Noah was righteous and blameless because he was a recipient of God's grace. He didn't earn favor in the eyes of God by his own goodness. He, too, was wicked. He owed everything to the fact that for some reason that is hidden from us, God determined to set his favor upon him.

Peter's words in Acts help us see the source and essence of the grace Noah was given, although Noah could not have identified it in this way. "We are all saved the same way, by the undeserved grace of the Lord Jesus" (Acts 15:11). And Paul helps us see that the grace given to Noah that led to his salvation is the same grace given to us that leads to our salvation. "God saved you by his grace when you believed. And you can't take credit for this; it is a gift from God. Salvation is not a reward for the good things we have done, so none of us can boast about it. For we are God's masterpiece. He has created us anew in Christ Jesus, so we can do the good things he planned for us long ago" (Ephesians 2:8-10).

We know what happened later in the life of Noah—how he lay naked in a drunken stupor and his sons had to spread a blanket over him to hide his shame. But this slip did not surprise God nor nullify his favor. Because of God's grace, this failure of Noah's was neither the defining moment nor the damning failure in his life. The Bible mentions it only in passing. The defining experience and saving grace of Noah's life was that he "found favor" with the Lord.

† *Gracious One, I know I never could have been good enough on my own to catch your eye and win your favor. Instead, when I was lost in my wickedness, you granted me your favor and grace. You began your work in me, empowering me to walk blamelessly before you.*

JANUARY 28

HE STOOD ALONE
IN OBEDIENCE TO GOD

Building the ark required careful planning and engineering as well as a century or so of sweat. There is no biblical evidence that Noah received any help in the work of building the ark. He worked alone, day after day, building the ark and warning the people of the judgment to come: "It was by faith that Noah built a large boat to save his family from the flood. He obeyed God, who warned him about things that had never happened before. By his faith Noah condemned the rest of the world, and he received the righteousness that comes by faith" (Hebrews 11:7).

Noah's life was shaped by his certainty that judgment was coming. And because of this certainty, he was willing to be counted a fool, willing to stand alone in his obedience to God.

The ministry of Jesus was also shaped by his certainty that judgment was coming. In fact, he described the time when he will appear to judge the earth in terms of Noah's times:

> When the Son of Man returns, it will be like it was in Noah's day. In those days before the flood, the people were enjoying banquets and parties and weddings right up to the time Noah entered his boat. People didn't realize what was going to happen until the flood came and swept them all away. That is the way it will be when the Son of Man comes. (Matthew 24:37-39)

Like Noah, Jesus stood alone in obedience to God, warning of the coming judgment. But rather than condemning the world through his obedience, Jesus saved the world through his obedience. "For God loved the world so much that he gave his one and only Son, so that everyone who believes in him will not perish but have eternal life. God sent his Son into the world not to judge the world, but to save the world through him" (John 3:16-17).

Noah's whole family was saved with him—not because of their own righteousness, but because of their connection to Noah. Likewise, those who will be saved in the coming judgment against sin will be saved solely by their connection to Jesus.

✝ *Jesus, even as you were doing your saving work, voices called out to mock you. Yet you did all God required to provide safe passage for me through the storm of judgment to come. I am safe, not because of my obedience—but because of yours.*

JANUARY 29
ARK OF SALVATION

By the time of Noah, humanity was consummately and constantly wicked. So God decided to destroy all humanity—except for one family. Hebrews 11 says that Noah was warned about things not yet seen. He had never seen a flood or a thunderstorm, and he may have never even seen a raindrop. But he believed God. Even though this was all new to him, he took God at his word that there would be judgment on the earth in the form of a flood.

Noah also believed that God would provide a way for him and his family to escape judgment. "Make yourself an ark," God instructed Noah (Genesis 6:14, NIV). So Noah began building at God's command and according to his instructions. Noah had confidence that, just as God promised, the ark would protect him and his family from the judgment that was about to fall on the earth in the form of raindrops. And sure enough, the storm came. "God wiped out every living thing on the earth. . . . The only people who survived were Noah and those with him in the boat" (Genesis 7:23).

Those who were saved and those who died all went through the Flood. But those who survived were in the ark, which sheltered them from the effects of God's divine displeasure toward sin. In this way, the ark provides a picture of how God, through Christ, rescues his own people in the midst of judgment.

Just as Noah and his family found the ark to be a place of safe refuge, "we who have fled to [Christ] for refuge can have great confidence as we hold to the hope that lies before us" (Hebrews 6:18).

Just as the ark was a place of absolute security, so our "real life is hidden [like Noah in the ark] with Christ in God" (Colossians 3:3).

Just as the ark bore the storm of God's judgment, "Jesus . . . is the one who has rescued us from the terrors of the coming judgment" (1 Thessalonians 1:10).

† *My Ark of safety and refuge in the storm of judgment, I have entered into you, hiding myself in the depths of your being to escape the pounding wrath that I know I deserve. I should be on the outside—shut out from your goodness and drowning in the flood of your justice. Yet you have invited me to enter in, so I come with joy and relief, filled with anticipation for the new world that awaits once the storm is over.*

My Bow

After the Flood, Noah's feet were again on the solid ground of earth, but the sound of rushing torrents must have left its echo in his ear. The next time he and his family saw clouds gathering and the sky growing dark, their fears surely flourished as they wondered, *Is God's judgment about to rain down again? Is he coming again to wipe out the world?*

So God spoke to Noah and his sons, making them a promise and setting out a sign that would quiet their fears: "I have placed my rainbow in the clouds. It is the sign of my covenant with you and with all the earth. When I send clouds over the earth, the rainbow will appear in the clouds, and I will remember my covenant with you and with all living creatures. Never again will the floodwaters destroy all life" (Genesis 9:13-15).

The "bow" that God placed in the sky is not merely a curve of light shining through the rain. This sign is an archer's bow, a weapon. The psalmist described God's bow this way:

> God is an honest judge.
> > He is angry with the wicked every day.
> If a person does not repent,
> > God will sharpen his sword;
> > he will bend and string his bow.
> He will prepare his deadly weapons
> > and shoot his flaming arrows. (Psalm 7:11-13)

By setting his "bow in the cloud" (Genesis 9:13, KJV), God is saying that even though humans are sinful, he won't destroy us. The bow is hung in the sky, not strung tight with arrows at the ready, but loose and hanging at the warrior's side. God is no longer at war.

God can hang up his bow for only one reason. It is not because Noah and his descendants will no longer sin, and it's not because God will now overlook sin. He can hang up his bow because its arrows have been spent on someone else. God chose to aim the arrows of judgment toward an innocent Christ rather than toward guilty sinners.

† *You have set your bow in the heavens not only as a sign to me of your mercy but also as a sign to yourself of your promise. So I need not fear a storm of judgment even though I know I deserve your arrows. You have spent your arrows on Christ and hung your bow in the heavens so you can pour out your mercy on me.*

JANUARY 31

He Ushers in a New Creation

When Lamech, an early descendant of Adam, was 182 years old, he became the father of a son. The name Lamech gave to his son expressed both his frustration with life under the Curse and his hope for relief from it. Lamech named his son Noah, which means, "rest" or "comfort" or "relief," saying, "May he bring us relief from our work and the painful labor of farming this ground that the LORD has cursed" (Genesis 5:29).

Though Lamech could not have articulated it in this way, what he longed for was the day of Christ, which would bring comfort and relief from the terrible curse humanity lives under. Giving his son a name that meant "rest" expressed his faith that God would one day give his people relief from the Curse and his hope that God would one day restore all that had been lost because of Adam's sin. Lamech died in that hope at the age of 777 without seeing his hope become reality.

In a way, however, Lamech got what he hoped for in his son Noah. Genesis records that after the flood stopped, the ark came to *rest* on the mountains of Ararat. Noah, via the ark, was granted rest. When Noah threw open the doors of the ark, he and his family entered into a new creation, wiped clean by the judgment of God.

But the new creation Noah brought in turned out to be no better than the old one. What Lamech hoped for in his son Noah came in his descendant Jesus. Jesus, like Noah, survived the storm of God's judgment, emerging unscathed. Jesus will one day welcome his family into a new environment, a new earth, where we will finally live at rest, free from the effects of the Curse.

Because we live on this side of the coming of Christ, we know that the Curse will not have the final word on creation. "Against its will, all creation was subjected to God's curse. But with eager hope, the creation looks forward to the day when it will join God's children in glorious freedom from death and decay" (Romans 8:20-21). Christ will return, throwing open the doors to his new world. Our Rest Giver will welcome us in, saying, "Look, I am making everything new!" (Revelation 21:5).

† *Maker of all things, you have made me into a new creation. My old life—enslaved to sin, riddled by the effects of the Curse—is gone. A new life—a life at rest in Christ—has begun!*

FEBRUARY 1
HE GATHERS HIS PEOPLE

In Genesis 10, we find a list of nations descended from Noah through his sons, Japheth, Ham, and Shem. They were being fruitful and multiplying as God instructed, but they weren't spreading out across the earth as God told them to. They were determined to cluster together to build a great city and make a great name for themselves:

> They said, "Come, let's build a great city for ourselves with a tower that reaches into the sky. This will make us famous and keep us from being scattered all over the world." But the LORD came down to look at the city and the tower the people were building. . . . The LORD scattered them all over the world. (Genesis 11:4-5, 8)

They should have remained one family worshiping the one true God. Instead they were scattered and ended up at war with their relatives. The sons of Japheth were dispersed to the ends of the earth, where they awaited the call of the gospel to the Gentiles. The sons of Ham became nations with names such as Cush and Canaan. These nations eventually went to war against Israel, the descendants of Shem.

But this scattering and warring was not the end of the story. One is coming who will gather up his people and bring them back. Christ will come to reverse the curse of this dispersion.

Genesis 10 lists seventy nations that came from the sons of Noah—nations that eventually covered the face of the earth. When Christ came, he sent out seventy disciples, two by two, to preach the gospel (Luke 10, NKJV). Here he began the regathering of all those who are his from every corner of the earth. And he will bring this regathering to a glorifying conclusion when he returns: "Everyone will see the Son of Man coming on the clouds with great power and glory. And he will send out his angels to gather his chosen ones from all over the world—from the farthest ends of the earth and heaven" (Mark 13:26-27).

† *You are the God who scatters and the God who gathers. I hear your call to be a worker in your harvest, to proclaim your gospel as you gather in all who are called to be yours from among every people and nation of the earth. How good of you to invite me into your gathering work.*

FEBRUARY 2

CONQUEROR OF BABYLON

In the first few chapters of Genesis, there is a steady movement eastward—away from God. Adam and Eve were sent out of the Garden, east of Eden (Genesis 3:24), and Cain settled east of Eden (Genesis 4:16). Genesis 11:2 tells us that after the great Flood, the descendants of Noah "migrated to the east [and] found a plain in the land of Babylonia and settled there."

The continued movement away from the Garden, where God was known, reflected the inward condition of their hearts—they were not interested in being restored to a right relationship with God. Far away from God, they demonstrated their unbelief and their love of this world as they began to build a tower. In doing so, they weren't merely turning their backs on God; they were seeking to set themselves up as his rivals. But God was not impressed. And from his heavenly dwelling he mocked them: "Look! . . . The people are united, and they all speak the same language. After this, nothing they set out to do will be impossible for them!" (Genesis 11:6). Then God brought upon them the very judgment they had feared, confusing their language and scattering them all over the world (Genesis 11:7-8).

In time God set up his own city: Jerusalem. Empowered by God, the Israelites established a city for God. But since the problem of sin wasn't taken care of, the people eventually rebelled, and God sent another city to conquer them. The name of that city? Babylon. The city that sought to set itself in opposition to God was used by God to purify his people.

The people of Jesus' day were hoping for a Messiah who would defeat the oppressing Babylons of the world for good, raising Jerusalem to its proper place of power and prominence. But Jesus had no intention of responding to the city of man by setting up a rival city here on earth. Jesus came to set up an everlasting city in a new heaven and a new earth, and we who are his are already citizens of that heavenly city.

The day will come when Christ will finally destroy Babylon, the city of men. John detailed that coming defeat in Revelation 18:21: "The great city Babylon will be thrown down with violence and will never be found again." The city that sets itself against God will be gone for good. And the new Jerusalem will have only just begun.

✝ *Conqueror of Babylon, you will not forever tolerate the evil and abomination of the city that sets itself against you. You will one day destroy this city forever, and we will live in the new Jerusalem.*

FEBRUARY 3
PRAISED WITH ONE VOICE

The people of Babel wanted to make something of themselves that would be impressive.

> They said, "Come, let's build a great city for ourselves with a tower that reaches into the sky. This will make us famous and keep us from being scattered all over the world."
>
> But the LORD came down to look at the city and the tower the people were building. "Look!" he said. "The people are united, and they all speak the same language. After this, nothing they set out to do will be impossible for them! Come, let's go down and confuse the people with different languages. Then they won't be able to understand each other." (Genesis 11:4-7)

They wanted to make a name for themselves, and they succeeded, but it wasn't the kind of fame they'd hoped for. Babel came to mean "mixed-up, confused," signifying meaningless babble. Then came Jesus. His death and his resurrection were followed by Pentecost, when "everyone present was filled with the Holy Spirit and began speaking in other languages, as the Holy Spirit gave them this ability" (Acts 2:4). Whereas God had once used divided languages as a judgment on human pride, at Pentecost he gave his people the ability to speak in other languages so they could proclaim the gospel to people of every nation gathered in Jerusalem.

The judgment of Babel was not God's last word, yet neither was Pentecost's tongues of fire. Zephaniah prophesied, "I will purify the speech of all people, so that everyone can worship the LORD together" (3:9). The day is coming when God will unify the language of his people so they can praise him with one voice and tongue. John was given a vision of that day: "I saw a vast crowd, too great to count, from every nation and tribe and people and language, standing in front of the throne and before the Lamb . . . shouting with a great roar, 'Salvation comes from our God who sits on the throne and from the Lamb!'" (Revelation 7:9-10).

† *Jesus, how I long for the day when I am in that holy crowd of worshipers from every nation, tribe, people, and language standing in front of your throne, lifting up to you the magnificent praise you deserve.*

FEBRUARY 4

FOLLOW ME TO A
PLACE I WILL SHOW YOU

It was no comfortable call that God gave to Abram. And the reality that Abram was a pagan idol worshiper when God called him (Joshua 24:2) makes his willingness to follow God's costly call all the more stunning—and more clearly a work of irresistible grace. "The LORD had said to Abram, 'Leave your native country, your relatives, and your father's family, and go to the land that I will show you'" (Genesis 12:1).

The writer of Hebrews wrote that Abram "went without knowing where he was going" (11:8). God called Abram to follow his voice into the unknown. This required a supreme act of faith and trust.

If the Jews in Jesus' day had really considered how the life of faith began for their father Abraham, they should have recognized a familiar voice in the call of Christ. Jesus bid his followers to give up control, predictability, ease, comfort, familiarity, and autonomy to follow him. Jesus said to his disciples, "If any of you wants to be my follower, you must turn from your selfish ways, take up your cross, and follow me. If you try to hang on to your life, you will lose it. But if you give up your life for my sake, you will save it" (Matthew 16:24-25). He was up-front about what following his call would cost: "You will be arrested, persecuted, and killed. You will be hated all over the world because you are my followers" (Matthew 24:9).

But Jesus also made a promise to those who will leave everything to follow him:

> "I assure you that when the world is made new and the Son of Man sits upon his glorious throne, you who have been my followers will also sit on twelve thrones, judging the twelve tribes of Israel. And everyone who has given up houses or brothers or sisters or father or mother or children or property, for my sake, will receive a hundred times as much in return and will inherit eternal life." (Matthew 19:28-29)

† *Lord, I want to live by faith, and I know that means I cannot always demand to know where and what and when and how in advance. How I long to be quick to follow you, willing to go anywhere and do anything in pursuit of being a part of your saving purposes in this world.*

FEBRUARY 5
THE BLESSING OF GOD

In the first eleven chapters of Genesis we see a steady spread of sin from its origin in the Garden of Eden. Five times God pronounced a curse on sin and sinners. But in Genesis 12 God began the process of re-creating for himself a people by pronouncing a fivefold blessing on Abram: "I will make you into a great nation. I will bless you and make you famous, and you will be a blessing to others. I will bless those who bless you and curse those who treat you with contempt. All the families on earth will be blessed through you" (Genesis 12:2-3).

These are the promises the entire nation of Israel was built upon. It was these promises they held on to and believed God would be faithful to when their circumstances seemed to give no evidence that they would come true. These promises to Abram encapsulated God's vision not only for the children of Israel but for all of humanity. They were an expression of his love flowing over and enriching a guilty, dying world, starting with Abram; expanding to the nation of Israel; moving on to Israel's greatest Son, Jesus Christ; flowing on to the church; and reaching out to the nations.

When the angel came to Mary and told her she would give birth to the Son of the Most High, she recognized this moment as God fulfilling his promise to Abraham (Luke 1:55). Her relative Zechariah understood it that way too, and he prophesied, "Praise the Lord, the God of Israel, because he has visited and redeemed his people. . . . He has been merciful to our ancestors by remembering his sacred covenant—the covenant he swore with an oath to our ancestor Abraham" (Luke 1:68, 72-73).

After the ascension of Jesus, Peter made it clear to those gathered at the Temple that the blessing God had promised so many years before to their father Abraham was fulfilled in Jesus: "You are included in the covenant God promised to your ancestors. For God said to Abraham, 'Through your descendants all the families on earth will be blessed.' When God raised up his servant, Jesus, he sent him first to you people of Israel, to bless you by turning each of you back from your sinful ways" (Acts 3:25-26).

† *Blessing of God, all my happiness is tied up with and produced by God's covenant grace extended to me in you. I need look no further or make further demands for blessing. You, Jesus, are the blessing of God in my life!*

ALL NATIONS WILL BE BLESSED THROUGH YOU

In Genesis 12, we read that God initiated a plan to bless the entire world by making a promise to one man—Abram. "I will make you into a great nation. I will bless you and make you famous, and you will be a blessing to others. I will bless those who bless you and curse those who treat you with contempt. All the families on earth will be blessed through you" (Genesis 12:2-3).

When God chose Abram to found a new nation, he made sure Abram knew that the Jewish nation was being created for the world, not just for themselves. Their mission was to "be a blessing," and their destiny was to serve all the other nations. With this promise to Abram, God commenced an amazing two-thousand-year history that would, in the fullness of time, bring forth Jesus as a Savior not only for Israel, but for the whole world.

When Simeon, who had been waiting and watching his whole life for the Messiah, held the infant Jesus in his arms, he saw Jesus as the fulfillment of God's promises to bless all the families of the earth. "He is a light to reveal God to the nations," Simeon said (Luke 2:32).

Paul wrote that the promise made to bless all the families of the earth through Abram was fulfilled through Christ.

> The Scriptures looked forward to this time when God would declare the Gentiles to be righteous because of their faith. God proclaimed this good news to Abraham long ago when he said, "All nations will be blessed through you." . . . Through Christ Jesus, God has blessed the Gentiles with the same blessing he promised to Abraham. (Galatians 3:8, 14)

John was given a vision of this promise becoming reality. He saw "a vast crowd, too great to count, from every nation and tribe and people and language, standing in front of the throne and before the Lamb" (Revelation 7:9).

God's purpose was and is and always will be to bless the world with the blessings promised to Abraham. And Christ was and is and always will be the fulfillment of those promises.

† *I may not be a child of Abraham by human bloodlines, but your blood, Jesus, has made it possible for me to be a child of Abraham by faith! How I long for the day when I will stand before your throne along with people from every nation. We will bless you and thank you for extending to us the blessings you promised to Abraham.*

FEBRUARY 7

SON OF ABRAHAM

From the first pages of the Bible, God makes promises in regard to the "offspring" or "descendants" of his people. Following Adam's sin, he said to Satan, "I will cause hostility between you and the woman, and between your offspring and her offspring" (Genesis 3:15). But then the one son of Adam and Eve who seemed to be the offspring through whom salvation would come was killed! And by the time of Noah, the whole world was corrupt. Even then, there was still hope for the world through this one family. But following the Flood, Noah's family became involved in sin too, which brought another curse on them and their descendants.

Later God renewed his promise to bring salvation through a future generation when he made a covenant with Abram. But Abram endangered the purity of his wife and their offspring by giving her to two pagan kings (Genesis 12, 20). He also attempted to raise up a descendant through his wife's servant, Hagar (Genesis 16), but the child of that union was not God's promised heir. Later, the chosen offspring seemed to be in jeopardy when God called Abraham to sacrifice his son. But God's promise prevailed.

The descendants of Abraham proved, however, to be a sinful lot. Isaac did everything he could to reverse God's choice of Jacob over Esau. Jacob was a deceiver and a rascal. Jacob ended up with twelve sons, who were not only willing to kill one another (as they were intending to do to Joseph) but were also willing to intermingle with the Canaanites, as Judah, the designated one through whom the Savior would come, did (Genesis 38:1-2).

Left to themselves, Abraham's descendants would have either killed each other off or intermingled with the heathen around them until there was no distinct line of Abraham through whom God's salvation would be accomplished. In order for God to bring about Israel's salvation and blessings, along with those of the world, it would have to come about through a very special offspring, because thus far the next generation always multiplied the sins of their ancestors. Israel's hope was in a very special Son. "God gave the promises to Abraham and his child. And notice that the Scripture doesn't say 'to his children,' as if it meant many descendants. Rather, it says 'to his child'—and that, of course, means Christ" (Galatians 3:16).

✝ *Blessed Descendant of Abraham, because of you, Abraham's blessings have become my blessings. I am grafted in to your family through faith.*

FEBRUARY 8

A PRIEST OF GOD MOST HIGH

Melchizedek doesn't seem to be an important person in the Old Testament. He appears in Genesis 14 and is referred to twice more in the Bible (Psalm 110; Hebrews 5–7). But in terms of helping us understand the unique superiority of Christ's priesthood, he paints an important picture.

Genesis 14 tells us that after Abram rescued his nephew Lot from the armies that took him captive when they invaded Sodom, Melchizedek gave Abram bread, wine, and his blessing. Scripture says he was acting as "a priest of God Most High" (14:18). Abram received Melchizedek's gifts and gave him his tithe, thus recognizing Melchizedek's higher spiritual rank.

Much later in Israel's history, King David reflected on this unique priest when he said that the Messiah would be "a priest forever in the order of Melchizedek" (Psalm 110:4). The writer of Hebrews uses this exact phrase to describe Jesus, saying that he was "designated by God to be high priest in the order of Melchizedek" (Hebrews 5:10, NIV). What does it mean to be a priest "in the order of Melchizedek"?

The writer of Hebrews is saying that Jesus is not a priest from the order of Levi, as other priests in the Temple were. Jesus is a priest from the order of (or we might say, "along the lines of") Melchizedek. This writer was trying to convince the Hebrew people that someone who wasn't even a descendant of Aaron was the perfect High Priest. Everybody knew that someone couldn't be a priest unless he was from the tribe of Levi, so the writer of Hebrews built his case by reminding his audience that hundreds of years before Aaron, there was a priest of God who was appointed by God and respected by Abraham, the father of their faith.

Jesus is not a priest by ancestry, like the Aaronic priests; he is a priest by appointment, like Melchizedek. Jesus is a priest because of who he is, not because of the family he came from. But the most important thing about the priesthood of Jesus that Melchizedek prefigured was that his priesthood was forever. When Melchizedek is described as being "without beginning of days or end of life" (Hebrews 7:3, NIV), the implication is not that he lived forever but that the order of priesthood in which he ministered is forever. For us this means that our salvation is as secure as Christ's priesthood is indestructible.

† *My Priest forever, I rest in knowing that long after everyone I depend on in this life is dead and gone, you will still be alive, serving as my Priest and making it possible for me to approach a holy God.*

FEBRUARY 9

YOUR SHIELD, YOUR VERY GREAT REWARD

When Abram heard that his nephew Lot had been carried off by a cadre of kings who overtook Sodom and Gomorrah, he led his own army to attack them and bring Lot and the other captives back. Afterward, in appreciation, the king of Sodom offered Abram all the goods he had recovered. But Abram refused. Instead, he offered a tenth of what he had to Melchizedek, king of Salem, the priest of God Most High.

Soon after, God spoke to Abram in a vision: "Do not be afraid, Abram. I am your shield, your very great reward" (Genesis 15:1, NIV).

God told Abram, "I am your shield," meaning, "You didn't lose any protection by not relying on the king of Sodom. I am your protection." He said he was Abram's "very great reward," meaning, "You didn't lose anything of value when you declined to divide the booty with the king of Sodom. By having me, you have the greatest treasure you could ever own."

All that God wanted to be to Abram is what he wants to be to all children of Abraham in Christ.

Christ is our shield. He stands between God, whose majesty has been legitimately offended, and the offender, who is deservedly perishing, and presents himself to receive each blow. All the blows fall on him. All the fury of an avenging God is spent on the breast of God's beloved Son. Because Christ himself is our shield, we can meet the wrath of God, the rage of Satan, the deathblows of self, and the soul-murdering world—and live.

Christ is also our very great reward. He is not merely our means to a reward. He *is* our reward. God meets all our needs "from his glorious riches, which have been given to us in Christ Jesus" (Philippians 4:19). While we experience Jesus as our shield, going before us and sheltering over us, we experience Jesus as our great reward as he makes his home within us.

> God wanted them to know that the riches and glory of Christ are for you Gentiles, too. And this is the secret: Christ lives in you. This gives you assurance of sharing his glory. (Colossians 1:27)

✝ *Shield of salvation, there is no place of safety but under your sheltering wings, so that is where I hide. Great Reward, there is nothing I lack if I have you, so in you I am content.*

41

RIGHTEOUSNESS THAT COMES BY FAITH

That righteousness comes by faith is evident from the very first family in the Bible. Of Abel we read, "It was by faith that Abel brought a more acceptable offering to God than Cain did. Abel's offering gave evidence that he was a righteous man" (Hebrews 11:4). According to the writer of Hebrews, Enoch's God-pleasing faith was evident in his belief that "God exists" (Hebrews 11:6). The first occurrence of the word *righteous* (*tsadiq*) in the Bible is when we are told, "Noah was a righteous man" (Genesis 6:9). Noah's righteousness was derived not from his being perfect (we know he wasn't!), but "by his faith Noah . . . received the righteousness that comes by faith" (Hebrews 11:7).

With this background, we realize that the kind of righteousness that comes through faith—through believing what God has said—was not new with Abram. Yet it is in Abram's story that we first find it stated clearly: "Abram believed the LORD, and the LORD counted him as righteous because of his faith" (Genesis 15:6). Abram is not described as *doing* righteousness. In fact, Abram's unrighteous exploits are not hidden in Scripture. But when God promised to bless Abram, Abram took God at his word and believed him.

Abram's faith was a settled conviction that God would do what he had promised, no matter what. What he might not have understood clearly was that every aspect of God's promised blessing would ultimately be enjoyed through his promised Savior. In fact, all the promises that followed in the Hebrew Scriptures are merely expansions, closer definitions, and identifications of the salvation held out to the whole human race in this promise of a Savior. Abram might not have been able to explain who Jesus was and what he would be like, but Jesus was the unseen substance of what Abram believed in. As Paul wrote, "All of God's promises have been fulfilled in Christ" (2 Corinthians 1:20).

The writer of Hebrews described those in the Old Testament who put their faith in God's promises: "All these died in faith, without receiving the promises, but having seen them and having welcomed them from a distance" (Hebrews 11:13, NASB). They couldn't see Jesus clearly through the distance of time, but they died in faith, believing in the One they could not see.

† *Jesus, I have never seen you with my physical eyes, but with eyes of faith I see you. I believe that you are real and that you are the substance of all God's promises to me. I need nothing else from God except you.*

HIS RIGHTEOUSNESS CREDITED TO YOUR ACCOUNT

Abram had good reason to doubt God's promises to him. It had been a long time since God had made his promises and there was still no offspring and no ownership of even the smallest piece of property in Canaan. Then God spoke again, renewing his promise of a son from Abram's own body and descendants as numerous as stars. At this point, Genesis reveals that something profound took place: "Abram believed the LORD, and the LORD counted him as righteous because of his faith" (Genesis 15:6).

Abram heard God's promise. He weighed it in his mind. And he believed it. He decided to risk everything and rest completely in what God had promised. Abram's faith was a settled conviction that God would do what he promised, no matter what. And this faith became the means by which he received something significant from God. Genesis says that "the LORD counted him as righteous." The word translated as *counted* is a bookkeeping term, which means "to credit" or "to put to one's account." In other words, the Lord deposited righteousness to Abram's account. This righteousness was not Abram's own goodness; it wasn't payment for something he had earned. It was a gift. But where did it come from?

God didn't just decide to pretend that something was true about Abram when it was not. This was no "cooking the books," but an actual deposit to Abram's spiritual bank account. Deposited into Abram's account was the righteousness of Christ. Abram could not have explained how this happened. He could not see Christ clearly. He simply took God's word for it. Perhaps this is why Jesus said, "Your father Abraham rejoiced at the thought of seeing my day; he saw it and was glad" (John 8:56, NIV). Abraham rejoiced at the thought of Jesus' coming because his perfect life and perfect sacrifice provided the substance to the deposit that had been made to Abraham's spiritual account.

All believers in the one true God—in the Old Testament era, in the New Testament era, and in every era—are saved the same way: by grace through faith. This grace that saves us is the gift of Christ's righteousness deposited to our account. It is available to each one of us when we choose to risk and rest our whole lives on God and his provision and promises.

† *I believe in your promises, Lord, and because of that, I believe that you have deposited the righteousness of Christ to my spiritual account. It's a gift. I haven't earned it, and I don't deserve it. This is why it's called grace—your righteousness given to me. Pure, amazing grace.*

FEBRUARY 12
HE BORE
THE COVENANT'S CURSE

Prompted by God's promise of the land of Canaan as his possession, Abram asked a reasonable question about such a difficult-to-imagine pledge: "O Sovereign LORD, how can I be sure that I will actually possess it?" (Genesis 15:8). Abram's humble request for assurance was followed in the next verse by a divine order: "Bring me a three-year-old heifer, a three-year-old female goat, a three-year-old ram, a turtledove, and a young pigeon."

Abram understood exactly what God was ordering him to do. This was a common custom in Abram's homeland, in which two parties solemnized a promise or covenant by killing an animal and dividing it in two so that the two covenanting parties could walk between the sundered body of the animal. The ceremony dramatized a self-imposed curse, should either of them break their pledge. In essence, as they walked between the carcasses, they were saying, "May this be done to me if I do not live up to my part of the covenant."

So Abram slaughtered and arranged the animals and heard God telling him what was ahead for his people. Then he saw God appear as a smoking firepot and a flaming torch passing between the halves of the carcasses. But Abram was not invited or allowed to walk between the pieces of the animals. God alone traversed the bloody path, making this unconditional, unilateral covenant. God alone made the promise and submitted himself to the Curse. God assumed the full responsibility for seeing that every promise of the covenant would be realized. He committed to submit himself to the Curse for our failure to live up to our obligation. He committed himself to die.

The day came when God, in the person of Jesus Christ, did indeed walk the bloody path, marked not with the blood of halved animals, but with his own blood. Paul wrote, "When he was hung on the cross, he took upon himself the curse for our wrongdoing. . . . Through Christ Jesus, God has blessed the Gentiles with the same blessing he promised to Abraham" (Galatians 3:13-14). By bearing the full consequences of the covenantal pledge to death, Christ delivered us from the curse of our inability to live up to the covenant so that we might become heirs of its blessings.

† *You who bore the covenant's curse, I look to the Cross and see your sundered body, broken in my place because of my inability to live up to your standard. There you took on the curse so that I might enjoy the blessings of God's covenant love.*

FEBRUARY 13

HE BROKE
THE CHAINS OF SLAVERY

God made a formal covenant with Abram, promising to bless him and bless the world through him. But then God said something that must have seemed to Abram to be completely out of line with his promise of blessing: "You can be sure that your descendants will be strangers in a foreign land, where they will be oppressed as slaves for 400 years" (Genesis 15:13).

Why would God ordain in the history of his people that they would become slaves for four hundred years? This part of Israel's history, along with all the rest, was necessary to put God's glorious nature on display for the world, as well as to enable us to grasp most fully the way God saves his people.

God wants us to understand that apart from him we are slaves—slaves to our old natures and our old father, the devil. But long ago—long before Abraham's descendants became slaves in Egypt—God had it in his heart to bring us out of this slavery and into a loving relationship as his children. His fatherly affection is what he expressed to the people as they eventually prepared to enter the Promised Land: "I will walk among you; I will be your God, and you will be my people. I am the LORD your God, who brought you out of the land of Egypt so you would no longer be their slaves. I broke the yoke of slavery from your neck so you can walk with your heads held high" (Leviticus 26:12-13).

When God broke the chains of physical slavery from the necks of his people in their exodus from Egypt, it provided a vivid picture of the way Jesus would lift the burden of slavery to sin and our futile efforts to save ourselves. But more than just lifting the chains of slavery away from us, Jesus offers a new way for us to relate to God—as adopted children who are provided for and smiled on. "God sent [Jesus] to buy freedom for us who were slaves to the law, so that he could adopt us as his very own children" (Galatians 4:5). Jesus has accomplished the freeing work of God so we can walk with our heads held high because of our connection to him through faith.

† *Spirit, you have kissed my guilty heart with the love of God, my Father. You help me see that my Abba Father is not barking orders or driving me along with a whip. He sent his own Son to buy my freedom so I can live in security under his smile.*

FEBRUARY 14
IN HIM WE POSSESS THE LAND

The land was part of the inheritance God promised to Abraham and his descendants forever: "I have given this land to your descendants, all the way from the border of Egypt to the great Euphrates River" (Genesis 15:18). "I will give the entire land of Canaan, where you now live as a foreigner, to you and your descendants. It will be their possession forever, and I will be their God" (Genesis 17:8).

We might expect, based on these promises, that Abraham left Ur, moved into Canaan, and made himself at home. But according to the writer of Hebrews, Abraham made his home in the Promised Land of Canaan "like a foreigner, living in tents" (11:9), as did his son and his son's son. In fact, the only land Abraham ever owned in Canaan was a cave in which he buried his wife, Sarah. And even when the children of Israel took possession of the land under the leadership of Joshua, their possession still fell short of God's covenant promise. The land promise made to Abraham could be ultimately fulfilled only by a place with unfettered, eternal fellowship with God. And obviously that cannot happen in the world we live in now, on an earth that we know is going to pass away.

But Abraham's faith did not consist in seeking ownership of Middle Eastern real estate. "Abraham was confidently looking forward to a city with eternal foundations, a city designed and built by God" (Hebrews 11:10). Describing people of faith like Abraham, Hebrews 11:13, 16 says,

> All these people died still believing what God had promised them. They did not receive what was promised, but they saw it all from a distance and welcomed it. They agreed that they were foreigners and nomads here on earth. . . . They were looking for a better place, a heavenly homeland. That is why God is not ashamed to be called their God, for he has prepared a city for them.

It is as we possess Christ that God's covenant is fulfilled. God "has blessed us with every spiritual blessing in the heavenly realms because we are united with Christ" (Ephesians 1:3).

† *Once I was apart from you, excluded from citizenship among your people, alienated from the covenant promises. I lived in this world without God and without hope. But now I have been united with you. One day you will lead me into the heavenly homeland, where you will live with your people forever.*

FEBRUARY 15
THE LORD IS WITH YOU

When most of us think of the Son of God coming to earth, we picture him as a baby in Bethlehem. And certainly that is right and true. It was then that the second member of the Trinity took on flesh to live among us. But he was not absent or inactive in Old Testament times. Throughout the Old Testament there are numerous times the angel of the Lord appeared, and while Scripture doesn't spell it out absolutely, because this unique angel promised what only God can do and performed what only deity can accomplish, it may be that the angel of the Lord was none other than the pre-incarnate Son of God.

When the angel of the Lord spoke, his words were perceived as being God's words. The angel of the Lord met Hagar in the desert, and Genesis says, "the LORD . . . had spoken to her" (Genesis 16:13, emphasis added). Abraham heard the voice of the angel of the Lord on Mount Moriah telling him not to plunge the knife into his son Isaac, saying, "*I* will certainly bless you" (Genesis 22:17, emphasis added), which is a promise from God himself. The angel of the Lord appeared to Moses in flames of fire from within a bush, and we are told that "*God* called to him from the middle of the bush" (Exodus 3:4, emphasis added). In fact, it was the presence of God himself that made the place Moses was standing "holy ground" (Exodus 3:5). After the angel of the Lord appeared to Manoah and his wife to tell them she would give birth to Samson, Manoah said, "We will certainly die, for we have seen God!" (Judges 13:22).

While God sent angels as his messengers in the New Testament, this wondrous and unique angel of the Lord did not appear. His absence might convince us that this revealer of God in the Old Testament was not a different being from the revealer in the New Testament. It was his form that was different. Rather than angelic form, he took on human form.

Why would the angel of the Lord appear on the stage of the world's earlier history? It must have been in order to reveal his Father to us—to prepare the way for his own coming in the flesh, and to outline in shadows the nature of his coming Kingdom. God was here in the form of his Angel, providing his loving guidance and careful protection, actively involved in the cares and affairs of undeserving men and women. He sees our need and he condescends to us. He cares. He comes.

† *Revealer of God, visit me with your holy presence. Fill me with wonder and praise for your love that extends from eternity past into eternity future.*

ALMIGHTY GOD

Abram was ninety-nine years old, and his wife, Sarai, still had not had the child God had promised. He found himself struggling to believe that God could still carry out his promise to make him the father of many nations. That is when the Lord appeared to him and revealed himself to Abram in a new way, using a new name: "I am El-Shaddai—'God Almighty'" (Genesis 17:1).

In identifying himself as El-Shaddai—God Almighty, God was assuring Abram that he has all the power he needs to do anything he wants to do, that his purposes cannot be thwarted by anything—including aging bodies. El-Shaddai can also be rendered "all-sufficient God," expressing the sufficiency of God to fulfill his promises. El-Shaddai is the God who is able to save, able to carry out his will, able to bestow his blessings on his people, able to cause a woman beyond the age of conception to conceive.

The prophet Isaiah said that the Messiah would be called "Mighty God" (Isaiah 9:6). Though he would possess human nature, he would exercise absolute power. So it makes sense that the people of Jesus' day did not immediately recognize Jesus as Messiah. He did not appear to be Almighty God. He was a human who got tired and hungry. They saw glimpses of the Almighty's power when he exercised authority over demons and sickness and even nature. But any hopes that he was indeed the Mighty God promised by Isaiah must have vanished when he was beaten, nailed to a cross, and sealed in a tomb.

Surely the almighty, all-sufficient God would not be this weak. The people did not realize that "although he was crucified in weakness, he now lives by the power of God" (2 Corinthians 13:4) and that "God's weakness is stronger than the greatest of human strength" (1 Corinthians 1:25).

Jesus was El-Shaddai—God Almighty—but he willingly submitted himself to the greatest power the world possesses: the power of sin and death. However, this power could not hold him. It only served God's purposes. For "Christ is the power of God" (1 Corinthians 1:24).

† *Jesus, I can do everything through you who gives me strength. In fact, your power works best in my weakness. So I will not boast about my strength—I will boast about my weaknesses. Then your power can work through me. For when I am weak, then I am strong through you.*

FEBRUARY 17
CHRIST PERFORMED A SPIRITUAL CIRCUMCISION

God commanded that Abram walk before him in obedience with a life-transforming thoroughness (Genesis 17:1). But then God announced with emphasis one specific requirement: "This is my covenant with you and your descendants after you, the covenant you are to keep: Every male among you shall be circumcised. . . . My covenant in your flesh is to be an everlasting covenant" (Genesis 17:10, 13, NIV).

God established this rite of circumcision as an outward, physical sign of the need for cleansing. By commanding that his people cut away a natural part of their bodies, God was illustrating the judgment a sinner undergoes that purifies. Circumcision was no mere badge of national membership in the Jewish nation, but a physical sign of a loving, cleansing, purifying, identifying, and defining relationship between God and his people.

This sign also pointed to a cleansing to come that would not only mark the body but change the heart. This ritual purification became an experienced reality when Christ provided the cleansing that circumcision pointed to. Jesus began by submitting himself to the rite of circumcision. "When the right time came, God sent his Son, born of a woman, subject to the law" (Galatians 4:4). In his circumcision on the eighth day, and later in his baptism by John, Jesus experienced this cleansing rite not for his own sake but for the sake of the sinful people he came to purify.

We experience what is symbolized in this old-covenant sign when our consciences are cleansed through the blood of the new and better covenant. We experience the circumcision of the heart that Moses spoke of (Deuteronomy 10:16) when the Holy Spirit gives us a heart that longs to please God in purity. "True circumcision is not merely obeying the letter of the law; rather, it is a change of heart produced by God's Spirit" (Romans 2:29). Paul said, "We who worship by the Spirit of God are the ones who are truly circumcised. We rely on what Christ Jesus has done for us. We put no confidence in human effort" (Philippians 3:3).

† *You have circumcised me, Jesus—not by a physical procedure but by a spiritual one. You have cut away my sinful nature and freed me from its enslavement. I am marked by you as yours forever.*

HIS COMING
CONFIRMS THE COVENANT

The writer of Hebrews, looking back through the Old Testament, wrote that God "bound himself with an oath, so that those who received the promise could be perfectly sure that he would never change his mind" (6:17). He saw that again and again God promised to confirm his covenant: "I will confirm my covenant with you," God said to Noah (Genesis 6:18). "I will confirm my covenant with you and your descendants after you, from generation to generation," he said to Abraham (Genesis 17:7).

How would this happen? God confirmed his covenant with tangible signs: "My covenant will be confirmed with Isaac, who will be born to you and Sarah," he told Abraham (Genesis 17:21). "Moses took the blood from the basins and splattered it over the people, declaring, 'Look, this blood confirms the covenant the LORD has made with you'" (Exodus 24:8). "David realized that the LORD had confirmed him as king over Israel and had greatly blessed his kingdom for the sake of his people Israel" (1 Chronicles 14:2).

God used numerous signs to confirm that he would fulfill his covenants with Noah and Abraham and Israel and David, and each of them served to point toward his most significant sign—the sending of his Son.

When the angel told Mary that the Son of the Most High would be born to her, she recognized that it was a confirmation of God's covenant with Abraham. "He made this promise to our ancestors, to Abraham and his children forever," she sang (Luke 1:55). Zechariah understood the angel's message to him the same way: "He has sent us a mighty Savior from the royal line of his servant David, just as he promised through his holy prophets long ago. . . . He has been merciful to our ancestors by remembering his sacred covenant—the covenant he swore with an oath to our ancestor Abraham" (Luke 1:69-70, 72-73).

But the most tangible confirmation of God's covenant through Christ came not by Christ's birth but by his death. "This is my blood, which confirms the covenant between God and his people," Jesus said the night before he was crucified (Mark 14:24). Jesus was the personal confirmation that God will live up to all he promised Noah, Abraham, Moses, David, and all their descendants.

† *Jesus, you are the guarantee that God will do everything he has promised. And since he did not spare even you, his own Son, but gave you up for us all, won't he also give us everything else?*

FEBRUARY 19
ABRAHAM REJOICED TO SEE HIS DAY

Jesus was in the midst of an interaction with the Pharisees that would end with their taking up stones to throw at him when he said something they couldn't make sense of: "Your father Abraham rejoiced as he looked forward to my coming. He saw it and was glad" (John 8:56).

But how could Abraham have seen Christ? And why did he rejoice? Perhaps it was when God told Abraham that his wife, Sarah, would give birth in her old age: "Abraham bowed down to the ground, but he laughed to himself in disbelief. 'How could I become a father at the age of 100?' he thought" (Genesis 17:17).

Sarah laughed too when she heard God's promise. She was long past the age of having children. So she laughed silently to herself, saying, "How could a worn-out woman like me enjoy such pleasure, especially when my master—my husband—is also so old?" (Genesis 18:12).

The idea of Sarah having a baby was laughable to Abraham and Sarah. But God had the last laugh. Sarah gave birth to a son they named Isaac, which means "laughter." Sarah declared, "God has brought me laughter. All who hear about this will laugh with me" (Genesis 21:6).

When Abraham held his son Isaac in his arms, he rejoiced. If God could give him a son in his old age, then all the promised blessings still to come were surely in the process of being realized. But Abraham's rejoicing must have been even greater when, on Mount Moriah, the angel called out for him to withhold the knife, and his son was given to him a second time. Hebrews 11:19 says, "In a sense, Abraham did receive his son back from the dead."

Abraham rejoiced because he realized that salvation would come through the offspring of the promise, his son Isaac. He rejoiced because he realized that God does the impossible. He looked forward to the day when the true son of Abraham, the Father's beloved Son, Jesus, would—for the joy set before him—endure the Cross and come back to life again like his own beloved Isaac had.

† *Just as Abraham looked forward to your day and was glad, we look back and are glad—thankful for the promise fulfilled, the sacrifice provided, the life resurrected. We also look forward to your day—the day when you will return in glory—and we are glad.*

HE MAKES THE IMPOSSIBLE POSSIBLE

Humanly speaking, it was impossible that Abraham and Sarah would have a child. Sarah had always been barren, and even if she hadn't been, now, in her nineties, she was far beyond childbearing years. So when she overheard one of the men God sent say, "I will return to you about this time next year, and your wife, Sarah, will have a son" (Genesis 18:10), she laughed to herself. The Lord asked Abraham, "Why did Sarah laugh? Why did she say, 'Can an old woman like me have a baby?' Is anything too hard for the LORD? I will return about this time next year, and Sarah will have a son" (Genesis 18:13-14).

While Abraham and Sarah thought it was impossible for Sarah to give birth to a son, what was truly impossible was for God to *not* fulfill his promise. God waited until it was humanly impossible for the child of the covenant to be born in order to show that covenant people are created not by human effort but by divine and sovereign grace.

In Luke 1 the angel Gabriel told the virgin Mary (just like God had told the barren Sarah) that she would give birth to a son. Mary asked, "But how can this happen? I am a virgin" (1:34). The angel told her that the Holy Spirit would come upon her and that even her barren relative Elizabeth had become pregnant. He concluded his surprising message by saying, "Nothing is impossible with God" (1:37). Here again, God worked where it was humanly impossible to bring forth a child of promise. Why? To show that the creation of a covenant people does not rely on human effort or decision. It is God's work, and nothing is impossible with God.

Later Jesus spoke these same words to his disciples that had been spoken to Abraham in Genesis 18 and to Mary in Luke 1. The rich young man had just gone away sad, unwilling to sell all he had to inherit eternal life. "It is easier for a camel to go through the eye of a needle than for a rich person to enter the Kingdom of God!" Jesus had said. To this, the disciples responded, "Then who in the world can be saved?" Looking at them intently, Jesus said, "Humanly speaking, it is impossible. But not with God. Everything is possible with God" (Mark 10:23-27).

✝ *God of the impossible, it is only by your power and grace that what is impossible on human terms—that a sinner like me could be made acceptable to you—could be possible. You and you alone have made it possible for me to be reborn. Only you bring life from barrenness.*

He Intercedes for Sinners

Abraham knew people in the wicked cities of Sodom and Gomorrah, and he cared about them despite their paganism and depravity. So when God told Abraham about his plan to destroy the city, Abraham interceded for them with God: "Surely you wouldn't do such a thing, destroying the righteous along with the wicked. Why, you would be treating the righteous and the wicked exactly the same! Surely you wouldn't do that! Should not the Judge of all the earth do what is right?" (Genesis 18:25).

God wanted someone to mediate, someone to intercede for Sodom. He wanted someone who knew the weaknesses of people and could sympathize to plead with him on their behalf. He appointed Abraham to that task to show Abraham something about himself, while at the same time showing us a picture of the mediating work of Christ.

It was Abraham's descendant Jesus who would perfectly intercede with God in a way that would uphold the righteousness and justice of God while also saving sinful people from experiencing the destructive wrath of God. Because of the work of our Mediator, God will not always deal with sinners the way he dealt with those in Sodom and Gomorrah. The Judge of all the earth has made a plan for guilty sinners who deserve nothing less than annihilation to be saved from it.

> God presented Jesus as the sacrifice for sin. . . . This sacrifice shows that God was being fair when he held back and did not punish those who sinned in times past, for he was looking ahead and including them in what he would do in this present time. God did this to demonstrate his righteousness, for he himself is fair and just, and he declares sinners to be right in his sight when they believe in Jesus. (Romans 3:25-26)

Should not the Judge of all the earth do what is right? Yes, he will. Yes, he has. Our righteous Judge has justly punished sin. Our righteous Mediator has absorbed that punishment in our place.

† *Judge of all the earth, I'm so grateful that you have made a way for me to be saved from the wrath and judgment I deserve. Instead, you have given Christ what I deserve, and you have given me the freedom and blessings he deserves. I gladly choose to rest in your righteous judgment, knowing that you will always do what is right by me, with me, and for me.*

HE DID NOT SPARE
EVEN HIS OWN SON

When Abraham heard God calling, he gladly replied, "Yes, . . . here I am" (Genesis 22:1). But that was before he knew what God was about to ask of him. This was the eagerness of one who didn't know how his faith was about to be tested. "Take your son, your only son—yes, Isaac, whom you love so much—and go to the land of Moriah. Go and sacrifice him as a burnt offering on one of the mountains, which I will show you" (Genesis 22:2).

One would think that Abraham would drag his feet, go back with questions, search for some sort of out. But "the next morning Abraham got up early" (Genesis 22:3) and set out on a heartbreaking journey of costly obedience, taking his beloved son up Mount Moriah to be sacrificed. Then, just before Abraham plunged the knife into Isaac as he lay on the altar, the angel of the Lord called to Abraham from heaven: "Don't lay a hand on the boy! . . . Do not hurt him in any way, for now I know that you truly fear God. You have not withheld from me even your son, your only son" (Genesis 22:12).

When we read this story, we can't help but wonder if God knew what he was doing, if he realized what he was asking. But of course he knew. Abraham's love for and joy in his son were but a reflection of God's love for his own Son. The Father said about Jesus, "This is my dearly loved Son, who brings me great joy" (Matthew 3:17). Jesus was the beloved Son of promise, whom God did not withhold from us. "God showed how much he loved us by sending his one and only Son into the world so that we might have eternal life through him" (1 John 4:9).

God did what Abraham did not have to do: he made his Son an offering for sin. "God loved the world so much that he gave his one and only Son, so that everyone who believes in him will not perish but have eternal life" (John 3:16). When Abraham raised that knife over his son Isaac, God stopped him. But at the Cross God plunged the knife into his Son. Likewise, Jesus, the Son, did what Isaac, the son, did not have to do: he experienced the pain of death at the hands of his Father—the death that we deserve. The object of the Father's love was not spared, so that we would be eternally spared.

✝ *You did not spare your own Son so that you could spare me. You took everything away from your own Son to give everything to me. You were harsh toward your own Son in order to be sweet to me. You poured out your wrath on your own Son at the Cross in order to pour out your grace on me. You sacrificed your own Son so that I would gain everything.*

FEBRUARY 23

HE CARRIED THE
WOOD FOR THE SACRIFICE

As startling as it is to hear and process God's instructions to Abraham to offer his son as a sacrifice, it is perhaps just as startling to witness Abraham's immediate obedience. "The next morning Abraham got up early. He saddled his donkey and took two of his servants with him, along with his son, Isaac. Then he chopped wood for a fire for a burnt offering and set out for the place God had told him about" (Genesis 22:3). As he chopped the wood, was Abraham thinking that those logs would consume his son, his hope? Did he imagine that the sticks he was picking up would fuel the fire in which his boy would be burned?

The ascent up Mount Moriah, the place of sacrifice, was too steep for the donkey, so "Abraham placed the wood for the burnt offering on Isaac's shoulders, while he himself carried the fire and the knife" (Genesis 22:6). Here we see a prophetic image of Jesus, who, "carrying the cross by himself . . . went to the place called Place of the Skull (in Hebrew, *Golgotha*)" (John 19:17).

Two times in the story of Abraham we read that the two of them "walked on together" (Genesis 22:6, 8). Abraham could not have offered Isaac without Isaac's consent and cooperation. If Isaac, as the bearer of the wood, was strong enough to carry the wood, surely he could have overpowered his father. But evidently he decided to obey his father whatever the cost, just as his father had decided to obey God whatever the cost.

Here, too, we see a prophetic picture of the Son's obedience to his Father. "Even though Jesus was God's Son, he learned obedience from the things he suffered" (Hebrews 5:8). Both the planning and the execution of our salvation were the work of the Father and the Son. "No one can take my life from me. I sacrifice it voluntarily," Jesus said. "For I have the authority to lay it down when I want to and also to take it up again. For this is what my Father has commanded" (John 10:18).

Like Isaac, Jesus went willingly, putting his trust in his Father. In order to save Isaac, God provided a ram. In order to save us, God provided himself.

† *I hear you inviting me to take up my cross and follow you. I know that the reason you suffered isn't so I would never have to suffer. You bore the cross, not so I could escape suffering altogether, but so I can endure it. I hear you inviting me into the fellowship of sharing in your suffering. May my obedience be as immediate as Abraham's and my trust in my Father be as complete as Isaac's.*

THE LAMB GOD PROVIDES

"Father?" Isaac said to Abraham as they walked up the mountain together.

"Yes, my son?" Abraham replied.

Then Isaac asked the question that must have pierced Abraham deep inside: "We have the fire and the wood," the boy said, "but where is the sheep for the burnt offering?"

"God will provide a sheep for the burnt offering, my son," Abraham answered (Genesis 22:7-8).

Abraham was so confident in God's promise to him that he believed God would provide what was needed. And sure enough, God did provide: "Abraham looked up and saw a ram caught by its horns in a thicket. So he took the ram and sacrificed it as a burnt offering in place of his son. Abraham named the place Yahweh-Yireh (which means 'the LORD will provide'). To this day, people still use that name as a proverb: 'On the mountain of the LORD it will be provided'" (Genesis 22:13-14).

There is an obvious progression in the Old Testament in terms of God's provision of a sacrifice for sin. First God provided one lamb for one person— Abraham offered a ram in place of his son Isaac. Next God provided one lamb for one household. This happened at the first Passover, when every family in the covenant community offered its own lamb to God. Then God provided one sacrifice for the whole nation. On the Day of Atonement, a single animal atoned for the sins of all Israel.

But all these lambs were just preparing us for the coming of Christ. They were signs pointing to salvation in Christ's sacrifice. Finally the day came when John the Baptist "saw Jesus coming toward him and said, 'Look! The Lamb of God who takes away the sin of the world!'" (John 1:29). This was God's plan for provision all along: one Lamb to die for one world. By his grace God has provided a lamb—"the Lamb who was slaughtered" (Revelation 13:8).

† *My Provider, you always give to me what you demand from me. Again and again I see that your demands are not burdensome but that in Christ you provide for me everything you require of me.*

FEBRUARY 25

PROMISED WITH AN OATH

As Abraham poised the blade of his knife to descend into his son Isaac, the angel of heaven called to him, saying,

> This is what the LORD says: Because you have obeyed me and have not withheld even your son, your only son, I swear by my own name that I will certainly bless you. I will multiply your descendants beyond number, like the stars in the sky and the sand on the seashore. Your descendants will conquer the cities of their enemies. And through your descendants all the nations of the earth will be blessed—all because you have obeyed me. (Genesis 22:16-18)

While God had repeatedly promised Abraham that he would make a great nation from him, now he swore an oath to do so. God was so pleased with Abraham's supreme act of faith that he did something he had never done before—he bound himself with an oath that he would keep his promise. The book of Hebrews helps us understand why God made this promise and oath to Abraham and the confidence this promise should give us:

> God has given both his promise and his oath. These two things are unchangeable because it is impossible for God to lie. Therefore, we who have fled to him for refuge can have great confidence as we hold to the hope that lies before us. This hope is a strong and trustworthy anchor for our souls. It leads us through the curtain into God's inner sanctuary. Jesus has already gone in there for us. He has become our eternal High Priest in the order of Melchizedek. (Hebrews 6:18-20)

What is "the hope that lies before us"? It is Jesus himself and the truth of his gospel. The hope we have fled to and taken hold of is sure. It centers on the promises of God, which are fleshed out for us in the ultimate blessing of Jesus Christ. This hope comes from the fact that we are *in* Christ, the Son who fulfilled Abraham's covenant, and that we will be *with* Christ and *like* Christ. Jesus is the foundation and substance of our hope.

† *I see that everything promised by God comes through you, Jesus. You are my only hope, and I'm taking hold of you. I'm waiting patiently for you. You are the Anchor for my soul who will provide security in the storms of this world and carry me safely into the next.*

THE BRIDEGROOM

If Isaac, the son of promise, was going to be the father of descendants as numerous as the stars in the sky, he needed a wife. And not just any wife. She needed to be from a family that followed after God and not a Canaanite, who might lead Isaac away from God. She also had to be willing to leave her family and relocate to Isaac's home. Abraham's servant knew that God had selected a bride for Isaac, so he waited by a well to discover God's choice. "Before he had finished praying, he saw a young woman named Rebekah coming out with her water jug on her shoulder. She was the daughter of Bethuel, who was the son of Abraham's brother Nahor and his wife, Milcah. Rebekah was very beautiful and old enough to be married, but she was still a virgin" (Genesis 24:15-16).

In her beauty, her purity, and her chosenness, Rebekah was a picture of the bride of Christ. And yet when we look at ourselves, we know that we are not from the right family—we were born children of the world. We are not pure virgins—we have given ourselves to many other lovers, spiritually speaking. And we are not even hospitable like Rebekah was to Abraham's servant, but wrapped up in our own needs and desires. So how can Rebekah picture the bride of Christ, his church?

To discover the answer, we must look ahead to another meeting at another well. Jesus came to a well in Samaria where there was a woman who was not from the right family but was of mixed heritage. She was exactly what Abraham had feared when he told his servant not to take a bride for Isaac from the people near where they had settled—people who had no regard for sexual purity. In fact, this woman had had five husbands and was now living with a man who was not her husband (John 4:1-29).

Jesus asked her for a drink, just as Abraham's servant had asked Rebekah for a drink. But unlike Rebekah, this woman at the well was slow to respond—not because she was inhospitable, but because she assumed she was disqualified from being the bride Jesus sought for himself.

Yet he came to her—an unchaste, disliked, mixed-race woman—and made her his own. He came to her though she had no water to give him, and he offered her the water of eternal life that only he can give.

† *Bridegroom seeking a perfect bride, I know I do not qualify to be the beautiful and pure bride that you seek. Yet you have offered yourself to me and bound yourself to me so that I can be your bride forever.*

FEBRUARY 27

HE GIVES US THE BLESSING OF THE FIRSTBORN

Long before Jacob and Esau were born, the Lord told Rebekah about the two sons in her womb: "Your older son will serve your younger son" (Genesis 25:23). God made it clear from the beginning that these two sons would not follow the pattern of the culture, in which the firstborn son typically enjoyed the favored status that brought a greater share of inheritance and honor. But Isaac seemed to fight this foretelling from the start. Esau was born before his brother and was a skillful hunter and outdoorsman—his father's favorite— while Jacob was a quiet homebody—his mother's favorite.

When it came time for Isaac to give the blessing of the firstborn, he was determined to give it to his older son, Esau. But Rebekah overheard Isaac sending Esau out to kill game to make a meal for the time of blessing, so she sent Jacob, dressed up as Esau, to visit blind Isaac instead. When Jacob hesitated, fearing that he would be cursed instead of blessed, Rebekah insisted: "Let the curse fall on me, my son!" (Genesis 27:13).

So Jacob went in, saying, "It's Esau, your firstborn son" (Genesis 27:19), and he succeeded in fooling his father. Jacob finally heard the words of blessing he had longed his whole life to hear. Jacob—the one who was not the firstborn son, the one chosen by God to receive the blessing from before he was born—received the blessing of the firstborn.

Jesus is the true firstborn son Jacob points to. "He is the image of the invisible God, the firstborn over all creation" (Colossians 1:15, NIV). From eternity past, Jesus was dearly loved by his Father and enjoyed the blessing of the firstborn. But when he hung on the cross, he relinquished his firstborn status and willingly took the Curse upon himself. He did what Rebekah offered to do when she said, "Let the curse fall on me!"

Jesus clothed himself in human flesh so he would look like us and live like us, and so he could die for us. In this way, he made it possible for us to one day be clothed in glorified bodies like his own and to receive the firstborn blessing he deserves. He has made us members of "the church of the firstborn, whose names are written in heaven" (Hebrews 12:23, NIV).

✝ *Here I am in your family—a family completely composed of firstborns! The Father loves me as his firstborn and has given me the inheritance of the firstborn! Jesus, you took the Curse upon yourself so that I can have this blessing.*

JACOB'S STAIRWAY

Jacob was fleeing the consequences of his own deceit when he set up camp and stopped for the night. As sleep overtook him, he began to dream. But this was no ordinary dream. God, who has spoken "many times and in many ways" (Hebrews 1:1), revealed himself to Jacob in this dream. "He dreamed of a stairway that reached from the earth up to heaven. And he saw the angels of God going up and down the stairway" (Genesis 28:12).

God repeated the blessing he had promised to Abraham. He would give Jacob the land he was lying on, and his descendants would be as numerous as the particles of dust. Above all, the Lord pledged his own presence to Jacob: "I will not leave you until I have finished giving you everything I have promised you" (Genesis 28:15).

This was the stairway that connected the worlds of deity and humanity. This was the stairway on which God came down. And it was the stairway to God's abode—the only way to enter the throne room of God.

Jesus referred to this stairway in Jacob's dream early in his ministry. As Nathanael approached, Jesus said, "Now here is a genuine son of Israel —a man of complete integrity" (John 1:47). Jesus was obviously comparing Nathanael favorably with his ancient ancestor Jacob, who was known as a schemer and deceiver. When Jesus told Nathanael that he saw him under the fig tree, Nathanael realized that Jesus knew his innermost thoughts. That's when Jesus hearkened back to Jacob's dream: "I tell you the truth, you will all see heaven open and the angels of God going up and down on the Son of Man, the one who is the stairway between heaven and earth" (John 1:51).

Jacob saw the stairway and knew it was the way to God, and yet that way was still not clear. Jesus made it clear. He is that stairway. He is the way. He is God come down, and he is the One through whom sinners can ascend to the presence of God. Jesus can lead us up this stairway only because he was lifted up on the cross. We can ascend to God only when we come to the foot of his cross.

† *Stairway to heaven, you planted yourself in the soil of this earth, and you rise up into the very throne room of God, providing me with solid footing to ascend from life on this earth into the presence of God.*

THE LOVING HUSBAND OF AN UGLY BRIDE

Jacob's uncle Laban had two daughters: Leah, who is described as having "weak" eyes or "no sparkle" in her eyes, and Rachel, who had "a beautiful figure and a lovely face" (Genesis 29:17). Jacob was smitten by Rachel's beauty and agreed to work for Laban for seven years to have her as his bride. But on the wedding night, knowing that Leah would be harder to find a husband for, Laban sent Leah in to Jacob. When Jacob woke up the next morning, he discovered that he had slept with Leah, not Rachel, and he was enraged. Laban agreed to give Rachel to Jacob too, if he would work another seven years. So Rachel and Jacob were married, and "he loved her much more than Leah. . . . When the LORD saw that Leah was unloved, he enabled her to have children, but Rachel could not conceive. So Leah became pregnant and gave birth to a son. She named him Reuben, for she said, 'The LORD has noticed my misery, and now my husband will love me'" (Genesis 29:30-32).

Every time another child came along, Leah named him in a way that evidenced her longing to be loved by her husband. She named her second son Simeon, believing that the Lord heard she was unloved, and her third son Levi, believing that her husband would finally feel affection for her. But she continued to be unloved by Jacob.

Then she had another son, and this time everything was different. She named him Judah, saying, "Now I will praise the LORD!" (29:35). Somehow Leah finally saw that God intended to provide her with a divine husband who would love her in a far more complete way than Jacob ever could. In fact, this loving husband would be a descendant of her son Judah.

Jesus is the loving husband of an ugly bride, the church—a bride that has not been imposed on him but chosen by him and cherished by him. He has seen her misery, and he loves her. He has sensed her desperation and has committed himself to her. He has looked deep into her ugliness and given her his own beauty so that when the time comes for the wedding feast of the Lamb, she will be a "bride beautifully dressed for her husband" (Revelation 21:2).

† *Loving Husband, there is no hiding my fault from you. Yet you are my husband who loves me! I am beautiful in your eyes because of the purity and beauty you have provided for me. Nothing I do can cause you to love me more. And nothing I do can cause you to love me less. Like Leah, I will praise the Lord, because you love me!*

MARCH 2

THE GLORY OF GOD
IN THE FACE OF CHRIST

Jacob was at the end of his rope, afraid that Esau was on his way to exact long-overdue revenge. That's when a man came to Jacob's camp and began a wrestling match with him that lasted all night. "When the man saw that he would not win the match, he touched Jacob's hip and wrenched it out of its socket. Then the man said, 'Let me go, for the dawn is breaking!' But Jacob said, 'I will not let you go unless you bless me'" (Genesis 32:25-26).

The truth is, Jacob had been trying to wrestle a blessing all his life. Through trickery and deceit, he had wrestled the words of affirmation and blessing out of his father that belonged to Esau. Then he wrestled the blessing of having Rachel as his wife from her father, Laban, by working for him for fourteen years. Now he was wrestling someone new. And as the cover of darkness gave way to light, we get a clue as to who it was.

This man said he must go because light was coming. Jacob knew that no human can look at the face of God in the light of day and live. His life was in danger, yet he begged the man to stay. Jacob had come to the place where the blessing of God meant more to him than life itself. "Jacob named the place Peniel (which means 'face of God'), for he said, 'I have seen God face to face, yet my life has been spared'" (Genesis 32:30).

Jacob recognized that his opponent was no mere man or ordinary angel. This was no less than the pre-incarnate Jesus—the One who would come to earth again one day in weakness to take the Curse upon himself so we can know the blessing of God. Paul said that we can "know the glory of God that is seen in the face of Jesus Christ" (2 Corinthians 4:6). Surely this is the face of the one Jacob held in his grip as he wrestled his holy opponent.

Jesus is the promise and conduit of the blessing of God in our lives. "All praise to God, the Father of our Lord Jesus Christ, who has blessed us with every spiritual blessing in the heavenly realms because we are united with Christ" (Ephesians 1:3).

✝ *Giver of the blessing I struggled to obtain, I have looked for the blessings of approval and acceptance in so many faces other than yours. But now I realize that yours is the blessing I long for. Jesus, you are the blessing of God in my life.*

MARCH 3

LOVED BY HIS FATHER, HATED BY HIS BROTHERS

By the time Joseph arrived in Jacob's family, there was already a houseful of siblings. But "Jacob loved Joseph more than any of his other children because Joseph had been born to him in his old age" (Genesis 37:3). The antagonism of Joseph's brothers toward this favored son grew into outright hatred, which led to their conspiracy to kill him. Ultimately they sold Joseph to slave traders instead and led Jacob to believe that a wild animal had killed him. Jacob's intense love for Joseph was demonstrated by his overwhelming grief. He refused to be comforted, declaring he would go to his grave in mourning.

Jesus was also the beloved Son of his Father. Three times a voice from heaven affirmed God's love for his Son. He said, "This is my dearly loved Son, who brings me great joy" (Matthew 3:17; Matthew 17:5; see also John 12:28).

The intensity of the love Jacob had for his son Joseph was matched by the intensity of the hatred Joseph's brothers had for him. Genesis 37:4 says, "His brothers hated Joseph because their father loved him more than the rest of them." Jesus, too, was hated by his physical half-brothers as well as his larger Jewish brotherhood for claiming God as his Father. "Even his brothers didn't believe in him" (John 7:5). "He came to his own people, and even they rejected him" (John 1:11).

In addition to being loved by their fathers and hated by their brothers, Joseph and Jesus were both conspired against by their enemies to be put to death. "When Joseph's brothers saw him coming, they recognized him in the distance. As he approached, they made plans to kill him" (Genesis 37:18). The hatred of Jesus' Israelite brothers provoked their evil plan to kill him. After watching Jesus heal on the Sabbath, "the Pharisees went away and met with the supporters of Herod to plot how to kill Jesus" (Mark 3:6).

Joseph was not put to death, though he was presumed dead based on the news from his brothers and the bloodstained robe presented to his father. But Jesus *was* put to death, and his bloodstained robe was simply gambled away (Matthew 27:35). Jesus, the beloved Son, was killed at the hands of his jealous brothers so that he might offer salvation to them.

† *Jesus, I catch glimpses of you in the life of Joseph, and I stand in awe of my sovereign God, who could ordain such a life for Joseph. Through him you provided for your people, and you point me toward your Sonship and salvation.*

HE LEFT HIS HOME OF PRIVILEGE TO BECOME A SLAVE

Joseph lived a life of privilege in the house of his father, Jacob. But his father's favor served only to kindle his brothers' resentment. "When Joseph's brothers saw him coming, they recognized him in the distance. As he approached, they made plans to kill him" (Genesis 37:18).

But rather than kill him, they sold Joseph into slavery and he was carted off to Egypt, where he became a slave in the house of Potiphar. What a contrast—to go from being the favored son in his father's house to being a slave in a foreigner's home! Joseph would never have willingly left the home of privilege he enjoyed with the father who loved him to become a slave in a foreign land. But he did foreshadow One who was willing to leave his home of heaven, where he enjoyed the love of his Father, to become a slave in a foreign place. Jesus willingly "gave up his divine privileges; he took the humble position of a slave" (Philippians 2:7).

As a servant, Joseph pleased his master, Potiphar, who gladly put him in charge of his entire household. So it was with the One Joseph foreshadowed, who was given all authority by his Father. Jesus said about his Father, "I always do what pleases him" (John 8:29). After being falsely accused, Joseph was cast into prison. It is possible that Potiphar didn't believe the accusation his wife had brought against Joseph. If he had, he would have ordered this Hebrew slave to be put to death. Here, too, Joseph prefigures Jesus, who was also falsely accused and arrested. And clearly Pilate did not believe Jesus was truly guilty even though he handed down the sentence of crucifixion.

Joseph, the innocent one, suffered severely. Psalm 105 says of Joseph, "They bruised his feet with fetters and placed his neck in an iron collar" (105:18). So too did Jesus, the innocent One, suffer severely. He was mocked and spit upon, scourged and crowned with thorns, and nailed to a cruel tree. But Joseph did not remain enslaved and imprisoned forever. He emerged from prison to an exalted place in the kingdom of Pharaoh. Jesus, too, emerged from the prison of death. "God elevated him to the place of highest honor" (Philippians 2:9).

✝ *How I want to have the same attitude you had, Jesus—willing to let go of your divine privileges to become a slave, humbling yourself in obedience to death. My knee bows before you, exalted Jesus, and my tongue confesses that you are Lord, to the glory of God the Father!*

MARCH 5

HE WAS COUNTED
AMONG THE REBELS

The night he was arrested, Jesus told his disciples, "The time has come for this prophecy about me to be fulfilled: 'He was counted among the rebels.' Yes, everything written about me by the prophets will come true" (Luke 22:37).

This prophecy about Jesus from Isaiah 53:12 was also foreshadowed in the experience of Joseph. Falsely accused of attempted rape, Joseph was put into prison. Sometime later, Pharaoh's chief cup-bearer and chief baker offended their royal master, and they were put into prison along with Joseph. While there, they each had dreams about the future, which Joseph interpreted. Joseph told one, "Within three days Pharaoh will lift you up and restore you to your position as his chief cup-bearer." But to the chief baker he said, "Three days from now Pharaoh will lift you up and impale your body on a pole" (Genesis 40:13, 19).

Just as Joseph, though completely innocent, was cast into prison, so Jesus was falsely accused, lied about, and unjustly sentenced to death. There Jesus was flanked by two notorious culprits. Luke 23:39 records that one of the criminals hanging beside him scoffed, "So you're the Messiah, are you? Prove it by saving yourself—and us, too, while you're at it!"

The other criminal protested, "Don't you fear God even when you have been sentenced to die? We deserve to die for our crimes, but this man hasn't done anything wrong." Then he turned to Jesus: "Remember me when you come into your Kingdom." Jesus replied, "I assure you, today you will be with me in paradise" (Luke 23:40-43).

Just as Joseph was the means of blessing to one companion but the pronouncer of judgment to the other, so Jesus gave life to the repentant thief while the other thief perished.

Joseph asked the cup-bearer to "please remember me" to Pharaoh because he was innocent. The thief asked Jesus to remember him when he came into his Kingdom because he knew he was guilty. Christ, the truly innocent One, had taken on his guilt. He was counted among the rebels, so that even rebels can be counted innocent.

† *Because of my sin, I was counted among the rebels. But Jesus, you have taken my place there. You were counted among the rebels so that one day I will be counted among that vast crowd, too great to count, standing in front of the throne and before the Lamb.*

MARCH 6

FRUITFUL IN SUFFERING

At the very beginning of his covenant relationship with his chosen people, God told them about the tremendous suffering that was ahead for them: "The LORD said to Abram, 'You can be sure that your descendants will be strangers in a foreign land, where they will be oppressed as slaves for 400 years'" (Genesis 15:13).

God's people would suffer. But it would not be wasted, meaningless suffering. It would be fruitful suffering. They would emerge from Egypt with great wealth and great in number. How would they become "strangers in a foreign land"? Through the suffering of Israel's beloved son, Joseph. Joseph suffered the abuse of his brothers' jealousy as they sold him off to a caravan of slave traders heading for Egypt. There Joseph worked as a slave until he suffered as a result of the false accusations from Potiphar's wife that put him in prison. He suffered being forgotten in prison for many years before he emerged to become second in command to Pharaoh. But when he was released, his suffering did not leave him embittered. In fact, he celebrated what God had done in his life through his suffering in the naming of his sons: "Joseph named his older son Manasseh, for he said, 'God has made me forget all my troubles and everyone in my father's family.' Joseph named his second son Ephraim, for he said, 'God has made me fruitful in this land of my grief'" (Genesis 41:51-52).

Joseph was able to look at his suffering and see that it was not wasted; it was fruitful. God was accomplishing something good through all the hardship and hurt he experienced.

Likewise, Jesus, the greater Joseph, was willing to suffer, confident that his suffering would bear much fruit. The writer of Hebrews captured the fruitful suffering of Jesus:

> Even though Jesus was God's Son, he learned obedience from the things he suffered. In this way, God qualified him as a perfect High Priest, and he became the source of eternal salvation for all those who obey him. (Hebrews 5:8-9)

† *I find myself in a land of grief where I have known suffering. But only you can make me fruitful in this land. Only as I abide in you can I be fruitful. So don't let my suffering be wasted; make me fruitful in my suffering.*

MARCH 7

FROM HIS FULLNESS
WE HAVE RECEIVED

Joseph interpreted Pharaoh's dream, which predicted a coming famine.
And when Joseph outlined a plan to Pharaoh for preparing for the famine,
Pharaoh not only accepted the plan but also put Joseph in charge. "Joseph
gathered all the crops grown in Egypt and stored the grain from the surrounding fields in the cities. He piled up huge amounts of grain like sand on
the seashore. Finally, he stopped keeping records because there was too much
to measure" (Genesis 41:48-49).

When the time of famine came and the hungry came to Egypt after
hearing about the storehouses of grain Joseph had laid up, Pharaoh sent
them to Joseph: "'Go to Joseph, and do whatever he tells you.' So with severe
famine everywhere, Joseph opened up the storehouses and distributed grain"
(Genesis 41:55-56).

Here, as in so many other ways, Joseph points us to the heart of the
ministry of Jesus—the One who dispenses bread to a perishing world. When
sinners, with a great hunger in their souls, cry out to God, what is God's
response? He points them to Jesus because "there is salvation in no one else!
God has given no other name under heaven by which we must be saved"
(Acts 4:12).

But while the plenty Joseph dispensed points us to Jesus, it also helps
us to see the infinite superiority of the sufficiency of Jesus. For many in
Joseph's time, coming to Egypt to be fed required an arduous journey. But
faith brings us in one moment to Christ's storehouses of grace. Perhaps there
were appointed hours when Joseph distributed grain, but the grace of Christ
is always at hand. Those who came to Joseph were required to purchase
their food. But we receive all in Christ without cost. We merely ask, and we
receive. The Egyptian granaries, though very full, were one day exhausted.
But "from his abundance we have all received one gracious blessing after
another" (John 1:16).

In Christ, the empty are filled; the impoverished are made rich; the weak
become strong; the faint are revived; the famished are fed.

† *Son of Joseph, gracious Provider, I come to you from a land where there is
no good thing to feed my hungry soul, confident that you have provision you
will gladly give me from your abundance.*

MARCH 8

SAVIOR OF THE WORLD

Jacob sent Joseph to his brothers out in the fields, but instead of welcoming him, they turned on him. Their rejection ultimately put Joseph in a position to be a blessing to the whole world. The day came when Joseph became a savior to those who came to him—including his brothers. Joseph's exaltation to power in Egypt positioned him to provide food to a famished and perishing world. "With severe famine everywhere, Joseph opened up the storehouses and distributed grain to the Egyptians, for the famine was severe throughout the land of Egypt. And people from all around came to Egypt to buy grain from Joseph because the famine was severe throughout the world" (Genesis 41:56-57).

Paul wrote that what happened to Joseph—being sent by his father, Jacob; rejected by his brothers; and eventually put in a position to bless the world—is exactly what happened when Jesus' brothers—the Jews—rejected the Son their Father sent. "They were disobedient, so God made salvation available to the Gentiles" (Romans 11:11). Jesus' rejection by the Jews was in the sovereign plan of God so that it might be clear that Jesus is the Savior of the whole world, not solely for the Jews. Yet Jesus, like Joseph, provides salvation to the brothers who rejected him. The day is coming when "all Israel will be saved" (Romans 11:26).

Joseph, the rejected Jew, was exalted to become the only savior for a starving world. Anyone who was hungry could go to Joseph for food. Likewise, Jesus, a rejected Jew, is the only Savior for a world that is famished and perishing. Anyone in the world who is hungry can go to him for food and find "God's abundant provision of grace and of the gift of righteousness [so that he may] reign in life through the one man, Jesus Christ" (Romans 5:17, NIV).

Just as people from all countries came to Joseph, so Jesus has called to himself people from all countries of the earth. One day all who have come to Jesus for salvation will celebrate in his presence, and this song will rise up: "You were slaughtered, and your blood has ransomed people for God from every tribe and language and people and nation" (Revelation 5:9).

† *Savior of the world, I have come to you with a hunger deep in my soul. This world has proven to be in a vast famine, devoid of nourishment. Only you can feed me from your plenty. Only you can offer the abundant provision of grace I need.*

MARCH 9
Our Guarantee

Judah guaranteed Benjamin's safety with his own life before they left for Egypt. Then Joseph had a silver cup planted in the sack of his youngest brother, Benjamin. And when it was found, Joseph said that Benjamin would have to remain in Egypt as a slave while the rest of the brothers could go back home. But Judah would not let this happen. "I personally guarantee his safety," Judah had told his father, Jacob. "You may hold me responsible if I don't bring him back to you. Then let me bear the blame forever" (Genesis 43:9).

So when Benjamin's sack was found to contain the silver cup, Judah pleaded with Joseph to be imprisoned in place of Benjamin. "My lord, I guaranteed to my father that I would take care of the boy. I told him, 'If I don't bring him back to you, I will bear the blame forever.' So please, my lord, let me stay here as a slave instead of the boy, and let the boy return with his brothers" (Genesis 44:32-33). Judah was willing to give up his family, his future, and his freedom to save Benjamin from slavery and his father from further grief.

Judah offered himself as the guarantee for Benjamin and was willing to take his place to make good on his promise. Hundreds of years later, One from the line of Judah would pledge himself to be the guarantee for the safety and security of his brothers, offering himself as a substitute for sinners so they could go free. "Jesus is the one who guarantees this better covenant with God" (Hebrews 7:22).

For Judah to be a guarantee for Benjamin meant that he would become a slave in Egypt the rest of his life. For Jesus to be our guarantee meant that he would become a sacrifice and give his life. Jesus' dignity and worth far exceed Judah's in offering himself as a guarantee. Judah was a sinner himself. But Jesus is our sinless surety. Judah's guarantee was temporary and for only one person, while Jesus is the eternal guarantee, not just for one person, but for a countless multitude of people who turn from sin to him.

The Lion of the tribe of Judah is not only our guarantee to free us from slavery and punishment but our guarantee of an eternal future enjoyed in the presence of God.

✝ *My Guarantee of everything that is good, it is your magnificent worth and incorruptible integrity that make your promise sure and your oath secure. You have offered yourself up to guarantee my freedom though it cost you your life. I know my future in you is secure. You have guaranteed it with your own life.*

MARCH 10
God Sent Me Here

When Joseph's brothers came to Egypt for grain, they did not recognize him. But when they were brought back to the palace because of the silver cup that had been stashed in their belongings, they fell before Joseph. Judah said, "Oh, my lord, what can we say to you? How can we explain this? How can we prove our innocence? God is punishing us for our sins" (Genesis 44:16).

Finally Joseph couldn't stand it any longer, and he said to his brothers,

> I am Joseph, your brother, whom you sold into slavery in Egypt. But don't be upset, and don't be angry with yourselves for selling me to this place. It was God who sent me here ahead of you to preserve your lives. . . . God has sent me ahead of you to keep you and your families alive and to preserve many survivors. So it was God who sent me here, not you! (Genesis 45:4-5, 7-8)

Joseph's brothers were clearly responsible for selling Joseph into servitude all those years ago. They had clearly committed a great evil against him. Yet Joseph saw the invisible hand of God behind their actions. He saw all of his suffering as part of God's plan of salvation. And so he forgave. And beyond forgiving, he provided everything those who had sinned against him needed for survival.

Jesus, too, suffered significantly due to the cruel and evil intentions of those who conspired against him, lied about him, and called for his death. These people were responsible for their cruel sin. Yet Jesus did not hold this against them. Like Joseph, he offered forgiveness to those who put him in such a place of pain. When Jesus was on the cross, he said, "Father, forgive them, for they don't know what they are doing" (Luke 23:34).

Jesus knew that ultimately those who nailed him to the cross were not the ones who put him there. So when he looked at those who drove the crowds and drove the nails, he could echo Joseph's words: "It was God who sent me here, not you!" (Genesis 45:8).

† *When I find myself in a place of deep suffering, I can trust that your sovereign hand is working behind the scenes, Lord. I can say to those who hurt me, "It was God who sent me here, not you!" And empowered by your Spirit, I can forgive.*

THE LORD IS MY SHEPHERD

When we read the Twenty-third Psalm, in which David wrote, "The LORD is my shepherd," we might think that David was writing from his personal knowledge of shepherding. But David was not the first person to call God his Shepherd. In fact, David was likely drawing on the words of Jacob, who at the end of his life said to Joseph's sons: "May the God before whom my grandfather Abraham and my father, Isaac, walked—the God who has been my shepherd all my life, to this very day, the Angel who has redeemed me from all harm—may he bless these boys" (Genesis 48:15-16).

Jacob had walked through many dark valleys—for the most part made dark by his own deceit. But at the end of his life, he could look back and rejoice that the Lord had been his Shepherd—pursuing him like a lost sheep, providing for him, caring for him. David, too, lived in a world full of dark valleys and sinister enemies. In Psalm 23, David was saying that, like Jacob, he had found himself in dark valleys and discovered there that the Lord was a shepherd to him. But while Jacob and David experienced the presence of the Lord as their Shepherd, protecting and caring for them, a far greater revelation of God as Shepherd was to come.

In Jesus we see the sacrificial nature of "the good shepherd" who "sacrifices his life for the sheep" (John 10:11). In Jesus we see the ongoing work of "the great Shepherd of the sheep" who will "equip you with all you need for doing his will" and "produce in you . . . every good thing that is pleasing to him" (Hebrews 13:20-21). In Jesus we see the generosity of our great Shepherd from whom we will receive "a crown of never-ending glory and honor" (1 Peter 5:4). We see the worthiness of our Shepherd—the "Lamb that looked as if it had been slaughtered," the Lamb who sits on the throne and gives us shelter so we will never again be hungry or thirsty or scorched by the heat of the sun. "For the Lamb on the throne will be their Shepherd" (Revelation 5:6; 7:15-17).

† *My good Shepherd, because I have you, I have all that I need. You lead me into rest and empower me. You guide me to live in ways that honor you. Even when I walk through darkness and difficulty, I don't have to be afraid, because I look up and find you right there. Your Cross has drawn me to you, and your Word keeps me close to you. You have invited me to feast on you, and you have poured out your Spirit on me. My life is overflowing with your goodness and mercy. Forever I will live safely within your fold.*

THE ONE TO WHOM THE SCEPTER BELONGS

When Jacob was near the end of his life, he summoned each of his twelve sons to his bedside, where he painted in broad strokes the future history of a nation yet to come into existence. In his blessing, he described how each son and his descendants would be a part of God's redemptive nation. And while God would work in and through all the tribes, the tribe of Judah would be preeminent in his saving purposes.

> Judah, my son, is a young lion
>> that has finished eating its prey.
> Like a lion he crouches and lies down;
>> like a lioness—who dares to rouse him?
> The scepter will not depart from Judah,
>> nor the ruler's staff from his descendants,
> until the coming of the one to whom it belongs,
>> the one whom all nations will honor. (Genesis 49:9-10)

God chose Judah's descendants as the tribe through whom the Messiah would come. The psalmist wrote, "[The Lord] rejected Joseph's descendants; he did not choose the tribe of Ephraim. He chose instead the tribe of Judah, and Mount Zion, which he loved" (Psalm 78:67-68). Matthew noted what we might think would have disqualified Judah from such an honor. In listing Judah's place in the ancestry of Jesus (1:2-3), Matthew included a reminder of the sin Judah committed with Tamar by naming her as the mother of Judah's son.

It has always been God's way to choose to use the weak, the foolish, the imperfect—even the shamefully sinful but ultimately repentant—in his redemptive plan. It is his glory to do so, and it will be into eternity. We see this pattern in Revelation 5:5, where John described the resurrected and ascended Jesus as "the Lion of the tribe of Judah." This Lion is perfect and sinless, but he is still marked by weakness. John's Lion is also "a Lamb that looked as if it had been slaughtered" (Revelation 5:6). This Lion-Lamb alone is worthy to sit on the throne. He is the One to whom the scepter belongs, the One worthy of blessing and honor and glory and power forever and ever.

† *Lion of the tribe of Judah, I see in you that there is hope for one like me who has failed and been forgiven. Your roar overcomes the evil that would damn me forever, and now I may worship you around your throne forever.*

PEOPLE FROM EVERY TRIBE

The twelve sons of Israel (Jacob) were Reuben, Simeon, Levi, Judah, Dan, Naphtali, Gad, Asher, Issachar, Zebulun, Joseph, and Benjamin. These were the ancestors of the original twelve tribes—ethnic Israel, the people of God, the recipients of all the promises of God.

Significantly, when Jesus began his ministry, he chose twelve men to be his disciples. Matthew listed them as Simon (also called Peter), Andrew, James and John (sons of Zebedee), Philip, Bartholomew, Thomas, Matthew, James, Thaddaeus, Simon (the zealot), and Judas Iscariot (Matthew 10:2-4). By choosing twelve disciples, Jesus not only signaled his mission to Israel but also indicated that he was raising up a new people to displace the nation that would reject him and his message. He told his disciples, "I assure you that when the world is made new and the Son of Man sits upon his glorious throne, you who have been my followers will also sit on twelve thrones, judging the twelve tribes of Israel" (Matthew 19:28). In other words, Jesus' disciples would be the leaders of the true remnant of God's people, who by embracing Jesus would bring judgment to all who had the advantages of the promises and yet rejected Christ.

Those represented by the twelve tribes and those represented by the twelve apostles unite in the church. In Revelation 21, the apostle John describes the ultimate gathering of all of God's people in the new Jerusalem. John describes twelve gates to the holy city that comes down from heaven. The gates have the names of the twelve tribes of Israel written on them, pointing to the fact that the heavenly city is the true Israel, with its splendor far exceeding anything the prophets had seen. John also describes the foundations, which are inscribed with "the names of the twelve apostles of the Lamb." It is the saving work of Jesus Christ, witnessed by the twelve apostles, that provides the foundation to the city where God's people will live forever.

Our eternal home will be populated by the true Israel—the people of God who come from the twelve tribes and those taught by the twelve apostles. This includes all those in both the Old and the New Testament eras who responded to God by faith and whose spiritual origin rests exclusively in God's grace.

† *Jesus, you have established a new people for yourself—all those who believe the testimony of the Twelve who spoke of your saving work. This is the foundation of my life now as well as my eternal life.*

MARCH 14

GOD INTENDED
IT ALL FOR GOOD

"God intended it all for good." Joseph was betrayed by his brothers, imprisoned by Potiphar, and forgotten by Pharaoh's cup-bearer. They were each responsible for evil done to Joseph. Yet Joseph clearly saw God behind the suffering inflicted by his brothers when he said to them: "You intended to harm me, but God intended it all for good. He brought me to this position so I could save the lives of many people" (Genesis 50:20).

Joseph's recognition of God's invisible hand working behind the scenes to accomplish something good out of his suffering provides a picture of God's sovereignty in the Crucifixion, using the most significant evil and suffering of all time to accomplish the greatest good of all time. Perhaps this is the only way we can make sense of Isaiah's prophecy about Jesus: "It was the LORD's good plan to crush him and cause him grief" (53:10).

When we look at the Cross of Christ, we see the most innocent victim, the most immense suffering, the greatest injustice, the most hurtful betrayal, the greatest physical and emotional agony. Surely the Cross was the greatest evil of all time. Yet it was also the most precious gift God has ever given, the greatest good ever accomplished. Because of the Cross, we don't get what we deserve—punishment for our sin. Instead, we get what we don't deserve—the mercy and forgiveness of God.

Paul spoke of God's plan for Jesus' suffering, which he intended for good since before the world began. "I decided that while I was with you I would forget everything except Jesus Christ, the one who was crucified. . . . His plan . . . was previously hidden, even though he made it for our ultimate glory before the world began" (1 Corinthians 2:2, 7). Paul also assured us that God will also use *our* suffering for our good. "God causes everything to work together for the good of those who love God and are called according to his purpose for them" (Romans 8:28).

If God can use something as evil as the Cross of Christ for such amazing good, we can begin to believe that he can and will use what we might label as evil in our lives for our ultimate good.

† *Almighty God, I will keep believing that Romans 8:28 is really true—that you can and will use everything, no matter how dark, for my ultimate good, because I am yours.*

MARCH 15

A SAVIOR BORN UNDER SENTENCE OF DEATH

Moses was born under a sentence of death. Feeling threatened by the growing number of Hebrews, Pharaoh ordered that all Hebrew baby boys be killed at birth. But Moses' mother put him in a basket, which she hid in the reeds on the Nile River. The basket was found by Pharaoh's daughter, and Moses was saved from the slaughter. He was born to be a savior of his people, and nothing could stop God's plan. This child, once doomed to death by Pharaoh's decree, would become the very instrument of Pharaoh's destruction and the means through which all Israel would escape their slavery in Egypt.

But while Moses was a savior, he was not *the* Savior. He was simply a prototype of the Savior to come. "Jesus deserves far more glory than Moses, just as a person who builds a house deserves more praise than the house itself" (Hebrews 3:3).

Like Moses, Jesus was born under a sentence of death. Herod the Great, a tyrant as wicked as any of the Pharaohs, felt threatened by the prophecies of a king born in Bethlehem. So he issued a decree for all Jewish baby boys in Bethlehem to be killed. But like Moses, Jesus was saved from the slaughter. He was born to save his people, and nothing could stop God's plan. Jesus and his family escaped to Egypt and eventually were brought out of Egypt into the land of Israel. Matthew applied a statement about the Exodus of the children of Israel to Jesus: "This fulfilled what the Lord had spoken through the prophet: 'I called my Son out of Egypt'" (2:15).

In his deliverance from a violent death in infancy and his years of quiet training; in his willingness to leave the palace of a king to deliver his people from bondage; in his meekness, his faithfulness, and his commitment to finishing the work God gave him to do, Moses was a picture of the better Savior to come. But the picture fell short. Moses sinned under provocation; Christ was without sin. Moses was unable to bear the burdens of the people alone; Christ bore the burden of our sins in his own body on the tree. Moses was unable to die for the sins of the people; "Christ died for our sins according to the Scriptures" (1 Corinthians 15:3, NIV). Moses was unable to bring the people into the Promised Land; Christ is able to bring us into a permanent Promised Land. "Now all glory to God, who . . . will bring you with great joy into his glorious presence . . . through Jesus Christ our Lord" (Jude 1:24-25).

† *My Savior, born under sentence of death, you have made me alive and will deliver me safe into the joy of your presence for eternity.*

THE BURNING BUSH THAT WAS NOT CONSUMED

Moses was tending his father-in-law's flock in the wilderness and came to Sinai, which the Bible describes as "the mountain of God." God was there at that great mountain and appeared to Moses in all his living, burning presence: "The angel of the LORD appeared to him in a blazing fire from the middle of a bush. Moses stared in amazement. Though the bush was engulfed in flames, it didn't burn up. 'This is amazing,' Moses said to himself. 'Why isn't that bush burning up? I must go see it'" (Exodus 3:2-3).

Moses may have seen a bushfire or two during his travels in the wilderness. But as he watched this bush, he realized that it was different. Though it was burning, it was not burned up. It just kept burning. Before God told Moses who he was, he *showed* him who he was. The burning bush revealed the very being of God, who, in his eternity and self-sufficiency, burns but is not consumed. Most significantly, the burning bush revealed to Moses the utter holiness of God. Then God himself called to Moses from the middle of the bush: "'Do not come any closer,' the LORD warned. 'Take off your sandals, for you are standing on holy ground'" (Exodus 3:5).

Standing in the presence of the magnificent holy God, Moses realized that he was a thoroughly unholy man. He had to keep his distance, or the fire might have consumed him. Later Moses would write, "The LORD your God is a devouring fire" (Deuteronomy 4:24). Because of God's infinite holiness, there was no way a sinful man could come near. At least not until God—the same God who appeared as a burning bush—was "found in appearance as a man" (Philippians 2:8, NASB). God came near in the person of Jesus, who shared "the power of a life that cannot be destroyed" (Hebrews 7:16) so that we can draw near to him. Though we were unholy and far away from God, "yet now he has reconciled you to himself through the death of Christ in his physical body. As a result, he has brought you into his own presence, and you are holy and blameless as you stand before him without a single fault" (Colossians 1:22).

† *Eternal, self-existing One, you burn with jealous love, but you are not consumed. You died, yet you did not rot in the grave. You are holy, yet you humbled yourself to come to people as unholy as I, offering yourself to make me holy so that I can draw near to you.*

MARCH 17

OUR LIBERATOR FROM SLAVERY

The Egyptians made the Israelites their slaves. They appointed brutal slave drivers over them, hoping to wear them down with crushing labor. To be a slave was to have no rights, no freedom, no dignity. Exodus 2:23 says that the Israelites "continued to groan under their burden of slavery. They cried out for help, and their cry rose up to God." So God said to Moses from the burning bush, "I have certainly seen the oppression of my people in Egypt. I have heard their cries of distress because of their harsh slave drivers. Yes, I am aware of their suffering. So I have come down to rescue them from the power of the Egyptians and lead them out of Egypt into their own fertile and spacious land" (Exodus 3:7-8).

Later God reminded the people as they prepared to enter the Promised Land, "I am the LORD your God, who brought you out of the land of Egypt so you would no longer be their slaves. I broke the yoke of slavery from your neck so you can walk with your heads held high" (Leviticus 26:13).

It is interesting that many years later Isaiah spoke in future terms when he prophesied, "In that day the LORD will end the bondage of his people. He will break the yoke of slavery and lift it from their shoulders" (Isaiah 10:27). Hadn't the Lord already done that?

In reality, the deliverance of the Israelites from their bondage to slavery in Egypt was not a one-time event but a model event. God's deliverance of his people from slavery to the Egyptians through his servant Moses served as a model or prefigurement of God's deliverance of his people from slavery to sin through his servant Jesus.

Jesus said, "I tell you the truth, everyone who sins is a slave of sin. A slave is not a permanent member of the family, but a son is part of the family forever. So if the Son sets you free, you are truly free" (John 8:34-36). While Moses led his people out of bondage to Egypt, the greater Moses, the greater Liberator, Jesus, has freed us from bondage to sin. As God chose to rescue the Israelites from the power of the Egyptians, so he has come to rescue us from the clutches of sin and death through our liberator, Jesus Christ.

† *Thank you, Jesus, my Liberator, for freeing me from the chains of slavery to sin that have only brought me misery. I gladly take your chains that bind me to you and bring me joy and rest.*

MARCH 18

He Came Down

The figures of speech in the Bible always point to a literal reality. And the reality with God is that he comes to his people. He responds to our needs. He intervenes. We see it over and over in the Old Testament.

God came down to rescue his people from slavery: "I have come down to rescue them from the power of the Egyptians and lead them out of Egypt into their own fertile and spacious land" (Exodus 3:8).

He came down to reveal himself to Moses: "The LORD came down in a cloud and stood there with him; and he called out his own name, Yahweh" (Exodus 34:5).

He came down to fill the Holy of Holies with his glorious presence: "When all the people of Israel saw the fire coming down and the glorious presence of the LORD filling the Temple, they fell face down on the ground and worshiped and praised the LORD" (2 Chronicles 7:3).

All these ways God came down pointed toward his coming down in the flesh to live with us and walk among us. "No one has ever gone to heaven and returned. But the Son of Man has come down from heaven," Jesus said (John 3:13). "I am the bread that came down from heaven" (John 6:41).

When we are told that Jesus came down to earth, the "coming down" refers not to his physical descent, but to his lowering himself, humbling himself. "He came down to the lowest level" (Philippians 2:8, NIRV). Just as he came down to rescue his people from slavery, to reveal himself, and to fill the world with his glorious presence, he came down in Christ to rescue his people from slavery to sin, to reveal himself in human form, to fill the world with his glorious presence.

And he will come again to do it all once more in the final consummation of his Kingdom. "The Lord himself will come down from heaven with a commanding shout" (1 Thessalonians 4:16). When he comes again, he will come down for good. He will make his home with his people for all eternity.

† *You are the God who comes! You have not just made me and then left me on my own. You intervene. You reveal yourself. You come so that I can know you and enjoy your glorious presence. So come in all your fullness into my life and into my very being, and make yourself at home.*

I Am Who I Am

When the Israelites were enslaved in Egypt, God charged Moses to confront
Pharaoh and demand that he let God's people go. But Moses was not interested. He was alone in the wilderness tending sheep when God spoke to him,
and he was looking for any excuse to refuse God's command. "If I go to the
people of Israel and tell them, 'The God of your ancestors has sent me to
you,' they will ask me, 'What is his name?' Then what should I tell them?"
God's response was, "I Am Who I Am. Say this to the people of Israel: I Am
has sent me to you. . . . This is my eternal name, my name to remember for
all generations" (Exodus 3:13-15).

God revealed himself to Moses in a way he had never done before with
any other person. He told Moses his personal name. The name was so holy
to God's people that they wouldn't even say it out loud. So when a man
came along taking this name upon himself, they were justly offended. Jesus
said, "I tell you the truth, before Abraham was even born, I Am!" (John 8:58).

If Jesus had wanted to claim only that he existed before Abraham, it
would have been simpler to say, "Before Abraham was, I was." But he was
claiming far more than that. And clearly the people who heard him understood what he was saying, since they took up stones to kill him for what
they heard as a blasphemous claim to deity.

Jesus, the "I Am," took these two words upon himself as his deepest identity—the ultimate expression of who he is. He took upon himself
the most divine name of God, saying, "That is *my* name: I Am."

God has always wanted his people to know him—not in a generic or
shallow way, but personally, as he truly is. So he has revealed himself, not
only through his name, but also through his glorious presence, through
the Law, and through his mighty deeds on behalf of his people. But these
revelations all led up to a definitive revelation in the person of Jesus. "Long
ago God spoke many times and in many ways to our ancestors through the
prophets. And now in these final days, he has spoken to us through his Son"
(Hebrews 1:1-2). The Son shares not only his nature but also his name.

† *Great I Am, there is no other God besides you. I stand amazed that you
have seen fit to reveal yourself to me.*

MARCH 20
HE REVEALS
GOD'S OWN NATURE

The people of Jesus' day thought they knew what God was like. The stories of the patriarchs, the demands of the law, the rituals of the Temple, and the preaching of the prophets had shaped their picture of God. The picture they had wasn't complete and had little detail or clarity.

Jesus brought clarity to what was unclear. He filled in the gaps about what God was like. In some ways, he finished the sentence that God had begun when he gave his name to Moses, saying, "I AM WHO I AM" (Exodus 3:14). Jesus said:

I am the living bread that came down from heaven. (John 6:51)

I am the light of the world. (John 8:12)

I am the gate. (John 10:9)

I am the good shepherd. (John 10:11)

I am the resurrection and the life. (John 11:25)

I am the way, the truth, and the life. (John 14:6)

I am the true grapevine. (John 15:1)

In a sevenfold series of progressive clarity, Jesus uttered the most concise and comprehensive expression of his character, his purpose, and his provision. And in telling us who *he* is, Jesus also told us important things about who *we* are. He showed us our need for him. Without him we starve spiritually. Without him we struggle in the darkness, which is anywhere he is not. Without him we have no protection from the forces of evil, no provision for our needs, no guidance for our future. Without him we have no hope beyond the grave, no knowledge of what is true, no source or security. Jesus said, "Unless you believe that I AM who I claim to be, you will die in your sins" (John 8:24).

✝ *Great I AM in the flesh, I see that you are everything I need. I want to feed on you, live in your light, enter into you, depend on you, live through the power of your unstoppable life, walk in your way, and be connected to you in a life-giving way. Who you are is everything to me.*

MARCH 21
ROD OF GOD

During his years as a shepherd in Midian, Moses had picked up a rod of wood. It was a long stick that he used as a shepherd's staff, a walking stick, and possibly even a weapon. Though it was an ordinary and unremarkable stick, God intended to use it in the hands of his servant to convince the Israelites that God had sent him to be their deliverer.

The LORD asked him, "What is that in your hand?"

"A shepherd's staff," Moses replied.

"Throw it down on the ground," the LORD told him. So Moses threw down the staff, and it turned into a snake! Moses jumped back.

Then the LORD told him, "Reach out and grab its tail." So Moses reached out and grabbed it, and it turned back into a shepherd's staff in his hand.

"Perform this sign," the LORD told him. "Then they will believe that the LORD, the God of their ancestors—the God of Abraham, the God of Isaac, and the God of Jacob—really has appeared to you." (Exodus 4:2-5)

Later Moses waved this rod over the Nile and saw it turn to blood. He stretched it over the streams, and frogs came up on the land. He struck the dust, and gnats came up from it. He raised his staff over the Red Sea to divide the water for the Israelites to pass through.

While this rod of God wielded the power of God to bring deliverance to his people, it was only a preview of how God would use another rod, in the person of Jesus, to bring a greater deliverance. Like Moses' rod, Jesus was ordinary and unimpressive. He was cast down on the ground, became a curse for us (Galatians 3:10-13), and then was restored.

And God is not finished working through his rod, Jesus Christ. Dictating a letter to John for the church in Thyatira, Jesus recalled the words of the psalmist: "You will break them with an iron rod and smash them like clay pots" (Revelation 2:27). Jesus is the rod of God who not only saves those who belong to God but also smashes those who reject God.

† *Rod of God, you wield the power in this world to deliver or demolish, to protect or plague, to comfort or cast away. How grateful I am that because I am yours, you use your power not against me, but for me.*

MARCH 22

FIRSTBORN SON

In God's instructions to Moses we see the heart of a Father who longs to be with his child. God commanded Moses to say these words when confronting Pharaoh: "This is what the LORD says: Israel is my firstborn son. I commanded you, 'Let my son go, so he can worship me'" (Exodus 4:22-23).

Here we see why God cared about what happened to the Israelites, why—out of all the nations of the world—he went to the trouble of rescuing them from slavery. The loving Father wanted to rescue his children so they could be together with him as a family. Later God described his longing through his prophet Hosea: "When Israel was a child, I loved him, and I called my son out of Egypt" (11:1).

But God's son Israel always proved a disappointment. God's son grumbled and complained and rejected the Father who loved him. The people of Israel simply couldn't live up to their Father's standard. Another Son was needed who would do his Father's business, accomplish his Father's purpose, display his Father's likeness, and demonstrate his Father's love.

From his earliest days, Jesus seemed to understand his unique purpose, as well as his unique relationship, as God's Son. When Jesus' parents found him lingering in the synagogue at age twelve, he said, "Did you not know that I must be about My Father's business?" (Luke 2:49, NKJV). Jesus was everything God had ever wanted in a Son. In his perfect obedience to his Father, he did what Israel could never do.

And because of what the Son of God accomplished in his obedience at the Cross, everyone who comes to him in faith becomes a true child of God. Paul called Jesus "the firstborn among many brothers" (Romans 8:29), because every believer is a child of God. Paul wrote to the Galatians, "You are all children of God through faith in Christ Jesus" (3:26).

God sent his Son to rescue us so we can one day be together as a family. "He died for sinners to bring you safely home to God" (1 Peter 3:18).

† *My loving Father, you have rescued me so we can be together as a family! I know the day is coming when, because of what your beloved Son has done, we will all be together in the place you are preparing for us. Rescued from this world. Safe with you. At home.*

MARCH 23

MIRACLES OF JUDGMENT, SIGNS OF MERCY

God's judgment against Egypt and her gods came in the form of ten plagues: blood, frogs, gnats, flies, disease, boils, hail, locusts, darkness, and death. One by one through the ten plagues, God defeated the gods and goddesses of Egypt (Exodus 12:12). The Egyptians worshiped the Nile River and called it "the father of the gods." The first plague, therefore, was blood in the Nile River. The Egyptians worshiped cows, so cattle disease was brought on the land. They even worshiped the sun, so the ninth plague brought darkness over the land.

The plagues were miracles of judgment. They are often referred to as signs—signs that showed the world that God is God and must be worshiped as God. Similarly, Jesus performed miracles throughout his ministry, which John called "signs" throughout his Gospel. But these were miracles of mercy, not judgment.

But while the plagues on the Egyptians showed that worship of the created order brings God's judgment, Jesus' miracles showed that with the Lord, all that is deadly in creation—illness, demonic forces, nature run amok, and even death itself—can be overcome by life. Jesus' signs were purely redemptive in focus. They showed that he had come not to judge but to save, not to express the wrath of God but to show the love of God (John 3:16-18; 12:47). As Jesus healed the disabled, fed the hungry, and raised the dead, he transformed and transcended the signs in Exodus. Water was turned into wine rather than blood. Instead of inflicting disease, Jesus healed disease and disfigurement. While the final plague in Exodus was the death of the firstborn, one of the final signs of Jesus recorded in the book of John was the raising of Lazarus to life.

Sadly, just as most of the Egyptians refused to worship God even though they'd seen his power in the plagues, most of the Israelites also refused to embrace Jesus. John wrote, "Despite all the miraculous signs Jesus had done, most of the people still did not believe in him" (John 12:37).

But some saw the signs and embraced the One they pointed to. "To all who received him, to those who believed in his name, he gave the right to become children of God" (John 1:12, NIV).

† *I see the signs that point to you, Jesus. In them I see your power and your compassion. Because I see the signs, I don't have to live in fear of your judgment. I can rest in your mercy and grace.*

MARCH 24

DEATH OF THE FIRSTBORN

Surely the most devastating plague of the ten that God brought on Egypt was the death of the firstborn. He warned, "Every firstborn son in Egypt will die, from the firstborn son of Pharaoh, who sits on the throne, to the firstborn son of the slave girl, who is at her hand mill, and all the firstborn of the cattle as well" (Exodus 11:5, NIV).

How could God bring about such a terrible plague? If we look at the whole story in the book of Exodus, we see that Pharaoh had issued a decree that all male Hebrew babies be killed. The Hebrew midwives were ordered to kill them immediately upon birth. So there was justice in this punishing plague.

But while we may be able to accept that God would punish the Egyptians with the death of their firstborn sons, it seems surprising that the Israelites were under the same sentence of death. The same night God brought death to every house in Egypt, he also visited the home of every Israelite family with the purpose of killing their firstborn sons.

All the previous plagues had left the Israelites unscathed. While chaos engulfed their oppressors, the Israelites watched from the safety of Goshen. While they might have thought that God was protecting them because they were more righteous than the Egyptians, this final plague made it clear that they, too, were sinners deserving death.

But while God justly delivered judgment, in his great mercy he also provided a way for his people to escape death. He told them to "slaughter their lamb . . . [and] take some of the blood and smear it on the sides and top of the doorframes of the houses. . . . When he sees the blood on the top and sides of the doorframe, the LORD will pass over your home. He will not permit his death angel to enter your house and strike you down" (Exodus 12:6-7, 23).

Though they deserved divine judgment, the firstborn Israelites were saved by grace through faith as they placed the blood of a lamb over their doorposts. Though there was no way they could see clearly what this pictured, they put the blood of the lamb over their doors in faith. God would one day offer the blood of his own firstborn as a sacrifice for sin. The death angel would not pass over him but strike him down.

† *Firstborn over all creation, because your blood was shed, the death angel cannot take my life from me. Your blood painted across my life marks me as forgiven, justified, saved, secure.*

MARCH 25

I WILL PASS OVER YOU

God was preparing to rain down his final judgment on the Egyptians, causing the death of the firstborn son in every home. But God also provided a way to be protected from this storm of death:

> On that night I will pass through the land of Egypt and strike down every firstborn son and firstborn male animal in the land of Egypt. . . . But the blood on your doorposts will serve as a sign, marking the houses where you are staying. When I see the blood, I will pass over you. (Exodus 12:12-13)

When God said he would "pass over" the houses marked by the blood of a lamb, it meant more than merely skipping over something to avoid contact. The Hebrew word used here means spreading the wings over and protecting. It tells us that God not only passed by the houses of Israelites but stood on guard, protecting those behind blood-marked doorways.

God established the feast of Passover to celebrate the protection he provided. He gave detailed instructions for the feast and the lamb that would be sacrificed, but it was not just so the people would look *back* and remember his provision of protection but also so they would look *forward* to his fuller provision of ultimate protection to come in Christ. All along, God intended to show us his mercy through "Christ, our Passover Lamb, [who] has been sacrificed for us" (1 Corinthians 5:7).

The Passover lamb chosen for the Israelites' feast had to be a choice male lamb in the prime of his life; Jesus was in the prime of his life as well: "Jesus was about thirty years old when he began his public ministry" (Luke 3:23). The lamb had to be physically flawless; Christ was "the sinless, spotless Lamb of God" (1 Peter 1:19). The Passover lamb had to be slain; Jesus, too, was "slaughtered, and [his] blood has ransomed people for God" (Revelation 5:9). The bones of the lamb could not be broken; when Jesus was crucified, "they saw that he was already dead, so they didn't break his legs" (John 19:33). John the Baptist saw Jesus as the Lamb from the very beginning, saying when he saw Jesus walking toward him, "Look! The Lamb of God who takes away the sin of the world!" (John 1:29).

† *God of wrath and mercy, see the precious blood of the Lamb of God covering my life, and pass over me. The blood of your own Son has written across my life: protected, covered, paid for, marked as mine.*

MARCH 26

CHRIST, OUR PASSOVER LAMB

Each spring people from all over the country would go to Jerusalem to sacrifice a lamb for the Passover feast. The day Jesus made his triumphal entry into Jerusalem was the very day herds of Passover lambs were being driven into the city. Later that week Jesus told his disciples, "As you know, Passover begins in two days, and the Son of Man will be handed over to be crucified" (Matthew 26:2). Ever since John the Baptist identified Jesus as the "Lamb of God," all of Jesus' ministry had been driving toward this day, this celebration of Passover, when Christ, "our Passover Lamb" (1 Corinthians 5:7), would be sacrificed.

God had given very specific instructions about the celebration of Passover and the lamb that would be slain for the feast:

> On the tenth day of this month each man is to take a lamb for his family. . . . The animals you choose must be year-old males without defect. . . . All the people of the community of Israel must slaughter them at twilight. . . . Eat the meat roasted over the fire, along with bitter herbs, and bread made without yeast. . . . Do not break any of the bones." (Exodus 12:3, 5-6, 8, 46, NIV)

The Passover sacrifice was to be a lamb free from all defects. Peter wrote that Christ was "a lamb without blemish or defect" (1 Peter 1:19, NIV). The lamb was to be slain by "all the people of the community of Israel," and though Jesus was condemned by Pilate, the Roman governor, it was the Jews who plotted and pleaded for his crucifixion. The paschal lamb was to be slain publicly. So Christ was put to death in the most public and ignominious way, crucified on a hill within sight of Jerusalem at the very time huge crowds were there to witness the scene.

No bones in the paschal lamb were to be broken. When the Roman soldiers came to break the bones of those crucified, they discovered that Jesus had already died, and so none of his bones were broken. The paschal lamb was to be roasted with fire. Christ, too, experienced the fire of God's wrath— intense and consuming.

✝ *Jesus, my Passover Lamb, you were slain not only for sacrifice but also for food. And unless I eat of your flesh, I have no part of your life, no protection from the fires of judgment. So I will gladly feed on you.*

MARCH 27
WE SAVOR HIS
DEATH AS OUR LIFE

God gave strict instructions about how the Passover lamb was to be eaten:

Roast the meat over a fire and eat it along with bitter salad greens and bread made without yeast. Do not eat any of the meat raw or boiled in water. The whole animal—including the head, legs, and internal organs—must be roasted over a fire. Do not leave any of it until the next morning. Burn whatever is not eaten before morning. (Exodus 12:8-10)

By ingesting the whole offering, the Israelites made total identification with the sacrifice God provided for their salvation. They took it in personally, completely. It became nourishment that sustained and satisfied them.

Just as the Passover lamb had to be eaten, so Christ, our Passover Lamb, needs to be eaten. Jesus said,

I tell you the truth, unless you eat the flesh of the Son of Man and drink his blood, you cannot have eternal life within you. But anyone who eats my flesh and drinks my blood has eternal life, and I will raise that person at the last day. For my flesh is true food, and my blood is true drink. Anyone who eats my flesh and drinks my blood remains in me, and I in him. (John 6:53-56)

In his Passion, Jesus' flesh was ripped and pierced; his blood flowed. By inviting us to eat of his flesh and drink of his blood, he's pointing us to the life-giving nourishment of his death. It is only as we partake of his death on our behalf that we become united with him in that death. This is the feast of salvation that we cannot merely admire. We must eat.

It isn't enough for the wine to be poured and the bread to be broken. It isn't enough that Jesus died. We must savor his death as our life, or we will never know what it means to live. It's not enough to be inspired by Jesus' beautiful life; we have to find a feast of satisfaction in his death.

† *Feast for my soul, I cannot afford to simply nibble at your teaching or feebly try to follow your example. I must partake of your death. So I come to your table with an aching hunger in my soul and partake of the feast of your dying sacrifice. This is salvation—the salvation feast in which I take your life into mine and live.*

THE UNLEAVENED BREAD

Passover was followed by the Feast of Unleavened Bread, which lasted for an entire week. The regulations for this feast were very specific: "Celebrate this Festival of Unleavened Bread, for it will remind you that I brought your forces out of the land of Egypt on this very day. . . . During those seven days, there must be no trace of yeast in your homes. . . . During those days you must not eat anything made with yeast" (Exodus 12:17, 19-20).

While unleavened bread reminded the Israelites of their hasty departure from Egypt, the command to get rid of yeast had another purpose. Jewish teachers had always understood yeast to represent the corrupting power of sin. As yeast ferments, it works its way all through the dough. Sin works the same way. It is always seeking to extend its corrupting influence through a person's entire life. For the Hebrews, putting away all the leaven symbolized breaking the old cycle of sin and starting out afresh from Egypt to walk as a new nation before the Lord.

When Jesus shared the Passover meal with his disciples the night he was arrested, "he took some bread and gave thanks to God for it. Then he broke it in pieces and gave it to the disciples, saying, 'This is my body, which is given for you. Do this to remember me'" (Luke 22:19).

Were their eyes opened that night to the significance of the unleavened bread they had eaten year after year during Passover? Jesus made it clear that the bread—made of pure grain untouched by yeast—was a foreshadowing of his sinless and incorruptible life. The practice of breaking the bread symbolized his broken body on the cross. The second piece of bread, which was traditionally wrapped in a linen cloth, hidden, and later brought back to the table, symbolized Jesus' body, wrapped in linen grave clothes, hidden in the tomb for three days, and resurrected. Christ not only had no corruption in his character, his physical body did not experience the ravages of death while in the grave. "[God] will not . . . allow [his] Holy One to rot in the grave" (Acts 2:27). It is his sinless life we feast on and his nature we partake of to escape the corruption of sin.

† *Sinless Bread of heaven, you brought the perfection of heaven into the corruption of this world. By your incorruptible life, you defeated the power of sin to damn my life through its corruption. Lord, as I feast on your life, your body, I find myself wanting to sweep sin out of my life and escape the corruption of this world.*

MARCH 29

A FEAST TO REMEMBER HIS DELIVERANCE FROM DEATH

When God gave Moses the instructions for the Passover meal, he made it clear that this was a feast they would celebrate annually to remember how God delivered them from their slavery in Egypt:

> This is a day to remember. Each year, from generation to generation, you must celebrate it as a special festival to the LORD. . . . When you enter the land the LORD has promised to give you, you will continue to observe this ceremony. Then your children will ask, "What does this ceremony mean?" And you will reply, "It is the Passover sacrifice to the LORD, for he passed over the houses of the Israelites in Egypt. And though he struck the Egyptians, he spared our families." (Exodus 12:14, 25-27)

Just as God gave his people a feast to remember his deliverance from death in the Passover, so Jesus instituted a feast to help us remember his deliverance from death through the Cross. He gave us this gospel feast when he celebrated Passover with his disciples for the last time and turned this Old Covenant celebration that looked back to the Exodus into a New Covenant celebration that would look back to the Cross:

> When the hour came, Jesus and his apostles reclined at the table. And he said to them, "I have eagerly desired to eat this Passover with you before I suffer. . . ."
> And he took bread, gave thanks and broke it, and gave it to them, saying, "This is my body given for you; do this in remembrance of me."
> In the same way, after the supper he took the cup, saying, "This cup is the new covenant in my blood, which is poured out for you." (Luke 22:14-15, 19-20, NIV)

In the Last Supper, Jesus endowed the Feast of the Passover with new meaning. Instead of celebrating God's past redemption, these elements now symbolized the redemption of Jesus Christ. He is the Lamb without defect. He is the broken Bread. He is the Cup of redemption. He is the One who has delivered us from the slavery of sin.

† *As I eat the bread and drink the cup of your supper, I do remember, Lord. I remember the beauty and perfection of your sacrifice. I remember the sufficiency of your blood. I remember that I am no longer a slave to sin. You have delivered me from its death.*

PILLAR OF CLOUD BY DAY, PILLAR OF FIRE BY NIGHT

When God brought his people out of Egypt, they didn't march directly into the Promised Land. Instead, they wandered in the desert for forty years. But they did not wander aimlessly or alone.

> The LORD was going before them in a pillar of cloud by day to lead them on the way, and in a pillar of fire by night to give them light, that they might travel by day and by night. He did not take away the pillar of cloud by day, nor the pillar of fire by night, from before the people. (Exodus 13:21-22, NASB)

This was no ordinary cloud in the sky. It was the visible manifestation of God's personal presence with them. He was there to guide them and pro-tect them in the form of this column of cloud. When the cloud moved, the people followed it. When it stopped, everybody stopped. The pillar of cloud by day changed to a pillar of fire at night. All night long the radiance from that cloud brightly illuminated the entire camp so that no night ever touched them.

Perhaps the Pharisees saw this connection when Jesus stood up in the Temple and said, "I am the light of the world. If you follow me, you won't have to walk in darkness, because you will have the light that leads to life" (John 8:12). Jesus had come to be a physical and personal manifestation of the presence of God in their midst; he was there to lead the people to the Promised Land of God's presence. But the Pharisees did not want to follow. They wanted to put out his light.

As we make our way in this world, we may long to have something as visible and tangible as a pillar of cloud or fire to show us when to move and where to go. But Jesus left us with something better—Someone far better—to guide us. Jesus promised, "When the Spirit of truth comes, he will guide you into all truth. . . . He lives with you now and later will be in you" (John 16:13; 14:17). The Holy Spirit is the column of cloud and fire sent to guide us, not from the sky around us, but from inside us.

† *Pillar of cloud and fire, you guide me by your Spirit. He guides me into truth as he illumines your Word and makes it understandable and unavoidable. I cannot make it through the wilderness of the world without your personal presence, and I would never want to be without you. Guide me. Illumine my path. Lead me through the wilderness to your Promised Land.*

MARCH 31

He Makes a Way for Us to Pass through Death

Guided by the pillar of cloud away from Egypt, the Israelites found themselves in a very vulnerable position—trapped between the impassable sea to the east, the mountains to the south and west, and Pharaoh's armies to the north.

> Moses told the people, "Don't be afraid. Just stand still and watch the LORD rescue you today. The Egyptians you see today will never be seen again. The LORD himself will fight for you. Just stay calm." . . .
>
> Then Moses raised his hand over the sea, and the LORD opened up a path through the water with a strong east wind. The wind blew all that night, turning the seabed into dry land. So the people of Israel walked through the middle of the sea on dry ground, with walls of water on each side! (Exodus 14:13-14, 21-22)

God had shown himself as Redeemer when his people were purchased out of Egypt by the blood of the Passover lamb. Now God showed himself as Savior as he demonstrated his power, ushering his people through the clutches of death.

In opening up the Red Sea to make a way through death for his people, God was showing how he would miraculously make a way through death for all those who come to him by faith through his Son, Jesus. Just as God destroyed the power of Pharaoh over the Israelites at the Red Sea, so the resurrection of Jesus broke the power of Satan over his people. And just as the sea the people feared became the means of their deliverance from the Egyptians, so the physical death we fear becomes the means of our deliverance into the Promised Land of God's presence. We need not fear physical death. Our Deliverer has raised his rod, and we can pass through on dry ground, unscathed. He is with us, getting us safely to the other side.

But we pass through on dry ground only because the waves of death flooded in on Christ at the Cross. The deep waters of death covered him, yet he emerged alive. In so doing, he made a way for us to pass through death.

† *When I come to my own Red Sea of death, may I look back and remember your sure and safe deliverance. May I look forward to the Promised Land of your presence, confident that you will bring me safely to the other side.*

APRIL 1
THE LORD WILL FIGHT FOR YOU

The Hebrew slaves didn't win their own liberation. It was initiated and accomplished by God.

The Israelites left Egypt burdened down by children, cattle, and cartloads of household goods. Meanwhile, Egypt's war chariots mobilized and quickly hemmed them in against the shore of the Red Sea. The Israelites were ready to give up and go back. "Why did you bring us out here to die in the wilderness?" they complained to Moses and Aaron. "Weren't there enough graves for us in Egypt? What have you done to us? Why did you make us leave Egypt?" (Exodus 14:11).

That's when Moses told them, "Stand still and watch the LORD rescue you today. The Egyptians you see today will never be seen again. The LORD himself will fight for you. Just stay calm" (Exodus 14:13-14). God himself, in the pillar of fire and cloud, drove back the Egyptians and held them at bay. Then God opened the sea so Israel could pass over on dry ground. The Egyptians attempted to pursue them but were destroyed by the returning waves.

On the far side of the sea Moses and the Israelites sang to Yahweh:

I will sing to the LORD,
    for he has triumphed gloriously;
he has hurled both horse and rider
    into the sea.
The LORD is my strength and my song;
    he has given me victory. (Exodus 15:1-2)

The Israelites' song of celebration was not about their own strength or cunning or accomplishment but about the victory accomplished by God and granted to them. Israel's great deliverance was God's work, not theirs.

In the same way, our deliverance is God's work. It's not something we do on our own or even contribute to! He comes to us and in spite of us; he saves us and leads us out of a life of slavery to sin into the Promised Land of his presence. "Thank God! He gives us victory over sin and death through our Lord Jesus Christ" (1 Corinthians 15:57).

† *My strong Deliverer, you have fought for me and delivered me from everything that seeks to enslave me. Keep me from longing to return to my old ways of alienation that only enslaved me and burdened me. Put your song of celebration on my lips and in my heart, and I will sing.*

APRIL 2

THE SONG OF
MOSES AND OF THE LAMB

Immediately after the children of Israel crossed through the sea on dry ground and Pharaoh's army was destroyed by the waters of judgment, Moses led the people in singing a song of deliverance:

> The LORD is a warrior;
>   Yahweh is his name!
> Pharaoh's chariots and army
>   he has hurled into the sea.
> The finest of Pharaoh's officers
>   are drowned in the Red Sea.
> The deep waters gushed over them;
>   they sank to the bottom like a stone. . . .
> The power of your arm
>   makes them lifeless as stone
> until your people pass by, O LORD. . . .
> You will bring them in and plant them on your own mountain—
>   the place, O LORD, reserved for your own dwelling,
>   the sanctuary, O LORD, that your hands have established.
> The LORD will reign forever and ever! (Exodus 15:3-5, 16-18)

This celebratory song was really only a foretaste of a coming day when this song of Moses will be sung again. Revelation 15 says that God's people will once again sing the song of Moses, but at that time it will combine with "the song of the Lamb." This new song will tell of a greater redemption for all of those who have placed their trust in the greater Moses, and the final destruction of all God's enemies—all who would harm and enslave his people.

Just as the Israelites praised God for who he is and what he had done as they stood safely on the other side of the Red Sea, so will all of God's children—gathered safely on the other side of this earthly existence—sing this song. Gathered around the throne of heaven, all who have been rescued from slavery to sin, all who have put their faith in the blood of the Passover Lamb, will sing into eternity with joy.

† *Yours is the song I want to sing, Lamb of God. My heart nearly bursts with anticipation of singing that song with all who have been redeemed! We'll finally be safe. Satan will have been destroyed. Your victory will be complete.*

APRIL 3
HE MAKES THE BITTER SWEET

The children of Israel walked out of Egypt and away from bitter slavery and hardship. But their songs of joy quickly turned into a chorus of complaint. "They traveled in this desert for three days without finding any water. When they came to the oasis of Marah, the water was too bitter to drink" (Exodus 15:22-23).

But God had not brought them this far to allow them to die of thirst in the desert. "So Moses cried out to the LORD for help, and the LORD showed him a piece of wood. Moses threw it into the water, and this made the water good to drink" (Exodus 15:25).

Just as God had cursed Egypt and made their drinkable water undrinkable by turning it into blood, the first miracle in the wilderness was to make this undrinkable desert water drinkable. Here we see the pattern of how God turns blessing into a curse for those who hate him, and turns a curse into blessing for those on whom he has set his love.

The woman at the well thought that she was cursed, not only by her race but also by her five failed marriages (John 4). She came to the well to quench her physical thirst, not knowing that Jesus waited for her with the promise of turning the bitterness of her life into sweet joy.

> [Jesus said to her,] "If you only knew the gift God has for you and who you are speaking to, you would ask me, and I would give you living water."
>
> "But sir, you don't have a rope or a bucket," she said, "and this well is very deep. Where would you get this living water?" . . .
>
> Jesus replied, "Anyone who drinks this water will soon become thirsty again. But those who drink the water I give will never be thirsty again. It becomes a fresh, bubbling spring within them, giving them eternal life." (John 4:10-11, 13-14)

It was not a piece of wood thrown down into the well that would make it possible for Jesus to offer this living water. It was a cross of wood on which Jesus would be lifted up. There he would experience the desperate thirst we deserve to experience forever so that he might be to us a fresh, bubbling spring.

† *Sweetness of God, Water of life, your Cross turns the bitterness in my life to sweetness. Your Cross is the remedy for the bitterness of my own bad choices, filling my life with a fresh, bubbling spring of life.*

APRIL 4
The Lord Who Heals

When the bitter water of Marah was healed (made sweet and drinkable) at God's command, God made the incident a sign of his covenant promise and a further revelation of his nature: "If you will listen carefully to the voice of the LORD your God and do what is right in his sight, obeying his commands and keeping all his decrees, then I will not make you suffer any of the diseases I sent on the Egyptians; for I am the LORD who heals you" (Exodus 15:26).

Healing is not just an activity that God chooses to do or not do. Healing is who he *is*; it is his very nature, reflected in his name. But while God is the Healer of his people, this healing will primarily be accomplished through his Anointed. During Jesus' three years of ministry on the earth, he gave the world a glimpse of the complete healing God intends to bring about for all of his creation.

As Jesus moved from town to town performing many miraculous healings, word began to get around, and more and more people came to him in search of his healing touch. But his healing ministry was not merely about healing people physically; in fact, every healing miracle pointed to Jesus' ability to heal our deeper spiritual sickness of sin.

When Jesus said to the blind man, "Go, for your faith has healed you" (Mark 10:52), it showed that he can remove the spiritual ignorance that keeps us from seeing who he really is. When he healed the man who had been demon possessed (Mark 5:19), he showed that he can free us from enslaving, dominating sin. When Jesus said to the paralyzed man, "Be encouraged, my child! Your sins are forgiven" (Matthew 9:2), he showed that he can take away the sin that cripples and incapacitates us. When he healed the woman who had hemorrhaged for twelve years (Mark 5:34), he showed that he can stop the waste of spiritual power and life. When Jesus said to the ears and mouth of the deaf and mute man, "Be opened!" (Mark 7:34), he showed that he can overcome our inability or refusal to hear from God and speak for God. And when Jesus brought Lazarus out of the tomb (John 11), he showed that he brings back to life what sin has put to death, just by the power of his word.

Through his healing ministry, Jesus showed that he indeed was the same God who identified himself to Moses and his people as, "I am the LORD who heals you."

† *O Lord who heals, I am sick with sin and desperate for your healing touch. Without it, I will surely die. Touch me and heal me.*

APRIL 5

TRUE BREAD FROM HEAVEN

It was a month after the children of Israel had left Egypt, and their food supplies had run out. Hunger pangs pushed the people to complain:

> "If only the LORD had killed us back in Egypt," they moaned. "There we sat around pots filled with meat and ate all the bread we wanted. But now you have brought us into this wilderness to starve us all to death."
> Then the LORD said to Moses, "Look, I'm going to rain down food from heaven for you. Each day the people can go out and pick up as much food as they need for that day." (Exodus 16:3-4)

For the next forty years, God fed his people in this way—six days a week, manna fell from heaven, as much as they could eat. The manna taught Israel to depend on God for all their needs. But manna did have certain limitations. It was only bread, so it could only meet physical needs, and only for a little while. The people got hungry again. This bread could not give them any lasting satisfaction. But it did teach them to look to God for their sustenance and salvation until he sent the true and living bread from heaven. That bread came in the person and work of Jesus.

When Jesus fed more than five thousand people from one boy's meager lunch basket, the people began to wonder if Jesus was the Messiah, whom they expected would perform feeding miracles like Moses. But Jesus set them straight about the real source of the manna as well as what the manna pointed to:

> Jesus said, "I tell you the truth, Moses didn't give you bread from heaven. My Father did. And now he offers you the true bread from heaven. The true bread of God is the one who comes down from heaven and gives life to the world."
> "Sir," they said, "give us that bread every day."
> Jesus replied, "I am the bread of life. Whoever comes to me will never be hungry again." (John 6:32-35)

The manna God provided in the desert was perishable; it only lasted for a day. But the true Bread from heaven is imperishable. It lasts forever. It feeds and nourishes and sustains forever.

† *Bread from heaven, you alone are what I need, and unless I feed on you day by day, I will perish.*

APRIL 6

That Rock Was Christ

Once again, the Israelites were in the wilderness and out of water. And once again, they complained to Moses, or more accurately, complained *against* Moses. Moses seemed to have adopted their complaining tone when he turned to God saying, "What should I do with these people? They are ready to stone me!"

> The LORD said to Moses, "Walk out in front of the people. Take your staff, the one you used when you struck the water of the Nile, and call some of the elders of Israel to join you. I will stand before you on the rock at Mount Sinai. Strike the rock, and water will come gushing out. Then the people will be able to drink." So Moses struck the rock as he was told, and water gushed out as the elders looked on. (Exodus 17:5-7)

God had brought his people to this place in the desert to test them, to see if they would trust him to care for them and meet their needs. So their complaint against Moses was ultimately a complaint against God, and it amounted to putting God on trial. Guilty of unbelief and rebellion, they refused to trust in the faithfulness of God. But rather than punish them for their rebellious unbelief, God offered himself to endure the punishment they deserved. God, the Judge, stood on the rock—identified himself with the rock—and told Moses to strike the rock. He received the blow that their rebellion deserved, and in so doing, provided them with a gushing stream.

Paul recognized this Rock. He saw that it was, in fact, the Savior who was standing on the Rock, the One who was struck with the rod of God's justice in place of guilty people:

> I don't want you to forget, dear brothers and sisters, about our ancestors in the wilderness long ago. . . . They drank from the spiritual rock that traveled with them, and that rock was Christ. (1 Corinthians 10:1, 4)

Long ago in the desert, God showed his people not only how he would execute just judgment against sinful rebellion, but how he would provide the water of life that quenches our thirst. Christ is the Rock who was struck for us. From him flows living water.

† *Rock of Christ, smitten for me, Fountain opened for me, you submitted to the blow of God's justice so that out of you living water would flow to me.*

APRIL 7

EVERY KNEE
WILL BOW AT HIS NAME

Throughout the Old Testament, we see over and over the passion God has for his own name. When we read about God's "name," it refers to his glorious, excellent character—his glory gone public. In other words, the name of God often refers to his reputation, his fame, his renown.

One of the first times we see God's passion for his own name is in the story of the Exodus when he told Moses to tell Pharaoh: "I have spared you for a purpose—to show you my power and to spread my fame throughout the earth" (Exodus 9:16).

Because of his confidence in God's love for his own name, Samuel assured the Israelites of God's continued care after they sinned by demanding a king: "The LORD will not abandon his people, because that would dishonor his great name" (1 Samuel 12:22).

And through his prophet Isaiah, God said,

Let all the world look to me for salvation!
    For I am God; there is no other.
I have sworn by my own name;
    I have spoken the truth,
    and I will never go back on my word:
Every knee will bend to me,
    and every tongue will confess allegiance to me. (Isaiah 45:22-23)

Paul recognized that this prophecy of Isaiah spoke not only of God the Father, but also of God the Son:

God elevated him to the place of highest honor
    and gave him the name above all other names,
that at the name of Jesus every knee should bow,
    in heaven and on earth and under the earth,
and every tongue confess that Jesus Christ is Lord,
    to the glory of God the Father. (Philippians 2:9-11)

† *My tongue will confess that Jesus Christ is Lord to the glory of God the Father! May your fame spread throughout the earth! I will not dishonor you by misusing your name. May my life bring only honor to your great name.*

APRIL 8

HE HAS SPOKEN
THROUGH HIS SON

Moses climbed the mountain where God spoke to him, giving instructions for the children of Israel to keep his covenant. Then the Lord told Moses to bring the people themselves to the foot of the mountain so they could hear God speak to Moses. They came to the very place where God had spoken to Moses from the flaming bush. But this time, it wasn't just a bush on fire—the whole mountain was in flames.

> All of Mount Sinai was covered with smoke because the LORD had descended on it in the form of fire. The smoke billowed into the sky like smoke from a brick kiln, and the whole mountain shook violently. As the blast of the ram's horn grew louder and louder, Moses spoke, and God thundered his reply. (Exodus 19:18-19)

The author of Hebrews described the terror of this scene and contrasted it with the new way God's people hear his voice:

> You have not come to a physical mountain, to a place of flaming fire, darkness, gloom, and whirlwind, as the Israelites did at Mount Sinai. For they heard an awesome trumpet blast and a voice so terrible that they begged God to stop speaking. . . . No, you have come to Mount Zion, to the city of the living God, the heavenly Jerusalem. . . . You have come to Jesus. (Hebrews 12:18-19, 22, 24)

Like the Israelites who gathered at the foot of Mount Sinai, we too hear God's voice. "Now in these final days, he has spoken to us through his Son" (Hebrews 1:2). And just as the Israelites were warned to listen to and obey God's voice, so the writer to the Hebrews warns us to listen, writing, "Be careful that you do not refuse to listen to the One who is speaking. For if the people of Israel did not escape when they refused to listen to Moses, the earthly messenger, we will certainly not escape if we reject the One who speaks to us from heaven!" (12:25).

God has given us his final, most exhaustive, most definitive word in the person of Jesus Christ. He is everything God wants to say to us.

† *Word of God, I hear your voice calling to me, "Repent, for the Kingdom of Heaven is near," "Follow me," "Come to me," "Remain in me." I hear your voice instructing me, "Go and make disciples." And I hear your voice assuring me, "I am with you always, even to the end of the age."*

APRIL 9

OUR SECURITY IN THE SHAKING

When God spoke on Mount Sinai, revealing himself in the law, the force of his holy presence caused the earth to shake. Exodus 19:18 says, "All of Mount Sinai was covered with smoke because the LORD had descended on it in the form of fire. The smoke billowed into the sky like smoke from a brick kiln, and the whole mountain shook violently." As God laid down the law to be our judge, the force of it shook the earth.

When Jesus came, he didn't condemn us, even though he had every right to do so. Instead, he came to fulfill the law in our place and to subject himself to God's judgment in our place. From the cross, "Jesus shouted out again, and he released his spirit. At that moment the curtain in the sanctuary of the Temple was torn in two, from top to bottom. The earth shook, rocks split apart" (Matthew 27:50-51). Why did the earth shake? Because the judgment of God was falling on Jesus to punish sin. The judgment you and I deserve for the things we've said and done and for our rejection of God fell on Jesus that day. And the force of the tremendous weight of that judgment shook the earth.

In the book of Hebrews, the writer says that "once again" there will be a shaking of the earth (12:26). This is the violent shaking described in Revelation 6:12, 15-17:

> I watched as the Lamb broke the sixth seal, and there was a great earthquake. . . . Then everyone—the kings of the earth, the rulers, the generals, the wealthy, the powerful, and every slave and free person— all hid themselves in the caves and among the rocks of the mountains. And they cried to the mountains and the rocks, "Fall on us and hide us from the face of the one who sits on the throne and from the wrath of the Lamb. For the great day of their wrath has come, and who is able to survive?"

The day is coming when Jesus will return, and this time he will come not to *bear* judgment but to *bring* judgment. Once again the judgment of God will shake the earth, and the only ones who will survive will be those who have hidden themselves in Christ.

† *My Security in the shaking, there is no place safe and secure apart from you, so I run to you and hide myself in you. And because I know that you have absorbed the judgment of God that I deserve, I rest secure.*

APRIL 10
THE PERFECT LAW KEEPER

The Ten Commandments were literally written in stone by the hand of God. But it would take a perfect human being to live up to them, someone who:

1. is always single-mindedly radical about God, never losing his "first love."

2. has pure and exalted thoughts of God, never giving his worship to anyone or anything less.

3. uses his words to communicate who God is in ways God is worthy of, never speaking in a flippant manner in regard to the Holy One.

4. always enjoys the worship of God so profoundly that he manipulates his schedule to make God central, never just fitting God in.

5. always overflows with gratitude toward his parents, never acting condescending or uncaring.

6. always breathes life into the people around him, never taking it from them.

7. reveres the institution of marriage, never violating the sacred boundary of sexual intimacy.

8. always looks for opportunities to meet the needs of others, never operating in me-first mode.

9. always guards other people's reputations, never gossiping.

10. is always content with the life God has given him because he has God, never resenting it when other people succeed.

Who could ever live up to this list? Certainly not the religious leaders who brought before Jesus a woman caught in adultery. Jesus turned to her accusers and said, "Let the one who has never sinned throw the first stone!" (John 8:7). One by one the accusers slipped away. Jesus, however, *could* have thrown a stone at her. He was the only one in the crowd—the only one in the history of humanity—who has never sinned. But instead of casting stones of condemnation, Jesus turns to all of us who can never live up to God's holy law and offers to us his own perfect record of righteousness.

† *My perfect Righteousness, I am grateful that you do not throw stones at my imperfections but instill in me the desire to conform my life to yours.*

EVERYTHING ELSE IS WORTHLESS

Over and over in the books of Exodus, Leviticus, and Numbers, we read detailed instructions from God followed by, "This is a permanent law for you, and it must be observed from generation to generation."

The apostle Paul came from a family where the laws of God were taken seriously. Paul described himself as "a real Hebrew if there ever was one!" (Philippians 3:5). He was the ultimate Israelite insider. His parents circumcised him seven days after his birth. He was a pure-blooded citizen, a descendant of the tribe of Benjamin, which, because of its history of faithfulness, was a source of extra pride. Paul had the best education available in Jerusalem under a famous rabbi as well as a track record of religious zeal as a Pharisee. He voluntarily bound himself to keep not only the laws of God, but also the hundreds of commandments that had been added to God's law by religious leaders over the years. Paul was so zealous for the law that he led the way in the pogrom against what he saw as deviants from Jewish law—Jewish Christians.

But then something happened to Paul. He saw the One toward whom the law had been pointing all along. And he saw his law-keeping and religious heritage through new eyes. He saw that although these things were not necessarily bad in themselves, they were working against him rather than for him, because they kept him from seeing his need for Christ.

> I once thought these things were valuable, but now I consider them worthless because of what Christ has done. Yes, everything else is worthless when compared with the infinite value of knowing Christ Jesus my Lord. For his sake I have discarded everything else, counting it all as garbage, so that I could gain Christ and become one with him. I no longer count on my own righteousness through obeying the law; rather, I become righteous through faith in Christ. For God's way of making us right with himself depends on faith. (Philippians 3:7-9)

True faith is not just believing biblical doctrines, important as that is. True faith is valuing Christ above all else. True faith, given by the Holy Spirit, fills our hearts with a deeper understanding of the superior worth of Jesus.

† *My greatest Treasure and highest Joy, give me a new set of values so that I can rightly measure your inestimable worth. Give me a new way of seeing what really matters and what is truly pleasing to you.*

APRIL 12
The True Altar

The children of Israel couldn't see God or meet with God on the mountain as Moses did—they would have been destroyed in God's holy presence. But God sanctioned a way for the people to approach him. It required an animal sacrifice offered on an altar built for God.

> Build for me an altar made of earth, and offer your sacrifices to me-your burnt offerings and peace offerings, your sheep and goats, and your cattle. Build my altar wherever I cause my name to be remembered, and I will come to you and bless you. (Exodus 20:24)

So that's what they did, dotting the desert landscape with altars, just as Abraham and Jacob had done throughout Canaan long before. An altar was a simple structure of stone marking the place where God met with his people as they placed their sacrifices for sin on the altar.

As the nation of Israel prepared to enter the Promised Land, they would need a more permanent place to worship. God wanted them to have a central place where they could come into his presence and offer sacrifices to him. No longer would small, simple altars be enough; something larger and grander was needed. God told Moses, "Have the people of Israel build me a holy sanctuary so I can live among them" (Exodus 25:8). With those words, God initiated the building of the Tabernacle. The Tabernacle replaced the altar as the primary location where God revealed his intimate presence to his people. But it also incorporated the sacrificial altar in its courtyard where sacrifices were burned before God.

The altar in this Tabernacle, like all the altars built before it, was a picture of the true Altar to come on which a better sacrifice would be offered. Jesus himself is the true Altar as well as the all-sufficient Sacrifice.

No altar constructed by humans could ever stand under the weight of the sin of all humanity. Only Jesus, the true Altar, who was both fully God and fully man, could bear the weight of sin fully and forever. Jesus was sufficient in himself to bear not only our sin, but also the flood of the wrath of God that poured out on him.

† *It is through you, Jesus, that I offer a continual sacrifice of praise to God, proclaiming my allegiance to his name. Only in you do I dare to enter and enjoy the presence of God. You make it safe for me to approach his holiness.*

APRIL 13

HE PITCHED
HIS TENT AMONG US

The Tabernacle was a giant tent, a portable sanctuary for God's presence with his people. God gave Moses detailed designs for the Tabernacle, saying, "Have the people of Israel build me a holy sanctuary so I can live among them. You must build this Tabernacle and its furnishings exactly according to the pattern I will show you" (Exodus 25:8-9). Since it was similar to the tents they lived in, it showed how close God was. This was the blessing of the covenant: God was with his people, and they were with their God. At the same time, since the Tabernacle was so elaborate, it reminded them that God was separated from them by his holy majesty.

Thousands of years before Jesus came to live among us, God purposed that there be a Tabernacle in order that there would be One who would fulfill the meaning of that Tabernacle and who would be the true Tabernacle for us. That's why John's wording is so significant when he wrote that "the Word became human and made his home among us" (John 1:14). The word John used for "made his home" is the Greek word for "putting up a tabernacle" (*skēnoō*). He is saying that Jesus "tabernacled among us," which means that "he pitched a tent among us."

Every detail of the Tabernacle pointed to some aspect of the character and work of Jesus. In fact, this Tabernacle had no meaning apart from Jesus Christ.

The Tabernacle was for use in the wilderness: "Jesus was led by the Spirit into the wilderness" (Matthew 4:1). The Tabernacle was outwardly humble and unattractive: "There was nothing beautiful or majestic about his appearance" (Isaiah 53:2). The Tabernacle was where God met with his people: "I am the way, the truth, and the life. No one can come to the Father except through me" (John 14:6). The Tabernacle was the center of Israel's camp, a gathering place for God's people: "When I am lifted up from the earth, I will draw everyone to myself" (John 12:32). The Tabernacle was where sacrifices for the sins of God's people were made: He "offered himself to God as a single sacrifice for sins, good for all time" (Hebrews 10:12). The Tabernacle was a place of worship: "'My Lord and my God!' Thomas exclaimed" (John 20:28).

† *True Tabernacle, you have pitched your tent among us, giving us direct access to God and inviting us into his very presence. In you I discover the glory of God, and I find a way to know, experience, and be transformed by that glory.*

APRIL 14

WHERE SINNERS FIND MERCY

God gave specific instructions for everything that would go inside the Tabernacle. In the innermost part of the Tabernacle, the Most Holy Place where God descended to dwell with his people, was the Ark of the Covenant.

> Have the people make an Ark of acacia wood—a sacred chest 45 inches long, 27 inches wide, and 27 inches high. Overlay it inside and outside with pure gold, and run a molding of gold all around it. . . . When the Ark is finished, place inside it the stone tablets inscribed with the terms of the covenant, which I will give to you. Then make the Ark's cover—the place of atonement—from pure gold. It must be 45 inches long and 27 inches wide. Then make two cherubim from hammered gold, and place them on the two ends of the atonement cover. (Exodus 25:10-11, 16-18)

The Ark of the Covenant was an earthly symbol of the heavenly reality of God's loving intentions toward his people. It pictured what would ulti-mately make it possible for him to be reconciled with sinners who seek him. God was above the Ark, in all his holiness, enthroned between the cherubim. Underneath him was the law of God that exposed Israel's sin. And in between was the mercy seat, where the high priest would sprinkle bull's blood to make atonement for his own sins, and then goat's blood for the sins of the whole community of Israel (Leviticus 16). In between a holy God and the law of God came the blood of the atoning sacrifice. In this way, when God came down to dwell with his people, he would not see them in light of the law that they had broken, but instead would see them through the saving blood of an atoning sacrifice.

The cross of Christ is our mercy seat. It is the place where the blood of an atoning sacrifice reconciles us to God by coming between his holiness and our law-breaking.

> For all have sinned and fall short of the glory of God, and are justified freely by his grace through the redemption that came by Christ Jesus. God presented him as a sacrifice of atonement, through faith in his blood. (Romans 3:23-25, NIV)

† *I come boldly to your throne, gracious God, confident that you see me not in the harsh light of the law, but covered by the atoning blood of Christ. There I receive mercy and find grace to help me when I need it most.*

APRIL 15

THE NEW AND LIVING WAY

God gave Moses detailed instructions about the curtain that would separate the Holy Place from the Most Holy Place in the Tabernacle where God's presence would dwell.

> Make a special curtain of finely woven linen. Decorate it with blue, purple, and scarlet thread and with skillfully embroidered cherubim. Hang this curtain on gold hooks attached to four posts of acacia wood. Overlay the posts with gold, and set them in four silver bases. Hang the inner curtain from clasps, and put the Ark of the Covenant in the room behind it. This curtain will separate the Holy Place from the Most Holy Place. (Exodus 26:31-33)

Moses did as he was instructed, and there the curtain hung for five hundred years. It announced that the way to approach God was not yet made known. And yet, because it was made of fabric rather than stone or metal, it was obviously temporary. A way of access into the presence of God would one day be revealed.

Matthew tells the dramatic story of when the curtain was finally opened. It happened on the day Jesus hung on the cross, when "Jesus shouted out again, and he released his spirit. At that moment the curtain in the sanctuary of the Temple was torn in two, from top to bottom" (Matthew 27:50-51). The writer to the Hebrews tells us exactly what this curtain and its dramatic rending pictured for us: "We have confidence to enter the holy places by the blood of Jesus, by the new and living way that [Christ] opened for us through the curtain, that is, through his flesh" (Hebrews 10:19-20, ESV).

For centuries the curtain hung in the Tabernacle and later in the Temple, speaking of the humanity of Christ, the Son of God. But the priests who looked at the curtain could not come close to God by merely looking at the beauty of the curtain. It had to be opened; his flesh had to be torn. And when it was, a new and living way to approach God was opened up.

† *I see the curtain torn from top to bottom and I know that it was you, God, who did it. Your hand tore through the flesh of Christ on the cross so that I can enter in. You have torn the curtain from top to bottom to show me that the work is complete. I can't add to it. I simply look up and see the mercy seat, and hear you welcoming me in.*

APRIL 16
LIGHT THAT LEADS TO LIFE

As with all the other furnishings in the Tabernacle, God gave Moses careful instructions for the golden lampstand:

> Make a lampstand of pure, hammered gold. Make the entire lampstand and its decorations of one piece—the base, center stem, lamp cups, buds, and petals. Make it with six branches going out from the center stem, three on each side. . . . Make the seven lamps for the lampstand, and set them so they reflect their light forward. . . . Be sure that you make everything according to the pattern I have shown you here on the mountain. (Exodus 25:31-32, 37, 40)

The golden lampstand had the obvious practical function of illuminating the Holy Place, enabling the priests to see what they were doing as they carried out their service to God. The lampstand stood for life because it was made in the shape of a tree, echoing the tree of life in Eden. And from the beginning it showed that as we approach God, we are coming into the light. "The LORD is my light and my salvation" (Psalm 27:1).

The prophet Isaiah connected this light with the Messiah, saying, "The people who walk in darkness will see a great light. For those who live in a land of deep darkness, a light will shine" (Isaiah 9:2). This light would be not only for the priests in the Tabernacle, but also for the whole human race.

John recognized this light when he saw it in the person of Jesus. "The one who is the true light, who gives light to everyone, was coming into the world" (John 1:9), he wrote. "His life brought light to everyone" (John 1:4). The life and light symbolized by the golden lampstand are now embodied in Jesus Christ, God's true Tabernacle. There is no more need of a lampstand because the reality has replaced the type.

And this is how it will be into eternity. John describes this at the end of Revelation when the new heavens and new earth come down. "The city has no need of sun or moon, for the glory of God illuminates the city, and the Lamb is its light" (Revelation 21:23).

† *Light that leads to life, I am drawn to your flame. You have called me out of suffocating darkness into the radiant light of yourself. Shine brightly in my life and through my life as only you can.*

OUR GREAT HIGH PRIEST

During the Israelites' time in the wilderness, Moses' older brother, Aaron, became Israel's first high priest. God appointed Aaron and his sons to be set apart and dedicated as priests (Exodus 28). The writer to the Hebrews described their role this way: "Every high priest is a man chosen to represent other people in their dealings with God. He presents their gifts to God and offers sacrifices for their sins" (Hebrews 5:1).

But priests were just men—men who sinned and had to offer sacrifices for themselves as well as for the people. They were men who were often seduced by the world to turn away from God, sometimes turning the work of the Temple into a travesty toward God. Tragically, it was Israel's high priest who led the charge in condemning and crucifying Jesus. Mark 14:61-62 records, "Then the high priest asked him, 'Are you the Messiah, the Son of the Blessed One?' Jesus said, 'I AM.'"

Caiaphas, the high priest, decided Jesus deserved to die for such blasphemy. Little did he know that Jesus was the fulfillment of what his own office merely pointed to, that Jesus would put an end to the priesthood and take its place as the one mediator between God and humanity.

Aaron and the high priests of Israel who followed him were a shadow and copy of the reality. Jesus is the reality. And knowing this reality makes a practical difference to us.

> Since we have a great High Priest who has entered heaven, Jesus the Son of God, let us hold firmly to what we believe. This High Priest of ours understands our weaknesses, for he faced all of the same testings we do, yet he did not sin. So let us come boldly to the throne of our gracious God. There we will receive his mercy, and we will find grace to help us when we need it most. (Hebrews 4:14-16)

Jesus, our great High Priest, made a way for us to enter the presence of God continually and confidently. We can draw near to God knowing we're wanted and welcome, not cowering in shame or fearing that we'll be rejected. Because of Jesus, we receive mercy for our past failures and grace to meet our present and future needs.

✝ *My great High Priest, because of You, I no longer have to relate to God from a distance. I can draw near, knowing that I'll be welcomed and accepted, not because of who I am but because of what you've done.*

APRIL 18

A PRIEST BETTER THAN AARON

Moses' brother, Aaron, had been a leader in Israel since Moses first told Pharaoh to let God's people go. Aaron had served as Moses' spokesman and performed miraculous signs. He had held the prophet's hands up in prayer and gone up the mountain with seventy elders of Israel to approach God. Then, when Moses went on up the mountain alone to hear from God, God said, "Call for your brother, Aaron, and his sons, Nadab, Abihu, Eleazar, and Ithamar. Set them apart from the rest of the people of Israel so they may minister to me and be my priests" (Exodus 28:1).

But while Moses was getting these instructions, Aaron was down with the people, making a golden calf and setting it up for the people to worship. In light of such heinous sin, how could Aaron ever be worthy to wear the righteous robes of priestly ministry? How would a sinner like Aaron be allowed to serve the holy God?

Aaron would have to be cleansed and consecrated for such service. In preparation for the priesthood, Aaron's body was washed with water (Exodus 40:12), symbolizing his consecration to God. Then he confessed his sins, placing his hands on the heads of a bull and two rams, which were sacrificed to make atonement. Through the cleansing water and the sacrificial blood, Aaron, a sinner, was set apart to serve. But it was not the water or the sacrificed animals that truly cleansed him. It was what that water and that sacrifice pointed toward. The Aaronic priesthood was purely a matter of God's grace in anticipation of what Christ would do, sprinkling us with his own "blood to make us clean" and washing us with "pure water" (Hebrews 10:22).

As Aaron was the head of a whole order of priests, so is Jesus Christ the head of a new order of priests—people who are not perfect but are forgiven, people who can enter the presence of God only by grace. This is, in fact, the goal of Christ's priestly ministry—to enable us, as unrighteous as we are, to serve the holy God. While we have not met and cannot meet the standards God has set for those who serve him as priests, Christ, the head of this new priesthood of believers, has met those standards fully. We find our sufficiency in him. Our great High Priest, Jesus, is marked by the perfection and holiness God demands.

† *I am not worthy to come before you in your holiness, God—I am well aware of my sinfulness. Yet Christ has invited me into his new Kingdom of priests and so I gladly come. I am not worthy, but he is! He cleanses me with his blood and washes me with his Word so that I can serve you.*

APRIL 19

In Naked Glory

Whenever the high priest performed his sacred duties, he did not act for himself alone, but for all the people before God. What he wore, therefore, was important. God gave very specific instructions for what the high priest would wear:

> Make sacred garments for Aaron that are glorious and beautiful. . . . These are the garments they are to make: a chestpiece, an ephod, a robe, a patterned tunic, a turban, and a sash. They are to make these sacred garments for your brother, Aaron, and his sons to wear when they serve me as priests. (Exodus 28:2, 4)

The high priest's ephod was made of fine linen adorned with richly colored thread. Two precious stones were attached to the shoulder pieces, and twelve more adorned the chestpiece. But the most important thing about the stones was what was written on them. Engraved on the precious stones were the names of the twelve tribes of Israel. So whenever the high priest put on his ceremonial robes, he, in a sense, lifted the people onto his shoulders and carried them into the presence of God with him.

The high priest's crowning glory was his turban, which had a golden medallion summarizing his whole priestly calling. It read, "Holy to the Lord" (Exodus 28:36-38). However, while the sign on his head said, "Holy to the Lord," his heart was far from holy. His outward ornamentation did not match his inward sanctification. Holy clothes don't make a man holy.

Every aspect of the priestly garments worn by Aaron and the other priests spoke to the perfect salvation God would provide through Jesus. On the cross, he carried us on his shoulders like the names on the precious stones on the shoulder pieces of the ephod, and he took our needs to heart, like the gemstones on the chestpiece (Exodus 28:9-21). He was robed in royal righteousness, and written across every aspect of his life was "Holy to the Lord." Our great High Priest, Jesus, did not need to wear any of the priestly garments. In fact, in doing his greatest priestly work on the Cross, Jesus hung in naked glory—glory that emanated from who he is, not what he wore.

† *Jesus, my great High Priest, you are glorious and beautiful, not because of what you wear but because of who you are and what you have done. I rest in knowing that you carried me on your shoulders, my needs are written on your heart, my righteousness is a gift of your own, and you are at work making me holy to the Lord.*

APRIL 20

THE ONE WHO HAS NEVER SINNED

Exodus tells us that the law was written in stone by the very finger of God, making it especially sacred and giving it divine authority. "When the LORD finished speaking with Moses on Mount Sinai, he gave him the two stone tablets inscribed with the terms of the covenant, written by the finger of God" (Exodus 31:18).

In the New Testament, we find Jesus being interrogated about this law. The religious leaders had set a trap for him, throwing a woman before him who had just spent the night with a man who wasn't her husband. "'Teacher,' they said to Jesus, 'this woman was caught in the act of adultery. The law of Moses says to stone her. What do you say?'" (John 8:4-5).

If Jesus had said, "Let her go," they could have accused him of breaking Moses' law. But if he gave them permission to stone her, he would have broken the Roman law, which did not allow death for anyone without the Roman government's approval. So what did Jesus do? "Jesus stooped down and wrote in the dust with his finger" (8:6). Then he stood up and said, "Let the one who has never sinned throw the first stone!" (8:7).

We wish we could look over his shoulder and read what he wrote in the dust. But we don't know. We do know, however, that the same finger that wrote in the dust in response to being interrogated about the law also wrote the law into the tablets of stone. Jesus is the Author of the law, and he is the only person who has ever kept the law perfectly. Therefore, he was the one person in the crowd around this woman who had never sinned. He was the only one who would have been justified in throwing stones at this guilty woman. He knew how much her sin would cost him on the cross, but he had no interest in throwing stones. He was going to the cross, and there he would take on her shame and guilt. The same finger that wrote into stone the law she had broken would write across her life—"Sinner saved by grace," "Deserved to be punished but received pardon," "Rescued from the hands of religion by the hands of a gracious God."

† *You have not come to condemn me, Jesus, but to save me from the sin that will destroy me. You have every right to dish out condemnation, yet you keep on lavishing your grace—grace that begets repentance, grace that gives me power to go and sin no more.*

APRIL 21
FOREVER INTERCEDING FOR US

While Moses was up on the mountain meeting with God, the people grew tired of waiting and made their own god in the form of a golden calf. Seeing their rebellion, God told Moses that he would destroy them and instead make Moses into a great nation. But Moses interceded on their behalf:

> "O LORD!" he said. "Why are you so angry with your own people whom you brought from the land of Egypt with such great power and such a strong hand? Why let the Egyptians say, 'Their God rescued them with the evil intention of slaughtering them in the mountains and wiping them from the face of the earth'? Turn away from your fierce anger. Change your mind about this terrible disaster you have threatened against your people! Remember your servants Abraham, Isaac, and Jacob. You bound yourself with an oath to them, saying, 'I will make your descendants as numerous as the stars of heaven. And I will give them all of this land that I have promised to your descendants, and they will possess it forever.'" (Exodus 32:11-13)

God heard Moses pleading and "changed his mind about the terrible disaster he had threatened to bring on his people" (32:14). Here Moses prefigured Jesus, who "is sitting in the place of honor at God's right hand, pleading for us" (Romans 8:34).

The writer of Hebrews explains that Jesus' intercession for his people is beyond that of Moses and the priests who served in the Temple.

> There were many priests under the old system, for death prevented them from remaining in office. But because Jesus lives forever, his priesthood lasts forever. Therefore he is able, once and forever, to save those who come to God through him. He lives forever to intercede with God on their behalf. (Hebrews 7:23-25)

Our future salvation depends not only on the past work of Christ, but also on the active work of Christ, who now and forever intercedes with God on our behalf.

✝ *My Intercessor, this very day I am being saved by your eternal intercession for me before the Father. And I know your prayers are answered because you pray for me perfectly on the basis of your perfect sacrifice.*

I WILL GIVE YOU REST

Moses went to the Tent of Meeting, where he could talk things over with God. God had said that the Israelites were still going to be able to go into the Promised Land even after the great sin of the golden calf, but there was a catch: God wasn't going with them. And to Moses, that was simply unacceptable. He would not settle for anything less than the very presence of God. He begged God to stay with him, reminding him of his promises to him and of his love for his chosen people. "The LORD replied, 'I will personally go with you, Moses, and I will give you rest—everything will be fine for you'" (Exodus 33:14).

God's rest can be pictured as a place where a bird can land and build its nest, a place to put down roots, a place where his people could let their guard down, a place to finally call home. And sure enough, that day finally came when "the LORD gave them rest on every side, just as he had solemnly promised their ancestors" (Joshua 21:44).

Yet the New Testament writer of Hebrews wrote to those living in the generation after Jesus that "God's promise of entering his rest still stands" (4:1). What is this rest that is still promised by God? This is the rest that Jesus himself described, the rest that is found only in him:

> Come to me, all of you who are weary and carry heavy burdens, and I will give you rest. Take my yoke upon you. Let me teach you, because I am humble and gentle at heart, and you will find rest for your souls. For my yoke is easy to bear, and the burden I give you is light. (Matthew 11:28-30)

The coming of Jesus was the greater fulfillment of God's promise to Moses. Here was God in the flesh offering himself personally, giving himself fully, opening his arms widely to welcome his people into real rest. Instead of withdrawing from those who break his law, Jesus came and offered to bear the heavy burden of law-keeping and obedience, echoing the words of promise Moses heard in the Tent that day: "I will give you rest."

† *You are my Rest, Lord Jesus. I come to you in my weariness, longing for the soul rest only you provide. I yoke my life to yours and find my burdens are light.*

APRIL 23

He Shows and Shares God's Glory

Moses was desperate for the favor of God and the presence of God as he prepared to lead God's people into the land of milk and honey. He had begged God to go with them, despite the people's sinfulness. God told Moses that he would do the very thing he asked for, but it wasn't enough for Moses. He wanted more. "Moses said, 'Now show me your glory'" (Exodus 33:18, NIV).

It was an audacious request—to be able to see the splendor and radiance of God that he had, till then, only seen in glimpses. He had glimpsed God's glory in the burning bush and in the cloud of God's presence. He saw it again at the Tent of Meeting where the pillar of cloud descended from heaven. But he knew there was more to see, so he asked God to let him see it.

> The LORD replied, "I will make all my goodness pass before you. . . . Stand near me on this rock. As my glorious presence passes by, I will hide you in the crevice of the rock and cover you with my hand until I have passed by. Then I will remove my hand and let you see me from behind. But my face will not be seen." (Exodus 33:19, 21-23)

Moses was able to see only a fleeting glimpse of God's glory. God would shield him from the withering, consuming intensity of his glory in its completeness that no sinful human can see and live. But the day did come when Moses met the same glorious God he had met on Mount Sinai; it happened on the Mount of Transfiguration in the person of God's Son. "Jesus' appearance was transformed so that his face shone like the sun, and his clothes became as white as light. Suddenly, Moses and Elijah appeared and began talking with Jesus" (Matthew 17:2-3).

Peter, James, and John saw it too, and John described it in his Gospel: "We have seen his glory, the glory of the Father's one and only Son. . . . No one has ever seen God. But the unique One, who is himself God, is near to the Father's heart. He has revealed God to us" (John 1:14, 18).

And the day will come when those who love him will not only see but also share in the glory of God in the person of Jesus Christ. "When Christ, who is your life, is revealed to the whole world, you will share in all his glory" (Colossians 3:4).

† *Jesus, you are the radiance of God's glory. When I look into your face— consider your work, listen to your words, observe your character—I see the glory of God.*

APRIL 24

COMPASSIONATE HEALER

Moses wanted to see God, to know God in a far more personal way than he had up to this point. So God told him to climb up Mount Sinai where he would show himself to Moses. But showing himself was not about showing Moses what he looks like, but rather, it meant revealing more of his infinite perfection. It was what the Lord told Moses about himself that helped Moses to know God more personally: "The LORD passed in front of Moses, calling out, 'Yahweh! The LORD! The God of compassion and mercy! I am slow to anger and filled with unfailing love and faithfulness'" (Exodus 34:6).

These words spoken to Moses became Israel's working definition of God. Whenever anyone wanted to know who God is and what he is like, they went back to this revelation.

God is compassionate. God cares. He sympathizes with our weaknesses and struggles. His heart is drawn to help us when we are in need. "The LORD is like a father to his children, tender and compassionate to those who fear him" (Psalm 103:13).

The Israelites needed a compassionate God. They needed someone to hear their cry of distress when they were groaning under their bondage to Pharaoh and when they were hungry and thirsty in the wilderness. They needed a compassionate God in the aftermath of exile.

In telling Moses that he was the God of compassion, he was not nearly finished revealing himself in this way. When God became flesh, our compassionate God became a God with skin who could hurt with us and help us. In Jesus, God reached out and touched us in our pain. "When he saw the crowds, he had compassion on them," Matthew 9:36 tells us. Out of his deep compassion, Jesus healed the sick and taught the truth. And he called those who want to follow him to be compassionate as well. "You must be compassionate, just as your Father is compassionate" (Luke 6:36).

✝ *Compassionate Healer who hears my cries of distress, the enemy might whisper to me that you are cold and uncaring, too distant to call upon in my time of need. But Jesus has shown me your compassion through his tears and through his touch. Your Spirit transforms my cold, self-centered heart so that I can reach out to others with the very compassion of God.*

THE GOODNESS OF GOD

Moses was desperate to know God in a deeper way than he had before. "Let me know your ways so I may understand you more fully and continue to enjoy your favor," he said to the Lord (Exodus 33:13).

And God responded to his request:

The LORD passed in front of Moses, calling out,

"Yahweh! The LORD!
     The God of compassion and mercy!
I am slow to anger
     and filled with unfailing love and faithfulness.
I lavish unfailing love to a thousand generations.
     I forgive iniquity, rebellion, and sin.
But I do not excuse the guilty.
     I lay the sins of the parents upon their children and
          grandchildren;
the entire family is affected—
     even children in the third and fourth generations."
          (Exodus 34:6-7)

We like the first part of this revelation, but the second part we're not so sure about. Yet God describes both parts as his goodness. God is not saying that he punishes innocent children for their parents' sins. God is saying, "If you hate me, if you refuse me as I am, I will give you exactly what you want—a life apart from me that is dominated by sin and its effects. I will visit your iniquity on you as long as you persist in it. But I would much rather visit my steadfast love on you." The goodness of God says, "There is no sin you can commit that I can't forgive." And the goodness of God also says, "My justice will never wink at your sin. I will by no means clear the guilty."

So how does the goodness of God forgive as well as punish? In Christ. God does not—in fact he cannot—overlook sin. God will punish every sin in one of two ways—either personally in our own experience in hell, or substitutionally in Christ's experience on the Cross. The goodness of God is not that he ignores sin. The goodness of God is that he doesn't demand our blood to pay for our sin. Instead, he gives his own.

† *Jesus, you are the goodness of God pouring over me and poured out for me. I see your goodness in your generous forgiveness as well as your perfect justice. Pour out your forgiveness on me and lavish your love on me.*

APRIL 26

ANOINTED BY THE HOLY SPIRIT

After the priests were washed with water and dressed in the priestly garments, God instructed that they be anointed with oil.

> Dress Aaron with the sacred garments and anoint him, consecrating him to serve me as a priest. Then present his sons and dress them in their tunics. Anoint them as you did their father, so they may also serve me as priests. With their anointing, Aaron's descendants are set apart for the priesthood forever, from generation to generation. (Exodus 40:13-15)

This special blend of oil and spices prepared specifically for this occasion was poured over the high priest's head and ran down onto his garments. The psalmist says that it "ran down his beard and onto the border of his robe" (Psalm 133:2). It was a visual representation of God pouring out his Spirit on the man, empowering him for his holy duties.

Though the anointing of Aaron and his sons took place hundreds of years before the earthly ministry of Jesus, it pictured exactly what happened when Jesus came. When Jesus went down to the Jordan River, "after his baptism, as Jesus came up out of the water, the heavens were opened and he saw the Spirit of God descending like a dove and settling on him. And a voice from heaven said, 'This is my dearly loved Son, who brings me great joy'" (Matthew 3:16-17). This was God anointing his great High Priest by a symbol of the Holy Spirit—the dove—showing that Jesus' ministry as a priest would always be a Spirit-filled ministry.

Jesus, who was fully God and yet fully human, willingly set aside many aspects of deity when he became flesh. His ministry was accomplished through the power of the Holy Spirit. This is why Jesus quoted Isaiah, saying that Isaiah's prophecy referred to him: "The Spirit of the LORD is upon me, for he has anointed me" (Luke 4:18).

The anointing of the Holy Spirit is no longer limited to Aaron's priesthood but is enjoyed by all believers. And the Holy Spirit is not only poured over us, he also lives in us. "He anointed us, set his seal of ownership on us, and put his Spirit in our hearts as a deposit" (2 Corinthians 1:21-22, NIV).

† *Holy Spirit, pour over me, fill me, set me apart for ministry to your people.*

APRIL 27

Unfading Glory

When Moses came down from Mount Sinai carrying the two stone tablets, he wasn't aware that his face had become radiant, shining with a supernatural light. But when the people of Israel saw it, they were afraid to come near him (Exodus 34).

Whenever Moses entered God's presence, he would leave his face uncovered and speak with God face-to-face, and would emerge radiating God's glory. But after a while the glory would fade. Paul says that "Moses . . . would put a veil over his face to keep the Israelites from gazing at it while the radiance was fading away" (2 Corinthians 3:13, NIV).

The glory shining from Moses' face was a reflected glory that was bound to fade away. It prepared us for and pointed us toward a glory that would be seen on the face of Jesus, a glory that was not reflected but inherent, a glory that will never fade away. The human flesh that Jesus poured himself into also veiled this glory. However, at one point in his ministry, Jesus did give his inner circle a glimpse of his intrinsic luminescent glory: "Jesus took Peter and the two brothers, James and John, and led them up a high mountain to be alone. As the men watched, Jesus' appearance was transformed so that his face shone like the sun" (Matthew 17:1-2).

For a brief moment, the veil of humanity was peeled back and Jesus' true essence was allowed to shine through. The glory that was always in the depths of his being rose to the surface and became visible. The disciples saw not only his prehuman glory, but also his future glory. In Revelation 1, John recounts for us the vision he was given of Jesus as he is now—still human yet glorified, as we will one day be. John says that "his face was like the sun in all its brilliance" (1:16). Jesus' glory does not fade away.

It is in the face of Jesus that we are able to see and know the glory of God. "For God, who said, 'Let there be light in the darkness,' has made this light shine in our hearts so we could know the glory of God that is seen in the face of Jesus Christ" (2 Corinthians 4:6).

† *Glorified Jesus, how I long to be transformed into your likeness with ever-increasing glory. As I gaze into your glorious face, you are changing me—taking away the darkness and giving me your own radiant countenance.*

APRIL 28
WHEN THE VEIL IS TAKEN AWAY

Moses put a veil over his face to keep the Israelites from seeing the fading of the glory of God that had radiated from his face. Yet there was a time he took off the veil: "whenever he went into the Tent of Meeting to speak with the LORD, he would remove the veil" (Exodus 34:34). Moses had unveiled access to Almighty God. When the veil was removed, he had an unfettered, transforming, freeing fellowship with God that was a taste of what is to come for all believers.

What is this veil and how is it taken away? Paul said that there is a veil that covers people's hearts when they are exposed to God's Word. They read the Bible, but they don't understand it. They hear the gospel, but they don't respond to it. The veil of sin keeps them from seeing the truth about God. "Satan, who is the god of this world, has blinded the minds of those who don't believe. They are unable to see the glorious light of the Good News. They don't understand this message about the glory of Christ, who is the exact likeness of God" (2 Corinthians 4:4). There is only one way the veil can be removed: "Only in Christ is it taken away. . . . Whenever anyone turns to the Lord, the veil is taken away. Now the Lord is the Spirit, and where the Spirit of the Lord is, there is freedom" (2 Corinthians 3:14, 16-17, NIV).

When we turn toward Jesus Christ, and the Holy Spirit does a regenerating, transforming work in our hearts, our eyes are opened. Only then is the veil taken away and we can finally see the glory of God in the face of Christ. No longer are we dull toward the things of God, but instead we come alive. No longer are we miserable under the condemnation of the law, but we begin to enjoy freedom in Christ.

When the veil is taken away, we finally begin to change. We begin to radiate the glory of God—perhaps not in a physical way as Moses did, but in even more beautiful ways. "All of us who have had that veil removed can see and reflect the glory of the Lord. And the Lord—who is the Spirit—makes us more and more like him as we are changed into his glorious image" (2 Corinthians 3:18).

† *Spirit, take away the veil from my eyes. Let me see the glory of God in all of its beauty. Bring me out from underneath the condemnation of your law into the glorious freedom of your grace. Fix my gaze on the face of Christ so that I might begin to look like him, think like him, love like him.*

APRIL 29
THE GRACE GIVEN UNDER MOSES

God gave Moses two stone tablets inscribed with the terms of the covenant to carry back to the people (Exodus 31:18). But by the time Moses got down the mountain, the people had already broken their covenant promise and made an idol. If the covenant had been based on absolute obedience or strict justice alone, that would have been the end of Israel.

But God's covenant has always been a covenant of grace. So after Moses, as mediator, pled with God not to destroy the people, God renewed his covenant.

God's covenant was not, and is not, based on the sinless perfection of God's people, but on the grace of God alone. When God said, "If you will obey me and keep my covenant, you will be my own special treasure from among all the peoples on earth" (Exodus 19:5), he was not saying that the people had to earn the blessings of the covenant through their behavior. Israel was to uphold their side of the covenant by loving God and by not allowing any other thing to take the place of affection that belonged to God. He said, "I lavish unfailing love for a thousand generations on those who love me and obey my commands" (20:6). Out of this love would flow obedience to his Word. This obedience would not earn God's favor, but would be evidence of God's favor. The people would receive forgiveness as they put their trust in the Forgiver, and benefit from the covenant's promises as they trusted the Promiser.

But how could a just God be so gracious and forgive so freely? Only because he looked forward to sending his Son and his sacrifice that would repair all the injury done to his honor through the disobedience of his people. There could have been no covenant with Abraham, no covenant with Moses, and no new covenant without the coming of Jesus Christ. Christ purchased what was freely given under Moses.

The obedience demanded in the covenant was the obedience of faith in the Covenant Giver. It is the same obedience required in the new covenant. Hebrews 5:9 says that Jesus "became the source of eternal salvation for all those who obey him."

† *Covenant Maker, Grace Giver, I see that the obedience you require is the obedience of faith. By faith, I receive your forgiveness for all the ways I have broken covenant with you. And by faith, I receive the merit of the perfect Covenant Keeper, the righteousness of Christ.*

APRIL 30
HIS EXODUS

The Exodus is a story of departure, an epic journey from slavery into salvation. In many ways, Israel's deliverance from Egypt set the pattern for the life of Christ. Certainly the pattern of the Exodus illustrates and illuminates Jesus' saving work. Jude went as far as to say that Jesus "delivered his people out of Egypt" (Jude 1:5, NIV).

So it is significant that a few days before Jesus' crucifixion, Moses would come down, along with Elijah, to talk with Jesus about what was about to happen:

> Jesus took Peter, John, and James up on a mountain to pray. And as he was praying, the appearance of his face was transformed, and his clothes became dazzling white. Suddenly, two men, Moses and Elijah, appeared and began talking with Jesus. They were glorious to see. And they were speaking about his exodus from this world, which was about to be fulfilled in Jerusalem. (Luke 9:28-31)

Moses and Elijah were talking with Jesus about *his* exodus, that is, they were talking about Jesus' coming crucifixion, resurrection, and ascension. Moses had been the faithful servant of God who led the exodus of God's people out of slavery. Elijah had been a prophet to God's people who challenged Baal's prophets and prayed down the fire of God. Their very presence with the transfigured Jesus affirmed to Peter, John, and James that Jesus was the fulfillment of the Old Testament prophecies and promises. That they were talking to him about his coming departure—his death, resurrection, and ascension—meant that this would be the zenith of redemption history, the story God had been writing in which Moses and Elijah had been key figures. While the exodus Moses led had been magnificent, and the miracles and ascension of Elijah had been dramatic—the ultimate deliverance of God's people, the ultimate demonstration of the miraculous power in the Resurrection, the ultimate ascension to heaven, the ultimate return in glory would be accomplished by Jesus.

† *Jesus, the One who leads me out of bondage to evil and self, the One who guides me through the wilderness of living in this world, the One who will bring me into your promised rest, you alone are my glorious Savior. I'm putting all my hopes in your glorious exodus and your glorious coming again.*

Leviticus

MAY 1
CONSUMED BY THE
FIRE OF THE LORD'S ANGER

Most of the sacrifices offered at the Tabernacle benefited both the offerer and the priests, in addition to being pleasing to God. Sometimes the offerer would eat some of the meat of the sacrificial animal, and most often the priest received a portion of it. But this was not the case in the burnt offering. Neither the offerer nor the priest ate any of the meat; it was all burned in the fire. This was sacrifice in its purest form—a very valuable animal was given up wholly to God. Neither the offerer nor the priest gained much materially from the offering. The sole benefit was being found acceptable to God, which, in the final analysis, is the ultimate benefit.

Bringing the burnt offering was a very personal experience, intended most certainly to make an impression on the Israelite making his sacrifice:

> Lay your hand on the animal's head, and the LORD will accept its death in your place to purify you, making you right with him. Then slaughter the young bull in the LORD's presence, and Aaron's sons, the priests, will present the animal's blood by splattering it against all sides of the altar. (Leviticus 1:4-5)

To make atonement for his sin and to gain God's acceptance, the offerer identified himself with the animal by laying his hand on the animal's head. When the animal died, it died for the offerer's sins—not so much for his specific sins (which were dealt with by other sacrifices), but rather for his general state of sinfulness.

Jesus fulfilled everything the burnt offering pointed to. The fire burned—the anger raged—until Christ suffered all the punishment for sin. For those who believe in him and trust in his sacrifice, no fuel remains. All is consumed. The fire died. The wrath expired. This is when Jesus uttered the wondrous words, "It is finished!" (John 19:30).

But for those who are not in Christ, the fire still burns. "He will come with his mighty angels, in flaming fire, bringing judgment on those who don't know God and on those who refuse to obey the Good News of our Lord Jesus. They will be punished with eternal destruction, forever separated from the Lord and from his glorious power" (2 Thessalonians 1:7-9).

† *My Sinless Substitute, you experienced the flames of God's anger for me so that I am not scorched. It is only because of your great love that I am not consumed.*

A PLEASING AROMA

In Exodus, Leviticus, and Numbers, as God gave instructions for the offerings, he described the smoke rising from the fire of the sacrifices as a pleasing aroma: "The priest will burn the entire sacrifice on the altar as a burnt offering. It is a special gift, a pleasing aroma to the LORD" (Leviticus 1:9).

The ancient Israelites did not understand what God was doing and why he was pleased with their sacrifices. The Israelites offered their burnt offerings in faith so that God's wrath could be avoided and his blessings received, waiting for this mystery to be made known.

The psalmist seemed to see beyond the shadow of the sacrifices into the substance of Christ when he wrote, seemingly speaking for the Messiah:

> Sacrifice and offering you did not desire,
>   but my ears you have pierced;
> burnt offerings and sin offerings
>   you did not require.
> Then I said, "Here I am, I have come—
>   it is written about me in the scroll." (Psalm 40:6-7, NIV)

In themselves, there was nothing pleasing or satisfactory in the various offerings prescribed in the ceremonial law. Neither the victim pouring forth its blood nor the fine flour rising in smoke from the altar could bring pleasure to God. They were pleasing to God because the offerings were made in faith and had the scent of the One who would come, the One who would eventually make them obsolete. In the shadow itself no genuine atonement was made. It was whom they pointed to—Christ alone—who made full atonement. Paul wrote that "Christ . . . loved us and offered himself as a sacrifice for us, a pleasing aroma to God" (Ephesians 5:2). On Golgotha, a transaction was made between God the Father and God the Son. And the single determinant of a sinner's relationship with God is that the sacrifice offered there was pleasing to him.

Christ's sacrifice was pleasing to the Lord because it demonstrated God's love in the most complete and perfect way possible. It was a tangible, unmistakable, worldwide demonstration of the way God loves sinners.

† *May my life be a Christlike fragrance rising up to you, God. May I be a living sacrifice that is pleasing and acceptable to you.*

LOOKING AHEAD

The Old Testament law, given throughout the Pentateuch, became a series of demands impossible to keep to perfection. So God instituted a series of sacrifices that would provide a picture of what God would do in the New Covenant that would make it possible for those who have broken God's law to be made right with him.

The sacrifices never could actually take away a person's sin or truly pay the debt for sin. The people of the Old Testament demonstrated faith in what God would do to take away sin by offering sacrifices. Those of us under the new covenant demonstrate faith in what God has done to take away sin by our belief and trust in Christ. We no longer need to offer sacrifices; we have seen the reality the sacrifices pointed to in the person and work of Christ, and we believe.

Paul helps us to see, however, that Christ's sacrifice was sufficient for those who had faith under the old covenant as well as for those of us who have faith under the new covenant:

> For God presented Jesus as the sacrifice for sin. People are made right with God when they believe that Jesus sacrificed his life, shedding his blood. This sacrifice shows that God was being fair when he held back and did not punish those who sinned in times past, for he was looking ahead and including them in what he would do in this present time. (Romans 3:25-26)

The writer to the Hebrews affirms that it was God's plan all along for the Old Testament sacrifices to point to the sacrifice of Christ. "For God's will was for us to be made holy by the sacrifice of the body of Jesus Christ, once for all time" (Hebrews 10:10).

While we no longer need to offer the variety of sacrifices, considering each of them as God prescribed helps us to understand in a deeper way the benefits that are ours in the once-for-all sacrifice of Christ. Each one pointed to a different aspect of Christ's sacrifice, and as the Old Testament believer would sacrifice the various offerings, he could grasp, to some degree, the particular blessing associated with each offering.

† *My once-for-all Sacrifice for sin, I sometimes settle for a small and limited view of your rich and glorious sacrifice, but I do not want to diminish your atoning work. I want to magnify who you are and what you've done.*

MAY 4

MY NOURISHMENT COMES FROM DOING THE WILL OF GOD

Grain was common in the ancient Near East, but it wasn't a common commodity in the camp of the Israelites. The Israelites could not raise wheat as they traveled through the desert. So the grain the Israelites were instructed to offer must have been a much more precious commodity than the cattle, which these shepherds had in abundance.

Assuming that the Israelites had grain with them in the camp, what would this grain have been for? Most likely it was taken with the Israelites for seed, and to sacrifice their seed to God was indeed an act of faith. This was the sacrifice of something precious.

The grain offering was most likely either wheat or barley that had been finely ground on a primitive grindstone, requiring significant effort on the part of the person who ground it. There was to be nothing rough or uneven in it. It could not have any yeast or honey, which were associated with corruption or spoiling, but was to include salt and frankincense, which were associated with preservation, purification, and a pleasing fragrance. The grain offering was also to be anointed with oil (Leviticus 2).

Whereas the burnt offering represented the value of Christ's work as our sin-atoning Substitute, the grain offering pictured his perfect human character and conduct, his obedience to God, and his finished work. There was nothing coarse or rough in the human nature of Jesus, no corruption or pride. He was both a pure and a pleasing sacrifice, anointed by the Holy Spirit to accomplish the work God gave to him to do.

Jesus himself spoke of accomplishing the work God gave to him as "meat" or "nourishment." The disciples had returned from their trip into Samaria to buy some food, and they urged Jesus to eat. But Jesus replied, "I have a kind of food you know nothing about. . . . My nourishment comes from doing the will of God, who sent me, and from finishing his work" (John 4:32, 34). Nothing moved Jesus from his purpose or even caused him to hesitate in his course of obedience. His character was perfectly formed like fine flour. Circumstances had no effect upon him. Company did not corrupt him. Sorrow did not sour him. Praise did not puff him up. His perfect obedience was received by God as a pleasing aroma.

† *Precious Jesus, you so purely and perfectly finished the work God gave you to do. And I know you will continue to be at work on me and in me until the day you return.*

MAY 5

HE HAS BROUGHT US PEACE

It is one thing to have your offense atoned for, burned away, as depicted by the burnt offering. But it is quite another to be welcomed back into relationship after the offense, to be smiled on, accepted. That is what the Israelites celebrated in the peace offering, which was more than a sacrifice—it was a festive meal. The whole burnt offering was given to God and consumed in the fire (except for the skin). Most of the grain offering was for the priests. But the peace offering was shared by the Lord, the priests, and the one who offered it (Leviticus 3).

The peace offering would follow the offering of guilt, or of atonement, as an expression of thanksgiving that the relationship between the worshiper and God had been healed, and that fellowship had been restored. The very act of the offering reminded the worshiper that the only way he had been able to come back into the fullness, the sweetness, the joy of fellowship and communion with God was through the blood of a perfect substitutionary sacrifice. Throughout the Old Testament, when the peace offering was given, it focused on the wholeness Israel was experiencing, or that which she had lost and longed for again. The offering was then an act of faith, looking forward to future wholeness or peace that God would grant his people.

We see evidence of the peace offering in the story Jesus told of two sons: one demanded his inheritance and wasted it living far away from his father; the other stayed home, close at hand, but far away in heart from his father. When the Prodigal Son returned home, the father gave instructions to "kill the calf we have been fattening. We must celebrate with a feast, for this son of mine was dead and has now returned to life" (Luke 15:23-24). Since the only meat Israelites ate from their cattle was that which was offered as a peace offering, the nature of the father's love in this story becomes even clearer. The meat for the feast would have been offered first as a peace offering, signifying that the son had been accepted by the father.

The peace offering points us to Jesus, whose blood makes it possible for us to be at peace with God. "Once you were far away from God, but now you have been brought near to him through the blood of Christ. For Christ himself has brought peace to us" (Ephesians 2:13-14).

† *Christ who is my peace, you have gone far beyond extending forgiveness; you have invited me to feast with you. You have put out the welcome mat, inviting me in at the cost of your own precious blood.*

126

MAY 6
HIS BLOOD
PURIFIES THE CONSCIENCE

Just as in other offerings, blood had to be shed in the sin offering. But in the sin offering, something unusual was done with the blood:

> The high priest will then take some of the bull's blood into the Tabernacle, dip his finger in the blood, and sprinkle it seven times before the LORD in front of the inner curtain of the sanctuary. The priest will then put some of the blood on the horns of the altar for fragrant incense that stands in the LORD's presence inside the Tabernacle. He will pour out the rest of the bull's blood at the base of the altar for burnt offerings at the entrance of the Tabernacle. (Leviticus 4:5-7)

By using the blood of the animal, God was demonstrating in a very dramatic fashion that it was the blood that atoned for Israel's sin; the blood cleansed the Tabernacle, the priests, the people, and the land from the defilement caused by the sin of the people.

The priest dipped his finger in the bowl of blood and sprinkled blood on the veil that concealed the Most Holy Place. Next the priest dipped his finger in the basin and smeared blood on each of the four horns of gold on the golden altar. From there he went to the bronze altar and poured out all the rest of the blood before the people.

Blood was everywhere—blood on the veil, blood on the horns of the altar, blood poured out. Everywhere the sinner looked—blood, blood, blood—an unavoidable statement not only about the pervasive nature of sin, but also about the need for a permanent remedy for sin. What was needed was a perfect sacrifice that would "once for all" not only cover sin, but wash away guilt and empower sinners to sin no longer.

This is the wonder of the once-for-all sacrifice of Jesus:

> Under the old system, the blood of goats and bulls and the ashes of a young cow could cleanse people's bodies from ceremonial impurity. Just think how much more the blood of Christ will purify our consciences from sinful deeds so that we can worship the living God. (Hebrews 9:13-14)

† *Cleanse my conscience with your blood, Jesus, so that I can worship God without the load of guilt and shame of what I've done and who I am. Only your blood can wash away my guilt.*

MAY 7
HE PROVIDES THE SURPLUS

Most of the sacrifices required the death of an animal to atone for sin. This was also part of the guilt offering, but there was another aspect to it:

> You must make restitution for the sacred property you have harmed by paying for the loss, plus an additional 20 percent. When you give the payment to the priest, he will purify you with the ram sacrificed as a guilt offering, making you right with the LORD, and you will be forgiven. (Leviticus 5:16)

The guilt offering asked for something beyond sacrifice; it required restitution. The guilty person had to confess his sin publicly, offer the blood sacrifice, and also make full restitution of what was defrauded, adding an additional 20 percent. It wasn't a cheap or easy repentance. It was a repentance that dearly cost the person who sinned. It required a righteousness that not only paid the debt for what was owed, but paid back more than what was taken.

The familiar demands of the guilt offering are likely what prompted Zacchaeus to say to Jesus, "I will give half my wealth to the poor, Lord, and if I have cheated people on their taxes, I will give them back four times as much!" To this Jesus responded, "Salvation has come to this home today, for this man has shown himself to be a true son of Abraham" (Luke 19:8-9). The evidence that Zacchaeus had found Christ was his eager willingness to engage in restitution to those he had defrauded.

While the guilt offering with its demands to demonstrate repentance through restitution tells us something about what our repentance should look like, it also demonstrates something significant about what Christ has done for us. The sacrificial death of Christ satisfied the claim against us for our sin, but Christ, as our guilt offering, did more than simply cover our debt. Christ also transfers to us the merit of his righteous life. Christ's *Cross* and his *life* are pictured for us in the guilt offering. His death paid the guilt penalty, while his righteous life supplied the surplus.

† *Christ, you alone are my guilt offering. Only by the death of one so valuable and perfect could payment for my sin be made. But that is not all. You also impart to me the merits of your obedient life. You go beyond paying the debt and bless me with all of the blessings that flow from being granted the right to claim your righteousness as my own.*

HE WASHES US WITH THE WORD

The ceremony of cleansing and robing Aaron were public rituals intended to teach Israel about God's holiness. "The whole community assembled at the Tabernacle entrance. Moses announced to them, 'This is what the LORD has commanded us to do!' Then he presented Aaron and his sons and washed them with water" (Leviticus 8:4-6).

This ceremonial washing indicated the moral purity required of a priest. But, of course, an external washing has no power to create an internal reality. Every day, for century after century, the priests were washed from head to toe, pointing to the need for a deeper, more pervasive and permanent cleansing that could not be accomplished by water.

Jesus told his disciples, "You are already clean because of the word I have spoken to you" (John 15:3, NIV). Jesus was saying that as water washes the body, so does the Word of God wash and cleanse the soul. The cleansing pictured by the external washing with water can become an ongoing, internal reality for all who are a part of his priesthood of believers as we wash ourselves daily with his Word.

The Word of God cleanses as it penetrates us and brings sin to the surface so it can be washed away. Its truth washes away our self-centered, people-pleasing, God-denying attitudes and actions so that the Spirit can fill us with Christ-centered, God-pleasing, God-dependent attitudes and actions.

In his great high priestly prayer, Jesus said of his own, "I have given them your word. . . . Make them holy by your truth; teach them your word, which is truth" (John 17:14, 17). Here is the fulfillment of what God intended all along in instituting the ritual washing of the priests. Jesus, the Word made flesh, is our great High Priest. We are washed as we hear his Word, receive his Word, live by his Word, and are changed by his Word. As his Word is applied to our hearts, as it penetrates our thoughts and shapes our perspectives, the cleansing that Christ accomplished on the cross becomes an internal reality in our day-to-day lives.

† *Jesus, I want to be more than declared clean in the legal sense. I want to be clean in an experiential sense. You have given me your Word, and it is living and active, penetrating and powerful. As I meditate on your Word, and as your Word convicts and corrects me, make me truly clean.*

MAY 9

CLEAN ON THE INSIDE

In Leviticus 11, Moses and Aaron spelled out instructions from God about foods that were "clean" and "unclean"; these rules defined what could be touched and eaten and what had to be avoided at the risk of becoming ceremonially "unclean." Every fish, bird, and insect was either clean or unclean, permitted or forbidden.

As we move through the Old Testament, the terms "clean" and "unclean" begin to describe people's internal condition rather than merely their external cleanliness. David wrote in Psalm 51:10: "Create in me a clean heart, O God." Ultimately, God promised that he would make the Israelites clean—something that never was possible through the Old Testament legal and sacrificial system. Ezekiel 36:25-27 spells this out:

> I will sprinkle clean water on you, and you will be clean. Your filth will be washed away, and you will no longer worship idols. And I will give you a new heart, and I will put a new spirit in you. I will take out your stony, stubborn heart and give you a tender, responsive heart. And I will put my Spirit in you so that you will follow my decrees and be careful to obey my regulations.

Even in Old Testament times, the prophets pointed toward a future ultimate and pervasive cleanness. That would come only through the New Covenant and its Mediator, Jesus Christ, whose blood cleanses us from all sin.

Jesus also spoke in terms of clean and unclean, particularly as the scribes and Pharisees disputed his disregard for the ceremonial traditions added to God's laws over the years: "It's not what goes into your body that defiles you; you are defiled by what comes from your heart," Jesus explained (Mark 7:15).

Jesus not only identified the real problem, he offered himself as the sole solution for our uncleanness. "But you were cleansed; you were made holy; you were made right with God by calling on the name of the Lord Jesus Christ and by the Spirit of our God" (1 Corinthians 6:11).

✝ *I call on the name of the Lord Jesus Christ to cleanse me. I see that from out of my heart come evil thoughts, greed, wickedness, deceit, envy, pride, foolishness, and on and on. Sin has utterly defiled me and only you can make me clean.*

MAY 10

HE TAKES UPON HIMSELF OUR SIN-SICKNESS

For the typical leper, the disease of leprosy probably started with just a few painful spots. Then the spots went numb. Slowly his body became a mass of ulcerated growths. The skin around his eyes and ears began to bunch; he lost his fingers and toes to unnoticed and untreated injuries. His eyebrows and eyelashes fell out, and his hair turned white. His rotting flesh gave off an unbearable odor.

The effects of leprosy on a person's body provide a vivid picture of the effects of sin on a person's soul. And just as it takes only one spot to indicate that a person's body is permeated with leprosy, one spot of sin in our lives reveals that the spiritual disease of sin has permeated our whole selves. Our thoughts, our emotions, and our wills have all become infected with sin. Like leprosy, sin infects the whole person, and it is ugly, loathsome, corruptive, contaminating, and alienating, and ultimately leads to death.

Because there was no cure for this terrible disease, God gave unbending instructions to those who suffered from leprosy to protect the rest of the community from it: "They must cover their mouth and call out, 'Unclean! Unclean!' . . . They must live in isolation in their place outside the camp" (Leviticus 13:45-46). So it was significant when a man with leprosy came and knelt in front of Jesus, begging to be healed. "If you are willing, you can heal me and make me clean," he said (Mark 1:40). What Jesus did in this interaction was perhaps more shocking than what he said. "Moved with compassion, Jesus reached out and touched him" (Mark 1:41). Jesus reached out and touched this man whom most people avoided. "I am willing," he said. "Be healed!" And instantly the leprosy disappeared and the man was healed.

In the Old Testament laws regarding the isolation of lepers, God was showing us how sin destroys and separates us from him. In healing the leper, Jesus showed that he can bring us back from the certain death and isolation caused by sin. As we see Jesus reaching out to touch the leper, we see a picture of the way Jesus reaches out to touch us in our guilt and alienation, taking upon himself our sin-sickness, and imparting to us his health, wholeness, and acceptance.

† *I came to you, Jesus, sick with the deadly disease that proves eternally fatal without your healing touch. And you were willing. You touched me, taking upon yourself my sin-sickness and imparting to me your health.*

MAY 11
ONE OUTSIDE THE CAMP

Under God's law, when someone who suffered from a skin disease became well, the person could be declared clean again so that he could return to his family and to the Temple through an unusual ceremony:

> Those who have been healed must be brought to the priest, who will examine them at a place outside the camp. If the priest finds that someone has been healed of a serious skin disease, he will perform a purification ceremony, using two live birds that are ceremonially clean, a stick of cedar, some scarlet yarn, and a hyssop branch. The priest will order that one bird be slaughtered over a clay pot filled with fresh water. He will take the live bird, the cedar stick, the scarlet yarn, and the hyssop branch, and dip them into the blood of the bird that was slaughtered over the fresh water. The priest will then sprinkle the blood of the dead bird seven times on the person being purified of the skin disease. When the priest has purified the person, he will release the live bird in the open field to fly away. (Leviticus 14:2-7)

The person with the skin disease was living as an outcast outside the camp. One bird was slaughtered and one freed, and the sick person was then welcomed back into the fellowship of God's people. Did that person think that the blood of a bird brought him back into God's presence? Or did he understand that this ritual was merely a shadow of a more significant sacrifice to come since "it is not possible for the blood of bulls and goats [and, we might add, birds] to take away sins" (Hebrews 10:4)?

Perhaps the restored sick person rightly wondered, *Could it be that I'm restored because the death I deserve has fallen on somebody outside the camp?* Because this is exactly what was being pictured for him in this process.

We are that leprous sinner. And the death we deserve fell on someone else outside the camp so that we could be restored to fellowship with God. Jesus became diseased in the eyes of the just God so that we could be healed. He died outside the gates of the city, and we've been welcomed into God's house.

† *Sacrifice of God, slain outside the camp so I can go in, the costliness of your sacrifice humbles me. So I receive your healing, and I enjoy the acceptance you have provided to me. Never again will my home be outside the camp. You have gone outside the camp so I can enter in.*

MAY 12

THE SCAPEGOAT

On the annual Day of Atonement, the high priest chose two goats as part of a special ceremony. "Aaron must slaughter the first goat as a sin offering for the people," Leviticus 16:15 instructs. The high priest was to sprinkle the goat's blood on the altar to cleanse it and make it holy. Then he turned to the live goat:

> He will lay both of his hands on the goat's head and confess over it all the wickedness, rebellion, and sins of the people of Israel. In this way, he will transfer the people's sins to the head of the goat. Then a man specially chosen for the task will drive the goat into the wilderness. As the goat goes into the wilderness, it will carry all the people's sins upon itself into a desolate land. (Leviticus 16:21-22)

One goat was killed to provide a picture of the death of a substitute for the sins of the people. The priest put his hands on the other goat—the scapegoat—and confessed the people's sins, ceremonially transferring their sins to the goat. Then the scapegoat was sent out into the wilderness to take the sin away from the community.

Both of these goats picture the work of Jesus: The slaughter of the first goat shows how the death of Christ satisfied the justice of God on our behalf. The transfer of sins to the second goat reveals how Christ bears the whole weight and load of our guilt—everything that the devil uses to accuse us—and carries it away from us. When Jesus died, he went into the wilderness of death, returning to Satan all the accusations he could use against any believer at any time. At the Cross, "the LORD laid on him the sins of us all" (Isaiah 53:6).

Jesus carried sin away to a remote place, as it were, far away from us. Now we can enjoy God's complete forgiveness. We don't have to live under a heavy weight of guilt and shame. "He has removed our sins as far from us as the east is from the west" (Psalm 103:12).

† *Scapegoat for sinners, because you have carried away my sin, I no longer have to live under the heavy weight of accusation and shame. You have given me a clean conscience so I can give myself to you, a living and holy sacrifice, the kind of sacrifice you will find acceptable, worshiping you in a way that is pleasing to you.*

THE SIN PURIFIER

Cleanliness is very important to God. He cannot tolerate the filthiness of sin in his presence. To help us understand this, God instructed the people of Israel to do an annual cleaning on the Day of Atonement—a day set aside to cleanse his dwelling place, the Most Holy Place in the Tabernacle, by making sacrifices for sin. It wasn't dust and dirt that God wanted cleaned out, but the uncleanness of his people's sinful attitudes and actions.

> On the tenth day of the appointed month in early autumn, you must deny yourselves. . . . On that day offerings of purification will be made for you, and you will be purified in the LORD's presence from all your sins. (Leviticus 16:29-30)

Only on this day once a year could the high priest enter the Most Holy Place. To prepare himself to step into God's presence, he carefully bathed himself, put on sacred linen garments, and presented a bull as a sin offering to purify himself and his family. The people of Israel fasted and prayed to God for forgiveness. The sacrifices offered would cover the impurity of their sin for another year, yet provided no permanent solution to the problem of sin. They only pointed to the permanent and wholly sufficient solution to come.

This day of cleansing foreshadowed and anticipated a greater cleansing of God's people and of his dwelling place—the hearts and lives of believers. A special Priest, Jesus—who did not need a cleansing ceremony for himself—would accomplish the day of cleansing to come. He was already perfectly clean.

> He is the kind of high priest we need because he is holy and blameless, unstained by sin. He has been set apart from sinners. . . . The law appointed high priests who were limited by human weakness. But after the law was given, God appointed his Son with an oath, and his Son has been made the perfect High Priest forever. (Hebrews 7:26, 28)

† *My pure and perfect High Priest forever, you have purified me with your blood and given me your own perfect righteousness. Because of your sacrifice, I am clean, and no one can accuse me. I am clean, and no sin can damn me.*

MAY 14

HIS GARMENTS OF WHITE LINEN

When the high priest entered the sanctuary area on the Day of Atonement, he put on a white linen tunic and linen undergarments reserved for that holy day.

> The purification ceremony will be performed by the priest who has been anointed and ordained to serve as high priest in place of his ancestor Aaron. He will put on the holy linen garments and purify the Most Holy Place, the Tabernacle, the altar, the priests, and the entire congregation. (Leviticus 16:32-33)

The high priests in the line of Aaron put on white linen garments to symbolize purity. These men were not pure in themselves, so they washed themselves in the water that represented the cleansing blood of Christ, and they covered themselves in this special linen garment that represented the perfect, all-encompassing righteousness of Christ.

This is the righteousness of the One who left the purity of heaven to be laid in the filth of a manger where he was wrapped, not in fine white linen, but in strips of cloth (Luke 2:7). The day would come when he would be wrapped in linen, but this would not be until the day of his death (John 19:40).

But Jesus left the linen wrapping that covered him in death in the tomb when he emerged to resurrection life. He rose from death, having accomplished everything necessary to provide the white linen garments of his own perfect purity to all who are soiled by the world.

The day is coming when all who have been willing to allow Jesus to cleanse them will be clean. This is what Jesus was saying to his disciples the night before his crucifixion when, as John tells us, he "got up from the table, took off his robe, wrapped a towel around his waist, and poured water into a basin. Then he began to wash the disciples' feet, drying them with the towel he had around him" (John 13:4-5).

"You don't understand now what I am doing, but someday you will," he said. "Unless I wash you, you won't belong to me" (13:7-8).

† *Wash me, Jesus, in the way only you can! Purify me for that day when all who are victorious will be clothed in the white linen garments of your righteousness, when you will announce before your Father and his angels that I am yours.*

MAY 15
LORD OF THE SABBATH

In Leviticus 23, God gave Moses an outline of the feasts and festivals that were to shape the yearly calendar of the nation of Israel. But before he introduced the list of feasts to be observed, he reiterated the fourth commandment—to observe the Sabbath, a pattern of rest following work that was established by God himself at creation. "You have six days each week for your ordinary work, but the seventh day is a Sabbath day of complete rest, an official day for holy assembly. It is the LORD's Sabbath day, and it must be observed wherever you live" (Leviticus 23:3).

Over the centuries between the time of Moses and the time of Jesus, as more and more rules were added to God's command, the Sabbath became more of a burden than the blessing God intended it to be. Into that atmosphere of rigid legalism, Jesus came with a message and a mission that would revive and fulfill God's original intentions for the Sabbath.

In Matthew 12, we read about Jesus and his disciples walking through grain fields on the Sabbath. Some Pharisees saw the disciples plucking heads of grain to eat and protested: "Look, your disciples are breaking the law by harvesting grain on the Sabbath."

Jesus responded by challenging their corruption of the Sabbath as God intended it and questioning them about Old Testament teachings they conveniently ignored that didn't serve their purposes. Then he said something that unveiled God's purpose in establishing the Sabbath in the first place: "For the Son of Man is Lord, even over the Sabbath!"

Jesus didn't come to abolish the Sabbath, but to dig it out from underneath the mountain of legalistic sediment heaped upon it and to give it back to God's people as a blessing rather than a burden. Against the harsh, unbending interpretation of the Pharisees, Jesus reminded all who heard him that God never intended his law to usurp mercy and compassion. But most significantly, as Lord of the Sabbath, Jesus is revealed as the focus and fulfillment of God's command to Sabbath rest. In Jesus we find rest for our souls—now and for eternity.

† *Lord of the Sabbath, I'm so glad you didn't come merely to reinforce the law, but to deliver people like me who can't keep the law. May I turn away from my work and my restlessness so that I can turn toward you and enjoy the Sabbath rest that can be found only in you.*

MAY 16

THE FIRST OF A GREAT HARVEST

Along with the Feast of the Passover and the Festival of Unleavened Bread, God called his people to annually celebrate the Festival of First Harvest (sometimes called Firstfruits). "When you enter the land I am giving you and you harvest its first crops, bring the priest a bundle of grain from the first cutting of your grain harvest" (Leviticus 23:10).

On this day, the first sheaf of harvested barley was brought to the Lord and waved before him. The grain was then left for the priest and for the poor as an act of thanksgiving for the Lord's provision and bounty. This offering was called a firstfruits offering because it was the first part of their crops. Instead of waiting until the full harvest was done and choosing from what was left over, the people were to bring the very best of what was gathered first, before they even knew if more would be harvested, before they knew they would have enough for themselves. The firstfruits offering was a step of faith, a way of trusting God with their first and best. It was an expression of their belief that God would take care of them, whether the rest of the harvest was much or little.

Jesus once described himself as a grain of wheat that fell to the ground and died, that it might spring to life and produce much fruit (John 12:23-24). Most certainly his listeners didn't understand what he was saying then, but after his resurrection it became clearer. God offered up his first and his best in giving his own Son. And because of his faithful offering, there will be a plentiful harvest—a harvest of believers who will be resurrected from their graves, just as Christ was resurrected from the grave.

The apostle Paul described the resurrection of Christ as the "firstfruits" of a greater resurrection day to come: "Christ has indeed been raised from the dead, the firstfruits of those who have fallen asleep. . . . Each in his own turn: Christ, the firstfruits; then, when he comes, all those who belong to him" (1 Corinthians 15:20, 23, NIV).

✝ *Firstfruits of the harvest, knowing that your resurrection life is but the firstfruits of all that is to come, I need not despair about the death that is all around me and in me. I put my hope and confidence in you, that when this seed of my earthly body goes into the ground, you will indeed raise it up again, giving me a glorified body fit for the eternal Kingdom of God.*

MAY 17
LORD OF THE HARVEST

To celebrate the giving of the Law at Sinai, God gave instructions for the Festival of Harvest, or Pentecost, fifty days after Passover:

> Present an offering of new grain to the LORD. From wherever you live, bring two loaves of bread to be lifted up before the LORD as a special offering. Make these loaves from four quarts of choice flour, and bake them with yeast. They will be an offering to the LORD from the first of your crops. (Leviticus 23:16-17)

The loaves of leavened bread waved before the Lord were significant as a rehearsal of something that God had in mind for a time in the future. Baked with yeast, the loaves represented sinful humanity, yet since they were "first-fruits," they represented redeemed or resurrected men. Centuries before it came to pass, the two loaves of this special offering symbolized the body of Christ made up of both Jewish and Gentile believers. It has always been God's intention to use his own special people as instruments to bring in a great harvest of humanity, and that is what began in earnest on the Day of Pentecost that followed Jesus' resurrection. This was the Day of Pentecost that the celebrations through the centuries had all pointed toward.

God chose the time when people from all over the world would be in Jerusalem on the Day of Pentecost to reap a spiritual harvest of souls (Acts 2:5, 36-37, 41).

Jews who had come to Jerusalem to offer God the firstfruits of the wheat harvest became the firstfruits of a great spiritual harvest. They represented the harvest to come, not just of the Jewish people, but also of the entire world.

✝ *Lord of the harvest, I know that the harvest is plentiful but the laborers are few. And I simply can't pray for you to send laborers without offering myself. Fill me with your Spirit, so I can boldly and clearly speak of you.*

MAY 18
A TRUMPET
ANNOUNCES HIS COMING

When a trumpet blasted in Old Testament times, it sounded an alarm, giving a warning to the people of Israel. The people in ancient Israel needed to be periodically awakened from their apathy and careless attitude toward God so they could prepare to welcome his presence in their lives. God appointed the Festival of Trumpets to blast them out of their spiritual laziness (Leviticus 23:24-25) and call them to repentance before God as the Day of Atonement approached.

Similarly, speaking of the day when the Messiah would come, the prophet Isaiah said, "In that day the great trumpet will sound" (27:13). Just as the trumpets that sounded during the Festival of Trumpets called God's people out of their apathy to look for him to act, so will the trumpet call of Christ awaken all who slumber spiritually when he comes to earth the second time.

Christ came quietly the first time, and many people rejected and ignored him. But he will not come quietly the second time. When he comes again, no one will be able to ignore him. Jesus described what that day will be like:

> The sign that the Son of Man is coming will appear in the heavens, and there will be deep mourning among all the peoples of the earth. And they will see the Son of Man coming on the clouds of heaven with power and great glory. And he will send out his angels with the mighty blast of a trumpet, and they will gather his chosen ones from all over the world—from the farthest ends of the earth and heaven. (Matthew 24:30-31)

Paul also spoke of this day when the sound of trumpets will blast us out of our complacency. "The Lord himself will come down from heaven with a commanding shout, with the voice of the archangel, and with the trumpet call of God" (1 Thessalonians 4:16). It will be too late to repent when this final trumpet blasts. For those who have longed for his coming, the trumpet will announce the fulfillment of the Day of Atonement. But for those who have refused to repent, the trumpet will usher in the Day of Judgment.

† *Trumpet of God, I hear your blast, awakening me, alerting me to your soon coming, announcing your arrival, calling me to repentance. Your trumpet call cannot be ignored. I will keep watch for you since I do not know what day you are coming. I long for you to be pleased with my life when you return.*

MAY 19
GOD'S HOME AMONG HIS PEOPLE

Camped in the desert, the twelve tribes of Israel set up their tents on the north, south, east, and west of the Tabernacle, and over the Tabernacle appeared the manifest presence of the Lord. God didn't want his people to forget how he provided for them and how his presence was with them in the wilderness in this way. So he established the Festival of Shelters, also called the Feast of Tabernacles. It revealed something important about his loving care for his own in the past, as well as his loving intentions for his own in the future.

> For seven days you must live outside in little shelters. . . . This will remind each new generation of Israelites that I made their ancestors live in shelters when I rescued them from the land of Egypt. I am the LORD your God. (Leviticus 23:42-43)

The Festival of Shelters pointed *back* to that time in the desert when God's presence was manifest among his people in the center of their camp in the form of a pillar of cloud by day and a pillar of fire by night. But it also pointed *forward* to the day John described when he wrote, "The Word became human and made his home among us" (John 1:14).

The Festival of Shelters also points toward another day when God's presence will be manifest among his people on the new earth—not in a cloud, and not temporarily, but in fullness of glory and for all time. John was given a vision of that coming day, and he described it in Revelation 21:3: "I heard a loud shout from the throne, saying, 'Look, God's home is now among his people! He will live with them, and they will be his people. God himself will be with them.'"

The day is coming when we will experience all of the promise that is celebrated in the Festival of Shelters. We'll finally live in our forever home where we will enjoy the presence of God in our midst. We'll remember how he rescued us from the land of our slavery to sin and brought us out of the wilderness of this world into the safety and security of our eternal home.

† *God who dwells among your people, as holy as you are, you have chosen to come close to me, interact with me, and dwell with me and within me by your Spirit. How I long for the day when I will see you face-to-face, when I will know you even as I am fully known.*

MAY 20

HE RESTORES OUR INHERITANCE

God put Adam and Eve into the Garden of Eden, and it was theirs to cultivate and rule over. But then sin wrought a cruel work that led to crushing exile: "So the LORD God banished them from the Garden of Eden" (Genesis 3:23). Sin forced them into a wilderness of weeds and woe, and ever since then, God has been working out his plan to restore us to our Eden heritage.

God was already hinting at how he would do this in the Old Testament establishment of the Year of Jubilee (Leviticus 25:8-55). Every fiftieth year Israel was to take the whole year off, cancel all debts, and return all family property that had been sold off to its original owners. It was a yearlong Sabbath rest of no toil. "Proclaim freedom throughout the land" (Leviticus 25:10)—that was everyone's job for a whole year.

The Year of Jubilee would have truly been a time of great joy. The downcast debtor was freed. All forfeited estates were returned. The oppressor could no longer oppress. No servant trembled at a lord's stern voice. The descendant reclaimed his father's fields. The ancient landmarks were rebuilt, and liberty resumed its sway. In every house—in every heart—there would have been a consciousness of relief. Sorrow and mourning would have fled away.

In his plan for the Year of Jubilee, God was foreshadowing for us the coming liberation of Christ. The gospel is true jubilee in every sense. We are poor debtors. There is nothing we can generate on our own to satisfy the vast amount that we owe. But our Lord frees us from our unpayable debt and we are welcomed home.

Jesus is our jubilee who restores our inheritance. He will bring us back to the land of our Father. One day we will be restored to the eternal Eden God planned for us all along. We'll walk in its lush perfection, never to be banished again. Our debts fully forgiven and our freedom fully granted, we'll enjoy our Father's fields of goodness forever. We'll have a sure estate anchored in God himself. All that he is—all that he has—will be our inheritance restored.

† *You, Jesus, are my jubilee! You are restoring to me what sin has robbed from me, making it possible for me to come back home into your presence forever.*

HUMBLE AND GENTLE

Moses' brother and sister, Aaron and Miriam, were criticizing Moses, questioning his choices and his unique status as a prophet of God. And in the middle of the account of this conflict, we find an insight into Moses' character, included in parentheses: "(Now Moses was very humble—more humble than any other person on earth)" (Numbers 12:3). Moses could have tried to justify and defend and prove himself in the face of unjust criticism. But he didn't. He chose instead to trust God, to wait on God, and to absorb the insults and criticism without fighting back. This is what it means to be humble.

But while Moses was incredibly humble and meek, he was not perfectly humble and meek. This grace of humility ebbed and flowed in his life. In fact, Moses wasn't allowed to enter the Promised Land of Canaan. Why? Because in a weak moment, Moses struck the rock of God—not in humility but in pride, not in restful trust but in impatient frustration (Numbers 20:9-12).

In his great speech to the people before they entered the land, Moses told them, "The LORD your God will raise up for you a prophet like me from among your fellow Israelites" (Deuteronomy 18:15). And interestingly, in one of the few times Jesus spoke about his own personal character, he pointed to a significant way he was like Moses. Jesus said, "Come to me, all of you who are weary and carry heavy burdens, and I will give you rest. Take my yoke upon you. Let me teach you, because I am humble and gentle at heart, and you will find rest for your souls" (Matthew 11:28-29).

When Jesus was insulted, accused, and brutalized, he didn't fight back or defend himself. He didn't demand to be understood or regarded. His humility was indeed our salvation. "He took the humble position of a slave. . . . He humbled himself in obedience to God and died a criminal's death on a cross" (Philippians 2:7-8).

† *Humble Jesus, how I long to live out an abiding sense of humility in this world that values pride and bravado, not humility and servanthood. I know that it is the death of selfish ambition and an increasing yieldedness to God that reveals the gospel at work in my life, shaping and forming me into your image.*

MAY 22
LOOK AND LIVE

God had just given the Israelites victory over the Canaanites. The Israelites should have been content; instead, they became impatient about getting to the land God had promised to them and started grumbling once again against God and Moses. God had had enough of their complaining. "So the LORD sent poisonous snakes among the people, and many were bitten and died" (Numbers 21:6).

The snakes had their intended effect and the people began to confess their sin. Then the Lord told Moses:

> "Make a replica of a poisonous snake and attach it to a pole. All who are bitten will live if they simply look at it!" So Moses made a snake out of bronze and attached it to a pole. Then anyone who was bitten by a snake could look at the bronze snake and be healed! (Numbers 21:8-9)

It was this picture from the past that Jesus put before Nicodemus, a Pharisee who came to Jesus in the middle of the night. Jesus was less interested in explaining himself than in offering himself to this seeker. Jesus wanted to impress on him the life-or-death decision he had to make. So Jesus recalled the familiar story, saying, "As Moses lifted up the bronze snake on a pole in the wilderness, so the Son of Man must be lifted up, so that everyone who believes in him will have eternal life" (John 3:14-15).

Jesus wanted Nicodemus to understand that we, too, have been bitten—not by a poisonous snake, but by the poison of sin. We too need a cure to break the curse or we face certain death. And just as God provided the cure to his people in the desert, so has he provided a cure to us. But the cure requires something of us. We have to look to Jesus.

Jesus invited Nicodemus to turn away from his learned religiosity and self-righteousness and look to him in repentance and dependence—a simple remedy, but one that required action. In its simplicity, this saving invitation becomes a stumbling block to many. But when we humble ourselves to look at Jesus lifted high on the cross, he breaks the power of the poison of sin and brings healing to our very souls.

✝ *Jesus, I have looked to you for life. You are the only remedy for the deadly curse of sin, and I continue to fix my gaze on you.*

THE BLESSING OF GOD

Balaam was a diviner—a person who read signs and omens to determine the future and performed rituals to change future events. Dreading the invasion of the Israelites, Balak, king of Moab, hired Balaam to curse Israel. But God allowed Balaam to say only what God told him to say. And to Balak's great frustration, God told Balaam to bless rather than curse Israel. Balaam tried to explain himself to Balak:

> God is not a man, so he does not lie.
>> He is not human, so he does not change his mind.
> Has he ever spoken and failed to act?
>> Has he ever promised and not carried it through?
> Listen, I received a command to bless;
>> God has blessed, and I cannot reverse it! (Numbers 23:19-20)

Balaam's words of blessing were a reflection of God's settled attitude and solid intentions toward his people. His promises to bless Israel and to bless the world through her will come to pass. But the people who received the promise had to wait, and waiting can be hard.

Waiting patiently for God to fulfill his promises is what it means to have faith. Saving faith is not just believing what God has done for us in the past through Jesus on the cross; saving faith is putting all our hopes in what God is going to do for us in the future because of what Jesus accomplished on the cross. Faith is putting all of our hopes in the promises of God and being willing to wait, trusting that "God's way is perfect. All the LORD's promises prove true" (Psalm 18:30). And we know that "Christ came as a servant to the Jews to show that God is true to the promises he made to their ancestors" (Romans 15:8).

Indeed God has settled his intentions toward his people—to bless them—and has provided this blessing through Christ. We can lift our voices along with Paul, saying, "All praise to God, the Father of our Lord Jesus Christ, who has blessed us with every spiritual blessing in the heavenly realms because we are united with Christ" (Ephesians 1:3).

† *Blessing of God, how good it is to know that you have settled your attitude toward me—that you intend to bless me—not because I have earned this favor, but because of your own character and your love for your own glory.*

MAY 24
BRIGHT MORNING STAR

Balak, the king of Moab, called on the renowned prophet Balaam in hopes he would deliver a curse on Israel. But while pagan prophets were paid to exert a measure of control over the gods, it was the Lord who controlled Balaam. Balaam's oracles declared that the Lord's blessing rested on Israel with different aspects of that settled blessing unfolding in the past, present, and future. His final oracle spans the entire sweep of human history, revealing that in the end, the Lord's people will be the only ones left standing in total triumph:

> I see him, but not here and now.
>> I perceive him, but far in the distant future.
> A star will rise from Jacob;
>> a scepter will emerge from Israel.
> It will crush the foreheads of Moab's people,
>> cracking the skulls of the people of Sheth.
> Edom will be taken over,
>> and Seir, its enemy, will be conquered,
>> while Israel marches on in triumph.
> A ruler will rise in Jacob
>> who will destroy the survivors of Ir. (Numbers 24:17-19)

At the birth of Jesus, a heavenly star indeed rose over Israel, but the baby King lay in a manger, not in a palace, and those drawn by the star were not Israelites but foreign wise men. King Herod, an Edomite by descent, was not instantly crushed by the coming of this new King but continued his rule. The rising of this star in Christ's first coming did not yet bring about the total destruction of the nations and the triumph of Israel.

The fulfillment of Balaam's prophecy and the clearest revelation of the identity of this star are found in John's record of the end of history in Revelation 22:16, where Jesus proclaims, "I, Jesus, have sent my angel to give you this message for the churches. I am both the source of David and the heir to his throne. I am the bright morning star."

† *Lord, your settled determination to bless your people has always been and will always be to bless us through your star, Jesus Christ. I see his star rising and I say, come, Lord Jesus!*

MAY 25

CALLED TO A LOVE RELATIONSHIP

The people of Israel spent forty years of wandering in the wilderness as punishment for their lack of faith when they first arrived at the Promised Land (Numbers 14:34). The older generation died and the nation was once again poised to enter the land. At that point, Moses began to teach the people what God wanted for them and from them as they prepared to live in the land he had given to them. Loving God became the first and greatest commandment in the law: "Listen, O Israel! The LORD is our God, the LORD alone. And you must love the LORD your God with all your heart, all your soul, and all your strength" (Deuteronomy 6:4-5).

From the very beginning, God called his people to a love relationship. He revealed himself to Moses, saying, "I lavish unfailing love for a thousand generations on those who love me and obey my commands" (Exodus 20:6). He called his people to delight in him and admire him above all else.

But to deeply love God, we must know him. So Jesus came into the world to make God knowable. In fact, Jesus became the measuring rod, the revealer, of whether or not a person truly loves God. Our love for God—or our lack of love—is revealed by whether or not we love Jesus. Jesus made it clear to the Jews who prided themselves in keeping the commandments that there was no way they could claim to have kept the first commandment and still reject him. "If God were your Father, you would love me," he said (John 8:42).

When the religious leaders asked Jesus which commandment was most important, he took them back to Deuteronomy. "'You must love the LORD your God with all your heart, all your soul, and all your mind.' This is the first and greatest commandment" (Matthew 22:37-38).

Jesus revealed something stunning to the people of his day. While God demanded obedience, what he really wants is obedience that flows from a heart of love. But this demands that his people have new hearts—hearts made soft by the Spirit of Christ.

† *Jesus, you came to reveal the true heart and nature of God to me. And only you can take away my heart of stony, self-seeking rule keeping and give me a heart that is soft and pliable so that I can love God with my whole heart in a way worthy of him.*

MAY 26

WE DIDN'T CHOOSE GOD; HE CHOSE US

The Old Testament tells us the story of the people God chose from all the peoples of the earth to showcase his redeeming work. But the reasoning and purpose behind his choice is not obvious in human terms.

> The LORD did not set his heart on you and choose you because you were more numerous than other nations, for you were the smallest of all nations! Rather, it was simply that the LORD loves you, and he was keeping the oath he had sworn to your ancestors. (Deuteronomy 7:7-8)

God didn't choose to set his affections on Israel because they had done anything to deserve it or because they were strong or numerous or impressive. He loved them because he chose to love them. And he loved them because he had promised Abraham and Isaac and Jacob that he would love them when he said, "This is the everlasting covenant: I will always be your God and the God of your descendants after you" (Genesis 17:7). His choosing was not random, and neither was it without meaning. His purpose in choosing them? "I created Judah and Israel to cling to me, says the LORD. They were to be my people, my pride, my glory—an honor to my name" (Jeremiah 13:11).

We see some of the same reasoning and purpose in Jesus' choosing of his twelve disciples. They were not impressive and had no prior inclination toward Christ. Jesus simply called them to follow him. And before he died he reminded them, "You didn't choose me. I chose you" (John 15:16).

The apostle Paul reveals that God's choice of who would be his began not with the choosing of Israel or with Jesus' choosing his disciples, but long before. And it was always centered in Christ himself. "Even before he made the world, God loved us and chose us in Christ to be holy and without fault in his eyes. God decided in advance to adopt us into his own family by bringing us to himself through Jesus Christ. This is what he wanted to do, and it gave him great pleasure" (Ephesians 1:4-5).

† *Gracious God, before the creation of the universe you thought of me. You fixed your gaze on me and chose me for yourself. You didn't choose me because I was already in Christ by my own doing, but that I might be in Christ. You didn't choose me because I chose you, but so that I might choose you. You didn't choose me because I was holy or good, but so that I might become holy and good.*

MAY 27

HE PASSED THE
TEST IN THE WILDERNESS

As God led Israel toward the Promised Land, his purpose was not rapid transportation; it was education. Moses told the Israelites exactly how God wanted to test them and what God wanted to teach them:

> The LORD your God led you through the wilderness . . . humbling you and testing you to prove your character, and to find out whether or not you would obey his commands. Yes, he humbled you by letting you go hungry and then feeding you with manna, a food previously unknown to you and your ancestors. He did it to teach you that people do not live by bread alone; rather, we live by every word that comes from the mouth of the LORD. (Deuteronomy 8:2-3)

The Israelites needed to learn to trust God and to be content with his provision. If they learned to be content with little, they would more easily appreciate the bounty of Canaan. God was teaching the Israelites that their full satisfaction could not come from any food, no matter how good it tasted; their full satisfaction would come only from knowing and serving God.

Over and over again the Israelites failed the test. Rather than living by every word that came from God, they rejected and questioned God's instructions. But where they failed the test, Jesus passed the test. Jesus was tested in the wilderness, not for forty years, but for forty days. Though he was desperately hungry, he did not complain against God.

> During that time the devil came and said to him, "If you are the Son of God, tell these stones to become loaves of bread."
> But Jesus told him, "No! The Scriptures say,
>
> 'People do not live by bread alone,
>   but by every word that comes from the mouth of God.' "
>   (Matthew 4:3-4)

Rather than resenting God, Jesus chose to depend on God. Rather than forgetting God's Word and giving in to temptation, he called on God's Word and won the battle against temptation.

☩ *Lord, you have tested me to find out whether or not I will obey your commands, and I have come up short again and again. But I am united to Jesus who was tested and did not fail. His obedience is mine by faith.*

HE TOOK UPON HIMSELF THE CURSE OF DISOBEDIENCE

Moses told the children of Israel that if they genuinely loved the Lord, their wholehearted devotion would be characterized by obedience. Presenting the truth in graphic terms and emphasizing the need for a radical decision, Moses pointed to two mountains which would stand on either side of them as they entered the land: Mount Gerizim and Mount Ebal. One typified blessing, the other cursing:

> Look, today I am giving you the choice between a blessing and a curse! You will be blessed if you obey the commands of the LORD your God that I am giving you today. But you will be cursed if you reject the commands of the LORD your God and turn away from him and worship gods you have not known before. (Deuteronomy 11:26-28)

God had taken the initiative by setting his love upon the Hebrews as his covenant people, but each individual was compelled to make his choice as well. That choice would determine his future—a future in which he got what he chose: either God's blessings or the curse of a life apart from him.

In Deuteronomy 28, God lists for the people the ways in which he would bless them for obedience, as well as catastrophe upon catastrophe awaiting those who chose not to obey.

> You will grope around in broad daylight like a blind person . . . oppressed and robbed continually, and no one will come to save you . . . hungry, thirsty, naked, and lacking in everything. . . . You will find no peace or place to rest. . . . You will live night and day in fear, unsure if you will survive. (28:29, 48, 65-66)

But the people simply couldn't obey, and they came under the curse of disobedience (which becomes much of the story of the rest of the Old Testament). Their only hope was that God himself would rescue them from the curse. And that's what he did. "Christ has rescued us. . . . When he was hung on the cross, he took upon himself the curse for our wrongdoing" (Galatians 3:13).

† *I was blind and lost, a sad victim of the ravages of sin. But because you took that curse upon yourself, now I have an inheritance and I have victory over sin—I belong to you! You have taken the curse of disobedience and given me the blessings of your perfect obedience!*

A KING TO RULE OVER US

There was a reason God inaugurated his relationship with Israel with no human king. He wanted to make it clear that only God should be King of Israel. And yet he knew the day would come when they would demand to have a king, and indeed his giving them a king would be part of his plan to make them into people who would submit to his kingly rule.

> You are about to enter the land the LORD your God is giving you. When you take it over and settle there, you may think, "We should select a king to rule over us like the other nations around us." If this happens, be sure to select as king the man the LORD your God chooses. (Deuteronomy 17:14-15)

God was faithful as their divine King. When they cried to him, he saved them. He gave them safety. That's what a king is for—to provide peace for the people. And what was their response? "Give us a king to judge us like all the other nations have" (1 Samuel 8:5). When the day came that Israel asked for a king, they were rejecting the truth that only God could be their king. "It is me they are rejecting, not you," God said to Samuel, the judge. "They don't want me to be their king any longer" (1 Samuel 8:7). God gave in to Israel's demand for a human king, but he did not change his mind about being the only true King of Israel.

Indeed God knew there needed to be a human king. For God to have a people to rule and to love, who were not alienated from him because of their sins, their king would have to die for them. God cannot die, but a man can die. So God planned not only that only he could be the rightful King of Israel, but that the rightful King of Israel would die in the place of the people.

Jesus was the God-man King who was always needed. He was the King who came to die for his people. In claiming to be the King of the Jews, he was far more than a human king. He was the God-man King God had always planned to send.

† *My God-man King, I need a king to rule over me, protect me, and provide me with peace. But no human king can do this with justice, mercy, and perfection into eternity. Come and rule over me. Rule my passions. Overrule my fleshly desires. Rout out the sin that seeks to destroy me and let me live in your peaceful presence.*

THE PROPHET MOSES PREDICTED

At the end of forty years of wandering in the desert, God spoke a word of assurance and instruction to his people. Moses said, "The LORD your God will raise up for you a prophet like me from among your fellow Israelites. You must listen to him" (Deuteronomy 18:15).

In part, this referred to a succession of prophets whom God would raise up in Israel. Yet none of the Old Testament prophets who followed Moses were quite like him. None had the unique face-to-face relationship with God that Moses had, or enjoyed the same communion with God Moses enjoyed. None performed the level of public miracles Moses performed.

Moses was speaking of another prophet to come who would enjoy unusually intimate fellowship with the Father as Moses did. He would work great miracles in public and be a lawgiver as Moses was. He would be a mediator who would offer himself so that his people could be saved, and a deliverer who would lead them out of bondage.

Jesus not only suggested that he was the fulfillment of the Prophet whom Moses spoke about, but also that he should be listened to. "Blessed are your eyes, because they see; and your ears, because they hear. I tell you the truth, many prophets and righteous people longed to see what you see, but they didn't see it. And they longed to hear what you hear, but they didn't hear it" (Matthew 13:16-17).

But it was when they saw Jesus feed more than five thousand people with a couple of fish and some bread that it began to become clear to the people of his day. "Surely, he is the Prophet we have been expecting!" they began to say (John 6:14). Later, after Jesus ascended into heaven, Peter confirmed the connection between Jesus, whom the Jews had crucified, and the prophet Moses had predicted. Addressing a crowd that gathered at the Temple, Peter reminded the people, "Moses said, 'The LORD your God will raise up for you a Prophet like me from among your own people.' . . . Starting with Samuel, every prophet spoke about what is happening today" (Acts 3:22, 24).

Jesus comes to us as this Prophet, giving us a message from God that must be heard and obeyed. "You must listen to him."

† *I'm listening, Prophet of God. How I long to hear your voice speaking into my life. I'm listening for instruction and direction, clarity and comfort. Speak to me, and I will listen.*

MAY 31

My Words in His Mouth

After hearing the voice of God at Sinai pronouncing judgment on them for their sin with the golden calf, the Israelites were afraid to hear God speak to them again. So Moses was the mediator.

> You said, "Don't let us hear the voice of the LORD our God anymore or see this blazing fire, for we will die."
>
> Then the LORD said to me, "What they have said is right. I will raise up a prophet like you from among their fellow Israelites. I will put my words in his mouth, and he will tell the people everything I command him." (Deuteronomy 18:16-18)

Instead of hearing God's thundering voice, they would hear God's Word from a prophet who was a man like them. And in the coming centuries, God raised up a number of prophets from among the Israelites who spoke God's words to his people. But still they waited for the unique and singular prophet God had promised. And when John the Baptist came powerfully preaching repentance, they thought maybe he was the prophet they had been waiting for. But John made it clear he was not the one but pointed to Jesus, saying,

> We are of the earth, and we speak of earthly things, but he has come from heaven and is greater than anyone else. He testifies about what he has seen and heard, but how few believe what he tells them! Anyone who accepts his testimony can affirm that God is true. For he is sent by God. He speaks God's words, for God gives him the Spirit without limit. (John 3:31-34)

Later, Jesus himself claimed to speak the words of God, saying, "I don't speak on my own authority. The Father who sent me has commanded me what to say and how to say it. And I know his commands lead to eternal life; so I say whatever the Father tells me to say" (John 12:49-50).

Jesus is the Prophet Moses promised, raised up by God, to speak the very words of God.

† *Prophet of God, you have the words of eternal life. You speak life into death, hope into despair, truth into delusion, meaning into futility, peace into panic. From your lips I receive wisdom and compassion and companionship and so much more. Give me ears to hear your word, Lord Jesus.*

JUNE 1
HE TOLD THEM IN ADVANCE

A prophet was God's mouthpiece, speaking for God and giving out God's message. But while being a true prophet meant that the person had a message from God, it didn't mean he always understood the meaning or the timing of the events predicted. The prophets struggled to learn the circumstances surrounding the time of the fulfillment of their prophecies, and they were also perplexed as to who would fulfill them and how that fulfillment would come about. Peter explained:

> This salvation was something even the prophets wanted to know more about when they prophesied about this gracious salvation prepared for you. They wondered what time or situation the Spirit of Christ within them was talking about when he told them in advance about Christ's suffering and his great glory afterward. (1 Peter 1:10-11)

The "Spirit of Christ within them" told the prophets exactly what to say about Christ's coming, his character, and the work he would accomplish, even though it might not have been clear to them.

When Jesus said of the Law and the Prophets, "I have not come to abolish them but to fulfill them" (Matthew 5:17, NIV), he was not saying simply that he fulfilled certain messianic predictions that are scattered throughout the prophetic writings. Instead, he was saying that *all* that the prophets spoke about is fulfilled in him.

But this was difficult for the people of Jesus' day to accept. There were certain things the prophets said about the Messiah that Jesus just didn't seem to fulfill. That's because in foretelling future events, the prophet resembled a traveler viewing a mountain range from afar. From far away, the range appears as one ridge of hills. But as he gets closer, he sees range behind range. Peaks that appeared from far off to be at the same distance from him are perhaps miles behind each other. So it is with prophecy. The prophet cannot tell the immense distances of time that separate one event from another. The prophets couldn't distinguish between Christ's first coming in humiliation and his second coming in glory.

† *My God, to you one day is as a thousand years, and a thousand years is as one day. You told the prophets in advance about your coming and now we long for your coming again.*

THE CURSED ONE

Although the Jews didn't practice crucifixion as a means of capital punishment, they did have a similar custom for expressing a high degree of contempt for certain outlaws. After a criminal had been put to death by some other means (i.e., the sword, stoning, etc.), the dead body would be strung up on a tree as a symbol of shame and dishonor. This public exposure gave the people an opportunity to express their venomous hatred for a despicable criminal as they hurled their insults and mockery at the strung-up victim. Hanging a body in public showed that that person was under God's curse as described in Deuteronomy 21:

> If someone has committed a crime worthy of death and is executed and hung on a tree, the body must not remain hanging from the tree overnight. You must bury the body that same day, for anyone who is hung is cursed in the sight of God. (21:22-23)

It was for this reason that Joshua impaled the king of Ai on a pole (Joshua 8:29) and the bodies of the five kings of the southern confederacy on five sharpened poles (Joshua 10:26-27). Interested in more than their execution, he wanted to expose them to public shame and ridicule.

Because they wanted this shame and ridicule to fall on Christ, the Jews cried out to Pilate, "Crucify him!" Knowing that the Roman idea of crucifixion was paramount to their practice of hanging on a tree, they would be satisfied with nothing less than having Jesus crucified. This would put him to shame and demonstrate that he was cursed by God.

What they did not understand, however, was that it was their shame Christ was bearing on the tree, their curse he took upon himself: "When he was hung on the cross, he took upon himself the curse for our wrongdoing" (Galatians 3:13).

While thousands of people died on crosses throughout history, only one has ever received the full measure of the curse of God while on a cross. There, the One with whom the Father was well pleased received in himself the curse of God—not for his own sin but for the sin of the truly guilty who will turn to him in faith and repentance.

† *You became a curse for me, Jesus. You received the humiliation I deserve, the rejection by God I deserve for my blatant disobedience against the God of the universe. Because of you, I will not be cut off from God; instead, I am welcomed in.*

JUNE 3
God's Secret Plan Revealed

Before the coming of Christ, people were saved by trusting in the mercy of God. They looked to his mighty deeds like the Exodus and to the blood sacrifices. They remembered the promises of a Redeemer and a Messiah. They believed God's promise that he would bless the nations through Israel, but they did not know how that would happen. "To this day the LORD has not given you minds that understand, nor eyes that see, nor ears that hear!" Moses said to the people as they prepared to finally enter the Promised Land (Deuteronomy 29:4). He continued, "The LORD our God has secrets known to no one. We are not accountable for them, but we and our children are accountable forever for all that he has revealed to us, so that we may obey all the terms of these instructions" (29:29).

There was plenty that Old Testament saints could not see or understand when it came to how God would fulfill his promises and enact his plans. But when Christ came, he lifted the veil so that all could see that *he* is the way God fulfills his promises, and *he* is the instrument through whom God will enact his plans for salvation. In Ephesians 1:9-13, Paul wrote:

> God has now revealed to us his mysterious plan regarding Christ, a plan to fulfill his own good pleasure. And this is the plan: At the right time he will bring everything together under the authority of Christ— everything in heaven and on earth . . . for he chose us in advance, and he makes everything work out according to his plan.
>
> God's purpose was that we Jews who were the first to trust in Christ would bring praise and glory to God. And now you Gentiles have also heard the truth, the Good News that God saves you. And when you believed in Christ, he identified you as his own by giving you the Holy Spirit, whom he promised long ago.

God has always had a plan. Colossians 2:2 says that God's secret plan is "Christ himself." What makes this secret plan so significant is that it is not just a secret we can know with our minds, but an experience we're invited to enter into. "This is the secret: Christ lives in you" (Colossians 1:27).

† *Christ, who lives in me, what a beautiful, magnificent, holy plan—a plan that will culminate when you return and bring everything together under your rightful rule. I will not resist your perfect plan for this world or for my life, but gladly submit myself to you.*

JUNE 4
HIS SPIRIT WILL CHANGE THE HEART

Moses gave God's law to God's people but it was immediately and repeatedly obvious that they could not obey. So Moses began to look forward to the day when God would give his people new hearts that would be empowered to obey God's law: "The LORD your God will change your heart and the hearts of all your descendants, so that you will love him with all your heart and soul and so you may live!" (Deuteronomy 30:6).

The Lord sent this promise not only through his prophet Moses, but also through Jeremiah—"I will put my instructions deep within them, and I will write them on their hearts" (Jeremiah 31:33), and Ezekiel—"I will put my Spirit in you so that you will follow my decrees and be careful to obey my regulations" (Ezekiel 36:27).

When Christ ascended and the Spirit descended at Pentecost, the Spirit brought God's law to his people in a new way. It was no longer external, written on tablets of clay, but became internal, written on the hearts of God's people, enabling and empowering them to fulfill the law's commands.

While in the economy of the old covenant, God's Spirit gave God's Word to his prophets, under the new covenant ushered in by Christ, all of the Lord's people possess the knowledge of God formerly experienced only by the prophets. This is exactly what Moses had longed for when he said, "I wish that all the LORD's people were prophets and that the LORD would put his Spirit upon them all!" (Numbers 11:29). At Pentecost, Moses' wish became the reality we now live under and enjoy.

The new heart is wrought by the Spirit's work of regeneration. In regeneration, the Spirit liberates a believer's will from its bondage to sin. He cleanses the contamination left behind by sin. The Spirit creates a new appetite for God and his Word. This is the radical change that penetrates a person deeply. It is the gift of a new heart.

† *Jesus, your Spirit is teaching me everything I need to know, and what he teaches is true. And as your truth sinks in, it is truly changing my heart. Your Spirit is transforming my mind so I can understand your plans and purposes, and he is changing my will so that I want to obey your commands. Your Spirit is giving me a heart made to love you completely!*

JUNE 5

He Did What the Law Could Not Do

The law God gave to his people through Moses was more than lists of dos and don'ts. It was a system of divine expectations regarding belief and behavior, which, if faithfully carried out, would bring God's richest blessing. In fact, life itself depended on keeping the law.

But God gave the law without giving the Holy Spirit to most Israelites, and so they were powerless to keep the law. Moses himself said, at the end of his life, "Take this Book of Instruction and place it beside the Ark of the Covenant of the LORD your God, so it may remain there as a witness against the people of Israel. For I know how rebellious and stubborn you are" (Deuteronomy 31:26-27).

So if the law would not give life, but only condemnation, why was the law given? Paul answered this question directly in the New Testament:

> God's law was given so that all people could see how sinful they were. But as people sinned more and more, God's wonderful grace became more abundant. (Romans 5:20)

> It was given alongside the promise to show people their sins. But the law was designed to last only until the coming of the child who was promised. (Galatians 3:19)

God gave the law so that we could look in it like we would look into a mirror and see the sin in our lives. And God devoted over a thousand years of history (from Moses to Christ) so that we could see our own failures in the failures of Israel. But his intention was never to leave us in this slavery to sin:

> The law of Moses was unable to save us because of the weakness of our sinful nature. So God did what the law could not do. He sent his own Son in a body like the bodies we sinners have. And in that body God declared an end to sin's control over us by giving his Son as a sacrifice for our sins. He did this so that the just requirement of the law would be fully satisfied for us, who no longer follow our sinful nature but instead follow the Spirit. (Romans 8:3-4)

† *The law came through Moses, but grace and truth came through you, Jesus. Because of you, I can look into your law and face the truth about myself. But rather than be defeated and disheartened by it, I am empowered to be changed by it through your grace.*

HISTORICAL
BOOKS

THE LAW CAN'T BRING US INTO THE LAND

When we look at Israel's history leading up to entry into the Promised Land, we see a picture of the experiences of the soul prior to conversion. In Exodus, as the Israelites were enslaved in Egypt, we see the natural self in bondage to sin and Satan. In Leviticus, as Moses detailed the required offerings, sacrifices, and cleansing rituals, we see God speaking, making known his holy requirements. In Numbers, the record of the Israelites' wanderings, the people of God are in a great howling wilderness, which is how the world appears to one who has been awakened by the Spirit. Then Deuteronomy teaches the strictness and spirituality of the law, which cuts into pieces all self-righteousness and reveals that Another than Moses must become the Captain of one's salvation if ever he is to enter into all that God has promised.

The people could not enter the land of Canaan until Moses was dead. Moses represented the law. Neither can we enter into the life God has promised to us merely by law keeping. Even our best efforts could never be good enough. "For no one can ever be made right with God by doing what the law commands. The law simply shows us how sinful we are" (Romans 3:20). We need someone else to take us beyond recognition of our guilt before God. We needed a Joshua. "For the law was given through Moses, but God's unfailing love and faithfulness came through Jesus Christ" (John 1:17).

Joshua, rather than Moses, led the Israelites into Canaan. He led them to victory, driving out their enemies; he was their advocate in time of defeat. He allotted them their inheritance within the Promised Land. And so it is Jesus, our Joshua, who leads us into the rest of salvation. He alone perfectly kept the law's demands. We cling to his merits, his perfect living out of the law that he imputes to us—and that alone enables us to enter in. He empowers us to gain victory and advocates for us before the Father. He gives us our inheritance that has been purchased with his own blood.

Paul wrote, "The law of Moses was unable to save us because of the weakness of our sinful nature. So God did what the law could not do. He sent his own Son" (Romans 8:3). The law simply couldn't bring us into the life God has for us. So he sent us his Joshua to lead the way.

† *Lord, I love your law—what it reveals to me about you and about myself. But in its light I see my need for your salvation! I need a Savior! And that is what you have provided to me in Jesus, who is full of grace and truth.*

OUR JOSHUA

Numbers 13 gives the names of the men Moses sent out to explore the land, and we are told that "Moses called Hoshea son of Nun by the name Joshua" (13:16). While *Hoshea* means "salvation," Moses changed his name to Joshua, which means, "Yahweh saves."

When the spies returned from exploring the land, most of them came back frightened. Only Joshua and Caleb came back ready to enter the land God gave them. However, they were overruled by the fearful Israelites, and God sent the entire nation wandering for forty years. Then, as they prepared to enter the land, Joshua was commissioned to become Moses' replacement. We read in Deuteronomy 34:9 that "Joshua son of Nun was full of the spirit of wisdom, for Moses had laid his hands on him."

Joshua—full of the spirit, given a name that celebrates the saving intentions of God, given the task of leading God's people into the Promised Land of rest—prefigures the One to come who would also be named "Yahweh Saves." The angel Gabriel told Joseph that Mary would give birth to a Son, given by God, and that they were to name him Jesus because "he will save his people from their sins" (Matthew 1:21).

Jesus, the greater Joshua, initiated his work of salvation in much the same way as the first Joshua—by crossing over the Jordan River through his baptism by John (Mark 1:9). God promised Joshua, "I will give you every place where you set your foot, as I promised Moses" (Joshua 1:3, NIV). But this promise was not solely for Joshua but for all God's people. "You will lead these people to inherit the land I swore to their forefathers to give them," God said (1:6, NIV). Jesus is the greater Joshua the promises were given to, not for the sake of himself alone, but so that all who are in him might possess the earth and be granted all the promises of God.

Joshua promised to perform his salvation and take the people of Israel into their land within the space of three days. "Get your supplies ready. Three days from now you will cross the Jordan here to go in and take possession of the land the LORD your God is giving you for your own" (1:11, NIV). Likewise, the greater Joshua accomplished our greater salvation when he suffered, died, and rose again in three days.

✝ *Jesus, my Joshua, I am weary from my own failed efforts of living up to the law, and you have come to lead me into the rest of salvation. Truly you are the Lord who saves.*

JUNE 8
I Will Be with You

After Moses died, the Lord promised Joshua: "Wherever you set foot, you will be on land I have given you. . . . No one will be able to stand against you as long as you live. For I will be with you as I was with Moses. I will not fail you or abandon you" (Joshua 1:3, 5). In effect, these verses reiterated an earlier charge Moses had given to Joshua:

> You have seen for yourself everything the LORD your God has done to these two kings. He will do the same to all the kingdoms on the west side of the Jordan. Do not be afraid of the nations there, for the LORD your God will fight for you. (Deuteronomy 3:21-22)

The Canaanites who occupied the land were fierce warriors, and it was clear that the people of Israel could never occupy the land in their own strength. The hand of their God, Yahweh, must deliver the land to them. Though the Canaanites would be tough fighters, the sovereign God promised to be with the Israelites and give them victory.

The same covenant promise that God gave to Joshua is reiterated in the New Testament and given to us, the people of God, through the greater Joshua, Jesus Christ. At the end of Matthew's Gospel, Jesus left his disciples with the following words:

> I have been given all authority in heaven and on earth. Therefore, go and make disciples of all the nations, baptizing them in the name of the Father and the Son and the Holy Spirit. Teach these new disciples to obey all the commands I have given you. And be sure of this: I am with you always, even to the end of the age. (Matthew 28:18-20)

Just as Israel was to enter Canaan confident in the power of God, we are to go into all the world, making disciples and teaching the nations not to depart from the Word of God. And just as God was with Joshua, so too the greater Joshua is with us. He will never leave us nor forsake us.

✝ *Christ who strengthens me, many enemies desire to keep me from enjoying the life of rest you have promised, and they loom large in my estimation. I am weak, but you are strong! With you, the Captain of my salvation, going before me and beside me, I can be strong and courageous. I can win the battle against sin in my life.*

JUNE 9

HE LEADS US
TO POSSESS THE LAND

As the Israelites prepared to cross over the Jordan, God said, "You will be on land I have given you" (Joshua 1:3). The Israelites were not entitled to the land of Canaan. They had done nothing to merit it, nor would their subsequent prowess in conquering the Canaanites earn it. But even though it was a gift, entering into possession of this gift would not come without effort on their part. The Jordan must be crossed, cities must be captured, battles must be fought, and the Canaanites must be conquered before Israel could enter into possession and enjoyment of their inheritance. The people would experience long marches, protracted campaigns, and much heavy fighting before they fully entered into possession of their heritage. It involved years of persevering effort.

God told the Israelites that he would drive their enemies out of the land he would give them. However, he said, "I will not drive them out in a single year, because the land would become desolate and the wild animals would multiply and threaten you. I will drive them out a little at a time until your population has increased enough to take possession of the land" (Exodus 23:29-30).

Certainly in contrast to the wanderings in the wilderness, living in Canaan brought real rest. In actual experience, however, their entrance into the land marked the beginning of years of hard fighting. So it is for those outside of Christ when they enter into his rest of salvation. That moment there is a new rest for the soul, yet the fierce battle between the flesh and spirit has just begun, and will, in fact, last a lifetime.

The apostle Paul understood the reality of this ongoing battle, the effort and perseverance required to truly possess all that God had given to him. But he also knew his Joshua would ultimately lead him into victory:

> I press on to possess that perfection for which Christ Jesus first possessed me. No, dear brothers and sisters, I have not achieved it, but I focus on this one thing: Forgetting the past and looking forward to what lies ahead, I press on to reach the end of the race and receive the heavenly prize for which God, through Christ Jesus, is calling us. (Philippians 3:12-14)

† *By faith I have received the inheritance you give to all of your children of a place in your Promised Land. But until that day I will fight the good fight. I intend to finish the race, to remain faithful.*

JUNE 10

By Grace, through Faith

Two spies made their way across the Jordan River and into Jericho to scout out the enemy territory. There, to avoid any kind of suspicion, they spent the night in the house of a prostitute named Rahab. Rahab had heard about the Israelites. But more significantly, she had heard about the God of the Israelites.

> "I know the LORD has given you this land," she told them. "We are all afraid of you. Everyone in the land is living in terror. For we have heard how the LORD made a dry path for you through the Red Sea when you left Egypt. And we know what you did to Sihon and Og, the two Amorite kings east of the Jordan River, whose people you completely destroyed. No wonder our hearts have melted in fear! No one has the courage to fight after hearing such things. For the LORD your God is the supreme God of the heavens above and the earth below. Now swear to me by the LORD that you will be kind to me and my family since I have helped you." (Joshua 2:9-12)

The spies agreed, telling Rahab to leave a scarlet rope hanging from her window so that she and her family would be spared when the Israelites overtook Jericho.

The writer to the Hebrews reveals that though Rahab was a notorious sinner, her grabbing hold of the promises of God revealed that she was a woman of great faith. She believed in the power of God and was willing to risk everything to become a part of the people of God (Hebrews 11:31). Rahab was delivered from the judgment that fell upon Jericho because she knew that Yahweh was the true and living God, and she believed he would give his people the land as he promised. Not only did she want to be saved from the judgment of God about to fall on Jericho, she wanted to get in on the promises of God that belong to those who live by faith. Because Rahab was justified through faith and her sins were forgiven, she lived the rest of her life as a citizen among God's people. Not only that, she married among these people and is included in the family line of Jesus Christ (Matthew 1:5)—the One in whom all of the promises of God are ultimately fulfilled.

† *Holy God, in your sight I stand in Rahab's place. I deserve your flaming judgment. But because I believe you will fulfill your promises, you have grafted me in to the people of God. You are not ashamed to call me yours.*

JUNE 11
HE GOES BEFORE US

Joshua gave clear instructions for crossing over the Jordan River and into the Promised Land:

> "When you see the Levitical priests carrying the Ark of the Covenant of the LORD your God, move out from your positions and follow them. . . . Purify yourselves, for tomorrow the LORD will do great wonders among you." . . .
>
> So the people left their camp to cross the Jordan, and the priests who were carrying the Ark of the Covenant went ahead of them. It was the harvest season, and the Jordan was overflowing its banks. But as soon as the feet of the priests who were carrying the Ark touched the water at the river's edge, the water above that point began backing up a great distance away at a town called Adam, which is near Zarethan. And the water below that point flowed on to the Dead Sea until the riverbed was dry. Then all the people crossed over near the town of Jericho. (Joshua 3:3, 5, 14-16)

God did something significant that day—"great wonders" as Joshua said. But the wonder was not so much the miracle of the Jordan River drying up for the people to cross over; the wonder was that the living God was among them, leading them, going with them.

The Ark of the Covenant went ahead of them. Inside this chest made of wood were the stone tablets inscribed with the terms of the covenant. On top of the Ark was the atonement cover where God promised to meet with his people. Here was where God made substitutionary provision so that through the shedding of blood to cover sin, he might be able to dwell with his people.

The Ark going before the people signified that God himself was establishing his presence in the world among his purified people. Here is a picture of the One to come, God-Become-Flesh, Jesus—God's provision to make atonement for the sins of the world—going before his people, establishing God's presence in the world. He is the way in which we enter into real and lasting relationship with God. He has gone before us to do all that is necessary to secure a place of rest for his people. "He entered into heaven itself to appear now before God on our behalf" (Hebrews 9:24).

† *Living God, I consecrate myself to you. Your cross goes before me, making a way for me to live in your holy presence.*

COMMANDER OF THE LORD'S ARMY

Israel crossed the Jordan River on dry ground and was camped at Gilgal, just a few miles from the gates of Jericho. It would not be long before the Lord granted his people a stunning victory. But first, Joshua would encounter a mysterious man who was none other than the pre-incarnate Christ:

> When Joshua was near the town of Jericho, he looked up and saw a man standing in front of him with sword in hand. Joshua went up to him and demanded, "Are you friend or foe?"
>
> "Neither one," he replied. "I am the commander of the LORD's army."
>
> At this, Joshua fell with his face to the ground in reverence. "I am at your command," Joshua said. "What do you want your servant to do?"
>
> The commander of the LORD's army replied, "Take off your sandals, for the place where you are standing is holy." (Joshua 5:13-15)

Just as the ground became holy when God appeared to Moses in the burning bush, the presence of the pre-incarnate Christ as the commander of the Lord's army made the ground Joshua was standing upon "holy."

In Revelation 19, John is given a vision of the same mysterious commander of the Lord's army who appeared to Joshua. This time the scene is not the forthcoming battle of Jericho, but the end of the age when that same commander comes to raise the dead, judge the world, and make all things new. Revelation says that "the armies of heaven, dressed in the finest of pure white linen, followed him on white horses. From his mouth came a sharp sword to strike down the nations" (19:14-15).

Just like in Jericho, the day is coming when all those who oppose or simply ignore God will face the Commander of the Lord's army in all his wrath. But for those who belong to Christ, the Commander of the Lord's army is even now preparing the way, so that we will receive our promised inheritance. That same Commander has laid down his life upon the Cross, taking upon himself that same wrath which is meted out upon his enemies, so that we, the people of God, will enter that good and bountiful land which the Lord has promised to us.

† *Commander of the army of the Lord, you have come to fight for me and grant to me the victory you have won on your Cross. I hide myself in you and wait for you to do your holy work.*

JUNE 13
HE EXECUTES
DIVINE VENGEANCE

When making his covenant with Abraham and telling Abraham about his descendants' coming captivity and deliverance, God said, "In the fourth generation your descendants will come back here, for the sin of the Amorites has not yet reached its full measure" (Genesis 15:16, NIV).

As the Israelites camped outside the border of Canaan forty years after leaving Egypt, the time had come. The sin of all those in Canaan had finally reached its full measure and the Israelites, led by Joshua, were about to become the tool God would use to bring judgment on them. In making war against the Canaanites, the Israelites were not exacting their own vengeance against an innocent people, but were, in fact, executing divine vengeance against a wicked people. "So Joshua and the Israelite army continued the slaughter and completely crushed the enemy. They totally wiped out the five armies except for a tiny remnant that managed to reach their fortified towns" (Joshua 10:20).

Just as the people of Noah's day had reached their full measure of rebellion and God sent the rain, and just as the people of Sodom and Gomorrah reached their full measure of rebellion and God sent burning sulfur, the Canaanites had finally reached their full measure of sin, and so God sent the Israelites to destroy them.

There is a time coming when the sin of humanity will once again reach its full measure. At that time, a greater Joshua will come, bringing just judgment upon the wickedness of the world. Jesus will execute God's righteous judgment against those who persist in refusing to repent.

> The Lord isn't really being slow about his promise, as some people think. No, he is being patient for your sake. He does not want anyone to be destroyed, but wants everyone to repent. But the day of the Lord will come as unexpectedly as a thief. Then the heavens will pass away with a terrible noise, and the very elements themselves will disappear in fire, and the earth and everything on it will be found to deserve judgment. (2 Peter 3:9-10)

† *Righteous Warrior against evil, I will escape the coming judgment you will surely bring only because you have borne it for me. Only you are worthy to bring the sword of judgment, and bring it you will, in perfect righteousness.*

JUNE 14

OUR REFUGE

Moses instructed the people, "When you cross the Jordan into the land of Canaan, designate cities of refuge to which people can flee if they have killed someone accidentally" (Numbers 35:10-11). And when Joshua led the people into Canaan, six cities spaced throughout the land were designated as cities of refuge (Joshua 20).

In most ancient cultures, someone who killed a person—even if it was by accident, in the heat of an argument, or perhaps in self-defense—would have been killed by the victim's relatives. God gave his people a way for justice to be done that was better than resorting to revenge. As soon as the killer realized what he had done, he could run to a divinely appointed place of safety—one of the cities of refuge. When the killer reached the city, he would run to the sanctuary and put his hands on the altar of God. He could not be touched until the elders had a chance to investigate his crime properly. If, after due process, they judged that the crime was indeed an accident, the perpetrator was allowed to live. However, if his crime was deliberate, not even the altar could save him.

Hebrews 10:1 tells us, "The old system under the law of Moses was only a shadow, a dim preview of the good things to come, not the good things themselves." Surely the city of refuge is a shadow, a dim preview of the good things to come in Christ. The city of refuge was a place where someone who had killed another could find mercy and safety. So Christ is a refuge for sinners seeking mercy. "Therefore, we who have fled to him for refuge can have great confidence as we hold to the hope that lies before us" (Hebrews 6:18).

When we flee to God's appointed place of refuge, which is the Cross, we are saved from the punishment we deserve. There, we take hold of the atonement offered for us on the altar of God, and the enemy can no longer touch us. There, our great High Priest seals our pardon by his own death so that we might never again fear punishment. We need live in fear no longer because he has pledged to "never again remember [our] sins and lawless deeds" (Hebrews 10:17).

† *Jesus, my blessed Refuge, I have come running to you, confessing my heinous crimes against your grace, falling on your mercy, seeking your full pardon. In you alone I find freedom from the law and absolution from guilt.*

JUNE 15
OUR PROMISED REST

The people had been camped at Moab for some time after Moses died. Joshua instructed the officers to get the people ready to march. They had broken camp many times before, but this time it was different. They weren't breaking camp only to wander further into the wilderness. This time they were finally entering the land to enjoy the rest that God had promised them so long ago. When we come to the end of Joshua's story, we find that, indeed, God did exactly what he promised:

> The LORD gave to Israel all the land he had sworn to give their ancestors, and they took possession of it and settled there. And the LORD gave them rest on every side, just as he had solemnly promised their ancestors. None of their enemies could stand against them, for the LORD helped them conquer all their enemies. (Joshua 21:43-44)

For these nomads who had wandered through the desert with no homes for forty years, rest meant coming into the land, building a home, establishing a family, cultivating the land, and raising a large number of animals—enjoying what we might call a normal life. While all these things involved a great deal of manual labor, it was rest in the sense that the people could live in peace, without wandering, without fear of attack.

And yet, Israel's rest in the land of Canaan, while real, was not that rest which God had ultimately promised to his people: "If Joshua had succeeded in giving them this rest, God would not have spoken about another day of rest still to come. So there is a special rest still waiting for the people of God" (Hebrews 4:8-9).

That "special rest" that is "still waiting" is found only in Jesus Christ, the greater Joshua, who has achieved the victory—in his doing and in his dying—that will allow us to rest from our labors. The rest won for us by Jesus will one day be realized when we cross over—not the Jordan River, but into the presence of God. There at last, in the true Promised Land, glorious beyond measure because of the presence of God in all his glory, we will be forever safe from all of our enemies.

† *Jesus, you are my rest in the here and now, and for all eternity. And because of who you are and what you have done, I need not fear that day when I cross over into your Promised Land. That will be a glorious day, when all the struggles of life finally give way to ultimate rest in your presence.*

JUNE 16

The Judge Who Saves

After the death of Joshua, the writer of Judges narrates the sad next chapter in the story of God's people: "They abandoned the LORD, the God of their ancestors, who had brought them out of Egypt. They went after other gods, worshiping the gods of the people around them. And they angered the LORD" (Judges 2:12).

But God was not done with his people. Even though he was angry, God sent a series of deliverers to rescue them from their enemies:

> Then the LORD raised up judges to rescue the Israelites from their attackers. . . . Whenever the LORD raised up a judge over Israel, he was with that judge and rescued the people from their enemies throughout the judge's lifetime. For the LORD took pity on his people, who were burdened by oppression and suffering. (Judges 2:16, 18)

For the next three hundred years, Israel's national life was a miserable roller-coaster ride of sinking in sin and oppression, crying out to the Lord and being delivered by a judge, then falling back into sin. The stories of Ehud, Gideon, Samson, and the other judges are stories of savior-judges whom God sent to rescue Israel from their enemies and from themselves.

Each of the judges God sent pointed toward the great Savior-Judge to come. In Jesus, the God who takes pity on his people took on flesh. Luke wrote that as Jesus entered Jerusalem, "He began to weep," saying, "How I wish today that you of all people would understand the way to peace" (Luke 19:41-42). The first time Jesus came, he saved by *experiencing* judgment, not by exercising it. To save God's people to the uttermost, Jesus experienced the judgment of God on our behalf. "God sent his Son into the world not to judge the world, but to save the world through him" (John 3:17).

But it would be a mistake to assume that judgment has been altogether discarded. At the second coming of Jesus, he will come to judge. "He will come with his mighty angels, in flaming fire, bringing judgment on those who don't know God and on those who refuse to obey the Good News of our Lord Jesus" (2 Thessalonians 1:7-8).

† *Judge who endured the judgment I deserve, Savior who provides the rescue I don't deserve, I lift up my eyes to see your salvation and wait for you to bring your saving work to its full consummation.*

HE USES THE WEAK
THINGS OF THE WORLD

Throughout the Old Testament we find cycle after cycle of obedience that led to victory for God's people, only to be followed by disobedience that brought judgment. This was where the Israelites were in Judges 6: "The Israelites did evil in the LORD's sight. So the Lord handed them over to the Midianites for seven years" (6:1).

During those seven years, the Israelites had to hide themselves in mountain dens and caves, living as refugees and fugitives in their own Land of Promise. But God was not done delivering his people. In the midst of this dark and dangerous time, the angel of the Lord appeared to Gideon, calling him a "mighty hero" (6:12) and instructing him, "Go with the strength you have, and rescue Israel from the Midianites. I am sending you!" (6:14).

"But Lord," Gideon replied, "how can I rescue Israel? My clan is the weakest in the whole tribe of Manasseh, and I am the least in my entire family!" (6:15).

Gideon was startled that God would address him as a "mighty hero" and choose him to be a rescuer. He knew he possessed no extraordinary strength or battle know-how. But that was not what God needed to accomplish victory, and neither did he need a large army. In fact God would soon whittle down Gideon's army to only three hundred soldiers so that there would be no question that God gave the enemy into Gideon's hands.

Gideon didn't know that God had chosen him to demonstrate something about himself—that he chooses to use what is weak and humble to accomplish his grand purposes. In fact, his chosen method to accomplish his most important purpose in the world—reconciling the world to himself—was to *become* weak. He chose to set aside the strength and power that had been his since before the foundation of the world to become flesh, to become vulnerable to death. And he intends for us to reflect something of him as we not only accept, but also embrace, weakness. "My power works best in weakness," the Lord said to Paul, which enabled Paul to say, "So now I am glad to boast about my weaknesses, so that the power of Christ can work through me" (2 Corinthians 12:9).

† *Almighty God, can you really use someone as weak as me to accomplish your purposes in this world? Choosing to be weak goes against everything the world tells me about how to succeed and get ahead. Give me the grace I need to be weak so your power can work through my life.*

JUNE 18

An Inward, Intrinsic Holiness

Samson is the only person in the Old Testament whose conception was announced by an angel (Judges 13:3), very much like the angel's announcement of Jesus' conception. "His hair must never be cut. For he will be dedicated to God as a Nazirite from birth," instructed the angel to Samson's mother (13:5).

A Nazirite was a person who was entirely consecrated to God. As part of his consecration, a Nazirite drank no wine and allowed his hair to grow, untouched by a razor. His long hair made him stand out from the crowd so that when people saw him, they likely said, "That man is God's man, a Nazirite, set apart."

Though outwardly he conformed to the Nazirite vow by never cutting his hair, inwardly Samson was committed to his own pleasure and appetites. Though God endowed him with supernatural strength, Samson had little mental force and even less spiritual power. His whole life was a mix of miracles and follies as he was easily overcome by temptation, enticed, and led astray. Though Israelites were commanded not to intermarry with the people of the land, Samson persisted over his parents' objections and married a Philistine woman. As he was on his way to the wedding party, he scooped honey out of the dead lion he had earlier killed, even though Nazirites were forbidden from touching a dead body. Samson's visit to a prostitute and later liaison with Delilah revealed the reality of Samson's heart. He simply couldn't live up to his pledge and calling. He couldn't rule himself or his passions.

Samson's birth, under the terms of the Nazirite vow, pointed to the coming of the Nazarene of the tribe of Judah who would fulfill in every respect the law of consecration in ways that no Nazirite ever could. Samson kept only the outward purity of the Nazirite vow (and broke even that in the end); true and inward purity would appear in the final Judge of Israel. While Samson practiced an outward nonconformity that separated him to God, Jesus was set apart by an infinite inward holiness and perfect obedience.

† *Holy Jesus, I find myself powerless on my own to rule my passions and discipline my desires. I don't want to settle for outward conformity that is betrayed by an inner reality in my heart and life. Cleanse me. Purify me. Set me apart for service to you in my innermost being. Implant in me a longing for your holiness.*

THE GREATER SAMSON

In the period of the judges, God raised up warriors of the covenant to deliver his people from their oppressors. The role of judge as a divinely endued and appointed deliverer anticipated the Judge who was yet to come. Samson's story specifically shows us that victory comes through apparent defeat, and that God can deliver his people through one Champion whose victories in life are crowned by his conquest in death.

In the final, climactic story of Samson's life, Samson's lover, the infamous Delilah, nagged Samson until he revealed the secret of his strength and thus betrayed his Nazirite vow. She cut his hair, and the Philistines were finally able to overpower him. They gouged out his eyes, bound him with chains, and forced him to grind grain in the prison. But before long, his hair began to grow back. One day, when the Philistines were celebrating and making fun of him, he asked to be led to the two central pillars of the pagan temple.

> Then Samson put his hands on the two center pillars that held up the temple. Pushing against them with both hands, he prayed, "Let me die with the Philistines." And the temple crashed down on the Philistine rulers and all the people. So he killed more people when he died than he had during his entire lifetime. (Judges 16:29-30)

Samson's story shows us that God can bring judgment on the foes of his people through one man equipped by the Holy Spirit. Through the death of his mighty judge, God worked deliverance for his people.

Clearly Samson's story is not in the Bible so that young men will emulate him. Neither is it there primarily as a negative example to warn us away from indulging in temptation and sinful passions. Samson foreshadows the mighty Savior, set apart to God, filled with the Holy Spirit, handed over and bound by Gentile oppressors, and mocked as helpless. Samson foreshadows Jesus, who willingly gave up his life, and in his death wrought deliverance for all who believe.

† *Mighty Savior, I praise you for the victory you won through apparent defeat. I thank you that you were willing to die to destroy your enemies. I confess to you that my commitment to you, like that of Samson, falls far short of my calling. I cry out to you to fill me with your Spirit anew, and instill in me a passion for holiness.*

COVER ME

As a penniless widow from Moab recently relocated into the land of Israel, Ruth had limited prospects for marriage to say the least. But her mother-in-law had an idea:

> One day Naomi said to Ruth, "My daughter, it's time that I found a permanent home for you, so that you will be provided for. Boaz is a close relative of ours, and he's been very kind by letting you gather grain with his young women. . . . Go to the threshing floor. . . . Be sure to notice where he lies down; then go and uncover his feet and lie down there. He will tell you what to do." . . .
>
> Around midnight Boaz suddenly woke up and turned over. He was surprised to find a woman lying at his feet! "Who are you?" he asked.
>
> "I am your servant Ruth," she replied. "Spread the corner of your covering over me, for you are my family redeemer." (Ruth 3:1-4, 8-9)

Ruth's glimmer of hope was Boaz, a relative of her late husband. Perhaps he would be willing to be her family redeemer. Also called a kinsman-redeemer, this person was a relative who could redeem a poor man's inheritance by marrying the man's widow. However, he was not obligated to do so. If the kinsman-redeemer chose not to help, the widow would probably live in poverty.

When Ruth said to Boaz, "Spread the corner of your covering over me, for you are my family redeemer," she was boldly asking Boaz for a pledge from him to marry her. This same expression is used for God's relationship with Israel: "I spread the corner of my garment over you" (Ezekiel 16:8, NIV). And it is what we, too, want and need from God—for him to spread his garment of righteousness over our filthy rags.

As the penniless foreigner Ruth cast herself at Boaz's feet, so we, alienated from God, unworthy and needy, cast ourselves at the feet of Jesus. As she was dependent on the kindness and mercy of Boaz, we have no other hope than the mercy of God. We need a covering; we need to be brought under the covering of the One who can provide to us peace and security. We need a Bridegroom with integrity who will take us to himself.

† *My Kinsman-Redeemer, I brought you nothing but my need, and you have spread your robe of righteousness over me and drawn me close. How I need for you to provide for me, protect me, accept me.*

HE HOLDS THE KEYS OF DEATH

On an annual visit to the Tabernacle, Hannah had prayed to God for a son. She made a promise that if God granted her a son, she would give him back to God, to serve God an entire lifetime (1 Samuel 1:11). Now she had returned to keep her promise. She brought her longed-for son, Samuel, to the Tabernacle to leave him there under the care of Eli.

But before she left, she offered a prayer of praise. Her psalm doesn't concentrate on her sorrow at leaving her son behind, on her suffering, or even on her blessings. Instead, it focused on her God. Out of her suffering and exaltation, she came to see God more clearly, and as a result she praised him for who he is and what he does. Her psalm speaks of God as holy, faithful, omniscient, gracious, powerful, sovereign, and as the great reverser of circumstances. Celebrating God's sovereign favor in her life and in the world, Hannah sang, "The LORD gives both death and life; he brings some down to the grave but raises others up" (1 Samuel 2:6).

Here Hannah expressed a profound truth about the power and person of God—that he is in control of life and death. And we discover later, when Jesus appears to John on the island of Patmos, that God has put this control into the hands of his Son. Appearing in his glorified humanity, radiant and powerful, Jesus said to John, "Don't be afraid! I am the First and the Last. I am the living one. I died, but look—I am alive forever and ever! And I hold the keys of death and the grave" (Revelation 1:17-18).

Calling himself "the First and the Last," Jesus is saying, "Everything started with me, and everything will end with me. You find your starting point and your ending place completely in me."

What does it mean that Jesus holds "the keys of death and the grave"? The person who holds the keys opens, closes, and controls access. Jesus is saying that he is in charge of life and death, and of the place we go when we die. No one goes there unless and until Jesus opens that door. He holds the keys because he died and went there himself and emerged with the keys in his hand. Because Jesus holds the keys, we can be confident that he will open the door at just the right time, waiting to meet us on the other side.

† *Living One who holds the keys of death and the grave, I hear you telling me not to be afraid. And because it is you who holds the keys to death, I know that I need not fear. My life and my death are under your loving control.*

JUNE 22

HANNAH'S HOPE

The theme of Hannah's prophetic prayer appears at the end of her psalm:

> He thunders against them from heaven;
>> the LORD judges throughout the earth.
> He gives power to his king;
>> he increases the strength of his anointed one. (1 Samuel 2:10)

In her prayer, Hannah introduced the "king" to whom God will give strength—and at the point in which she prayed this prayer, Israel had never had a king. She also expressed the promise that God "increases the strength" or "exalts the horn" of his "anointed one" or "Messiah."

Some see the prediction that "[God] thunders against them from heaven" as fulfilled in 1 Samuel 7:10, when God delivered Israel from the Philistines at the battle of Mizpah by bringing on a violent storm with severe thunder and lightning. But that can't be the ultimate meaning because the thunder is parallel with "the LORD judges throughout the earth," which is much more universal in scope than one mere battle with the Philistines during a violent thunderstorm.

The thunder from heaven finally came as Jesus stood before a crowd of Israelites a short time before he was crucified:

> "Now my soul is deeply troubled. Should I pray, 'Father, save me from this hour'? But this is the very reason I came! Father, bring glory to your name."
>
> Then a voice spoke from heaven, saying, "I have already brought glory to my name, and I will do so again." When the crowd heard the voice, some thought it was thunder, while others declared that an angel had spoken to him.
>
> Then Jesus told them, "The voice was for your benefit, not mine. The time for judging this world has come." (John 12:27-31)

Just as Hannah had prophesied in her prayer, God's voice thundered from heaven as the time had finally come for judging the world. And no wonder Jesus' soul was deeply troubled. The judgment for the world was about to fall on him.

✝ *I hear the thunder of your voice warning of the coming judgment. But I am not afraid. I have found my rest and peace and hope in the Anointed One.*

JUNE 23
THE FAITHFUL PRIEST

Neither of Eli's two sons, Hophni and Phinehas, could succeed their father as high priest. They abused the privileges of their office by making themselves fat with the meat of sacrifices that did not belong to them and by sleeping with the women who served at the entrance of the Tabernacle (1 Samuel 2:14, 22). So God sent an unnamed prophet to Eli to tell him that his sons would die and God would raise up another priest: "I will raise up a faithful priest who will serve me and do what I desire. I will establish his family, and they will be priests to my anointed kings forever" (2:35).

In the midst of all the sin of Eli and his household, God promised to raise up a priest who would not compromise his office or render it defunct through his own personal sin. The badge of this priest would be his faithfulness.

God raised up many faithful servants to serve at his altar down through the years, but they all found their culmination in Christ, who was the only completely faithful Priest. Only of Christ could it be said that he always did what God desired. "He was full of unfailing love and faithfulness" (John 1:14). Only in Christ could the priestly office bear the weight of God's purposes of salvation.

Not only did God say he would raise up a faithful priest, but he promised that he would establish his family forever. In the covenant with Abraham, God had promised to make Abraham's descendants more numerous than the stars in the sky or the sand on the seashore (Genesis 22:17). It was his intention to establish a people that would be his own—his family. The same promise is repeated in the covenant with David—that his house, or family, would not only continue, but would always rule on the throne (2 Samuel 7:16).

Here is the purpose of God's grace—he will build a house for the faithful Priest, and that house will remain before the Anointed One (who is also the priest) forever. The writer of Hebrews points to Christ as the One who fulfilled this promise: "Christ, as the Son, is in charge of God's entire house" (Hebrews 3:6).

† *My faithful Priest, you have made me a part of your family, your household of faith, your royal priesthood, and given me a heart to serve before you gladly. However, I know I cannot remain faithful. But you can. So hide me in your faithfulness so that I might serve you with freedom and gladness.*

THE KING OF THE JEWS

Samuel, the judge and priest of Israel, was growing old and so appointed his sons to be the next judges over Israel. But rather than promoting justice, his sons were greedy and perverted. So the elders of Israel met with Samuel. "'Look,' they told him, 'you are now old, and your sons are not like you. Give us a king to judge us like all the other nations have'" (1 Samuel 8:5).

God had been a faithful divine King who protected and cared for his people. But they didn't want him as their king—they wanted a human king so they could be like all the other nations. Samuel described the demands a king would make on them, and warned that the day would come when they would beg for relief from the king they now demanded. Nevertheless, Samuel followed God's instructions to anoint Saul to be their king.

But God had his own sovereign purpose in giving in to the people's sinful demand for a human king. Over the coming centuries under a series of kings, the people would discover for themselves that only God should be their king. A long line of human kings would fail them again and again until finally a King would come who was not only a man but also God. This King would rule in righteousness. In this way God would prove that only God can be King of Israel.

God also planned that the rightful King of Israel would die for his people. That's the only reason we as sinful subjects are not put to death for our offenses—because we have a King who died for us and rose again to rule over us.

Each of the Gospel writers wanted to make sure that Israel recognized Jesus as the God-man King that God had always intended to give them. Each included Jesus' response to Pilate's question before his crucifixion, "Are you the king of the Jews?" to which Jesus answered, "You have said it" (Matthew 27:11; Mark 15:2; Luke 23:3; John 18:33-34).

Indeed, Jesus is not just king of the Jews, but the King of all. He is seated at the right hand of the Father until all of his enemies are put under his feet and all his elect are gathered in from the peoples of the earth. And when he appears a second time, on his robe at his thigh this title will be written for all to see: "King of all kings and Lord of all lords" (Revelation 19:16).

✝ *I crown you as King of my life, Jesus. Take your rightful throne. Rule over my plans and my passions. Give me the joyful privilege of being your subject.*

JUNE 25
HE MADE HIMSELF SMALL

King Saul had instructions from the Lord to completely destroy the Amalekite nation. So he mobilized his army and killed *most* of the Amalekites. However, he captured the Amalekite king and brought him back as his prisoner, and he kept the best of the livestock, destroying only what had no value anyway. Then he "set up a monument to himself" (1 Samuel 15:12). Upon discovering these events, Samuel was not pleased.

> Samuel told him, "Although you may think little of yourself, are you not the leader of the tribes of Israel? The LORD has anointed you king of Israel. And the LORD sent you on a mission and told you, 'Go and completely destroy the sinners, the Amalekites, until they are all dead.' Why haven't you obeyed the LORD? Why did you rush for the plunder and do what was evil in the LORD's sight?" (15:17-19)

God saw Saul's partial obedience as utter disobedience and rejected him as king of Israel. Once Saul had been ordinary and small. And when he was anointed as king, God made him great. Yet Saul never embraced the greatness God bestowed upon him by choosing him to be king. Saul still thought little of himself and so continually sought to prove his greatness. By bringing home the plunder of the Amalekites, he increased his wealth. By imprisoning the Amalekite king rather than slaying him as God commanded, he made himself a king of kings. Saul sought to escape his smallness by taking for himself the wealth and power of the world—and he ended up dethroned.

A greater king of Israel would come in the person of Jesus. Though he was great, he was willing to make himself small. The God of the universe became an embryo in a maiden's womb. He was completely obedient to his Father. Rather than grasping for wealth and power, he set aside the privileges of deity to become a human with no monetary resources, no official position of power, not even a home to live in. But because he did all of this, rather than being dethroned as Saul was, he has been enthroned forever as King of kings. Rather than being rejected by God, he was received into heaven by God where he sits in the seat of honor at God's right hand.

✝ *Lord, I have set up so many monuments to myself hoping to draw attention to my own supposed greatness. Please develop in me the same attitude that was in Christ Jesus, who gave up his divine privileges and became small so that he might share his greatness with all who come to him.*

THE LORD'S ANOINTED

Since the days of Abraham, God had been working in and through the people from whom Christ would one day be born. But the time came when God singled out a specific man from whom Christ would come, and he sent Samuel to anoint him to set him apart for service.

> He was dark and handsome, with beautiful eyes. And the LORD said, "This is the one; anoint him." So as David stood there among his brothers, Samuel took the flask of olive oil he had brought and anointed David with the oil. And the Spirit of the LORD came powerfully upon David from that day on. (1 Samuel 16:12-13)

David was actually anointed three times. First, privately at Bethlehem in front of his family; second, by the men of Judah (2 Samuel 2:4); and third, by all the elders of Israel (2 Samuel 5:3). In some respects, the anointing of David was the anointing of Christ himself. Christ, the seed of David, was anointed in him so that both Christ's anointing and David's anointing are spoken of when the psalmist writes: "I have found my servant David. I have anointed him with my holy oil" (Psalm 89:20).

Like David, Jesus was anointed three times. Jesus was set apart from his very conception by the Spirit, as the angel told Mary, "The Holy Spirit will come upon you, and the power of the Most High will overshadow you" (Luke 1:35). He was publicly anointed at his baptism, when, "as he was praying, the heavens opened, and the Holy Spirit, in bodily form, descended on him like a dove" (Luke 3:21-22). His third anointing came when Jesus ascended into heaven to sit at the right hand of God. The writer to the Hebrews uses the words of the psalmist to celebrate this anointing. "But to the Son he says, 'Your throne, O God, endures forever and ever. You rule with a scepter of justice. You love justice and hate evil. Therefore, O God, your God has anointed you, pouring out the oil of joy on you more than on anyone else'" (Hebrews 1:8-9).

The night before he died, Jesus prayed, "I give myself as a holy sacrifice for them so they can be made holy by your truth" (John 17:19). Jesus, the Lord's anointed, was preparing himself to do what was necessary so that we, too, might experience this holy anointing from God that sets us apart.

† *Holy Spirit, come to me and anoint me, making me holy with the truth of God's Word. Convict me. Teach me. Cleanse me. Change me.*

JUNE 27

VICARIOUS VICTOR

A host of Philistine warriors were camped on one side of the valley and the armies of Israel were on the other. "Then Goliath, a Philistine champion from Gath, came out of the Philistine ranks" (1 Samuel 17:4). In Hebrew, Goliath is called, not "champion" as we read it in the English, but the "middleman," the "mediator." Goliath was the one man sent out by the Philistines to fight one man from the Israelite army. The entire army of each side would experience defeat or victory vicariously through the victory or defeat of their representative.

For forty days Goliath taunted the Israelites, who were too scared to send anyone out to meet him. That is, until David came to bring supplies to his brothers at the camp. While even the most seasoned soldiers were frightened of Goliath, David was not intimidated. In fact, he was infuriated that Goliath would dare to defy and diminish the God of the armies of Israel with his taunts.

So David went out to fight Goliath. One man carried the weight of the future of God's people but was confident in God's conquering power. One man killed the Philistine champion with a single smooth stone implanted deep into Goliath's forehead. One man's lone victory over God's enemy became a shared victory of God's people.

Just as the Israelites that day became victors through the victory of David, so we are victors through the victory of Christ (Romans 8:37). Because our Champion went into battle for us and applied his victory to us, it's not up to us to be strong enough or smart enough or good enough to win the fight against our enemy, sin. In fact, even the most beleaguered believer triumphs through Christ. He is the Victor who shares his victory with us.

We stayed behind where it was safe, and Jesus faced down the enemy that sought to enslave us. On our own, we accomplished nothing. And yet, our Champion has imputed his victory to us. "Thank God! He gives us victory over sin and death through our Lord Jesus Christ" (1 Corinthians 15:57).

† *My vicarious Victor, because you have fought and won the battle against sin and death for me, I can claim your victory as my own. My life is preserved, my freedom is assured, my enemy has been conquered.*

CLOSER THAN A BROTHER

Saul brought David into his court after David's great victory over Goliath. But Saul became murderously envious of David's military success and his growing popularity and, in fits of rage, repeatedly attempted to kill young David. But while the king resented and sought to kill David, Jonathan, the king's son, loved and protected David.

> There was an immediate bond between them, for Jonathan loved David. . . . Jonathan made a solemn pact with David, because he loved him as he loved himself. Jonathan sealed the pact by taking off his robe and giving it to David, together with his tunic, sword, bow, and belt. (1 Samuel 18:1, 3-4)

Jonathan, the oldest son of King Saul, was next in line to be king. So when he made a covenant of friendship with David, who had been anointed to become the next king, Jonathan surrendered his rights to the throne. In giving David his royal robe, tunic, sword, bow, and belt, he essentially transferred the rights to the throne to David. He committed himself to serve David to the death. Jonathan stripped himself of power and privilege and gave it all to David, so that David could be saved from Saul's wrath, protected from his enemy's sword, and enthroned in his rightful place of honor.

Like Jonathan, Jesus, our best heavenly Friend, bound himself to us in covenant love. He stripped himself of his royal garments so that he might give them to us. He made himself vulnerable to offer us protection. He left his rightful throne so that he might one day share it with us for all eternity. "Having loved his own who were in the world, he now showed them the full extent of his love" (John 13:1, NIV). Like Jonathan, Jesus was faithful to his friends to the death. Jesus said, "There is no greater love than to lay down one's life for one's friends" (John 15:13).

David was saved from death, protected from evil, and released to become the king all because of the sacrificial, to-the-death friendship of Jonathan. And we are saved, protected, and destined for glory, all because of the to-the-death friendship of Jesus who made the ultimate sacrifice for us.

† *My best heavenly Friend, you have bound yourself to me in to-the-death covenant love. And in you, I can begin to love others sacrificially, consistently, persistently.*

JUNE 29

HOMELESS OUTCAST

No doubt it would have been a simple matter for God to put forth his power, destroy King Saul, and give David rest from all who sought to harm him. David had already been anointed as Israel's next king. But David had deeper lessons of dependency upon God to learn. So rather than ascending the throne and making his home in the palace,

> David left Gath and escaped to the cave of Adullam. Soon his brothers and all his other relatives joined him there. Then others began coming— men who were in trouble or in debt or who were just discontented— until David was the captain of about 400 men. (1 Samuel 22:1-2)

The anointed king of Israel was, indeed, a homeless outcast—living in a cave, surrounded by a small army of needy devotees. He was hated and persecuted by Saul, who sought to kill him.

David's Lord, Jesus, the anointed King, was also a homeless outcast. He said, "Foxes have dens to live in, and birds have nests, but the Son of Man has no place even to lay his head" (Matthew 8:20).

Though David was an outcast, there were those who drew close to him. But it was not the captains of the army, the men of means, or those respected in the community who came to make their home with David in the cave of Adullam. The type of people who sought out David were distressed, in debt, and discontented.

For the most part, those who sought out Jesus were poor and needy; it was the lepers, the blind, the disfigured, and the outcasts who came to Jesus for help and healing. The rich and influential, the learned and the mighty, the leaders of the nation had no heart for him, while his small group of disciples were mostly simple fishermen.

But just as David became a captain, or leader, to all who came to him, so has God made "Jesus, through his suffering, a perfect leader, fit to bring" all who come to him to salvation (Hebrews 2:10).

† *Captain of my Salvation, I sought you in a sorry state—distressed by the depths of my own depravity, owing a debt I was bankrupt to pay, discontent with all the things of the world I had sought out to bring me peace and pleasure—and you became my Captain. You took me in and made me one of your own. And so you will take me with you into your Kingdom, where we will no longer be homeless outcasts. We'll be honored, and we'll be at home.*

JUNE 30

KING OF THE CITY OF GOD

David reigned for seven years over Judah in Hebron, but after being anointed king over all Israel, he cast his eyes toward Jerusalem, which had been called Jebus, as it was inhabited by the Jebusites.

> David then led his men to Jerusalem to fight against the Jebusites, the original inhabitants of the land who were living there. The Jebusites taunted David, saying, "You'll never get in here! Even the blind and lame could keep you out!" For the Jebusites thought they were safe. But David captured the fortress of Zion, which is now called the City of David. (2 Samuel 5:6-7)

Jerusalem was captured by David, and was made his royal residence; the Temple was erected upon one of its mounts. Thus the stronghold of the enemy was converted into a habitation of God and became the throne of his government upon earth. God was at work reconciling himself to the world in the muck of Canaanite civilization, declaring, "Here I will be known."

But Jerusalem would later be sullied by the likes of sinful men. King David would dishonor it with adultery and murder. It would become infamous for its child sacrifices and unlawful sorceries. It would mock the saintly integrity of Jeremiah and turn a deaf ear to the powerful preaching of Isaiah. It would twice be destroyed in judgment. Most significantly, this would be the city that rejected Jesus. So it is somewhat surprising that when we come to the end of God's story of redemption, we find that it is the "new Jerusalem" that comes down out of heaven for all of God's people to live in with God and with the Lamb. "He showed me the holy city, Jerusalem, descending out of heaven from God. . . . Nothing evil will be allowed to enter, nor anyone who practices shameful idolatry and dishonesty—but only those whose names are written in the Lamb's Book of Life" (Revelation 21:10, 27).

God is making out of our idol-loving, God-defying, Christ-rejecting city a holy city. This is what it means to be made new. God takes people like us—who worship idols of pleasure and pride—and remakes us into a city he wants to live in. This new city is none other than the church—the church made up of forgiven sinners.

† *King of Jerusalem, I long to live as a citizen of heaven, the new Jerusalem, the city of my God, drawing my identity and inheritance and sustenance from its King.*

JULY 1

HOLINESS THAT CAN BE SEEN AND TOUCHED

David wanted to bring the Ark to Jerusalem, so he and his men went to retrieve it. When the Ark of the Covenant needed to be moved, the priests were supposed to use poles, sliding them through the rings on each corner of the lid (Exodus 25:14). This allowed them to carry the Ark without touching it. Anyone who touched the Ark of the Covenant would die.

To see how serious God was about these regulations, we need only consider the tragic death of Uzzah, the man who touched the Ark. Rather than carrying it properly—on their shoulders using the poles—the priests loaded the Ark onto an ox cart.

> When they arrived at the threshing floor of Nacon, the oxen stumbled, and Uzzah reached out his hand and steadied the Ark of God. Then the LORD's anger was aroused against Uzzah, and God struck him dead because of this. So Uzzah died right there beside the Ark of God. (2 Samuel 6:6-7)

Because of God's holiness, people could not come near to see or touch him. If people were ever to be able to come close enough to touch him, the holy God would have to pour himself into flesh. And that is what he did. Jesus was God who could be touched. Matthew tells us what happened when someone dared to touch Jesus:

> A woman who had suffered for twelve years with constant bleeding came up behind him. She touched the fringe of his robe, for she thought, "If I can just touch his robe, I will be healed."
> Jesus turned around, and when he saw her he said, "Daughter, be encouraged! Your faith has made you well." And the woman was healed at that moment. (Matthew 9:20-22)

Jesus was God become man to walk among us. People could look at him and live. They could be touched by him. His touch brought life and health, not death. John wrote of him, "We proclaim to you the one who existed from the beginning, whom we have heard and seen. We saw him with our own eyes and touched him with our own hands. He is the Word of life" (1 John 1:1).

† *Holy God with hands that can be held, a breast that can be laid upon, feet that can be anointed, because I am hidden in you, I dare to approach you. I have no fear of death, only expectation of eternal life.*

HIS ROYAL THRONE WILL LAST FOREVER

Kingdoms rise and kingdoms fall. They have throughout history. But God made a promise to David of a kingdom and a throne that would never end. "I will raise up one of your descendants, your own offspring, and I will make his kingdom strong. . . . I will secure his royal throne forever. . . . Your kingdom will continue before me for all time, and your throne will be secure forever" (2 Samuel 7:12-13, 16).

In one sense, David's son Solomon was that descendant. But obviously Solomon's throne did not last forever. The kingdom can never be secure in the hands of a sinner. The fulfillment of God's covenant with David is found in "someone greater than Solomon" (Matthew 12:42).

> He will be called:
> Wonderful Counselor, Mighty God,
>   Everlasting Father, Prince of Peace.
> His government and its peace
>   will never end.
> He will rule with fairness and justice from
>   the throne of his ancestor David
>   for all eternity. (Isaiah 9:6-7)

In Isaiah's prophecy we find the promise that ultimately *God himself* will come as king and sit upon the throne.

How and when will he come? The angel Gabriel, who appeared to Mary, said about the son in her womb, "The Lord God will give him the throne of his ancestor David. And he will reign over Israel forever; his Kingdom will never end!" (Luke 1:32-33). Beyond any shadow of a doubt, the promise to David that his descendant would rule forever is fulfilled in Jesus Christ.

In the book of Revelation, John saw the throne of Jesus, established for all eternity: "I saw a throne in heaven and someone sitting on it" (4:2). John identified it as David's throne, saying, "One of the twenty-four elders said to me, 'Stop weeping! Look, the Lion of the tribe of Judah, the heir to David's throne, has won the victory'" (5:5).

† *My King on the throne, when circumstances cause me to wonder if anyone is in control of what's happening in this world, it is good to know that you are on your throne, and that your throne will last forever. Reign in this world, and reign in my life!*

HE WILL BUILD A
HOUSE FOR MY NAME

After King David had been given rest from all his enemies in Canaan, and after he had finished building his famed cedar palace, he told the prophet Nathan that he wanted to build a house for God. Nathan's first reaction was to applaud and encourage David's plans. But that night, God warned Nathan that what he had told David was his own opinion and not a divine instruction. So Nathan then delivered a word from God that was decisive.

> The LORD declares that he will make a house for you—a dynasty of kings! For when you die and are buried with your ancestors, I will raise up one of your descendants, your own offspring, and I will make his kingdom strong. He is the one who will build a house—a temple—for my name. And I will secure his royal throne forever. (2 Samuel 7:11-13)

On one hand, God was declaring that David's son Solomon would be the one to build a house for God. But Solomon can't be the only son referred to here, because his kingdom did not last forever. There must be another descendant, another offspring, whose throne will be secure forever. Far beyond Solomon, who would build a house made of stone, God was promising his greater Son, Jesus, who would build a house made of living stones—the lives of his elect. Peter wrote to those coming to Christ, "You are living stones that God is building into his spiritual temple" (1 Peter 2:5).

God was giving David much more than he could have ever imagined. Instead of having David build a "house" for the Almighty, God planned to make a "house" out of David. He was part of the same promise and plan that had been given to Abraham, Isaac, and Jacob.

God promises a spiritual house, an eternal home, for people from all nations and all times. "So now you Gentiles are no longer strangers and foreigners. You are citizens along with all of God's holy people. You are members of God's family. Together, we are his house, built on the foundation of the apostles and the prophets. And the cornerstone is Christ Jesus himself" (Ephesians 2:19-20).

† *Master Builder, I don't deserve to be a part of the house you are building for God, but you have made me into a living stone, into a part of your grand plan for your world. In this world where foundations crumble so easily, I find my security in being built into your house, where you are the cornerstone.*

HE SAVES US
BY RULING OVER US

"Your house and your kingdom will continue before me for all time, and your throne will be secure forever" (2 Samuel 7:16).

In this passage the unfolding purpose of God takes a big step forward. We now discover that the blessing God promised Abraham—protection, reward, inheritance, descendants, homeland—comes down to us in the form of a kingdom.

God promised King David that his dynasty was no passing phase. His royal line would turn out to be the "happily ever after" of the whole story. The Messiah would come as the royal son of David. He will bless us by reigning over us.

Jesus' ministry began with the angel's announcement of his Kingdom: "The Lord God will give him the throne of his ancestor David. And he will reign over Israel forever; his Kingdom will never end!" (Luke 1:32-33). When he began his ministry, Jesus said, "The Kingdom of Heaven is near" (Matthew 4:17). He taught us to pray, "May your Kingdom come soon" (Matthew 6:10). Jesus made it clear that God is building a Kingdom and inviting us in. Jesus inaugurated his Kingdom when he came the first time, and he'll bring it to fullness when he comes again.

Jesus offers us the safety of living in his Kingdom and the blessing of being subject to him as the King. But the reality is that many of us resist the reign of a king. As long as God presents himself to us as our Father, we're okay with that. Who doesn't want to be loved? We're okay with God as our Guide and Defender and Provider and even our Judge, because we long for God to intervene in the evil world we live in. But when God says that he wants to *rule* over us, that's hard for us. We simply don't see the blessing that could be ours if we lived life under God's rule.

But God sets the terms for who are welcome in his Kingdom, and Jesus announced those terms: "Anyone who obeys God's laws and teaches them will be called great in the Kingdom of Heaven" (Matthew 5:19).

† *King Jesus, I don't want to be ruled or controlled by anything or anyone but you. You are the rightful King of this world and of my life. Your authority in my life is not a burden I resist, but a blessing I cherish. Rule my heart and make me submissive to your commands.*

JULY 5
GOD'S KINDNESS TOWARD US

Life was good for the king in Jerusalem. David had defeated and subdued his enemies, and his sons served as priestly leaders. Then he remembered the covenant he had made with his dear friend Jonathan, promising to care for Jonathan's family in the event of his death (1 Samuel 20:14-15). Jonathan and his father, King Saul, had died in battle, so David summoned a man who had been one of Saul's servants, asking, "Is anyone in Saul's family still alive—anyone to whom I can show kindness for Jonathan's sake?" (2 Samuel 9:1).

The servant Ziba replied, "Yes, one of Jonathan's sons is still alive. He is crippled in both feet" (9:3).

When David sent for Mephibosheth, Jonathan's crippled son, to be brought to the palace, Mephibosheth most likely assumed it meant he was going to be put to death to solidify David's claim to the throne. As the last remaining son and grandson of the previous royal line, he must have been terribly afraid. But David said, "I intend to show kindness to you because of my promise to your father, Jonathan. I will give you all the property that once belonged to your grandfather Saul, and you will eat here with me at the king's table!" (9:7).

The kindness David showed to the family of his archenemy pictures for us how God deals in grace with undeserving sinners. Mephibosheth, whose name means "a shameful thing," received favor, not because of any personal worthiness he possessed, but wholly on account of a covenant promise that had been made before he was born.

So it is with those toward whom God shows his kindness. God rescues us from our shame, not because of what we've done, but based on his covenant with Christ made before the foundations of the world, wherein he promised to extend mercy to all who belonged to his "house." We could not come to him on our own, yet he invited us and brought us in. And he lavishes on us an inheritance and a seat at his table. Why has our King done this? "So God can point to us in all future ages as examples of the incredible wealth of his grace and kindness toward us, as shown in all he has done for us who are united with Christ Jesus" (Ephesians 2:7).

† *King of heaven, you have sought me and found me in a shameful condition in a desolate place, and have brought me into your house. I don't deserve your kindness, yet you have lavished it on me through Christ.*

189

BECAUSE OF HIS MERCY

David had sinned—adultery, murder, lying—and he thought he had gotten away with it. Several months had passed, yet David seemed to have no remorse. But the Bible tells us, "The LORD was displeased" (2 Samuel 11:27). So God sent the prophet Nathan to David. Nathan told David a parable designed to help David see the evil he had done by committing adultery with Bathsheba and by having her husband, Uriah, killed. And when David saw himself in Nathan's parable, his heart was broken by its own corruption.

David confessed his sin and was forgiven and justified in the presence of God. Later he put this life-saving, heart-purifying experience into poetry:

> Have mercy on me, O God,
>> because of your unfailing love.
> Because of your great compassion,
>> blot out the stain of my sins.
> Wash me clean from my guilt.
>> Purify me from my sin. (Psalm 51:1-2)

David knew and loved God's Word. As he penned this psalm in the agony of his guilt, he recalled the words of God's revelation of himself from Exodus 34: "Yahweh! The LORD! The God of compassion and mercy! I am slow to anger and filled with unfailing love and faithfulness. I lavish unfailing love to a thousand generations. I forgive iniquity, rebellion, and sin" (34:6-7).

David understood that there are some who are guilty and never turn to God for forgiveness. But there are some who are guilty, and by a mysterious act of mercy on the part of God, are not counted as guilty, but instead are forgiven. David sought to lay hold of the mercy of God by faith, even though that mercy remained to him a mystery.

What David couldn't see clearly became clear: "When God our Savior revealed his kindness and love, he saved us, not because of the righteous things we had done, but because of his mercy. He washed away our sins, giving us a new birth and new life through the Holy Spirit. He generously poured out the Spirit upon us through Jesus Christ our Savior" (Titus 3:4-6).

† *Have mercy on me, O God, because of your unfailing love. I feel the weight and contamination of my sin, and I am helpless to escape its heaviness or wash away its stain. I fall on your mercy. And I know it is through Christ that you will pour out your mercy on me.*

JULY 7

HE CROSSED
THE KIDRON VALLEY

While David had been forgiven of his sin with Bathsheba, God told him that there would still be consequences for his sin. "I will cause your own household to rebel against you" (2 Samuel 12:11). That day came when David's son Absalom staged a rebellion against the king. So David and his loyal followers left the city.

It was a heartbreaking sight—the aged King David forsaking his palace in Jerusalem with but a small retinue, fleeing from his own son. "Everyone cried loudly as the king and his followers passed by. They crossed the Kidron Valley and then went out toward the wilderness" (2 Samuel 15:23).

In this sad scene, David foreshadowed Jesus in one of the most bitter episodes of his Passion. Both were rejected kings, leaving the city of Jerusalem and crossing the Kidron Valley with their little companies of devoted followers, betrayed by someone close to them who had joined forces with their enemies.

Jesus was in the upper room with his disciples, pouring out his heart to them, praying for them, promising the coming of an Advocate who would help them. And then John tells us: "After saying these things, Jesus crossed the Kidron Valley with his disciples and entered a grove of olive trees" (John 18:1).

The Kidron Valley lay between the bases of the Temple hill and the Mount of Olives. The sewage of the city, as well as the filth from the Temple sacrifices, continually emptied into the brook that flowed through the Kidron Valley. In a sense, it was the place in which the filthy sins and iniquities of the people were being washed away from before God's face.

It was over this foul brook that David passed on his way to the wilderness and over which Jesus passed on his way to Gethsemane. Christ must have seen in this filth-filled brook a picture of the mire into which he was about to sink. The Holy One was about to be encompassed with all the guilt and filth of sin belonging to his people. Unlike David, whose heart was heavy knowing that he was experiencing the judgment on his own sin, Jesus' heart was heavy knowing that he was about to experience the judgment of God for the sin of the world.

† *I am repulsed by the stench of the Kidron Valley. Yet it is my pollution that has filled it, my sin that causes its stench. You, most Holy One, were willing to cross this valley, enduring its mire, so that I can know the pleasure of being cleansed and pure.*

DEVOTION POURED OUT

Along with a few of his faithful warriors, David camped in a cave near Bethlehem. Bethlehem was occupied by Israel's enemies, the Philistines. David was thirsty, and he mentioned to three of his most devoted men that he missed the water he grew up drinking from the well in Bethlehem.

> So the Three broke through the Philistine lines, drew some water from the well by the gate in Bethlehem, and brought it back to David. But he refused to drink it. Instead, he poured it out as an offering to the LORD. "The LORD forbid that I should drink this!" he exclaimed. "This water is as precious as the blood of these men who risked their lives to bring it to me." So David did not drink it. (2 Samuel 23:16-17)

David did not ask his men to get him a drink, but they were so devoted to him that to hear his desire expressed was enough to inspire them to break through enemy lines and risk their lives to get him a drink from Bethlehem's well. But when they gave the water to David, he likened it to their blood, which they risked to get it. Expressing his unworthiness of such a sacrifice, David poured it out before the Lord as a drink offering.

The day would come, however, when David would betray the devotion of his loyal soldier Uriah and have him murdered. So while David was a great king and worthy of devotion, he was not the king God's people needed most—a king who would not only be worthy of our sacrificial devotion, but who would, in fact, pour his own life out as a drink offering.

Jesus is the water from Bethlehem, poured out for us. While David's soldiers snuck into Bethlehem at risk of their lives for the one they loved and served, Jesus, the One from Bethlehem, set his face to go to Jerusalem—not merely at risk of his life but to face certain death, not to satisfy the momentary thirst of one man, but to satisfy the spiritual thirst of all people. While David poured out the water, likening it to the blood of his men, Jesus poured out his own blood, inviting us to drink, saying, "This is my blood, which confirms the covenant between God and his people. It is poured out as a sacrifice for many" (Mark 14:24).

✝ *As I take the cup to drink, I realize that it holds the evidence of the ultimate devotion by you, my King—devotion until death. And I drink freely and gladly, yet humbled by the cost at which it came.*

GREATER THAN SOLOMON

As David's son Solomon ascended the throne of Israel, he knew that he would need great wisdom in order to rule the people well. So he asked God for wisdom, and God gave it to him. "God gave Solomon very great wisdom and understanding, and knowledge as vast as the sands of the seashore," says 1 Kings 4:29. And soon word got around.

> When the queen of Sheba heard of Solomon's fame, she came to Jerusalem to test him with hard questions. . . . Solomon had answers for all her questions; nothing was too hard for him to explain to her. When the queen of Sheba realized how wise Solomon was, and when she saw the palace he had built, she was overwhelmed. (2 Chronicles 9:1-4)

Evidently the people who heard Jesus deal with the questions of his day had a similar reaction. "The people were amazed at his teaching, for he taught with real authority—quite unlike the teachers of religious law" (Mark 1:22).

But, of course, those teachers of religious law didn't exactly appreciate the comparison, and they began looking for a way to discredit Jesus. That's when Jesus said, "The queen of Sheba will also stand up against this generation on judgment day and condemn it, for she came from a distant land to hear the wisdom of Solomon. Now someone greater than Solomon is here—but you refuse to listen" (Matthew 12:42).

What was Jesus saying? Why will the queen of Sheba stand up and condemn the generation who rejected Jesus? Jesus is suggesting that the queen of Sheba would condemn them for their foolishness and arrogance. They had the epitome of wisdom and understanding in their midst, and instead of learning from him, they loathed him. Instead of being amazed by him, they were offended by him. Instead of receiving him, they rejected him.

When Jesus said, "someone greater than Solomon is here," it was at once a stunning claim and an incredible understatement. It was also an unavoidable indictment. We are responsible for how we respond to the Wisdom of God in the person of Jesus Christ. "For our benefit God made him to be wisdom itself" (1 Corinthians 1:30).

† *Wisdom of God, I turn to you with all of my questions about how this life works, and I am amazed at the answers you show me in your Word. Thank you for opening my eyes to see you in your glorious wisdom so that I will not be condemned with those who reject you.*

HE WILL RAISE THE TEMPLE

It took Solomon seven years to build God's Temple with a labor force of 30,000 men from all Israel. They quarried large blocks of high-quality stone and shaped them to make the foundation of the Temple.

> The LORD gave this message to Solomon: "Concerning this Temple you are building, if you keep all my decrees and regulations and obey all my commands, I will fulfill through you the promise I made to your father, David. I will live among the Israelites and will never abandon my people Israel." (1 Kings 6:11-13)

But God's people did not obey all his commands, so eventually the Lord withdrew his presence from the Temple, and "Nebuzaradan, the captain of the guard and an official of the Babylonian king, arrived in Jerusalem. He burned down the Temple of the LORD" (2 Kings 25:8-9). The Temple was rebuilt after God's people returned to Jerusalem from exile, but it never regained its former glory. By the time Jesus came, Herod's reconstructed Temple had become a place where empty religion and profiteering replaced true worship and prayer. This angered Jesus, and when he drove out those who sullied his Father's house, the religious leaders demanded,

> "What are you doing? If God gave you authority to do this, show us a miraculous sign to prove it."
>
> "All right," Jesus replied. "Destroy this temple, and in three days I will raise it up."
>
> "What!" they exclaimed. "It has taken forty-six years to build this Temple, and you can rebuild it in three days?" But when Jesus said "this temple," he meant his own body. After he was raised from the dead, his disciples remembered he had said this, and they believed both the Scriptures and what Jesus had said. (John 2:18-22)

Jesus' opponents, obsessed by the old order, could think only of the bricks and mortar. But the Temple in Jerusalem had always been a preview of the temple to come in Jesus himself. It was his body, the true Temple, that was raised in three days to give us life for all the days to come.

† *The hour is here when true worshipers worship the Father in spirit and truth. No pilgrimage to Jerusalem is needed, only a searching heart following after the true Temple, Jesus Christ.*

HE IS ABLE TO SAVE COMPLETELY

The Ark of the Covenant had been staying "inside the special tent David had prepared for it" (2 Samuel 6:17). Now that Solomon had built the glorious Temple, the priests carried the Ark there and placed it in the Most Holy Place. When it arrived, Solomon prayed a prayer of dedication:

> Hear the cry and the prayer that your servant is making to you today. May you watch over this Temple night and day, this place where you have said, "My name will be there." May you always hear the prayers I make toward this place. May you hear the humble and earnest requests from me and your people Israel when we pray toward this place. Yes, hear us from heaven where you live, and when you hear, forgive. (1 Kings 8:28-30)

Solomon asked God to hear the prayers of the people directed toward the Temple. He prayed that what was falsely believed of all the idol temples around—that the gods there heard their prayers—would be true in Jehovah's Temple. He prayed that God, who now dwelt in his Temple, would hear the prayers of his people and forgive their sin.

Though Solomon could not have known it, his words were prophetic. He was asking that those who looked to the Temple of God would have their prayers answered. The Temple and all its parts—the sacrifices and priests and Most Holy Place—pointed to Christ. While in that day God met his people in the Temple, now God meets us in Jesus Christ. And so as Solomon encouraged the people to pray toward the Temple, so the writer to the Hebrews instructs us to "fix our eyes on Jesus, the author and perfecter of our faith, who for the joy set before him endured the cross, scorning its shame, and sat down at the right hand of the throne of God" (12:2, NIV).

We turn to Jesus and pour out our requests because "he is able to save completely those who come to God through him, because he always lives to intercede for them" (7:25, NIV). And we turn to him to pour out our confession, knowing that his grace is sufficient to atone for our sin and that he has the authority to forgive sin (Matthew 9:6).

† *I need not look to any holy site or temple on this earth for you to hear my prayers, Lord. You have asked me only to go to a secret place. I can pray in full confidence that you hear because Christ has opened up a new and living way for me to approach your holy throne.*

PROPHET OF FIRE

Elijah was known as the prophet of fire. Fire accompanied many of his most memorable acts—always showing the people the power of his God.

Elijah challenged Baal's prophets to a contest on Mount Carmel as a way to demonstrate the identity of the true God. He set up the contest by having sacrifices prepared and set on two altars. He would pray to God and the 850 prophets would pray to Baal. "The god who answers by setting fire to the wood is the true God!" (18:24). The prophets of Baal prayed all day in vain. Then Elijah saturated his sacrifice with water. Sure enough, the fire of the Lord came down and consumed the burnt offering and the wood, along with the stones, the saturated dust, and the water in the trench (18:38).

Later, Elijah called down the fire of God on the king's men who came to arrest him (2 Kings 1). And at the end of Elijah's earthly existence, rather than dying, he was caught up into heaven in a chariot of fire (2 Kings 2).

John the Baptist came in "the spirit and power of Elijah" (Luke 1:17). Like Elijah, he was a hairy man who wore a leather belt. Like Elijah, he vigorously called God's people to repentance. And like Elijah, John the Baptist expected fire to fall on God's enemies, saying:

> Even now the ax of God's judgment is poised, ready to sever the roots of the trees. Yes, every tree that does not produce good fruit will be chopped down and thrown into the fire.
>
> I baptize with water those who repent of their sins and turn to God. But someone is coming soon who is greater than I am—so much greater that I'm not worthy even to be his slave and carry his sandals. He will baptize you with the Holy Spirit and with fire. . . . He will clean up the threshing area, gathering the wheat into his barn but burning the chaff with never-ending fire. (Matthew 3:10-12)

John the Baptist was looking for fire, so he was confused when Jesus seemed to bring blessing rather than judgment. John didn't understand that Jesus came the first time to offer forgiveness rather than bring down fire. But the day is coming when Jesus will "come with his mighty angels, in flaming fire, bringing judgment on those who don't know God and on those who refuse to obey the Good News of our Lord Jesus" (2 Thessalonians 1:7-8).

† *My God, you are a Consuming Fire. I ought to be consumed by your holy fire. But instead, your fire came down on your own Son, consuming all of the sin placed on him. So I will never be burned in the fires of your judgment.*

JULY 13
THE MIRACLE WORKER

After Elijah was taken into heaven, Elisha's miracles demonstrated that God's great power was now with him. And while Elijah's miracles had been associated with death and destruction, Elisha's miracles were works of healing and restoration. The work of Elijah was chiefly a protest against evil, while the work of Elisha was an almost continuous testimony to the readiness of God to respond to the call of need. Just as Elijah, the prophet of fire, prefigured the fiery ministry of John the Baptist, Elisha, the miracle worker, prefigured the miraculous works of Christ.

When a wealthy woman from Shunem brought to Elisha the news that her son was dead, she begged Elisha to come. Elisha prayed and lay down on the child's body, and his body began to warm with life (2 Kings 4). Similarly, a synagogue leader came and knelt before Jesus, saying, "My daughter has just died, . . . but you can bring her back to life again if you just come and lay your hand on her." Jesus did not have to be begged to come, but went in and simply took the girl by the hand, and she stood up (Matthew 9:18-25)!

In the midst of a famine, a man brought Elisha a sack of fresh grain and twenty loaves of barley bread. There were one hundred people to feed but "when they gave it to the people, there was plenty for all and some left over" (2 Kings 4:42-44). Similarly, the disciples brought Jesus five loaves and two fish. Five thousand men, plus women and children, were fed as much as they wanted, and there were twelve baskets of leftovers (Matthew 14:13-21).

Many more of Elisha's miracles anticipated Jesus' ministry. But while Elisha went through various rituals and prayed to God to bring about his miracles, Jesus did not have to pray to God for his miracles to happen. He just said the word, and they happened. Elisha healed lepers (2 Kings 5), just as Jesus did. He caused an iron ax head to float on water (2 Kings 6:1-7), similar to Jesus' walking on water. He opened the eyes of his servant to see the spiritual realities surrounding him (2 Kings 6:17), and Jesus opened the eyes of the blind to see the reality of who he was. Elisha saw an unseen army of the Lord, just as Jesus was completely aware of the unseen army of God all around him as he faced the Cross. But Jesus refused to call on this unseen army of angels to save him from death. He anticipated the greatest miracle—the miracle of resurrection.

✝ *Worker of miracles, Giver of life and sight and sustenance, your miracles reveal your power, your compassion, your identity as Lord. With a word, you bring life from death, sight from blindness, plenty from little.*

THE MAN OF GOD WHO IMPARTS LIFE

The wealthy woman from Shunem was so kind to Elisha, showing such hospitality. She even built a little room for Elisha to stay in whenever he passed by. On one visit, Elisha promised that she and her husband would have a son—and they did. But when the child was still young, he died suddenly. The heartbroken mother went to find Elisha. When he heard her plight, he went with her back to her home, where she had laid the boy in Elisha's own bed.

> When Elisha arrived, the child was indeed dead, lying there on the prophet's bed. He went in alone and shut the door behind him and prayed to the LORD. Then he lay down on the child's body, placing his mouth on the child's mouth, his eyes on the child's eyes, and his hands on the child's hands. And as he stretched out on him, the child's body began to grow warm again! (2 Kings 4:32-34)

Elisha stretched himself out over the boy, uniting with him in every way, overpowering death and imparting life from God.

Just over the hill from Shunem is the village of Nain where, hundreds of years later, Jesus arrived. As he approached the village, a funeral procession was coming out, carrying the dead body of a young man, followed by his weeping mother.

> When the Lord saw her, his heart overflowed with compassion. "Don't cry!" he said. Then he walked over to the coffin and touched it, and the bearers stopped. "Young man," he said, "I tell you, get up." Then the dead boy sat up and began to talk! And Jesus gave him back to his mother. (Luke 7:13-15)

These people remembered what Elisha had done for the Shunemite woman and they said, "A mighty prophet has risen among us," and "God has visited his people today" (7:16). In fact, God incarnate had come. And just as Elisha identified himself with the dead boy mouth to mouth, eyes to eyes, hands to hands, Jesus identified with us in every way. "For he raised us from the dead along with Christ and seated us with him in the heavenly realms because we are united with Christ Jesus" (Ephesians 2:6).

† *Man of God who became human to identify with my humanness, you have spread out your arms to me and invited me to become united with you in your death and in your life. In you I live and move and exist.*

JULY 15

THE ANTIDOTE TO DEATH

In the northern kingdom of Israel where Elijah and Elisha ministered, the people, including their leaders, had abandoned the Lord and his Word and had begun to worship Baal. "Elisha now returned to Gilgal, and there was a famine in the land" (2 Kings 4:38).

What land did Elisha return to? The land of promise. The land God swore to give to Israel, the land on which God had promised to "send rain at the proper time from his rich treasury in the heavens" (Deuteronomy 28:12) if they obeyed. But he had also promised, "the skies above will be as unyielding as bronze, and the earth beneath will be as hard as iron" if they did not obey (28:23). So the real problem causing the famine was the spiritual famine of a godless and idolatrous society. And in this famine, we see not only a mighty act of God's provision but also a picture of his power over the poison of sin.

Elisha instructed his servant to make some stew for the rest of the group (2 Kings 4:38). "One of the young men went out into the field to gather herbs and came back with a pocketful of wild gourds. He shredded them and put them into the pot without realizing they were poisonous" (4:39). The pot became an illustration of the world, a "stew" of humankind's ideas, religions, and attempts to satisfy their spiritual appetites. Then they poured out the stew for the men to eat, and they all quickly began to experience stomach cramps.

"After they had eaten a bite or two they cried out, 'Man of God, there's poison in this stew!'" But Elisha knew the antidote. "Bring me some flour," Elisha said. Then he threw it into the pot and said, "Now it's all right; go ahead and eat" (4:40-41).

As Elisha pitched the flour into the pot, we see Jesus Christ, the Bread from heaven, who is the antidote to death, the One who quenches the poison of sin. "God sent his Son into the world not to judge the world, but to save the world through him" (John 3:17).

Only Jesus can feed us in the midst of the famine of truth in this world. And we are no longer sick only because he absorbed the poison of sin for us. He promised, "Anyone who feeds on me will live because of me. I am the true bread that came down from heaven" (John 6:57-58).

† *Jesus, Bread of Life, only you can feed me in the midst of the famine and poisons of this world. Either I feed on you or I will starve.*

JULY 16
FAITH IN HIS FINISHED WORK

Naaman was an important man, the general of all the armies of Aram. But though Naaman had respect and influence and success, he also had a great problem: he had leprosy. Having heard about Israel's great God from a young captive from Israel who served in his household, Naaman went to see the prophet of God, Elisha, to seek healing. "Elisha sent a messenger out to him with this message: 'Go and wash yourself seven times in the Jordan River. Then your skin will be restored, and you will be healed of your leprosy'" (2 Kings 5:10).

The very idea sent Naaman stalking away in anger. He thought himself far too important to do something so silly, so simple, as dipping himself in the muddy Jordan River. But his servants pleaded with him, "If the prophet had told you to do some great thing, would you not have done it?" (5:13, NIV), and he relented. One, two, three times, four, five, six times, and his skin was still leprous. But then, after he came out of the water the seventh time, his skin was like that of a young child—indeed, he had been born again; he had become a new creation.

Then Naaman wanted to pay the prophet something to show his gratitude. But Elisha refused any gifts. He wanted to show Naaman that this God could not be bought.

Prideful people have always sought to obligate God through their great wealth or good deeds. But salvation comes only to those who are willing to humble themselves and receive by faith the wealth and goodness of another—Jesus Christ. The only "great thing" God wants is for us to turn to him in humble faith and obedience, recognizing that we can do nothing to save ourselves. The "great thing" is simply to rest completely in the great finished work of Christ on the Cross.

Many will come to him at the judgment, Jesus said, and plead all the great things they did for God. Yet Jesus will say, "I never knew you. Get away from me" (Matthew 7:22-23). Why? Because they were determined to accomplish their own salvation through the "great things" they did for God. They were unwilling to simply rest in the finished work of Christ.

† *I've heard the Word of the Lord telling me to humble myself and offer you only my need, yet I so easily slip back into what seems to make more sense— that I be required to do some great work for you in order to be loved and accepted by you. Make me willing to rest in your great work alone.*

JULY 17

HE PRESERVES A REMNANT

Hezekiah was reigning in the southern kingdom when Assyria's King Sennacherib, who had defeated the northern kingdom, turned his sights on the southern kingdom and besieged Jerusalem. And when King Hezekiah cried to the Lord for help, the prophet Isaiah brought a message of hope, saying, "A remnant of my people will spread out from Jerusalem, a group of survivors from Mount Zion" (2 Kings 19:31).

In the midst of disaster and destruction, idolatry and indifference, God has always preserved for himself a remnant of people whom he has kept faithful in their embrace of his covenant. On the ark, there was Noah and his family, a faithful remnant. Among the children of Israel in the desert, there were Joshua and Caleb. In Elijah's day, there were the 7,000 who had not bowed the knee to Baal. Jeremiah and Isaiah's prophecies are full of expectations that "a remnant of the house of Judah will take root below and bear fruit above" (2 Kings 19:30, NIV) and assurance that God promised to "forgive the remnant" he spared (Jeremiah 50:20).

The remnant of those faithful to God and preserved by God throughout the Old Testament continues in the New Testament as those who, by God's grace, see and embrace Jesus as the fulfillment of God's covenant promises. These are the "few" Jesus spoke of in his Sermon on the Mount when he said, "The highway to hell is broad, and its gate is wide for the many who choose that way. But the gateway to life is very narrow and the road is difficult, and only a few ever find it" (Matthew 7:13-14).

It was this faithful remnant that Jesus prayed for as he prepared to go to the Cross and eventually leave this world.

I have revealed you to the ones you gave me from this world. They were always yours. You gave them to me, and they have kept your word. (John 17:6)

Throughout all generations since Christ, there remains a faithful remnant. They "have remained faithful because of God's grace—his undeserved kindness in choosing them. And since it is through God's kindness, then it is not by their good works. For in that case, God's grace would not be what it really is—free and undeserved" (Romans 11:5-6).

† *How I long to remain faithful to you, Father, over the long haul of my life. But I know I cannot do this in my own power. It will only be by your grace and your keeping, which you have promised to provide.*

We Will Dwell with Him in Perfect Safety

Jerusalem had become the capital of the southern kingdom. It had been taken over the centuries by the Egyptians and the Assyrians, retaken by the kings of Israel, and then taken by Nebuchadnezzar, the king of Babylon:

> The entire Babylonian army . . . tore down the walls of Jerusalem on every side. Nebuzaradan, the captain of the guard, then took as exiles the rest of the people who remained in the city. (2 Kings 25:10-11)

Ancient cities were surrounded by thick, strong stone walls. The walls provided protection from enemies, and security and safety to all who lived within the walls. So when the Babylonian army broke down the walls of Jerusalem, it put an end to safety and security for Jerusalem's inhabitants. They were carried off to exile in Babylon.

God's people have always needed a city to live in with walls that are impenetrable by their enemies, where they can live in peace and safety and without fear. But no human king could ever construct such a city. No wall built by human hands could ever provide security that would last.

The writer to the Hebrews says that the country God's people have longed for is "a heavenly homeland" and that God "has prepared a city for them" (Hebrews 11:16). The apostle John was given a vision of this city, and he saw that it is a city with walls—magnificent, beautiful, impenetrable walls "made of jasper," built on foundation stones "inlaid with twelve precious stones." And because these walls provide such solid security for the new Jerusalem, "nothing evil will be allowed to enter, nor anyone who practices shameful idolatry and dishonesty—but only those whose names are written in the Lamb's Book of Life" (Revelation 21:18-19, 27).

It is the saving work of Jesus, the slain Lamb of God, that provides the foundation for an eternity of peace and safety from the enemies of sin and Satan. All those whose names are written in his book—all those who have come alive to Jesus Christ—will live with him forever in his city, surrounded by beautiful, impenetrable walls.

† *Builder of the walls around the city of God, how I long to live in the place you have gone to prepare for me. No more attacks from my enemies of pride and lust and greed. No more being carried off into captivity by my selfishness and fear. With you I will dwell in perfect safety.*

JULY 19

LET YOUR ANGER
FALL AGAINST ME

First Chronicles records many of David's victories over his enemies, and then we read in 21:1: "Satan rose up against Israel and caused David to take a census of the people of Israel." Counting was a way of measuring and celebrating his success. But David was far from being alone in this folly. Ever prone to remove their eyes from Jehovah in the unbelief of self-confidence, the people of Israel were proud of their own resources and numbers. So after they had completed ten months of counting, the Lord sent a plague upon Israel, and in ten hours 70,000 people died. David had taken pride in the thousands in his nation, and his thousands were drastically reduced. Then God sent an angel to destroy Jerusalem.

> David looked up and saw the angel of the LORD standing between heaven and earth with his sword drawn, reaching out over Jerusalem. So David and the leaders of Israel put on burlap to show their deep distress and fell face down on the ground. And David said to God, "I am the one who called for the census! I am the one who has sinned and done wrong! But these people are as innocent as sheep—what have they done? O LORD my God, let your anger fall against me and my family, but do not destroy your people." (1 Chronicles 21:16-17)

The dreadful spectacle of the avenging angel about to fall upon the holy city deeply affected David. He had confessed and repented of his sin of calling for a census, but now he poured out his heart in humble contrition and earnest supplication, taking the entire blame on himself. He not only shouldered the guilt but was willing to bear the retribution. His willingness can be compared to that of Moses, who interceded when God planned to destroy his people after they had worshiped a golden calf. Moses asked God to forgive them and, if not, to erase Moses' name out of his book (Exodus 32:32).

But God would not allow Moses or David to suffer in the stead of all Israel. None could fill that awful and honorable place of substitution but the greater Moses, David's Son and Lord. While God stayed his hand of justice and did not let his anger fall on Jerusalem, God did not stay his hand at Calvary. There his anger fell on the one mediator between God and man—Jesus Christ.

† *Greater David, the hand of justice was not stayed when you welcomed God to let his anger fall against you rather than on your people. Because you exhausted God's anger against sin, I have received an abundance of mercy.*

PRINCE OF PEACE

In the ancient Near East, the building of a palace or a temple often commemorated the culmination of a king's military campaign. David had fought battles and conquered his enemies, and he was now ready to build a great Temple for God. But that was not to be.

> David sent for his son Solomon and instructed him to build a Temple for the LORD, the God of Israel. "My son, I wanted to build a Temple to honor the name of the LORD my God," David told him. "But the LORD said to me, 'You have killed many men in the battles you have fought. And since you have shed so much blood in my sight, you will not be the one to build a Temple to honor my name. But you will have a son who will be a man of peace. I will give him peace with his enemies in all the surrounding lands. His name will be Solomon, and I will give peace and quiet to Israel during his reign. He is the one who will build a Temple to honor my name. He will be my son, and I will be his father. And I will secure the throne of his kingdom over Israel forever.'" (1 Chronicles 22:6-10)

Each in his own way, both of these kings, David and Solomon, were forerunners of Jesus. Like David, Jesus is a royal warrior who defeated Satan once and for all. But like Solomon, he is also the Prince of Peace—building his temple with living stones. Christ is building his church made up of men and women who are no longer at war with God, but at peace with him because of what was accomplished when the warrior-king Jesus conquered all his enemies at the Cross.

> Since we have been made right in God's sight by faith, we have peace with God because of what Jesus Christ our Lord has done for us. Because of our faith, Christ has brought us into this place of undeserved privilege where we now stand, and we confidently and joyfully look forward to sharing God's glory. (Romans 5:1-2)

† *Prince of Peace, you are building a temple where God will live forever with his people. Though I have brought dishonor to your name, you are using me, along with my brothers and sisters in Christ from all ages, to build a temple that will honor your name.*

JULY 21

WHOLEHEARTED DEVOTION TO GOD

David was not allowed to build the Temple, but it was his great joy to lay the groundwork for its construction. He gathered craftsmen, provided building materials, and organized Temple officials. David called on the people to make their offerings for the building of the Temple, and "the people rejoiced over the offerings, for they had given freely and wholeheartedly to the LORD" (1 Chronicles 29:9). David prayed that this devotion would not die, but would continue in the hearts of the people and in their new king, Solomon:

> I know, my God, that you test the heart and are pleased with integrity. All these things have I given willingly and with honest intent. And now I have seen with joy how willingly your people who are here have given to you. O LORD, God of our fathers Abraham, Isaac and Israel, keep this desire in the hearts of your people forever, and keep their hearts loyal to you. And give my son Solomon the wholehearted devotion to keep your commands, requirements and decrees and to do everything to build the palatial structure for which I have provided. (1 Chronicles 29:17-19, NIV)

David's efforts were not about a mere building. He wanted God's people to know and experience God's presence in their midst as he took up residence in his Temple. But their devotion did not last. Their hearts became divided and their worship became empty. And eventually God's presence withdrew from the Temple itself. Even Solomon, David's son, lost his wholehearted devotion to keeping God's commands. His foreign wives turned his heart away from God and toward idols.

The reality is that we cannot be totally consecrated or wholeheartedly devoted to God. This is why we need the One greater than Solomon—the only person who has ever loved the Lord his God with all of his heart, mind, and strength, without fail. He is the only One who has lived in holiness, without which no one will see the Lord. He is the only One who has truly given his all to build God's Temple. He is the only One who is worthy of the presence of the Lord.

† *Devoted Son of God, you are worthy of the presence of the Lord, yet you made yourself an outcast of heaven. You experienced the abandonment of God so that I, unworthy, unconsecrated, halfhearted, disobedient, might be welcomed into God's very presence.*

JULY 22

HOW MUCH MORE THE BLOOD OF CHRIST

The nation had strayed so far from God that the Temple had fallen into disrepair. In the process of repairing the Temple, the priest "found the Book of the Law of the LORD that was written by Moses" (34:14). When the Law was read to young King Josiah and he realized how far the people of Israel had fallen away, he determined to obey all the commands of God, including the celebration of Passover.

> Then Josiah provided 30,000 lambs and young goats for the people's Passover offerings, along with 3,000 cattle, all from the king's own flocks and herds. . . . The administrators of God's Temple . . . gave the priests 2,600 lambs and young goats and 300 cattle as Passover offerings. The Levite leaders . . . gave 5,000 lambs and young goats and 500 cattle to the Levites for their Passover offerings. . . . The Levites then slaughtered the Passover lambs and presented the blood to the priests, who sprinkled the blood on the altar while the Levites prepared the animals. (2 Chronicles 35:7-9, 11)

Gallon upon gallon of blood served as an unavoidable megaphone, shouting about the seriousness of sin and reminding the people that sin both brings and demands death. The blood was like a constantly flashing neon sign in the window of the Israelites' minds: *Sin brings death . . . sin brings death . . . sin brings death.* That megaphone of sacrifice also pointed to the need for a perfect sacrifice. The blood of all those animals could not atone for sin. What was needed was a more efficacious sacrifice, the offering of a more precious blood that would put an end to animal sacrifice. Jesus was that perfect sacrifice. Our sin was dealt with by his death.

> Under the old system, the blood of goats and bulls and the ashes of a young cow could cleanse people's bodies from ceremonial impurity. Just think how much more the blood of Christ will purify our consciences from sinful deeds so that we can worship the living God. (Hebrews 9:13-14)

† *Christ, the perfect sacrifice for sins, you knew that the blood of bulls and goats only reminded us of sin, but it did not take it away. So with your own blood—not the blood of goats and bulls—you entered the Most Holy Place once for all time and secured our redemption forever!*

FAITHFUL

The chronicler needed to explain the failure of Israel as a kingdom. So he started and ended his narrative by describing the unfaithfulness of Israel's rulers:

> So Saul died because he was unfaithful to the LORD. He failed to obey the LORD's command, and he even consulted a medium. (1 Chronicles 10:13)

> Likewise, all the leaders of the priests and the people became more and more unfaithful. They followed all the pagan practices of the surrounding nations, desecrating the Temple of the LORD that had been consecrated in Jerusalem. (2 Chronicles 36:14)

Over and over again, Israel's prophets, priests, and kings were unfaithful. God's people longed for someone to rule over them who would not chase after idols, who would persevere in loving God's law, who would rule with righteousness that would last. But no human has the power to be that faithful.

That's why we need Jesus. He is the faithful leader the people of God have always longed for. In fact, at the end of history, in the book of Revelation, Jesus is called by the name Faithful. "Then I saw heaven opened, and a white horse was standing there. Its rider was named Faithful and True, for he judges fairly and wages a righteous war" (Revelation 19:11).

Jesus is faithful even to those who are repeatedly unfaithful to him. "If we are unfaithful, he remains faithful" (2 Timothy 2:13). But he also empowers us by his Spirit to become faithful like he is. "The fruit of the Spirit is . . . faithfulness" (Galatians 5:22, NIV). It is his faithfulness at work in us that will allow us to enjoy hearing him one day say to us: "Well done, my good and faithful servant. You have been faithful in handling this small amount, so now I will give you many more responsibilities. Let's celebrate together!" (Matthew 25:21). And when we doubt that this will ever happen, we remember, "The one who calls you is faithful and he will do it" (1 Thessalonians 5:24, NIV).

† *Faithful and True, I am holding on to your promise that you will keep me strong to the end so that I will be blameless on the day when you bring everything into the light. How I long to hear your "well done" on that day. It's your Spirit at work inside me that makes me confident that that day will surely come.*

STUDENT AND TEACHER

Ezra came from a long line of priests, going all the way back to Aaron himself, the first high priest. He was a scribe living among the exiles in Babylon when he received special permission to return to Jerusalem, the holy city of God, and was provided with everything he needed to rebuild the burned Temple and reestablish worship there. Ezra had the hand of God on him, but he was also diligent in doing his part to be used by God among his people: "Ezra had determined to study and obey the Law of the LORD and to teach those decrees and regulations to the people of Israel" (Ezra 7:10).

To know, understand, obey, and teach God's law was Ezra's heart commitment, the direction of his life, the settled intention of his soul. Much later, Jesus would perfectly fulfill Ezra's agenda: studying the law from beginning to end, doing it with perfection.

Having set aside the privileges of deity, Jesus had to learn the Torah. And from his earliest days, like Ezra, Jesus' heart and energy were attuned to studying the Word of God. At just twelve years old, Jesus was discovered "in the Temple, sitting among the religious teachers, listening to them and asking questions. All who heard him were amazed at his understanding and his answers" (Luke 2:46-47). Repeatedly in his ministry he expressed frustration at those who resisted his message, saying, "Haven't you read the Scriptures?"

Also, like Ezra, Jesus determined to obey the law of the Lord. His obedience was not automatic; it was authentic. He did not come to abolish the law but to accomplish its purpose (Matthew 5:17).

And finally, like Ezra, Jesus taught the Scriptures to the people of Israel. Out on a hillside, from the front of a boat on the water, and in the Temple, Jesus taught with freshness, authority, power, and clarity so that those who heard him said that they had never heard teaching like it.

While Ezra pointed those he taught to the law of God and the God of the law, Jesus pointed to himself as the fulfillment of all that the law taught and as the One who came from God and was God. He said, "As it is written in the Scriptures, 'They will all be taught by God.' Everyone who listens to the Father and learns from him comes to me" (John 6:45).

✝ *Teacher, you said that the student who is fully trained will become like the teacher. And that is what I want most in this life—to know, obey, and rightly handle your Word of truth.*

JULY 25
I WILL BUILD MY CHURCH

Nehemiah, an Israelite in exile from his homeland, was comfortable in the palace in Persia serving as the king's cup-bearer when his brother and some fellow travelers brought him news of current conditions back in Jerusalem. "They said to me, 'Things are not going well for those who returned to the province of Judah. They are in great trouble and disgrace. The wall of Jerusalem has been torn down, and the gates have been destroyed by fire'" (Nehemiah 1:3).

Years earlier, Ezra had returned to Jerusalem with a group of exiles and rebuilt the Temple. But without the wall, the city was still virtually defenseless. So when Nehemiah heard this, he sat down and wept. In fact, for days he mourned, fasted, and prayed. God allowed Nehemiah to return to Jerusalem with the blessing of the king. When he arrived, he discovered that even the grim description his brother had given him did not fully capture the reality of the disgraced and destroyed city. Jerusalem was a fallen and charred heap of rubble. Giant stones lay half-buried, embedded in the earth.

Nehemiah was determined to lead the people in rebuilding the wall. But his detractors scoffed, saying, "Do they actually think they can make something of stones from a rubbish heap—and charred ones at that?" (Nehemiah 4:2). But this is exactly what God did—for Nehemiah and for us. God sent his Son to rescue us from the rubbish heap so that we might become living stones, built together into a place where God chooses to dwell.

Built beautifully in the Garden of Eden, our lives have been dismantled and broken down by sin. We are in ruins. And so God sent a Builder greater than Nehemiah, a Restorer greater than Nehemiah, One whose heart is broken like Nehemiah's over the ruined state of the people he loves and the place in which he intends to live. Jesus came to us, planting himself in the muck and mire of earth so he might do the work necessary to reclaim us from the wreckage. He will build his church, made up of living stones, and the powers of hell will not be able to penetrate its walls (Matthew 16:18).

† *You are building your church—not with fresh-cut stones, but with charred and ruined stones—with people who have been ruined and scarred by sin. Joined by faith with you, we are transformed into living stones, being built into a spiritual temple and a city in which you are delighted to dwell.*

I CANNOT COME DOWN

Sanballat and Tobiah, governors over the area surrounding Jerusalem, were displeased that someone had come to help the people of Israel. So they hindered the rebuilding of the wall at every turn. When there were no gaps left in the wall and all that remained was to set the doors in the gates, they sent a message to Nehemiah, asking him to come down from his workplace on the wall to meet with them. But Nehemiah knew it was a plot to harm him and stop the work, so he sent messengers to them, saying: "I am doing a great work and I cannot come down. Why should the work stop while I leave it and come down to you?" (Nehemiah 6:3, ESV).

Nehemiah's enemies did everything they could to divert his attention and destroy his character, but he pressed on. "They were just trying to intimidate us, imagining that they could discourage us and stop the work," Nehemiah said. "So I continued the work with even greater determination" (6:9).

Amidst significant opposition, Nehemiah left the king's palace to do a great work out of his love for God and God's people. Similarly, Jesus left the palace of heaven to give himself to a great work of restoring a people for God. He, too, faced significant opposition to his rebuilding work. His enemies also called for him to come down.

> The people passing by shouted abuse, shaking their heads in mockery. "Ha! Look at you now!" they yelled at him. "You said you were going to destroy the Temple and rebuild it in three days. Well then, save yourself and come down from the cross!"
>
> The leading priests and teachers of religious law also mocked Jesus. "He saved others," they scoffed, "but he can't save himself! Let this Messiah, this King of Israel, come down from the cross so we can see it and believe him!" (Mark 15:29-32)

But Jesus did not come down. His willingness to be bound by nails and mocked by his enemies shouted out to us through the ages, saying, "I am doing a great work and I cannot come down!"

† *Great Rebuilder and Restorer, I praise you that you did not come down! You stayed there, accomplishing your redeeming work until you cried out, "It is finished!" And because your work is completed, I can live safely inside your walls where no enemy can harm me.*

JULY 27

REMEMBER THIS IN MY FAVOR

When word came to Nehemiah about the condition of Jerusalem, his heart was broken and his memory of God's promises was pricked. As he prayed, he asked God to remember his promise to his people about his city:

> Please remember what you told your servant Moses: "If you are unfaithful to me, I will scatter you among the nations. But if you return to me and obey my commands and live by them, then even if you are exiled to the ends of the earth, I will bring you back to the place I have chosen for my name to be honored." (Nehemiah 1:8-9)

God did remember his promise and granted Nehemiah success in his restoration work on the wall, in the city, and in working with Ezra for the restoration of worship and celebrations as God had commanded. And throughout the process, Nehemiah continued to call upon God to remember:

> Remember, O my God, all that I have done for these people, and bless me for it. (5:19)

At the end of his life, Nehemiah was still calling upon God. "Remember this in my favor, O my God," Nehemiah said (13:31). He entrusted all that he had done to God, and asked to be counted among the righteous at the final judgment.

In the final words of Jesus, we hear an echo of Nehemiah's plea. Jesus had come to the ruins of earth and made it his life's work to restore God's people. He walked in Herod's Temple and saw that it, too, was forsaken. Just as Nehemiah drove corrupt priests from the Temple, Jesus drove out the corruption of the Temple. Just as Nehemiah spoke God's word to the people, Jesus taught the truth of God. And just as Nehemiah entrusted himself to God's remembrance, so did Jesus entrust himself to God, saying, "Father, into your hands I commit my spirit" (Luke 23:46, NIV). But it is not for his own benefit Christ asks God to remember what he has done, but for ours. God remembers what Christ has done, and we receive his favor.

✝ *Father, remember me with favor—not any favor I might have endeavored to earn through good works, but the favor granted to me through Christ. On the day of final judgment, may my labors for you be the evidence of your favor at work in and through my life.*

JULY 28
INTERCEDING ON OUR BEHALF

When King Xerxes signed the edict to annihilate all the Jews in the kingdom, he didn't know that Queen Esther was herself a Jew. She had kept her family background and nationality secret as Mordecai, her cousin, had told her to. But now Mordecai urged her to go into the king's presence to beg for mercy and plead with him to save the lives of her people. "If you keep quiet at a time like this, deliverance and relief for the Jews will arise from some other place, but you and your relatives will die. Who knows if perhaps you were made queen for just such a time as this?" Esther replied, "I will go in to see the king. If I must die, I must die" (Esther 4:14-16).

God's covenant people needed a mediator—someone willing and able to go and plead their case where they could not go—into the presence of the king. Esther knew what this bold, uninvited approach would likely cost her. Her comfortable life in the palace could be gone in an instant, and she could well lose her life. But Esther took her life in her hands, risking everything for her people. She asked for her life and the lives of her people to be spared. And the king did as she requested.

We, too, need a mediator willing to go before God, the great King, to intercede for our very lives. We need a deliverer who identifies with us and stands in for us as our representative. We can't simply saunter into the King's presence to plead our own case. His edict to punish sin has gone out through-out his world—"This is my rule: The person who sins is the one who will die" (Ezekiel 18:4)—and it cannot be reversed.

But our Mediator has gone to our King asking that the sentence of death be passed down, not on us, but on him. Jesus knew his time had come. "Now the time has come for the Son of Man to enter into his glory," Jesus said. "Now my soul is deeply troubled. Should I pray, 'Father, save me from this hour'? But this is the very reason I came!" (John 12:23, 27).

Jesus stepped forward, not to plead for his life but to offer his life. He stepped forward not at the risk of his life but at the certain cost of his life. To stand before the throne to intercede for us not only risked his death, it required his death.

✝ *You have approached the great King in my stead, Jesus, knowing that it would cost you your life. You left the palace of heaven with no desire to protect yourself, but with every intention of offering yourself so that my life might be spared. And now you intercede for me before the throne.*

POETRY
AND
WISDOM

THE SUFFERING OF A RIGHTEOUS MAN

The book of Job is the story of the suffering of a righteous man. "There once was a man named Job who lived in the land of Uz. He was blameless—a man of complete integrity. He feared God and stayed away from evil" (Job 1:1).

Job's righteousness didn't mean that he was without sin. To be "blameless" is not the same as to be "guiltless." If someone is "blameless," it means that no matter how horrible his offenses may have been, all the charges against him have been dropped. Absolutely no blame attaches to him because the very one he offended has exonerated him. Job had "the righteousness that comes from God and is by faith" (Philippians 3:9, NIV). This blamelessness was available to him only because of what Christ would do when "God made Christ, who never sinned, to be the offering for our sin, so that we could be made right with God through Christ" (2 Corinthians 5:21).

In Job, a righteous man who suffered significantly, we see glimpses of the One to come, a truly righteous man, a guiltless man, who suffered so that we might be deemed blameless before God. But there are differences between Job, the righteous man who suffered, and Jesus, the Righteous One who suffered. In the face of his suffering, Job boldly and openly grumbled, "I am disgusted with my life. Let me complain freely. My bitter soul must complain" (Job 10:1). But Jesus endured beating and mocking and false accusation without complaint. Whereas Job justified himself, saying, "I will defend my integrity until I die" (Job 27:5), Jesus remained silent "when the leading priests and the elders made their accusations against him" (Matthew 27:12). Job determined to put his hope in God *even if* God killed him (Job 13:15). Jesus entrusted himself to God, knowing that it was God's plan from before the foundations of the world that he would die.

Job's hopes were centered in his anticipation of resurrection. "And after my body has decayed, yet in my body I will see God!" (Job 19:26). And so were Christ's. "'The Son of Man must suffer many terrible things,' he said. 'He will be rejected by the elders, the leading priests, and the teachers of religious law. He will be killed, but on the third day he will be raised from the dead'" (Luke 9:22). Job's resurrection became reality only through the resurrection of the Righteous One, who died so that Job might live.

† *Righteous One, I see your suffering and I know that it was for me, so that you might make me blameless before my holy God.*

JULY 30
SATAN MUST ASK PERMISSION

As Satan came before God in the story of Job, he had been roaming around the earth. He was looking for an opportunity—an opportunity to defeat God, to prove himself more powerful than God. He wanted to be worshiped as God. Satan was convinced that Job was faithful to God only because God had supernaturally blessed and protected him, and he asserted that if that protection were to be lifted, Job would curse God.

"'All right, you may test him,' the LORD said to Satan. 'Do whatever you want with everything he possesses, but don't harm him physically'" (Job 1:12). And later God readjusted the boundaries, saying, "All right, do with him as you please . . . but spare his life" (2:6). Satan asked permission to harm Job in a desire to destroy his faith, but God granted that permission in order to develop Job's faith. Job and his friends had no idea that this drama was behind Job's suffering. They had no perception of a personalized supernatural evil. Perhaps Job had been kept in the dark because the knowledge of such a powerful enemy would be too terrifying without the full revelation of the saving victory of Jesus on the Cross.

It's not until Satan came out of the shadows to tempt Jesus in the wilderness that the face of evil was unmasked. Throughout the Gospels we see Jesus asserting his authority over Satan and his demons. A legion of demons begged to be allowed to enter into a herd of pigs rather than sent to the bottomless pit, and Luke records that "Jesus gave them permission" (Luke 8:32).

In Luke, we once again find Satan asking permission to harm one of God's own, hoping to bring the faith of the faithful to ruin. Jesus said to Peter, "Simon, Simon, Satan has asked to sift each of you like wheat. But I have pleaded in prayer for you, Simon, that your faith should not fail" (22:31-32). Jesus was about to be arrested and ultimately crucified, and Peter was about to deny Christ. Jesus explained to Peter that Satan himself was involved in what was about to happen. Peter would need assurance that God was in ultimate control. God intended to use Satan's dirty tricks to serve his own purposes for the disciples' good. Though Peter would fail, his faith would not. He would fall away, but he would be restored. It was not greatness Peter needed to experience, but grace, and this was soon to come.

† *I place my life in your hands, Jesus, knowing that if you allow the evil one to bring temptation or suffering into my life, while he may mean to destroy my faith, you will use it to develop my faith.*

THE ONE WHO EXISTED FROM THE BEGINNING

In verse after verse of beautiful poetry, Job spoke in amazement at the wonder of Almighty God. And as he did, he painted a stunningly accurate portrait of the Son of God, Jesus, who would one day walk the earth:

> He alone has spread out the heavens
>   and marches on the waves of the sea.
> He made all the stars—the Bear and Orion,
>   the Pleiades and the constellations of the southern sky.
> He does great things too marvelous to understand.
>   He performs countless miracles. . . .
> If he snatches someone in death, who can stop him?
>   Who dares to ask, "What are you doing?" (Job 9:8-10, 12)

Surely Job spoke far more than what he knew, and far more than his first readers could have understood, since every aspect of his description of God pointed to the Incarnate Son of God. Since God alone "marches on the waves of the sea," when we see that Jesus "came toward them, walking on the water" (Matthew 14:25), we recognize him for who he is. Since God "made all the stars," it makes complete sense that he would set a star in the sky to announce his becoming flesh. Since God "does great things too marvelous to understand" and "performs countless miracles," we understand why Jesus would do many miracles—so that we would believe he is his Father's Son (John 10:38). Since God's words and works are beyond human questioning, we know Jesus was speaking the words of God when "no one dared to ask him any more questions" (Mark 12:34).

The apostle John proclaimed Jesus as, "the one who existed from the beginning, whom we have heard and seen. We saw him with our own eyes and touched him with our own hands" (1 John 1:1). The same God who made the universe and stands absolutely above and outside it—perfect, uncreated, and inscrutable—entered his own creation in the historical person of Jesus, making himself visible, understandable, available.

† *Incarnate God, I see in you the eternal God, and like Job, I cover my mouth, recognizing that I could never presume to define you with mere words or confine you to terms I can manage or master. You are God, and I am yours.*

AUGUST 1

A MEDIATOR
BETWEEN US AND GOD

Job wanted to take God to court so that he could be proven innocent, but Job knew that was impossible. God is too powerful, too perfect, for Job to accuse.

> God is not a mortal like me,
> so I cannot argue with him or take him to trial.
> If only there were a mediator between us,
> someone who could bring us together.
> The mediator could make God stop beating me,
> and I would no longer live in terror of his punishment.
> Then I could speak to him without fear,
> but I cannot do that in my own strength. (Job 9:32-35)

Job hit upon the idea of an arbitrator, a mediator between himself and God. In fact, that has always been God's plan from before the foundations of the earth—that he would submit himself to binding arbitration, that he would make peace with sinful humanity through a Mediator.

Only a Mediator who is fully God and yet fully man could bring God and people together. Only such a Mediator could be a perfectly fair and impartial representative of each party. Of course, Job had no clue as to how his outrageous proposal of a mediator would, in the fullness of time, come into glorious reality. Though we might expect Jesus, being God, to be biased in God's favor, the Cross reveals in agonizing clarity that Jesus didn't come to take sides, but to bring reconciliation.

Job's vision of a heavenly advocate foreshadows the truth expressed more fully in 1 Timothy 2:5: "For there is only one God and one Mediator who can reconcile God and humanity—the man Christ Jesus."

Whoever dares to become a mediator to negotiate peace between two parties can become a target of both. That's how it would be for Christ himself. "God knew what would happen, and his prearranged plan was carried out when Jesus was betrayed. With the help of lawless Gentiles, you nailed him to a cross and killed him" (Acts 2:23). Jesus, crucified by men, crushed by God, has become our blessed Mediator, granting us peace with God.

† *Most blessed Mediator, you have put yourself between me and God and made peace. I no longer need to live in terror of his punishment. I can speak to him without fear. I have peace with God because of what you have done.*

NO OTHER HOPE

Satan knew that Job was faithful to God, but Satan was convinced that Job was faithful only because God supernaturally protected and blessed him. Satan taunted that if Job's comfortable life were taken away, Job would turn on God. Satan wanted to prove that Job loved God only for what he could get from him.

God knew better. He knew that Job would be faithful to him no matter what, so he gave Satan permission to rob Job of his wealth, his children, and his health. When we read Job's story, as he agonized over his losses and argued with his so-called "friends" who were convinced that his suffering was his fault, we wonder if Job was slipping. At times we wonder if he will, in fact, pass this painful test. But then we read these words, and we know that indeed God won his wager with Satan: "God might kill me, but I have no other hope. I am going to argue my case with him" (Job 13:15).

Even if God himself should strike him dead, Job declared, he would still trust God with his life and his future. He would continue crying out to God in faith that he would be heard by God and ultimately vindicated.

What is perhaps most amazing about Job's confident testimony is that he offered it in a time when death held no promise for the believer in God. The Old Testament place of the dead, Sheol, was understood as a dark and murky place—not as a place that took one into the bright and glorious presence of God. This was before Jesus Christ arrived in person to burst through the gates of Sheol to free the dead along with the living.

God must have given Job eyes of faith to see beyond his limited Old Testament understanding of life beyond death. His eyes of faith enabled him to place his faith in the One who would say, "I hold the keys of death and the grave" (Revelation 1:18). Job's sure faith enabled him to share Paul's confidence that "nothing can ever separate us from God's love. Neither death nor life. . . . No power in the sky above or in the earth below—indeed, nothing in all creation will ever be able to separate us from the love of God that is revealed in Christ Jesus our Lord" (Romans 8:38-39).

† *Jesus, you stand before the limitations of life and death, giving me hope of a life beyond this one, where I will see you and know you face-to-face. But I will not need to argue my case with God when I get there. You are my intermediary who has settled my case with God. You are my sure and certain hope.*

AUGUST 3
MY REDEEMER LIVES

Job's vision of the future life was obscure at first, and we hear him asking the hopeful question, "Can the dead live again? If so, this would give me hope through all my years of struggle, and I would eagerly await the release of death" (Job 14:14). Somewhere along the way, as Job pursued God in the agony of his suffering, God clearly revealed the answer to Job so that he spoke of resurrection life with firm confidence:

> But as for me, I know that my Redeemer lives,
>   and he will stand upon the earth at last.
> And after my body has decayed,
>   yet in my body I will see God! (Job 19:25-26)

The Hebrew word translated "Redeemer" is *go'el,* and it had two general applications. It was used to refer to the next of kin who intervened to maintain the rights or preserve the continuity of the family (as it is used in the book of Ruth, referring to Boaz). But in daily usage, its primary meaning was "to buy back, recover." This is the prophetic vision Job had of Jesus himself—his Restorer, his Redeemer.

Job envisioned a day when his *Go'el* would restore his long-dead body and remake it into a body fit for the new heaven and new earth, where the Redeemer would live with redeemed humanity. Job longed for the day when he would gaze with his eyes upon his God-Redeemer standing "upon the earth." It was not the thought of his soul resting with God in a far-off heaven that brought him such intense anticipation, but the thought of seeing God-in-glorified-flesh standing in victory on a renewed earth.

God gave Job the prophetic ability to see not the first coming of Christ, but the Second Coming, when "the Lord himself will come down from heaven with a commanding shout" (1 Thessalonians 4:16). He could see with eyes of faith the renewal that Paul described clearly when he wrote, "Our earthly bodies are planted in the ground when we die, but they will be raised to live forever. . . . Thank God! He gives us victory over sin and death through our Lord Jesus Christ" (1 Corinthians 15:42, 57).

† *My Redeemer, the day is coming when all of those who are in Christ will have exactly what Job's aching heart longed for. Even after our physical bodies have long been in the grave, we will be resurrected, glorified, so that we can see you with our eyes and enjoy you forever!*

AUGUST 4
GOD'S ROYAL SON

Psalm 2 has four speakers. The first voices we hear are the enemies speaking against the Lord God and his anointed One. The second strophe records the calm words of God's assurance in the midst of the opposition: "For the Lord declares, 'I have placed my chosen king on the throne in Jerusalem, on my holy mountain'" (2:6).

Then the chosen king speaks: "The king proclaims the LORD's decree: 'The LORD said to me, "You are my son. Today I have become your Father"'" (2:7).

And finally the psalmist (David) exhorts, "Submit to God's royal son" (2:12).

Who is this chosen king to whom God says, "You are my son"? In a sermon at Antioch, Paul said, "This is what the second psalm says about Jesus: 'You are my Son. Today I have become your Father'" (Acts 13:33).

From the very first line of Mark's Gospel, "This is the Good News about Jesus the Messiah, the Son of God," it is clear that establishing Jesus' identity as the Son of God was Mark's clear aim. Throughout his Gospel, Mark emphasized Jesus' healings, exorcisms, raising of the dead, and his teachings that created wonder, awe, amazement, and fear. It's as if Mark wanted his readers to ask along with the disciples, "Who is this man? . . . Even the wind and waves obey him!" (Mark 4:41).

Jesus' identity as the Son of God was affirmed at his baptism when a voice from heaven spoke to Jesus, saying, "You are my dearly loved Son, and you bring me great joy" (Mark 1:11). It was heard again at the Transfiguration, saying, "This is my dearly loved Son. Listen to him" (9:7). Voices from hell affirmed that Jesus was the Son of God too. "Whenever those possessed by evil spirits caught sight of him, the spirits would throw them to the ground in front of him shrieking, 'You are the Son of God!'" (3:11). Jesus finally said it clearly himself when, during one of his trials, the high priest asked him, "Are you the Messiah, the Son of the Blessed One?" And Jesus said, "I AM" (14:61-62). But perhaps the most climactic identification of Jesus' identity as God's Son took place at the Crucifixion. "When the Roman officer who stood facing him saw how he had died, he exclaimed, 'This man truly was the Son of God!'" (15:39).

† *It is as I gaze on your Cross that deep in my spirit I say, "Truly you are the Son of God!"*

THE ANOINTED ONE

In Psalm 2 God declares, "I have installed my King on Zion, my holy hill" (2:6, NIV). Though history makes no mention of a king of Israel being anointed on Zion, Zion is named as the royal seat of the Anointed One.

The believers who gathered in Jerusalem after the death, resurrection, and ascension of Jesus recognized that they had just seen the fulfillment of Psalm 2, that Jesus was the Anointed One referred to in that psalm. When Peter and John returned to the believers after being jailed by the religious leaders for healing a crippled man and preaching about Jesus, the believers prayed, lifting back to God his own words from Psalm 2, declaring that they were now fulfilled:

> O Sovereign Lord, Creator of heaven and earth, the sea, and everything in them—you spoke long ago by the Holy Spirit through our ancestor David, your servant, saying,
>
> "Why were the nations so angry?
>   Why did they waste their time with futile plans?
> The kings of the earth prepared for battle;
>   the rulers gathered together
> against the LORD
>   and against his Messiah."
>
> In fact, this has happened here in this very city! For Herod Antipas, Pontius Pilate the governor, the Gentiles, and the people of Israel were all united against Jesus, your holy servant, whom you anointed. But everything they did was determined beforehand according to your will. (Acts 4:24-28)

After this prayer, the meeting place shook, and they were all filled with the Holy Spirit. Then they preached the Word of God with boldness. Their boldness came not from their own strength, but from their confidence that Jesus was indeed the Anointed One who was conspired against but also was established forever by God. Death and the Cross had been overcome by resurrection and life, establishing Jesus as the ultimate Victor and reigning King over his rebellious enemies.

† *King Jesus, your defeat of your enemies is sure. By faith, I claim your victory as my own. Through you, the enemies of sin and death are soundly defeated in my life.*

HIS CORONATION CELEBRATION

In writing Psalm 2, King David, himself a "chosen king," was given prophetic eyes to see the day when the Messiah would take his seat at the right hand of Yahweh. He will be enthroned on Mount Zion, having rebuked his enemies. He will be both Sovereign and Son.

> For the Lord declares, "I have placed my chosen king on the throne
> in Jerusalem, on my holy mountain."
> The king proclaims the LORD's decree:
> "The LORD said to me, 'You are my son.
> Today I have become your Father.
> Only ask, and I will give you the nations as your inheritance,
> the whole earth as your possession.'" (2:6-8)

David may not have had a complete knowledge of all that God was planning to do, but he certainly must have understood that this promise went far beyond the bounds of his own reign or that of any human king. Another King would come who would sit on his throne. This King will not rule Israel only, but the whole earth will be his.

This chosen King took his throne when Jesus ascended into heaven and sat down at the right hand of the Father. The events of the Day of Pentecost were the coronation celebration of his taking his rightful throne. The sound from heaven like a mighty windstorm, the tongues of fire, and the sudden ability to speak other languages—these astonishing signs were like the fireworks display at a king's coronation. The coming of the Spirit was evidence of Christ's enthronement, just as the Resurrection was evidence of Christ's atonement. Peter celebrated Christ's enthronement, saying to all who were gathered in Jerusalem that day:

> God raised Jesus from the dead, and we are all witnesses of this. Now he
> is exalted to the place of highest honor in heaven, at God's right hand.
> And the Father, as he had promised, gave him the Holy Spirit to pour
> out upon us, just as you see and hear today. . . . So let everyone in Israel
> know for certain that God has made this Jesus, whom you crucified, to
> be both Lord and Messiah! (Acts 2:32-33, 36)

† *You are enthroned in the highest heaven, and the whole earth belongs to you! Blessing and honor and glory and power belong to the One sitting on the throne and to the Lamb forever and ever.*

AUGUST 7

CHILDREN WILL GIVE YOU PRAISE

The main point of Psalm 8 is clear from the first and last verses: that God's name—I AM WHO I AM—is majestic everywhere. Adding to the majesty of his name is the reality that God will silence his foes with what comes out of the mouths of infants:

> O LORD, our Lord, your majestic name fills the earth!
>   Your glory is higher than the heavens.
> You have taught children and infants
>   to tell of your strength,
> silencing your enemies
>   and all who oppose you. (8:1-2)

The crowds spread their cloaks on the road in front of Jesus as he entered Jerusalem. This is what people did when kings were crowned (2 Kings 9:13). All the people—including the children—were shouting words from Psalm 118, "Praise God for the Son of David!" (Matthew 21:9). "But the leaders were indignant. They asked Jesus, 'Do you hear what these children are saying?'" (21:15-16).

The religious leaders were asking Jesus a question designed to shame him into keeping the children quiet. They were saying, *Jesus, you know that they are ascribing to you a messianic title in that singing. You are letting those little children think that you are the Messiah.* These leaders, who a few minutes earlier had been overseeing the dove selling and crooked money exchanges in the Temple, were now suddenly concerned about reverence for God?

Jesus' reply in Matthew 21:16 referred to Psalm 8: "Haven't you ever read the Scriptures? For they say, 'You have taught children and infants to give you praise.'"

Because Psalm 8 is about the majesty of Yahweh's name, when Jesus quoted it, he was suggesting that he is worthy of this same praise by children and infants. At the same time he was suggesting that those who opposed him—the religious leaders—were in reality the enemies of Yahweh, who would be silenced.

✝ *O Lord, our Lord, your majestic name fills the earth! Your glory is higher than the heavens. I will glory in your glory. I will celebrate your strength. I will long for the day when the silencing of your enemies is fully realized.*

AUGUST 8
THE ONLY ANSWER TO OUR WICKEDNESS

The Old Testament doesn't exactly gloss over the reality of the sin in the human heart. Genesis 6:5 told us that "the LORD observed the extent of human wickedness on the earth, and he saw that everything they thought or imagined was consistently and totally evil." As centuries passed, and even after humanity "started over" after the Flood, not much seemed to change. David (who knew what it was to have a heart seeking after God as well as a heart that was broken by his own sinfulness) put it into poetry in Psalm 14:2-3:

> The LORD looks down from heaven
>   on the entire human race;
> he looks to see if anyone is truly wise,
>   if anyone seeks God.
> But no, all have turned away;
>   all have become corrupt.
> No one does good,
>   not a single one!

And the prophet Jeremiah wrote, "The human heart is the most deceitful of all things, and desperately wicked. Who really knows how bad it is?" (Jeremiah 17:9).

Christ's coming and Christ's dying provided the only hope for sinners who are totally evil, corrupt, and desperately wicked—which is everyone ever born. Paul explained it this way:

> When we were utterly helpless, Christ came at just the right time and died for us sinners. . . . And since we have been made right in God's sight by the blood of Christ, he will certainly save us from God's condemnation. (Romans 5:6, 9)

We are not basically good people who occasionally do bad things; we are thoroughly bad people who occasionally do good things. The good news of the gospel is that Jesus came to save bad people by taking their punishment and giving them his own perfect goodness.

† *I like to think I am good, Lord, but the closer I come to you, the clearer I see myself in your light. Your Word exposes my innermost thoughts and desires, which are stained by sin. My only hope is that Christ died for me, a sinner through and through. He has made a way for me to face the reality of my sin without fear of condemnation.*

AUGUST 9
HE WILL NOT
ROT IN THE GRAVE

After Jesus rose from the dead, he appeared numerous times to the disciples and "took them through the writings of Moses and all the prophets, explaining from all the Scriptures the things concerning himself" (Luke 24:27). It began to dawn on the disciples with increasing clarity what Jesus meant when he said, "The Scriptures point to me!" (John 5:39). They must have gone back to the writings of Moses and David and the prophets, reading them with new eyes, seeing clearly what had been fuzzy and unclear before. And they emerged from their studies prepared to make those connections for their fellow devout Jews who had not recognized Jesus as the fulfillment of all that the Scriptures pointed to and promised.

Fresh from this study with Jesus, on the Day of Pentecost Peter stood before the crowds in Jerusalem, quoting the words of David: "My body rests in safety. For you will not leave my soul among the dead or allow your holy one to rot in the grave" (Psalm 16:9-10).

Then Peter did something with the psalm that must have seemed outrageous to those who had read that same psalm all their lives: he said that David wasn't really talking about himself but about Jesus:

> Dear brothers, think about this! You can be sure that the patriarch David wasn't referring to himself, for he died and was buried, and his tomb is still here among us. But he was a prophet, and he knew God had promised with an oath that one of David's own descendants would sit on his throne. David was looking into the future and speaking of the Messiah's resurrection. He was saying that God would not leave him among the dead or allow his body to rot in the grave. (Acts 2:29-31)

It had dawned on Peter that the words from Psalm 16 went beyond anything that David experienced. David *did* die and was buried! David's flesh *did* see corruption. Peter recognized the voice of the Messiah speaking prophetically in the voice of his ancestor David.

✝ *Holy, Risen One, because you live, I will live. Because you conquered the grave, my soul will not be left among the dead. And though my flesh may rot and decay, I believe in your promise that you will take my weak, mortal body and change it into a glorious body like your own.*

AUGUST 10

HORN OF SALVATION

Several times in the Psalms and elsewhere in the Old Testament, a "horn" or "horn of salvation" is mentioned:

The Lord is my rock, my fortress and my deliverer;
  my God is my rock, in whom I take refuge.
He is my shield and the horn of my salvation, my stronghold.
    (Psalm 18:2, NIV)

Surely your enemies will perish;
all evildoers will be scattered.
You have exalted my horn like that of a wild ox. (Psalm 92:9-10, NIV)

Here I will make a horn grow for David
  and set up a lamp for my anointed one. (Psalm 132:17, NIV)

The kind of horn meant here is not a musical instrument, but the deadly weapon of the wild ox. It is a sign of strength and a means of victory. This strength flows out of David and yet finds its source in God himself. It is this horn that Zechariah celebrated in song at the birth of his son John:

Praise be to the Lord, the God of Israel,
  because he has come and has redeemed his people.
He has raised up a horn of salvation for us
  in the house of his servant David
(as he said through his holy prophets of long ago). (Luke 1:68-70, NIV)

Filled with the Holy Spirit, Zechariah prophesied about the day when the Messiah will literally destroy his enemies and gather his people into his land to rule in peace. This is surely what Jesus will do when he comes a second time. But it is not just this future work that Zechariah celebrated. Zechariah prophesied that this horn of salvation will "enable us to serve him without fear in holiness and righteousness before him all our days" (1:74-75, NIV). God's aim in raising his Horn of Salvation is not merely to liberate an oppressed people, but to create a holy and righteous people who live before him without fear because they trust in him.

✝ *Horn of Salvation, Strength of my life, Rescuer, Redeemer, God has raised you up and I worship you in all your strength and beauty! You have remembered your holy covenant and shown me mercy. Your goodness enables me to serve you without fear.*

AUGUST 11
GOD'S GRAND "YES!"

From Genesis through Malachi, the Old Testament is a book of promises. God promises that the seed of the woman will crush the head of the serpent. He promises he will never destroy the earth again after the Flood. He promises to bless the whole world through Abraham's descendant. He promises to give his people a home of their own where they can live at peace. He promises a king who will rule with justice. He promises to pour out his Spirit. He promises to heal and restore and renew and protect and provide and put right.

The psalmist sang, "All the LORD's promises prove true" (Psalm 18:30). While the Old Testament makes promises about Christ, the New Testament is the story of how God has kept and will keep all of the promises he has made. And every promise of God relies on Jesus for its fulfillment. Paul said it this way: "For all of God's promises have been fulfilled in Christ with a resounding 'Yes!' And through Christ, our 'Amen' (which means 'Yes') ascends to God for his glory" (2 Corinthians 1:20). Who Jesus is, what he has done, and what he will do is the sum and substance of the fulfillment of the promises of God.

Jesus is the Deliverer, the Mediator, the Ruler, the Reconciler, the Restorer, the Rescuer, the Light, the Beauty, the Joy that God has promised to us.

Jesus brings us into the close and nourishing relationship God has pledged to share with us. Jesus opens the way to enjoy the forgiveness God promised to extend to us. Jesus is the holiness we are given through faith so we can answer God's invitation into his presence. Jesus is the life that is given to us so we do not have to fear the grave.

And Jesus will still be God's "yes" to all of his promises yet to be fulfilled. He will return to us to resurrect our bodies from the grave. He will bring us into the new heaven and new earth he has prepared for us. He will be the source of our joy and satisfaction forever as we worship around his throne.

† *Jesus, God's grand "yes" to me, I refuse to demand that you fulfill your promises here and now in limited and physical ways. Instead, I see that you—in yourself—are the fulfillment of everything God has promised. I rest in knowing that into eternity, I'll still be enjoying God's faithfulness in giving you to me.*

AUGUST 12

THE HEAVENS PROCLAIM THE GLORY OF GOD

In Psalm 19, David recounts the way the creation speaks of its Maker: "The heavens proclaim the glory of God. The skies display his craftsmanship" (19:1).

The heavens shout the glory of God, and no one escapes hearing this voice. And while the glory of God spoken by the heavens is good news for those who believe and are destined to share in it, it is devastating to those who do not believe and are destined to be destroyed by it.

Paul wrote that "God shows his anger from heaven against all sinful, wicked people who suppress the truth by their wickedness. . . . Through everything God made, they can clearly see his invisible qualities—his eternal power and divine nature. So they have no excuse for not knowing God" (Romans 1:18, 20).

How does God show his anger from heaven? He showed it in the Garden when Adam and Eve sinned, and immediately the sentence of death was passed, the earth was cursed, and they were thrown out of Paradise. This was lesson number one in "God hates sin." The rest of the Old Testament is filled with occurrences of God's judgment upon sinners—the Flood, the destruction of Sodom and Gomorrah, the plagues of Egypt. At the same time, and in the same instances, these stories recount God's mercy for sinners—Noah and his family in the ark, Lot escaping the fate of Sodom, the Israelites rescued from Egypt. But the most significant demonstration of God's anger from heaven and his mercy for sinners came when the full fury of the wrath of God was poured out on his Son on the cross.

But still a day of anger from heaven awaits those who have not hidden themselves in Christ. On that day, "the Son of Man . . . will appear in the heavens, and there will be deep mourning among all the peoples of the earth. And they will see the Son of Man coming on the clouds of heaven with power and great glory" (Matthew 24:30). The time for mercy will have passed. John wrote about that final show of God's anger from heaven: "I saw in heaven another great and marvelous sign: seven angels with the seven last plagues—last, because with them God's wrath is completed" (Revelation 15:1, NIV).

† *Creator of the universe, the heavens declare the glory of your love and the glory of your wrath. Your perfect justice demands that evil be punished, and I'm grateful to know it will be. But mostly I'm grateful that you have chosen to pour out on me the mercy I don't deserve rather than the wrath I do deserve.*

ABANDONED BY GOD

Whatever David's personal experience of suffering, the agony he gave words to in Psalm 22 surely transcended it. Jesus must have been meditating on this psalm, written a thousand years before he was born, as he hung on the cross. In it he found the words that gave utterance to his own agony of soul: "My God, my God, why have you abandoned me? Why are you so far away when I groan for help?" (22:1).

David wrote these words at a time when he felt utterly abandoned by God. But when we hear Jesus speak these words centuries later, we recognize that Jesus not only *felt* abandoned by God, that abandonment was a reality. There would be no rescue from the Cross or from death for Jesus. God turned away from him, not because of his own sin, but because of our sin placed on him. "At about three o'clock, Jesus called out with a loud voice, *'Eli, Eli, lema sabachthani?'* which means 'My God, my God, why have you abandoned me?'" (Matthew 27:46).

At the Cross, Jesus became sin for us. And because God cannot look upon sin, the Father had to turn away. Out of hatred for sin and love for sinners, the Father had to abandon his beloved Son. Yet he was not abandoned for good. Once the wrath of God had burned itself out in the very heart of Jesus, he spoke again from the cross, shouting, "Father, I entrust my spirit into your hands!" (Luke 23:46). The price for sin was paid and the relationship restored. David also wrote about this prophetically in Psalm 16, describing the restoration and reunion that was ahead for Jesus with his Father following the alienation and abandonment. "You will not abandon me to the grave. . . . You will fill me with joy in your presence" (Psalm 16:10-11, NIV).

Though it pains us to think of God turning away from his own Son, we must see that it is good news for us. Because God abandoned Jesus on that day, we need never fear that he will abandon us. Though we, like David, may *feel* abandoned, God has promised, "I will never abandon you" (Hebrews 13:5).

† *Abandoned One, I am the one who deserves to experience this agonizing abandonment by God. I'm the one who has sinned. Yet you bore not only my sin, but also the abandonment of your Father that I might experience his presence forever.*

OUR RESCUER
WHO WAS NOT RESCUED

In Psalm 22, David spoke more of Christ than of himself:

> Everyone who sees me mocks me.
>> They sneer and shake their heads, saying,
> "Is this the one who relies on the LORD?
>> Then let the LORD save him!
> If the LORD loves him so much,
>> let the LORD rescue him!" (22:7-8)

This is the precise speech that was hurled at Jesus on the cross. Though his accusers sought to discredit him with their insults, they proved that Jesus was who they said he was not.

> People passing by shouted abuse, shaking their heads in mockery. "Look at you now!" they yelled at him. "You said you were going to destroy the Temple and rebuild it in three days. Well then, if you are the Son of God, save yourself and come down from the cross!"
> The leading priests, the teachers of religious law, and the elders also mocked Jesus. "He saved others," they scoffed, "but he can't save himself! So he is the King of Israel, is he? Let him come down from the cross right now, and we will believe in him! He trusted God, so let God rescue him now if he wants him! For he said, 'I am the Son of God.'" (Matthew 27:39-43)

After his resurrection, two of Jesus' followers on the road to Emmaus expressed their disappointment in the death of Jesus. "We had hoped he was the Messiah who had come to rescue Israel," they said (Luke 24:21). But indeed, the way Jesus would rescue Israel was to refuse to be rescued himself. "Jesus gave his life for our sins, just as God our Father planned, in order to rescue us from this evil world in which we live" (Galatians 1:4). "He is the one who has rescued us from the terrors of the coming judgment" (1 Thessalonians 1:10).

✝ *My Rescuer, you could have been rescued from the agony of the Cross so easily, yet you chose instead to rescue me by what you accomplished there.*

AUGUST 15
I Am Thirsty

In several psalms, David, by divine inspiration, went far beyond his own experience to anticipate the suffering of the One who was to come.

> My life is poured out like water,
>> and all my bones are out of joint.
> My heart is like wax,
>> melting within me.
> My strength has dried up like sunbaked clay.
>> My tongue sticks to the roof of my mouth.
>> You have laid me in the dust and left me
>>> for dead. (Psalm 22:14-15)

> They give me poison for food;
>> they offer me sour wine for my thirst. (Psalm 69:21)

What neither David nor his ancient readers could completely grasp is that these laments go far beyond the psalmist to speak of the Messiah who would come centuries later. They are a preview to the final scene of the Cross. In the Gospel of John, we read about Jesus' ravaging thirst after spending hours hanging on the cross in the hot Judean sun: "Jesus knew that his mission was now finished, and to fulfill Scripture he said, 'I am thirsty.' A jar of sour wine was sitting there, so they soaked a sponge in it, put it on a hyssop branch, and held it up to his lips" (John 19:28-29).

It is interesting that Jesus said that he was thirsty, because though he had been whipped and beaten and nailed to the cross, he had never complained about the physical torture and agony. So when he said, "I am thirsty," perhaps he was not talking about a physical thirst, even though he must have been desperately thirsty. More likely, he was speaking as our substitute, as the One who became sin for us, who felt the agonizing pain every sinner deserves to feel forever. In those hours, he was living the parable he told of the rich man in hell, with no one to bring him water (Luke 16:24). Jesus experienced the unquenchable thirst and scorching fire of hell itself so we won't have to. He experienced the agonizing thirst of eternal punishment on behalf of all those who turn to him for the living water of life.

✝ *I deserve that unquenchable, unremitting, agonizing thirst that you experienced on the cross in my place. But instead of punishing me with this desperate thirst, you have provided streams of living water.*

AUGUST 16
NOT ASHAMED TO CALL US FAMILY

Psalm 22 begins with a prophetic cry of abandonment, moves into a lament and a desperate call for help, and then bursts into a vow of praise: "I will proclaim your name to my brothers and sisters. I will praise you among your assembled people" (22:22). The writer of Hebrews attributed these words in Psalms to Jesus, revealing that David, by inspiration of the Holy Spirit, went far beyond his own experience in penning them:

> God, for whom and through whom everything was made, chose to bring many children into glory. And it was only right that he should make Jesus, through his suffering, a perfect leader, fit to bring them into their salvation. So now Jesus and the ones he makes holy have the same Father. That is why Jesus is not ashamed to call them his brothers and sisters. For he said to God, "I will proclaim your name to my brothers and sisters. I will praise you among your assembled people." (Hebrews 2:10-12)

Jesus is not ashamed to call us family. But it is nothing about us that takes away the shame; it is everything about him. He is the One who is a "perfect leader," the only one fit to bring us into our salvation. And because he knew he would do this, he was willing not only to call us brothers and sisters, but to descend from generations of fathers and mothers who, apart from him, would only bring him shame.

Even the "heroes" of Jesus' genealogy have serious moral failures. Abraham twice lied about being married to Sarah and exposed her to violation to save his own skin. Jacob manipulated to steal his brother's birthright. Tamar was the Canaanite widow who, disguised as a prostitute, solicited her father-in-law, Judah, and bore a child by him. Rahab was a Canaanite prostitute. David committed adultery with Bathsheba and then had her husband murdered to cover his tracks. Solomon lost his spiritual moorings for many years because of sexual compromise and materialism.

But long before he took on human flesh, Jesus celebrated that he would praise God in the midst of imperfect people—people whom he refuses to keep at a distance but actually welcomes into his own family.

✝ *My Brother, Jesus, your love for sinners goes far beyond my understanding—that you would condescend not only to walk among us, but also to become one of us and make us into your own family.*

AUGUST 17
JESUS PAID IT ALL

David knew that his sin had caused him to run up a big debt with God. The man after God's own heart had turned away from God and gone after his own pleasure apart from God, leading to adultery and murder. And because God is perfectly just, David knew that the debt for his sin had to be paid for him to be at peace with God. But he also knew that he could not pay it—not with any amount of good works, not even with all the wealth at his disposal as king of Israel. And yet he celebrated, with a seemingly settled understanding, that his enormous debt had somehow been cleared: "Oh, what joy for those whose disobedience is forgiven, whose sin is put out of sight! Yes, what joy for those whose record the LORD has cleared of guilt, whose lives are lived in complete honesty!" (Psalm 32:1-2).

When David celebrated that the long tab he had run up by his sin had been covered and would not be counted against him, it was no small celebration! God had removed David's sins from his spiritual ledger. David was given a clean slate. But how? Was his debt merely written off, overlooked?

David's debt was not merely ignored. Someone else paid it. "For you know that God paid a ransom to save you from the empty life you inherited from your ancestors. And the ransom he paid was not mere gold or silver. It was the precious blood of Christ" (1 Peter 1:18-19).

Like David, we have racked up a big debt of sin that must be paid. At the Cross Jesus said, "Hand the bill to me—I'll pay it. It's a debt that you owe, but I will pay it with my own life's blood." When King David said, "Oh, what joy for those whose disobedience is forgiven," he was celebrating that God had forgiven him on the basis of, and in anticipation of, full payment for sin by Christ on the cross. David received this payment on his behalf by faith. He could not see the Cross clearly, but he believed God's promise to forgive his sin on the basis of the One who would come and make full forgiveness possible. He looked forward to the Cross in faith, just as we look back to the Cross in faith. It is clearer to us than it was to David. We know that truly Jesus paid it all.

† *My debt to God was large and I was bankrupt, unable to pay anything toward it. And you, Jesus, in your grace, paid my debt. What a gift! What freedom and joy! Now I understand David's great joy. I don't have to work to earn God's forgiveness. It was given to me as a gift when I turned to you in repentance.*

AUGUST 18

BETRAYED BY A FRIEND

Throughout the Psalms, David entreated God to give him victory over his enemies. But in Psalm 41, David lamented that even his friends were against him: "Even my best friend, the one I trusted completely, the one who shared my food, has turned against me" (41:9).

David may have been referring to Absalom, the son who had eaten at his own table and who violently turned against him. Whoever the friend-turned-foe, David saw himself as a righteous sufferer facing opposition from malicious enemies who brought false charges against him. And Jesus, conscious of his identity as the Son of David, used these words of David to identify himself the same way.

> It was time for supper, and the devil had already prompted Judas, son of Simon Iscariot, to betray Jesus. . . . Jesus replied [to Peter], "A person who has bathed all over does not need to wash, except for the feet, to be entirely clean. And you disciples are clean, but not all of you." For Jesus knew who would betray him. . . . [Jesus said,] "This fulfills the Scripture that says, 'The one who eats my food has turned against me.' I tell you this beforehand, so that when it happens you will believe that I Am the Messiah." (John 13:2, 10-11, 18-19)

Jesus repeatedly said that the Old Testament Scriptures pointed to him and that he must fulfill them. Here he used the words of the psalmist not only to identify with his ancestor David, but also to make it clear that Judas's betrayal did not catch him by surprise. In fact, it had always been in the sovereign plan of God. Just as Jesus' life and death were prefigured in Scripture, so were the actions of his enemies.

But it is interesting that Jesus did not quote the entire verse from Psalm 41. He did not include the first part of the verse that says, "Even my best friend, the one I trusted completely," because Jesus had always known that Judas had never truly been a trusted friend, that he had the heart and intentions of a betrayer. Yet even as Judas betrayed him, Jesus called him "friend:" "My friend, go ahead and do what you have come for" (Matthew 26:50).

† *Friend of sinners, I have the heart of a betrayer, and yet you call me friend. I have eaten at your table from your hand, enjoyed your friendship and your blessings. You have given me eyes to see my sin and made me willing to repent. So instead of being damned, I've been redeemed.*

AUGUST 19
WASH ME WITH YOUR BLOOD

David's sin was heinous—he committed adultery with Bathsheba and then had her husband murdered to cover it up. After Nathan the prophet confronted him, David was deeply aware of his sin. His great sin would require great mercy. Perhaps nowhere else in the Bible do we find a prayer more full of faith than David's plea to God in Psalm 51:

> Have mercy on me, O God,
>   because of your unfailing love.
> Because of your great compassion,
>   blot out the stain of my sins.
> Wash me clean from my guilt.
>   Purify me from my sin. . . .
> Purify me from my sins, and I will be clean;
>   wash me, and I will be whiter than snow. (51:1-2, 7)

Though David could not see how God would do it, David's prayer expressed jubilant faith that God could and would indeed provide the cleansing agent required to purge him of the filthiness of his sin.

John wrote, "The blood of Jesus, his Son, cleanses us from all sin" (1 John 1:7). The blood of Jesus reached back to cover David's sin and all the sins of God's people before his death, and it reached forward to cover all sin that occurred and continues to occur after his death. That's the value and power and necessity of Jesus' blood.

The blood of Jesus goes beyond wiping away our legal guilt. The writer to the Hebrews says, "Our guilty consciences have been sprinkled with Christ's blood to make us clean" (10:22). Though we usually think of blood as something that causes stains rather than removes them, the blood of Jesus can cleanse the stains of a guilty conscience. We no longer have to carry around the guilt of what we've done and who we've been. The blood of Jesus is sufficient to make us completely clean before God. With his own blood, Jesus writes in large red letters across our lives, "Forgiven! Clean! Mine!"

✝ *I bless you, Lord Jesus, for your blood spilled for me that cleanses me and makes it possible for me to live free of a conscience that condemns me. But I long for more than your pardon; I long for purity. I long for the power that flows from your blood, the power that is applied by your Spirit who sanctifies me through and through.*

AUGUST 20

BROKEN FOR YOU

Even though everything about Jewish life revolved around the Temple and the sacrifices offered there, King David recognized that these sacrifices were merely pointing to something greater, to a more costly, significant, and sufficient sacrifice for sin: "You do not desire a sacrifice, or I would offer one. You do not want a burnt offering. The sacrifice you desire is a broken spirit. You will not reject a broken and repentant heart, O God" (Psalm 51:16-17).

Brokenness. This is what God requires of sinners. To become brokenhearted over our sin and to turn to God in repentance paves the way to receive his forgiveness. Yet there must be a greater brokenness that will pay the price to make forgiveness possible. And that is what Jesus offered as the once-for-all sacrifice for sin. "Jesus took some bread and blessed it. Then he broke it in pieces and gave it to the disciples, saying, 'Take this and eat it, for this is my body'" (Matthew 26:26).

Because Jesus was broken, we can be whole. As we enter into his brokenness, it becomes ours. And because he lives again, so will we.

Jesus said that if a grain of wheat does not fall into the ground and if its outer shell is not broken, it does not produce a harvest (John 12:24). He was speaking of his own brokenness, the brokenness of his body that would demonstrate his supreme usefulness in the work of salvation. Yet his brokenness was not the end. It was the beginning. Out of his brokenness, he burst forth in resurrection. Because "Christ was raised as the first of the harvest" (1 Corinthians 15:23), we have hope beyond the brokenness of life in this world.

> Our earthly bodies are planted in the ground when we die, but they will be raised to live forever. Our bodies are buried in brokenness, but they will be raised in glory. They are buried in weakness, but they will be raised in strength. They are buried as natural human bodies, but they will be raised as spiritual bodies. (1 Corinthians 15:42-44)

† *Beautiful Jesus, broken for me, I take and eat the bread, taking your brokenness into myself. I receive the gift of your brokenness on my behalf. And I celebrate the sure hope that just as your brokenness led to greater life, so will the brokenness and death of my body be a precursor to the greater and eternal life you will give me!*

AUGUST 21
HE HELPS US OVERCOME THE DISTANCE

David began Psalm 61 asking God to hear his prayer, "From the ends of the earth, I cry to you for help" (61:2). Perhaps David was far away physically from Jerusalem, far away from where the Ark of God was located when he cried out. Or perhaps David just sensed in his heart that he was far away from God, and longed to have that sense of nearness restored.

Most of us know what it is to feel distant from God, to have an at-the-ends-of-the-earth experience in which we feel that God is far away. In this psalm, David shows us how to overcome the distance that intrudes in our relationship with God. "I cry to you for help when my heart is overwhelmed. Lead me to the towering rock of safety, for you are my safe refuge, a fortress where my enemies cannot reach me" (61:2-3).

David cried out to the God he knew as a Rock of safety, a Refuge, a Fortress. He knew that God was not a faraway, uncaring deity, but a caring and capable Protector whom he could run to in the midst of his alienation.

More than that, he seems to have recognized that God's promises of safety and refuge would find their fulfillment in a King who would be greater than he was. This King would not be a distant deity but a King who will come to his people. He will not live in a palace. In fact, he will not even have a home. He will not be served, but will serve. He will not be crowned in honor, but crowned with thorns in disgrace. He will not wear a robe but will be hung naked on a cross. A sign will hang on his cross that says, "King of the Jews" but it will be posted in ridicule, not respect.

This is what it will cost our true King to come to our aid when we cry to him for help. This is what it will cost to have our alienation from God eradicated and our nearness to God restored. This is how good our King Jesus is—he overcame the distance between heaven and earth, between God and man, to come to our aid.

When we join ourselves to King Jesus, we too can overcome the distance between ourselves and a holy God. Because of Jesus we not only have the hope of feeling closer to God, we have an open invitation to boldly draw near to God (Hebrews 7:19).

† *My towering Rock of safety, my safe Refuge, my Fortress, I am hiding in you where my enemies of self-centeredness and pride and self-sufficiency cannot alienate me from you. You draw me close and hold me tight. How good it is to know that I am under your protection forever.*

ENTHRONED IN GOD'S PRESENCE

David seems to have been praying for himself in Psalm 61, crying out for God to listen to his prayer, asking God to be his safe refuge, his sanctuary, his shelter. But then he switched from the first to the third person: "Add many years to the life of the king! May his years span the generations! May he reign under God's protection forever. May your unfailing love and faithfulness watch over him" (61:6-7).

Was David referring to himself, or to some other king? "Add many years to the life of the king!" could easily be understood as a prayer for an earthly king. "May his years span the generations!" could also apply to David perhaps, by stretching things a little. But not, "May he reign under God's protection forever"—at least not if it is understood literally.

This is not the only time David talked about another king whose kingdom would last forever. God sent Nathan to David with a promise that a descendant of his would sit upon his throne forever, saying, "When you die and are buried with your ancestors, I will raise up one of your descendants, your own offspring, and I will make his kingdom strong. He is the one who will build a house—a temple—for my name. And I will secure his royal throne forever" (2 Samuel 7:12-13).

Some of this promise was fulfilled in Solomon, David's immediate successor, who did indeed build the great Temple for God in Jerusalem. But Solomon did not fulfill the "forever" part, which David seems to have recognized since he responded by saying, "You speak of giving your servant a lasting dynasty! Do you deal with everyone this way, O Sovereign LORD?" (7:19).

David knew that nothing that is merely human lasts forever. So if God was promising a forever kingdom, it must be a kingdom established and maintained by a divine Messiah, who is God become man.

At the end of Psalm 61, David switched back to praying for himself, saying, "I will sing praises to your name forever as I fulfill my vows each day" (61:8). David understood that a forever king is worthy of day-by-day honor and obedience now. He is worthy of songs of praise now and into eternity.

† *My Forever King, I am so often shortsighted about my commitments to you and the responsibilities you've entrusted to me to build your eternal Kingdom. Fill my heart and my mouth with songs of praise that will honor you into eternity!*

AUGUST 23

PASSION FOR GOD'S HOUSE

It is clear that Psalm 69, like every other psalm, has its origins in the personal experience of the psalmist. With its deep expression of personal failing as well as personal zeal, it is clearly grounded in David's human experience. David felt overwhelmed by enemies. God's glory was at stake and he was jealous for it. His suffering was not only undeserved, it was endured precisely as a representative of God. Yet as we read the psalm, we soon lose sight of David. It does not seem to be about him exclusively.

"Passion for your house has consumed me," wrote David (69:9). And whether or not they read it as prophecy before they followed Jesus, his disciples clearly recognized it as such when Jesus cleared the Temple:

> In the Temple area he saw merchants selling cattle, sheep, and doves for sacrifices; he also saw dealers at tables exchanging foreign money. Jesus made a whip from some ropes and chased them all out of the Temple. He drove out the sheep and cattle, scattered the money changers' coins over the floor, and turned over their tables. Then, going over to the people who sold doves, he told them, "Get these things out of here. Stop turning my Father's house into a marketplace!"
>
> Then his disciples remembered this prophecy from the Scriptures: "Passion for God's house will consume me." (John 2:14-17)

When the disciples heard Jesus call the Temple "my Father's house," they remembered the words of Psalm 69:9. It became clear to them that David's words and actions were a foreshadowing of Christ's words and actions.

Jesus' act of cleansing, which occurred at the center of the place so laden with sacred meaning—the Temple—was far more than the reform of a decadent system of worship. Jesus was bringing an end to a way of life and thought. Israel's institutions were to be replaced. The whole business of sacrifice would become unnecessary now that he, the perfect, once-for-all sacrifice, had come.

† *Jesus, I see your zeal for the purity of your Father's house and find that my heart has become tolerant of perversion, casual about my worship, and I know that this temple of mine must be cleansed. Drive out my compromise and religious emptiness. Chase away my cynicism and exploitation. Give me a heart that is pure and passionate to worship you.*

WORSHIPED BY KINGS

Psalm 72 contains a description of an exalted King and of the blessings of his reign. His Kingdom will be universal, eternal, securing perfect peace. And through this King, all nations will be blessed and bring him praise. The psalmist (Solomon) prophetically saw a glimpse of when this King would be born, even as he described the nature of his Kingdom when it is fully consummated: "The eastern kings of Sheba and Seba will bring him gifts. All kings will bow before him, and all nations will serve him" (72:10-11).

Kings from the most uncivilized, the most distant, and the most opulent nations will pay homage to this King of kings. The prophet Isaiah saw a glimpse of this event, too, when he wrote of the Messiah, "All nations will come to your light; mighty kings will come to see your radiance" (60:3).

Matthew wrote his Gospel with a focus on helping his Jewish readers to see Jesus as the King they had been waiting and longing for. Matthew alone recorded the story of the kings who came to worship the infant Jesus:

> Some wise men from eastern lands arrived in Jerusalem, asking, "Where is the newborn king of the Jews? We saw his star as it rose, and we have come to worship him." . . . And the star they had seen in the east guided them to Bethlehem. . . . They entered the house and saw the child with his mother, Mary, and they bowed down and worshiped him. Then they opened their treasure chests and gave him gifts of gold, frankincense, and myrrh. (Matthew 2:1-2, 9, 11)

Matthew did not give us a lot of detail about the men themselves. He was most interested in telling us that Gentiles came to worship the Jewish Messiah and that they gave him kingly gifts. He wanted us to see that Jesus is the King the psalmist and Isaiah saw.

The apostle John helps us to see that these kings who came to Bethlehem were but a glimpse of all who will one day bow before Jesus in the new Jerusalem: "The nations will walk in its light, and the kings of the world will enter the city in all their glory" (Revelation 21:24).

† *King of kings, you are worthy of my most reverent worship, worthy of my most costly gifts. Therefore I bow low before you in anticipation of the day when every knee will bow and acknowledge you as King.*

HE SPEAKS IN PARABLES

In Psalm 78, Asaph announced his intentions to teach the next generation about the wonders God had done among his people by recounting the history of Israel's disobedience and God's repeated mercy to them. It seems that Asaph did not plan to offer a straight accounting of history:

> O my people, listen to my instructions.
> Open your ears to what I am saying,
> for I will speak to you in a parable.
> I will teach you hidden lessons from our past—
> stories we have heard and known,
> stories our ancestors handed down to us. (78:1-3)

Asaph invited his listeners to hear him speak in parables and hidden lessons, yet the seventy-two verses of the psalm don't seem like a typical parable—they seem to run very parallel to Israel's history. But there is a hidden meaning to the nation's travails, a hidden purpose in her story that is only partially revealed by Asaph's teaching. Deep knowledge of the ways of God means more than knowing the facts of history. It means also grasping the unfolding patterns to see what God is doing.

Matthew wrote that Jesus' teaching was the fulfillment of Psalm 78:

> Jesus always used stories and illustrations like these when speaking to the crowds. In fact, he never spoke to them without using such parables. This fulfilled what God had spoken through the prophet:

> "I will speak to you in parables.
> I will explain things hidden since the creation of the world."
> (Matthew 13:34-35)

Jesus solves the riddle and answers the question left unanswered in Asaph's psalm. He is the answer to Israel's repeated disobedience, for his work will give them hearts that want to obey. He is the culmination of Israel's history, for it has all led to his coming. He is the fulfillment of God's good intentions toward his people. He is the hidden secret, and he shares that secret with us as he reveals himself to us.

† *You are revealing to me the hidden lessons of Israel's history as I see that you are where the story was leading all along.*

THE TARGET OF GOD'S ANGER

The psalmist understood God's response to Israel's disobedience as object lessons about God's anger.

> His anger rose against Israel,
> for they did not believe God
>   or trust him to care for them. . . .
> They angered God by building shrines to other gods;
>   they made him jealous with their idols.
> When God heard them, he was very angry. (78:21-22, 58-59)

But the psalmist also wrote of God restraining his anger:

> Yet he was merciful and forgave their sins
>   and did not destroy them all.
> Many times he held back his anger
>   and did not unleash his fury! (78:38)

Later, David added to our understanding when he celebrated God's restraint of his righteous anger with song in Psalm 103:

> The LORD is compassionate and merciful,
>   slow to get angry and filled with unfailing love.
> He will not constantly accuse us,
>   nor remain angry forever.
> He does not punish us for all our sins;
>   he does not deal harshly with us, as we deserve. (103:8-10)

But how can our righteous, just God do anything other than "deal harshly with us, as we deserve"? On what basis can he drop his accurate accusation against us and show us mercy?

The too-good-to-be-true reality of the gospel is that "God chose to save us through our Lord Jesus Christ, not to pour out his anger on us" (1 Thessalonians 5:9) even though we deserve it. Instead, Jesus, his beloved Son, became the target of his anger. His anger was poured out on Christ so that he might pour out his love and forgiveness on us.

† *By my very nature I was subject to your anger, O God. But you are so rich in mercy that even though I deserve to be the target of your anger, you instead poured out your anger on Christ. What grace! In the ages to come, you will point to me as an example of the wealth of your grace toward sinners.*

HE FILLS THE EMPTINESS

From the first day of Creation, when he created everything from nothing, God has been filling nothingness with his goodness. His very nature is to fill emptiness with his fullness. He longs to satisfy us with himself. "For it was I, the LORD your God, who rescued you from the land of Egypt. Open your mouth wide, and I will fill it with good things" (Psalm 81:10).

God kept his promise to fill the mouths of his people by sending Jesus. Mary recognized this, singing in her Magnificat, "He has filled the hungry with good things and sent the rich away with empty hands" (Luke 1:53). John understood that Jesus was the fullness of God sent in human flesh, a fuller and more complete revelation than had ever been revealed in the Law and the Prophets. "From his abundance [or fullness] we have all received one gracious blessing after another," he wrote. "For the law was given through Moses, but God's unfailing love and faithfulness came through Jesus Christ. . . . He has revealed God to us" (John 1:16-18).

No one who was around Jesus could miss the fact that he came to fill God's people with good things. When the wine ran out at the wedding, Jesus had the pots filled with water and turned it into wine (John 2). When Peter's nets were empty, he told the fishermen to let their nets down again, and "this time their nets were so full of fish they began to tear!" (Luke 5:6). He multiplied a boy's small lunch so that thousands were fed and they "filled twelve baskets with scraps left by the people who had eaten from the five barley loaves" (John 6:13).

Paul tells us that Christ is not finished with his filling work. "God has put all things under the authority of Christ and has made him head over all things for the benefit of the church. And the church is his body; it is made full and complete by Christ, who fills all things everywhere with himself" (Ephesians 1:22-23). Paul continued, saying that Jesus ascended "so that he might fill the entire universe with himself" (4:10). The day is coming when Christ's purpose will be accomplished in every sphere of the universe.

† *My heart, my life, my whole being is empty if you do not fill me, Jesus! I am opening my mouth wide, asking you to fill me with good things—your word, your Spirit, your truth, your ways, your very life.*

SALVATION IS FOUND
IN NO ONE ELSE

The Bible speaks of salvation in terms of the past, present, and future. There is a sense in which we *were saved* (from before the foundation of the world); we *were being saved* (by the work of God in history); we *are saved* (having been justified by faith); we *are being saved* (by being sanctified or made holy); and we *will be saved* (from the wrath to come). This salvation—past, present, and future—is completely God's doing. We can do nothing to save ourselves and we contribute nothing to our own salvation. God plans the work of salvation, executes the work of salvation, and sustains the work of salvation.

> Sing a new song to the LORD,
>   for he has done wonderful deeds.
> His right hand has won a mighty victory;
>   his holy arm has shown his saving power!
> The LORD has announced his victory
>   and has revealed his righteousness to every nation!
> He has remembered his promise to love and be faithful to Israel.
>   The ends of the earth have seen the victory of our God.
>   (Psalm 98:1-3)

While God did great works of salvation in the lives of his people in the Old Testament, their hope was that God's salvation would be revealed in a greater, more pervasive and eternal way. The prophets spoke of God's salvation not only in terms of what he would do but of someone he would send. The angel announced his birth and his very identity in terms of the important work of salvation he would accomplish: "The Savior—yes, the Messiah, the Lord—has been born today in Bethlehem, the city of David!" (Luke 2:11).

To be saved means to be rescued from some calamity. God saves us from the ultimate calamity—coming under his judgment. The complete salvation of God will be accomplished through Christ "who rescues us from the coming wrath" (1 Thessalonians 1:10, NIV). "For God did not appoint us to suffer wrath but to receive salvation through our Lord Jesus Christ" (1 Thessalonians 5:9, NIV).

† *My Savior, salvation is found in no one else. So I turn to you to save me, and I know you will—it is who you are. You are the source of eternal salvation for all who obey you.*

SHEEP IN NEED OF A SHEPHERD

Over and over again, David described God as a shepherd and his people as
sheep. "The LORD is my shepherd" (Psalm 23:1); "Please listen, O Shepherd
of Israel" (80:1); "We are his people, the sheep of his pasture" (100:3). When
the Bible says we're sheep, it's not a compliment. Sheep are helpless and
dumb. They get confused and lost: "We all, like sheep, have gone astray"
(Isaiah 53:6, NIV).

But though we'll always be sheep who go astray, there is a way back into
the safety and supply of the fold of God. It is provided for us in the Shepherd
God intended for us to have all along. The New Testament says that Jesus is
the *good* shepherd (John 10:11), the *great* Shepherd (Hebrews 13:20), and the
Chief Shepherd (1 Peter 5:4, NIV).

Peter described our situation this way: "Once you were like sheep who
wandered away. But now you have turned to your Shepherd, the Guardian of
your souls" (1 Peter 2:25). In its essence, salvation is turning to the Shepherd
of our souls.

When Jesus comes a second time, Peter says that he will come as a
Shepherd, promising, "When the Great Shepherd appears, you will receive
a crown of never-ending glory and honor" (1 Peter 5:4). And in the age to
come, after the Second Coming, long into eternity, Jesus will still be our
Shepherd, providing for our every need:

They will never again be hungry or thirsty;
    they will never be scorched by the heat of the sun.
For the Lamb on the throne
    will be their Shepherd.
He will lead them to springs of life-giving water.
    And God will wipe every tear from their eyes.
    (Revelation 7:16-17)

This is the way it was always meant to be—the Great Shepherd caring for us,
his flock. And this is the way it will be forever.

† *Great Shepherd of my soul, I was made to be shepherded by you each day as
I live life amongst the dangers of this present world and into eternity as I live
in the world remade by you. I will never stop needing your tender care, never
stop enjoying your comforting presence.*

PRICELESS TREASURE

From the beginning of time, humans have had difficulty discerning what is beautiful and valuable from what is ugly and worthless. Over and over again we have traded what is good and glorious and given by God to bless us for what is destructive and diminishing and intended to damn us. The psalmist described how God's people did this in the desert when "they traded their glorious God for a statue of a grass-eating bull" (Psalm 106:20).

The people of Jesus' day had the same problem. The Son of God stood before them and they did not recognize how beautiful and valuable he was. Standing in a boat at the water's edge, Jesus told a story about two people who recognized an object's true value.

> The Kingdom of Heaven is like a treasure that a man discovered hidden in a field. In his excitement, he hid it again and sold everything he owned to get enough money to buy the field.
>
> Again, the Kingdom of Heaven is like a merchant on the lookout for choice pearls. When he discovered a pearl of great value, he sold everything he owned and bought it! (Matthew 13:44-46)

Though most who heard the parable had a hard time understanding its meaning, Jesus was telling them that *he* is a priceless treasure, a valuable pearl. It is worth trading everything you own to have him.

It is only as the Spirit of God works in us that we can see the true value of things, and most importantly, the truly magnificent value of Christ. This is what the psalmist was saying when he wrote, "I would rather be a gatekeeper in the house of my God than live the good life in the homes of the wicked" (Psalm 84:10). The writer saw it as a good trade to give up the stuff of this world for a relationship with God. Paul also recognized the value of Christ and so was willing to trade anything and everything to have him. "Everything else is worthless when compared with the infinite value of knowing Christ Jesus my Lord. For his sake I have discarded everything else, counting it all as garbage, so that I could gain Christ and become one with him" (Philippians 3:8-9).

† *Jesus, priceless Treasure, how my value system needs an overhaul. I so often value the things of this world that are worthless, passing away, and I devalue what is worthwhile, priceless, eternal. Only your Spirit can give me a heart and eyes to see your beauty and worth.*

AUGUST 31
SEATED AT GOD'S RIGHT HAND

Three distinct persons are involved in the conversation of Psalm 110. There is Yahweh, the speaker; David, the recipient of the message; and the One whom David calls "my Lord" and whom he understands to be his sovereign.

> The LORD said to my Lord,
> "Sit in the place of honor at my right hand
> until I humble your enemies,
> making them a footstool under your feet."
> The LORD will extend your powerful kingdom
> from Jerusalem;
> you will rule over your enemies. (110:1-2)

This Lord is a royal person, a King. And if the God of the universe has invited this Sovereign to take such a distinguished seat alongside himself, he must be no less than the promised Messiah. He is also a Priest: "The LORD has taken an oath and will not break his vow: 'You are a priest forever in the order of Melchizedek'" (110:4).

According to Psalm 110, "my Lord" is a King-Priest who has a throne appointed by God, a priestly office that no one else has yet fully occupied. This is to be filled by the King-Priest forever, with a worldwide Kingdom that will enjoy a full and final victory over every form of evil.

While the Jews might well have believed Psalm 110 to be messianic, they never expected it to be used as Jesus used it. After Jesus was arrested, he was brought before the high priest, who asked Jesus under oath to declare whether or not he was the Christ, the Son of God. When Jesus answered this question, he employed the words of Psalm 110 along with Daniel 7:13: "Jesus replied, 'You have said it. And in the future you will see the Son of Man seated in the place of power at God's right hand and coming on the clouds of heaven'" (Matthew 26:64).

With these words, Jesus not only affirmed that he is the Messiah, but asserted that he will judge his enemies when he returns to the earth to possess his throne.

† *My Lord, my Priest, my King, only you are fit to be seated at the place of honor at the right hand of God. There you serve as priest, making intercession for all who are yours. Though I cannot now see you seated in this place of honor with my eyes, the day will come when all will see.*

SEPTEMBER 1
HIS ENEMIES
HUMBLED BENEATH HIS FEET

In the ancient world, a victorious king would place his foot on the neck or back of an enemy as a symbolic act of domination. This is the prophetic image David depicts in what seems to be a Spirit-enabled overhearing of a conversation between Jehovah and the Messiah: "The LORD said to my Lord, 'Sit in the place of honor at my right hand until I humble your enemies, making them a footstool under your feet'" (Psalm 110:1).

Mark wrote that at the Ascension, "when the Lord Jesus had finished talking with them, he was taken up into heaven and sat down in the place of honor at God's right hand" (Mark 16:19). He is the Lord seated at the right hand of God. And there he waits.

How do we know he waits? And what is he waiting for? The writer to the Hebrews explained, "Our High Priest offered himself to God as a single sacrifice for sins, good for all time. Then he sat down in the place of honor at God's right hand. There he waits until his enemies are humbled and made a footstool under his feet" (Hebrews 10:12-13). He's waiting for this day that his Father talked to him about, the day when everything he died to accomplish will be accomplished. While Christ has done everything required to defeat his enemies, and though his Kingdom has been inaugurated, that Kingdom is yet to be consummated.

While he waits, his enemies are not yet subdued. But they will be. That is not in question. Otherwise he would not sit. He sits because all is safe. There is no cause for alarm, even though sin and death still wield a great deal of power in this world. The day is coming, the last day, when the enemies of Christ—those who have trampled on Christ, his Word, his ways, and his people—will themselves be trampled on. Jesus, at rest and enthroned in divine glory, will put his foot upon their necks, and his victory will be complete.

† *Enthroned Sovereign, established Victor, when I begin to wonder if evil will have its way forever in this world, I look up and see you there, poised to bring an end to your enemies and the terror they inflict on those you love. I am waiting with you, waiting for you, for that coming day.*

SEPTEMBER 2
REJECTED STONE

The first part of Psalm 118 is the song of a procession of Jewish worshipers as they wound their way up the hill to the Temple in Jerusalem. When the people arrived at the Temple gate, the leader would sing, "Open for me the gates where the righteous enter, and I will go in and thank the LORD" (118:19). And the people inside the gates would reply, "These gates lead to the presence of the LORD, and the godly enter there" (118:20). Then together they would sing songs of praise to the Lord God. At the heart of this beautiful Hebrew processional song of worship are the words: "The stone that the builders rejected has now become the cornerstone" (118:22).

The Jewish people applied this reference to Abraham and David, as well as to Israel herself. She was small and despised, hated and held in contempt by the Gentile nations. But what was relatively true of Israel was completely true of Jesus. The Jewish "builders"—the teachers of the law, priests, Pharisees—rejected Christ with disdain. He did not fit their ideal of how God would build his Temple. He was a stone hewn from a quarry other than themselves, not according to their preferences or expectations.

In Matthew 21:33-46 Jesus told the parable of a landowner who planted a vineyard, rented it out to tenant farmers, and went on a journey. When harvesttime came, the landowner sent his servants to collect his share of the crop, but the farmers beat one of the servants, killed another, and stoned a third. Then he sent his son, thinking, "They will respect my son." However, the farmers took the heir and killed him. Jesus concluded his parable with the familiar words from Psalm 118:22: "The stone that the builders rejected has now become the cornerstone."

With this parable, Jesus exposed the guilt of the religious leaders. It was not immoral living or inhumanity toward other people that was their greatest sin. Their crime across the centuries was rejection and refusal to listen to the many prophets of God who came to them. Worst of all, they had rejected and were plotting to kill God's own Son. Jesus gave them a warning that is still to be heeded today: "Anyone who stumbles over that stone will be broken to pieces, and it will crush anyone it falls on" (Matthew 21:44). Jesus is either the cornerstone on which we build our lives, or he becomes the stone of judgment under which we are crushed.

† *My Chief Cornerstone, I will not reject you; I will not stumble over you. I choose to build my life on you and align my life with yours.*

SEPTEMBER 3
HE GREW IN WISDOM

Isaiah prophesied that the Messiah would become wise by listening to God's word.

> The Sovereign LORD has given me his words of wisdom,
>> so that I know how to comfort the weary.
> Morning by morning he wakens me
>> and opens my understanding to his will.
> The Sovereign LORD has spoken to me,
>> and I have listened. (50:4-5)

The psalmist wrote of a person with greater insight than his teachers: "Yes, I have more insight than my teachers, for I am always thinking of your laws. I am even wiser than my elders, for I have kept your commandments" (Psalm 119:99-100).

This is exactly what we see in the twelve-year-old Jesus, when his parents found him "in the Temple, sitting among the religious teachers, listening to them and asking questions. All who heard him were amazed at his understanding and his answers" (Luke 2:46-47).

Here we have a glimpse into the mystery of how the divine nature and human nature of Jesus united in one person. Though he was God, Jesus still had to learn the Torah through study and meditation. When Paul wrote that Jesus "gave up his divine privileges" (Philippians 2:7), one of those privileges was his omniscience. So when Jesus asked questions of the religious teachers in the Temple, he was not pretending not to know. This was the process by which he "grew in wisdom" (Luke 2:52).

But the approval and favor of the religious leaders would not last. Whereas the religious leaders in the Temple were amazed at Jesus' depth of understanding when he sat with them in the Temple at age twelve, they would one day resent it when he began to teach in the Temple at age thirty. Rather than answering his questions, they would question his authority. Rather than listen to him, they would conspire against him. Rather than smile on him, they would spit on him. Rather than sit with him, they would condemn him. But even this would fulfill everything he had read about in the Scriptures.

† *You who grew in wisdom, speak to me as I open up your Word and make me wise.*

SEPTEMBER 4

HE CAME TO CALL SINNERS

Real faith is honest. Real faith struggles. And it is real faith we hear from the psalmist as he cried out to God: "From the depths of despair, O LORD, I call for your help. Hear my cry, O Lord. Pay attention to my prayer" (Psalm 130:1-2).

What are these depths of despair? They are deeper than simply depression and gloom. Deeper than awareness of sin and guilt. The psalmist was overwhelmed with a sense of God's disapproval, God's disfavor, God's frown rather than God's smile. He had sunk down into depths of distance from God and darkness toward God.

He knew that God forgives, for he wrote in verse 4: "You offer forgiveness." But he didn't feel personally forgiven. He believed that God forgives sin, but he wasn't at all sure that God would forgive *his* sin. In fact, he felt forsaken by God. And that is a deep pit. He was crying out for God to rescue him from the depths of his God-forsakenness. Yet even as he gave voice to the struggle within, the psalmist broke through to hope: "O Israel, hope in the LORD; for with the LORD there is unfailing love. His redemption overflows. He himself will redeem Israel from every kind of sin" (130:7-8).

Our greatest hope when we find ourselves in the depths of despair over our sin is that "he himself will redeem Israel from every kind of sin." In fact, we can't really welcome this redemption until we come to the place of true desperation. That was the problem of the religious leaders of Jesus' day—they did not sense that they needed forgiveness or a Savior. God's answer to every sinner's desperate cry for forgiveness from God stood in front of them, and instead of rejoicing in him, they rejected him.

"I came not to call the righteous, but sinners," Jesus said (Mark 2:17, ESV). Jesus did not come to help righteous people fine-tune their righteousness, but to help sinners come back to God. It is through his finished work on the cross that we can come back to the smile of God. From the depths we cry out for help and are met with generous forgiveness through Christ.

† *Long before I knew to call out to you for forgiveness, you were calling me to yourself, offering yourself to me. You have heard my cry and answered, and so I put my hope in you.*

HE CANCELED
THE RECORD OF DEBT

We like to keep a record of debts—knowing who owes how much to us. That way, in time, we can be sure to get repaid. But God is not like us. In fact, reading what the psalmist wrote about God, we might think that God doesn't keep records at all: "If you, O Lord, should mark iniquities, O Lord, who could stand? But with you there is forgiveness, that you may be feared" (Psalm 130:3-4, esv).

Of course, the marvelous truth that God is not keeping a record of our wrongs does not mean that he has gone soft in his sense of justice, refusing to require payment. That's not the case at all. The reason God will not require us to repay our debt to him is because someone else has already paid our debt on our behalf. God enforced strict justice, demanding that full payment be made—but not by us. Christ stepped in as our substitute and paid what we owed. That's why God can offer us forgiveness. In fact, it's the only way for us to be forgiven.

Paul described it this way: "He canceled the record of the charges against us and took it away by nailing it to the cross" (Colossians 2:14). God took from the court of law the file folder with all of the damning evidence against us—the names and dates and details of our wrongs—and nailed it to the cross where payment was exacted from Jesus so that payment can never be exacted from us.

Peter came to Jesus and asked how often he should forgive someone who sinned against him. Jesus responded by telling a story about a man with an impossible-to-pay debt that was forgiven. "His master was filled with pity for him, and he released him and forgave his debt" (Matthew 18:27). Peter probably didn't realize that Jesus was describing himself as that master filled with pity. He paid our impossible-to-pay debt so that we might be released from the debtor's prison of eternal punishment. "Oh, what joy for those whose disobedience is forgiven, whose sins are put out of sight. Yes, what joy for those whose record the Lord has cleared of sin" (Romans 4:7-8, quoting Psalm 32:1-2).

† *My debt for my sin looms large before me, Jesus. But through eyes of faith I can see that your forgiveness looms larger. It is big enough—your payment was great enough—to cover my sin and set me free.*

THE WAY

The book of Proverbs is not addressed to us, the reader. Through reading the book, we get to listen in on a father giving advice to his son about how to live life, avoid pitfalls, and achieve success. Over and over, the father points out to the son that two "ways" or two "paths" are open to him, and that he will have to choose one or the other.

One choice is the way of wisdom, which leads to life in its fullest sense. God is with those who are on this path; he protects them from danger. "He guards the paths of the just and protects those who are faithful to him" (Proverbs 2:8).

The other choice is the way of folly. This path is called "dark" (2:13) and "crooked" (2:15). Its dangers include evil people who take pleasure in doing wrong, and hidden snares that may appear good but ultimately only bring harm. Most significant, however, is this path's destination—death and destruction. "There is a path before each person that seems right, but it ends in death" (14:12).

Jesus also spoke often of two choices, two ways of living, two paths. In the Sermon on the Mount, he talked about two roads, warned that people cannot serve two masters, and described two builders, one who was wise and one who was foolish. "You can enter God's Kingdom only through the narrow gate," Jesus said. "The highway to hell is broad, and its gate is wide for the many who choose that way. But the gateway to life is very narrow and the road is difficult, and only a few ever find it" (Matthew 7:13-14).

Whereas Proverbs describes a way of wisdom that leads to life and to God, Jesus defined that way in much more personal terms. He said, "I am the way, the truth, and the life. No one can come to the Father except through me" (John 14:6). The decision, as Jesus made clear, is not merely a matter of behavior or companions, but a choice about how we respond to him, whether or not we will choose him as our path, our life.

† *Path to life, Way of wisdom, I turn to run in your direction, knowing that only as I walk in you will I find joy and peace, satisfaction and security. Your Word is a lamp to my feet as I walk this path, enabling me to see your beauty and your worth, convincing me of the folly of any path that takes me in another direction.*

SEPTEMBER 7
WISDOM PERSONIFIED

In the pages of Proverbs, Wisdom is personified as a woman who calls out to the son, inviting him into a mentoring relationship with her so she can impart instruction, understanding, good judgment, and discernment. She promises success, insight, strength, and wealth. She describes being the architect of the creation of the world and dwelling with God from all eternity. But most importantly, she says that whoever finds her finds life.

While this Wisdom is good and pure and life-giving, she does not tolerate rejection. "They rejected my advice and paid no attention when I corrected them," she says. "Therefore, they must eat the bitter fruit of living their own way, choking on their own schemes" (1:30-31). She knows that those who reject her head down a dangerous path.

When we come to the New Testament, we discover exactly whom Lady Wisdom was pointing us toward. We see it from the earliest accounts of Jesus, when he stayed behind in the synagogue to discuss theology with the teachers of the law. Even though he was only twelve years old, "All who heard him were amazed at his understanding and his answers" (Luke 2:47). Jesus "grew in wisdom and in stature and in favor with God and all the people" (2:52). Throughout his teaching ministry, one of Jesus' primary teaching methods was the parable. The Greek word translated as "parable" in the New Testament is a translation of the Hebrew word for "proverb." In other words, Jesus was a teacher of wisdom.

The Gospels demonstrate Jesus' wisdom, and Paul went a step further, asserting that Jesus was the very incarnation of God's wisdom. Twice Paul identified Jesus with God's wisdom. To the Corinthians he wrote: "For our benefit God made him to be wisdom itself" (1 Corinthians 1:30). And to the Colossians he proclaimed that in Christ "lie hidden all the treasures of wisdom and knowledge" (Colossians 2:3).

The Wisdom who beckons us into relationship and offers us understanding and wealth is none other than Jesus Christ. And he does not tolerate rejection. "All who reject me and my message will be judged on the day of judgment by the truth I have spoken" (John 12:48).

✝ *Hidden Wisdom of salvation, I hear you calling to me, offering me everything I need for life and godliness if I will come to you and listen to you. So teach me everything you have for me. Impart your wisdom generously to me and make me wise like you.*

HE GIVES LIFE MEANING

The temporary nature and frustrations of this world can lead to the conclusion that life is meaningless. "'Everything is meaningless,' says the Teacher, 'completely meaningless!'" (Ecclesiastes 1:2). It is as if the Teacher picked life up in his hands and turned it over and over to see it from every angle. He became convinced that our lives are futile because nothing we do will last. "The wise and foolish both die. The wise will not be remembered any longer than the fool. In the days to come, both will be forgotten" (2:16). The apostle Paul seemed to echo this aching reality, writing that the whole creation has been "subjected to futility" (Romans 8:20, ESV). Futility defines life in our broken world.

Can anything make life worth living? Is there a way to overcome life's futility? Can we find meaning and a way to invest this capital called "life" in something that will have significance? The answer is a resounding yes. Paul wrote: "Always work enthusiastically for the Lord, for you know that nothing you do for the Lord is ever useless" (1 Corinthians 15:58). For Paul, living meant living for Christ (Philippians 1:21). Jesus came to a world cursed with meaninglessness and futility and offered purpose and significance.

One day God will reveal the true value of how we've invested our lives:

No one can lay any foundation other than the one we already have—Jesus Christ. Anyone who builds on that foundation may use a variety of materials—gold, silver, jewels, wood, hay, or straw. But on the judgment day, fire will reveal what kind of work each builder has done. The fire will show if a person's work has any value. If the work survives, that builder will receive a reward. (1 Corinthians 3:11-14)

Clearly, some work survives, but only when it is built on the foundation of Jesus himself. He is the foundation for building a life that will matter for eternity. He invites us into his cause, the work of building his Kingdom. He energizes our lives with a sense of purpose as we realize that every moment of our lives can belong to Christ and bring glory to Christ.

† *Dear One who gives my life meaning, I know that my life is fleeting, like a breath that is here today and gone tomorrow. But you infuse my little life with significance now and forever. Serving you and seeking you fills my days with purpose and my future with promise.*

SEPTEMBER 9

DON'T CHASE AFTER THE WIND, COME AFTER ME

Nine times in Ecclesiastes, the Teacher says that all of life—everything under the sun—is fleeting, empty, elusive—a "chasing after the wind" (1:14, NIV). Understanding wisdom and folly—chasing after the wind. Work and achievement—chasing after the wind. Storing up wealth and seeking power—chasing after the wind. The Teacher concludes that death is actually better than life (7:1) because life is ultimately meaningless. At the end of his book, the Teacher makes no real progress in understanding or finding meaning in life, but he does come to a singular conclusion: "Now all has been heard; here is the conclusion of the matter: Fear God and keep his commandments, for this is the whole duty of man" (12:13, NIV).

But where does this conclusion leave the person who has tried and failed to fear God and keep his commandments? The Teacher's catalog of meaninglessness exposes humanity's desperate need for something solid and lasting, something significant. And the answer became clear only when the One "greater than Solomon" came (Matthew 12:42). To all those who have grown weary chasing after the wind, Jesus issued his own call—to *come after him*. Jesus speaks to all who have despaired of finding any joy, satisfaction, or meaning in life by telling them how to find it:

> If anyone would come after me, he must deny himself and take up his cross and follow me. For whoever wants to save his life will lose it, but whoever loses his life for me will find it. What good will it be for a man if he gains the whole world, yet forfeits his soul? Or what can a man give in exchange for his soul? (Matthew 16:24-26, NIV)

Over and over again, Jesus revealed that life in his Kingdom works the opposite of the way things work in the world. He said we must be poor if we want to be rich, mourn if we want to be happy, give everything away if we want to have everything, die so we can live. Only in the shadow of his Cross does this begin to make sense—as his death was the way to life. Only as we embrace his resurrection can we begin to believe that as we die to ourselves, we too will find life.

✝ *In a world of endless emptiness and meaninglessness, I find that as I come after you, deny myself, and take up my cross to follow you, I am finding joy and life. How can this be? It doesn't make sense on the world's terms. But your wisdom is not of this world, and it is in you I am finding life.*

SEPTEMBER 10
BECAUSE HE FIRST LOVED US

Though the surface meaning of the Song of Songs is clearly concerned with human sexuality, throughout all ages Christians have seen in it a metaphor of the intimate love relationship Christ has with his bride, the church. Jesus is not pictured here as King or High Priest or Prophet, but as a Bridegroom and Lover of his bride. From Song of Songs we learn about the emotional intimacy and exclusivity of our relationship with the God of the universe. Throughout this book we hear this repeated refrain:

My lover is mine, and I am his. (2:16)

I am my lover's, and my lover is mine. (6:3)

I am my lover's, and he claims me as his own. (7:10)

Though God is infinitely above us, he delights in us and in giving himself to us. His is not the fleeting love of a human suitor who may or may not love us tomorrow, but the secure love of One who has claimed us as his own for eternity and given us all that he owns. And indeed he has the power to hold us tight to himself, to preserve us, so that Jesus said of us, "No one can snatch them away from me" (John 10:28). God has come to us in Christ to draw us to himself so that he can love us:

All who confess that Jesus is the Son of God have God living in them, and they live in God. We know how much God loves us, and we have put our trust in his love. . . .

Such love has no fear, because perfect love expels all fear. If we are afraid, it is for fear of punishment, and this shows that we have not fully experienced his perfect love. We love each other because he loved us first. (1 John 4:15-16, 18-19)

Jesus has demonstrated his love for us by making the first move toward us, and calling us to himself. He has loved us best by taking our judgment upon himself so that we need not fear. And when we begin to grasp the goodness of his love for us, we find that we can "love our Lord Jesus Christ with an undying love" (Ephesians 6:24, NIV).

† *Jesus, I love you because you first loved me and drew me to yourself. And now you hold me safe and secure in your love so that nothing and no one can come between us.*

A BEAUTY NOT HER OWN

The beauty of his bride overcomes the Bridegroom in Song of Songs.

> You are altogether beautiful, my darling,
>> beautiful in every way. . . .
> You have captured my heart,
>> my treasure, my bride. . . .
> Your love delights me,
>> my treasure, my bride. (4:7, 9-10)

Here is a picture of how the Bridegroom, Jesus, sees his bride, the church. To him she is not merely beautiful, but "altogether beautiful." But how can he see her this way, since we know that in reality, she is not lovely at all, but impure and marred by the lingering effects of sin?

The Bridegroom sees that his bride has a perfect beauty that is not her own. He sees her in himself, washed in his sin-atoning blood and clothed in his own meritorious righteousness. It is his own perfect excellence that he admires, as it is his holiness, his purity, and his perfection that she wears as a garment. This is the way Christ loves his church, his bride. He has done everything necessary to wipe away her impurity, to provide her with his own beauty.

> He gave up his life for [the church] to make her holy and clean, washed by the cleansing of God's word. He did this to present her to himself as a glorious church without a spot or wrinkle or any other blemish. Instead, she will be holy and without fault. (Ephesians 5:25-27)

Into eternity, Jesus will celebrate the beauty of his bride. When the apostle John saw the end of all things, he "saw the holy city, the new Jerusalem, coming down from God out of heaven like a bride beautifully dressed for her husband" (Revelation 21:2). The church is made up of imperfect people transformed into a beautiful bride through a beauty not her own. She has been transformed—made beautiful—by the beauty of Christ, her Bridegroom.

† *My Bridegroom, how I want to be beautiful to you, to have the beauty that comes from within, the unfading beauty of a gentle and quiet spirit, the beauty of a deep trust in you. This is not a beauty I can achieve on my own apart from you. I need your beauty to transform my inner ugliness.*

MAJOR
PROPHETS

HE SPOKE TO THE PROPHETS

Peter explained how the Old Testament prophets knew what to write about the future of Israel and the coming of Messiah. "No prophecy in Scripture ever came from the prophet's own understanding, or from human initiative. No, those prophets were moved by the Holy Spirit, and they spoke from God" (2 Peter 1:20-21).

Peter also wrote that the prophets "wondered what time or situation the Spirit of Christ within them was talking about" (1 Peter 1:11). In other words, Christ himself—the Spirit of Christ, hundreds of years before his own birth and death and resurrection—informed the prophets about what was to come. It was the Spirit of the pre-incarnate Christ who "told them in advance about [his own] suffering and his great glory afterward" (1:11).

Why does this matter? This means that Christ was not a powerless victim at the hands of men. The Cross was not a good plan gone bad. The Cross *was* the plan. Christ contemplated his suffering and death, as well as the glory to follow, long before he came to earth and lived it.

The Spirit of Christ spoke to Isaiah several hundred years before he became flesh and inspired Isaiah to write about his suffering—that he would be despised and rejected (53:3); pierced, beaten, and whipped (53:5); mocked and spat upon (50:6). Likewise, the Spirit came to David and whispered into his heart and mind, inspiring him to pen the words Jesus would one day say in his greatest moment of suffering, "My God, my God, why have you abandoned me?" (Psalm 22:1).

Christ himself impressed on the prophets that he would be a suffering Messiah. Only "afterward"—after the suffering—would he come into his "great glory." He also spoke to the prophets of that future time, enabling Isaiah to describe the day to come when "the wolf and the lamb will live together" (11:6), when the Messiah will come in power rather than in weakness and will "rule with a powerful arm" (40:10). He allowed Isaiah to see the glory of the day when "no longer will you need the sun to shine by day, nor the moon to give its light by night, for the LORD your God will be your everlasting light, and your God will be your glory" (60:19).

† *Spirit of Christ who spoke to the prophets about your suffering and great glory afterward, I need to be reminded that to follow in your footsteps is to share in the fellowship of your suffering, knowing that I will one day also share in your glory.*

SEPTEMBER 13
ONE SITTING ON THE THRONE

Several of the Old Testament prophets were given the privilege of seeing beyond this world into the very throne room of God. Isaiah tells us exactly when he saw into God's throne room. God, in grace, allowed Isaiah to see that there is a greater throne than that of the nation's king, and a greater King sitting on that throne.

He was sitting on a lofty throne, and the train of his robe filled the Temple. Attending him were mighty seraphim, each having six wings. With two wings they covered their faces, with two they covered their feet, and with two they flew. They were calling out to each other,

"Holy, holy, holy is the LORD of Heaven's Armies!
    The whole earth is filled with his glory!" (Isaiah 6:1-3)

John's Gospel helps us understand what and who Isaiah saw, explaining that Isaiah "saw the future and spoke of the Messiah's glory" (John 12:41). Ezekiel saw this same glorious God who resembled a man:

Above this surface was something that looked like a throne made of blue lapis lazuli. And on this throne high above was a figure whose appearance resembled a man. From what appeared to be his waist up, he looked like gleaming amber, flickering like a fire. And from his waist down, he looked like a burning flame, shining with splendor. All around him was a glowing halo, like a rainbow shining in the clouds on a rainy day. This is what the glory of the LORD looked like to me. (Ezekiel 1:26-28)

Daniel also saw a vision of the throne, where God sits to judge. "His clothing was as white as snow, his hair like purest wool" (Daniel 7:9).

We too will one day see this One sitting on the throne with our eyes. But it is even better than that. On that day, we'll be invited to sit with him on his throne. Jesus promised, "Those who are victorious will sit with me on my throne, just as I was victorious and sat with my Father on his throne" (Revelation 3:21).

† *Holy, holy, holy are you, who sit on the throne! Blessing and honor and glory and power belong to the One sitting on the throne and to the Lamb forever and ever!*

SEPTEMBER 14

A BURNING COAL

God pulled back the curtain for Isaiah and allowed him to look into the heart of ultimate reality—right into the throne room of heaven. Prior to this vision, Isaiah had been very hard on those around him as he pronounced judgment on their sinfulness. Seeing the holiness of God on the throne, however, made Isaiah agonizingly aware of his own sin. "It's all over!" he said. "I am doomed, for I am a sinful man. I have filthy lips, and I live among a people with filthy lips" (Isaiah 6:5). Just then, a seraph dove straight for Isaiah, holding a live coal from the altar—the place of sacrifice, atonement, and forgiveness. He touched Isaiah's dirty mouth with the burning coal, and said, "See, this coal has touched your lips. Now your guilt is removed, and your sins are forgiven" (6:7).

Isaiah was forever changed by this experience. The holy coal touched this guilty sinner and, instead of hurting him, it healed him. This outward sign helped him to understand how his sin would be dealt with so he would not be doomed. It showed him that Someone would ultimately pay for his sin. He didn't know who it was, but even as the burning coal touched his lips, he learned what this holy sacrifice would do and what it would cost.

The coal from the altar symbolized the finished work of Christ on the cross. When the burning coal touched Isaiah's lips, the future finished work of Christ was applied to him. The burning coal is a picture of grace—because grace is not a casual indifference to sin. In fact, real grace punishes sin. It punishes not the guilty one, but our holy substitute, the Innocent One.

Isaiah's sin had to be *burned* away; but it was Jesus who was burned with the fire of God's judgment. Yet because Jesus is holy and righteous, the fire of God's judgment did not harm him; it only burned away the sin, our sin. And that frees us to live under grace. This holy sacrifice is continually being applied to us, touching us and cleansing us.

† *Holy Fire of God that burns away my sin and takes away my guilt, seeing your holiness brings my own sinfulness into glaring view. But when I see it, I know I am not doomed. I know that I'm forgiven and my guilt is gone.*

SEPTEMBER 15
GOD WITH US

The kings of Israel and Syria came up against King Ahaz to make war against Judah, against the house of David. Isaiah went to Ahaz to prophesy that these kings would not succeed in defeating him. God invited Ahaz to ask for a sign of confirmation, but Ahaz refused, saying that he did not want to test the Lord. Then Isaiah said:

> All right then, the Lord himself will give you the sign. Look! The virgin will conceive a child! She will give birth to a son and will call him Immanuel (which means "God is with us"). By the time this child is old enough to choose what is right and reject what is wrong, he will be eating yogurt and honey. For before the child is that old, the lands of the two kings you fear so much will both be deserted. (Isaiah 7:14-16)

Isaiah was clearly talking about a child who would be born during Ahaz's lifetime, a child who would be alive when the kings of Israel and Syria were defeated. Yet when Matthew wrote his Gospel, he cited this verse as a prophecy that Jesus fulfilled:

> This is how Jesus the Messiah was born. His mother, Mary, was engaged to be married to Joseph. But before the marriage took place, while she was still a virgin, she became pregnant through the power of the Holy Spirit. . . . All of this occurred to fulfill the Lord's message through his prophet:

> "Look! The virgin will conceive a child!
>   She will give birth to a son,
> and they will call him Immanuel,
>   which means 'God is with us.'" (Matthew 1:18, 22-23)

This is one of several places in Matthew's Gospel in which he cites an Old Testament passage that is clearly about something or someone else, and says that Christ fulfilled it. Matthew wanted his readers to know that ultimately all the Scriptures are about Christ and find their ultimate fulfillment in him.

Indeed Isaiah's prophecy had a prior partial fulfillment in a child born as a sign to Ahaz. But the true, final, total fulfillment of his prophecy is in Christ alone. Only Jesus could be "God with us."

† *Immanuel, the joy and meaning in my life is that you are with me. At some point I will let go of everything and everyone, but not you.*

LIGHT OF THE WORLD

Isaiah was lamenting over Israel. The people had rejected God's guidance and rejected his Word. They were in a state of intense darkness. But God was not finished with his people. Through his prophet God promised a coming triumphant brightness that the Israelites had never seen before:

> There will be a time in the future when Galilee of the Gentiles, which lies along the road that runs between the Jordan and the sea, will be filled with glory.
>
> The people who walk in darkness
> will see a great light.
> For those who live in a land of deep darkness,
> a light will shine. (Isaiah 9:1-2)

In his Gospel, Matthew wrote,

> When Jesus heard that John had been arrested, he left Judea and returned to Galilee. He went first to Nazareth, then left there and moved to Capernaum, beside the Sea of Galilee, in the region of Zebulun and Naphtali. This fulfilled what God said through the prophet Isaiah. (4:12-14)

Later, Jesus made it clear that he is the great light Isaiah wrote about. Jesus was teaching in the Temple in front of four great candelabra fueled by four golden bowls of oil. As darkness fell, four youths of priestly lineage climbed ladders to light the great torches. Suddenly an enormous blaze of light pierced the darkness, illuminating the streets and squares in the city of Jerusalem. It was perhaps at the very moment of the lighting of these candelabra that Jesus stood up and cried out, "I am the light of the world. If you follow me, you won't have to walk in darkness, because you will have the light that leads to life" (John 8:12). Jesus' startling words proclaimed that he was the one this festival ritual pointed to, that he was the Light for which the nation had been waiting.

† *Light of the world, shine your light into the darkness of my spirit. Light my way by your Word.*

A CHILD IS BORN, A SON IS GIVEN

Isaiah's ministry was one of comfort. To the people of Judah who were living in a time of moral and spiritual darkness, Isaiah brought a promise that assured them that comfort was coming. But it would come in an unexpected form—comfort would arrive in the form of a child, a son: "For a child is born to us, a son is given to us" (Isaiah 9:6).

God's answer to everything that had terrorized his people was a child. Even though this child would be mighty God and bear the weight of the world on his shoulders, he did not take the throne in power the first time he came. Instead, he came in weakness, in smallness, as a baby.

In his human nature, Jesus entered this world just like every other human—by being born as a baby. Yet, in his deity, he was not born, but given, from the heart and presence of the Father. "For God loved the world so much that he *gave* his one and only Son, so that everyone who believes in him will not perish but have eternal life. God *sent* his Son into the world not to judge the world, but to save the world through him" (John 3:16-17, emphasis added).

Jesus was *born to us* in full humanity, *given to us* in full deity, sent to us with a magnificent and holy purpose. Jesus' own awareness of having been sent with a purpose and a mission seems to have developed alongside his consciousness of being the Son of his Father from a young age. At age twelve, when he lingered at the Temple listening to the religious leaders teach and asking them questions about the Torah, his parents didn't know what to think.

The Son given to us found himself at home in the Temple, which he called "my Father's house" (Luke 2:49). Later, when he was baptized, a voice from heaven said, "This is my dearly loved Son, who brings me great joy" (Matthew 3:17). From then on, nothing and no one could derail him from the purpose for which he had been given to us: "My nourishment comes from doing the will of God, who sent me," Jesus said, "and from finishing his work" (John 4:34).

✝ *Child who was born, how amazing that you would reduce yourself to a woman's womb and be born like those you came to save. Son who was given, how generous is the Father to give his beloved Son to a world who would reject and crucify him. I open my arms and my heart to receive this incredible gift.*

HE TOOK THE
INITIATIVE TO MAKE PEACE

All the promises of the Old Testament depended on the coming of the Messiah who would rule as king in the line of David. Isaiah said this king would not make war, but would bring peace.

> The government will rest on his shoulders.
>   And he will be called:
> Wonderful Counselor, Mighty God,
>   Everlasting Father, Prince of Peace.
> His government and its peace
>   will never end. (Isaiah 9:6-7)

Isaiah also saw how the Messiah would bring this peace. "The punishment that brought us peace was upon him" (53:5, NIV). This peace would not come through waging war against his enemies, but by laying down his life for them. It would not come through the demonstration of overwhelming power, but through the agony of crushing weakness.

When the angel appeared to the shepherds to tell them about the baby born in Bethlehem, he was not alone. He brought an army with him—not an army of soldiers, but an army of angels. And they didn't come to make war; they came to announce peace. "Suddenly, the angel was joined by a vast host of others—the armies of heaven—praising God and saying, 'Glory to God in highest heaven, and peace on earth to those with whom God is pleased'" (Luke 2:13-14).

Jesus didn't come the first time to destroy his enemies. He came to turn enemies into friends. Deep in our hearts, all of us were once at war with him. But he reached out to us, taking the initiative to make peace. God himself gives us the grace to overcome our natural resistance toward him so that we can experience peace with him. He gives us the faith to trust in him, making us one of "those with whom God is pleased."

Jesus brought peace not through subjugation or negotiation, but through offering himself up to death. "For since our friendship with God was restored by the death of his Son while we were still his enemies, we will certainly be saved through the life of his Son" (Romans 5:10).

✝ *O Prince of Peace, even though I had declared war on God deep in my heart, you have declared peace to me. Though I have done nothing to deserve your favor, you have granted it to me in your grace so that I can enjoy the peace given to those with whom God is pleased.*

THE ROOT AND
OFFSPRING OF DAVID

A glimmer of hope. That is what Isaiah offers. He had just finished describing the devastation of judgment on God's people. In his prophecy, God had swung his axe and there were bare stumps as far as the eye could see. But wait. "Out of the stump of David's family will grow a shoot—yes, a new Branch bearing fruit from the old root" (Isaiah 11:1).

David was, of course, a "shoot" out of the stem of his father, Jesse, the last and the least of the eight shoots that appeared in Jesse's lifetime. He soon became the preeminent shoot of his day and generation. But the Shoot of whom Isaiah prophesied wholly eclipsed him.

How can someone be both "the Root" and "the Offspring" of the same person? This is not the only time Jesus pointed to this significant paradox about his personage. Jesus posed this very question to the Pharisees:

> Why do the teachers of religious law claim that the Messiah is the son of David? For David himself, speaking under the inspiration of the Holy Spirit, said,

> "The LORD said to my Lord,
> sit in the place of honor at my right hand
>   until I humble your enemies beneath your feet."

> Since David himself called the Messiah "my Lord," how can the Messiah be his son? (Mark 12:35-37)

No one was able to answer Jesus' question. It was a paradox that they were unable to understand. But in Revelation, Jesus spelled it out clearly. Harking back to Isaiah's prophecy, Jesus identified himself as the Branch that has grown out of the old root: "I am the Root and the Offspring of David" (Revelation 22:16, NIV). But notice that he says he is not only the Shoot or Offspring, he is the Root. Jesus is both his ancestor in his divine nature, and his descendant in his human nature. The promise God made to his people will be fulfilled. That glimmer of hope will become a reality in the fruitful Shoot, Jesus Christ.

† *Jesus, you are the Root of my very existence. All life that will live forever flows out of your life. Where there is dryness and deadness in my life, you bring forth new life, a new bud of hope, a new flourish of fruitfulness.*

OUR BANQUET HOST

In Isaiah 25, the prophet described a future day when God will prepare a great banquet for those who trust in him: "In Jerusalem, the LORD of Heaven's Armies will spread a wonderful feast for all the people of the world. It will be a delicious banquet with clear, well-aged wine and choice meat" (25:6).

The doors to this banquet of salvation were thrown open at the inauguration of Jesus' ministry when he told this story.

> A man prepared a great feast and sent out many invitations. When the banquet was ready, he sent his servant to tell the guests, "Come, the banquet is ready." But they all began making excuses. One said, "I have just bought a field and must inspect it. Please excuse me." Another said, "I have just bought five pairs of oxen, and I want to try them out. Please excuse me." Another said, "I now have a wife, so I can't come."
>
> The servant returned and told his master what they had said. His master was furious and said, "Go quickly into the streets and alleys of the town and invite the poor, the crippled, the blind, and the lame." After the servant had done this, he reported, "There is still room for more." So his master said, "Go out into the country lanes and behind the hedges and urge anyone you find to come, so that the house will be full. For none of those I first invited will get even the smallest taste of my banquet." (Luke 14:16-24)

Jesus' fellow Israelites sitting around the table could not have missed his uncomfortable message: He is the Host, the feast is the Kingdom of God, and the invitation refers to the covenant promises of the Old Testament. The Jews were the invited guests who were constantly making empty excuses not to come.

But many did come and will one day enjoy the ultimate fulfillment of the banquet Isaiah foresaw. Even now, Jesus, our Host, is looking forward to this banquet. The night he instituted his Last Supper, he said, "I will not drink wine again until the day I drink it new with you in my Father's Kingdom" (Matthew 26:29).

† *My Banquet Host, how I long for the day when I will drink with you in our Father's Kingdom! You have granted me the right to eat and drink at your table in your Kingdom. And I will drink deeply of your salvation.*

SEPTEMBER 21

HE WILL SWALLOW
UP DEATH FOREVER

The hopeful promises in Isaiah 25 are precious to anyone who has ever experienced the sorrow of death: "He will remove the cloud of gloom, the shadow of death that hangs over the earth. He will swallow up death forever! The Sovereign LORD will wipe away all tears" (25:7-8).

Isaiah used a word for "swallow" that is equivalent to making a thing disappear. He was saying that death will be destroyed so thoroughly that there will be no trace left of it. Paul tells us exactly when and how Isaiah's prophecy, along with part of Hosea 13:14, will be fulfilled:

When our dying bodies have been transformed into bodies that will never die, this Scripture will be fulfilled:

"Death is swallowed up in victory.
O death, where is your victory?
    O death, where is your sting?"

For sin is the sting that results in death, and the law gives sin its power. But thank God! He gives us victory over sin and death through our Lord Jesus Christ. (1 Corinthians 15:54-57)

Jesus will swallow up death in victory. What will this victory look like? It will look like resurrection. And in one of the few references to the hope of bodily resurrection in the Old Testament, Isaiah clearly celebrated it: "But those who die in the LORD will live; their bodies will rise again! Those who sleep in the earth will rise up and sing for joy!" (26:19).

Jesus will call all who are his from out of their graves. He is "the resurrection and the life" (John 11:25). He said,

I assure you that the time is coming, indeed it's here now, when the dead will hear my voice—the voice of the Son of God. And those who listen will live. . . . Indeed, the time is coming when all the dead in their graves will hear the voice of God's Son, and they will rise again." (John 5:25, 28-29)

† *My only hope in this world plagued with death is that you, Jesus, have defeated it and that one day you will swallow it up so that it can never hurt me or those that I love ever again. My hope in the face of rampant death is your promise of resurrection life.*

SEPTEMBER 22
THE LORD SAVES

Isaiah's name in Hebrew means "The LORD saves." His very identity announced God's intentions toward sinners. It said that God does everything—first to last—that is involved in bringing people from death in sin to life in glory. God plans, achieves, and communicates redemption. He calls and keeps. He justifies, sanctifies, glorifies.

Isaiah prophetically looked into the future and saw this salvation coming, a day he longed to see and experience himself: "In that day the people will proclaim, 'This is our God! We trusted in him, and he saved us! This is the LORD, in whom we trusted. Let us rejoice in the salvation he brings!'" (Isaiah 25:9).

God's way of bringing salvation to sinners may seem obvious and understandable to us, but it was not so obvious and understandable to the generations before Christ. It was not clear even to Isaiah and the other prophets who proclaimed its sure coming. "This salvation was something even the prophets wanted to know more about when they prophesied about this gracious salvation prepared for you," Peter wrote (1 Peter 1:10). The prophets had to trust in God's word to them, the promise that salvation would surely come from God.

Simeon, the man who was at the Temple when Joseph and Mary brought the infant Jesus to be circumcised, knew salvation when he saw it. He took the child in his arms and praised God, saying, "Sovereign Lord, now let your servant die in peace, as you have promised. I have seen your salvation" (Luke 2:29-30). Simeon was one of the first to connect salvation with the infant Savior and to proclaim that the promise and prophecies had become reality.

Though the prophets lived in different places and at different times in Israel's history, they all conveyed the same essential message. They declared that by God's gracious determination and design a costly redemption of sinners had been undertaken and would be accomplished. This would be done not by our *earning* our salvation, but by the holy and beloved Son of God *providing* that salvation for us.

† *Savior, I need to be saved from sin and Satan and judgment. And I need to be saved for the joy to come in your presence where I will live in the light of your glory forever and ever.*

SEPTEMBER 23

CORNERSTONE

In several places in the Old Testament, God describes his Son by using the metaphor of a building's cornerstone—a stone set in the foundation of a building's structure that all other stones are set in reference to. "Look! I am placing a foundation stone in Jerusalem, a firm and tested stone. It is a precious cornerstone that is safe to build on" (Isaiah 28:16).

Isaiah prophesied that this cornerstone could provide a safe foundation for Israel, but he also said that this stone could be a stumbling block. "To Israel and Judah he will be a stone that makes people stumble" (8:14). So which is it? Safety or snare? Secure foundation or stumbling block?

Jesus made it clear that he is the cornerstone spoken of by the prophet Isaiah. Our response determines our experience of him as either a safe foundation to build a life on or a stumbling block that sends us to our doom. Speaking to a group of leading priests and elders who confronted him while he was teaching in the Temple, Jesus asked if they had ever read in the Psalms: "The stone that the builders rejected has now become the cornerstone" (Psalm 118:22). Then Jesus said, "I tell you, the Kingdom of God will be taken away from you and given to a nation that will produce the proper fruit. Anyone who stumbles over that stone will be broken to pieces, and it will crush anyone it falls on" (Matthew 21:43-44).

The religious leaders of Jesus' day were unable to recognize the foundation stone of salvation that God had placed in Jerusalem—Jesus himself. All who build their lives on the foundation of the person and work of Christ will rest in safety. But while Jesus is a stone of safety, he is also a snare, a stumbling block. Those who reject Christ—those who choose to build their lives not on the rock of Christ but on the sinking sand of their own goodness—will be crushed by the stone rather than secured by it. "I am placing a stone in Jerusalem that makes people stumble, a rock that makes them fall," Paul wrote, quoting Isaiah. "But anyone who trusts in him will never be disgraced" (Romans 9:33; cf. Isaiah 8:14; 28:16).

✝ *Jesus, my Cornerstone, you have made me a living stone for the spiritual house that you are building called your church. Everything about my life is determined in reference to you. You are the cornerstone that is safe to build my life on.*

THE MESSIAH WE'VE BEEN EXPECTING?

Hell, fire, and brimstone—that's what John the Baptist proclaimed, using Old Testament passages that say the Messiah will set things straight. He will judge iniquity. He will rain down unquenchable fire on the wicked. This is what John preached until he was put into prison.

Then John heard of Jesus' preaching and his deeds, and he was perplexed. Isaiah prophesied that when the Messiah came, he would "proclaim that captives will be released" (61:1). How could Jesus be the Messiah if John was sitting in prison?

> So [John] sent his disciples to ask Jesus, "Are you the Messiah we've been expecting, or should we keep looking for someone else?"
>
> Jesus told them, "Go back to John and tell him what you have heard and seen—the blind see, the lame walk, the lepers are cured, the deaf hear, the dead are raised to life, and the Good News is being preached to the poor. And tell him, 'God blesses those who do not turn away because of me.'" (Matthew 11:2-6)

Jesus took John's disciples directly to Isaiah. While John had focused on Isaiah's prophecies about the judgment the Messiah would bring, Jesus pointed him to the parts of those passages that stress the servanthood of the Messiah. John had embraced, "Your God is coming to destroy your enemies. He is coming to save you" (35:4), but he missed the next verses: "And when he comes, he will open the eyes of the blind and unplug the ears of the deaf. The lame will leap like a deer." And furthermore, Jesus added, "the dead are raised to life." It's as if Jesus was saying, "I've done more than even Isaiah predicted I would do. I'm raising the dead."

Then Jesus referred to Isaiah 61:1: "The Spirit of the Sovereign LORD is upon me, for the LORD has anointed me to bring good news to the poor." John would recognize Isaiah's prophecy in Jesus' response. It answered his question. No, he did not need to look for someone else. John's proclamation had been true, his ministry had not been in vain. Jesus was indeed the Messiah.

† *Jesus, you are so good to meet me in my doubts and to answer them. You speak to me through your Word, reassuring me that you are trustworthy and true and that you will do everything you have promised to do.*

A VOICE IN THE WILDERNESS

God's people were in exile—defeated, bitter, and disillusioned, thinking that God had failed them. In this seemingly hopeless situation, Isaiah heard a prophetic voice:

> Listen! It's the voice of someone shouting,
> "Clear the way through the wilderness
>   for the LORD!
> Make a straight highway through the wasteland
>   for our God!
> Fill in the valleys,
>   and level the mountains and hills.
> Straighten the curves,
>   and smooth out the rough places." (Isaiah 40:3-4)

Isaiah's prophecy reflected the custom that when an eminent ruler was about to visit a city, the citizens would construct a smooth, broad road so he could enter the city with due pomp and dignity. In the same way, someone would go before the Messiah-King to prepare the road ahead of him so the people could welcome their King.

John the Baptist was a powerful preacher. He called people to repentance, and many responded to his message. He became so popular that he drew people away from the Temple and its teachers. Instead, people were flocking out into the wilderness by the Jordan River to hear John preach and to be baptized. So the Jewish religious leaders sent some priests and Temple assistants out to where he was to ask, "Who are you?"

John replied in the words of the prophet Isaiah:

> "I am a voice shouting in the wilderness,
>   'Clear the way for the LORD's coming!'" (John 1:23)

John knew that while his baptism was a formal call for people to repent and turn from their old ways, there was something incomplete about it. It necessitated a fulfillment, a life-giving baptism in the Spirit by the One who would inaugurate God's rule. John was merely a voice calling, a prophet preparing the way for the One to come, King Jesus.

✝ *I have heard the voice shouting to clear the way for the Lord in the wilderness of my life. I know it is a call to humble repentance, a call to clear away everything that would keep me from welcoming you, King Jesus.*

GLORY REVEALED

Glory is to God what brightness is to the sun or wetness is to water. It is his essential property that flows out of who he is. So whenever God reveals himself, it is his glory we see. And there are many ways in which we see his glory. The heavens display the glory of God. In some sense, everything God made reveals his glory.

God also revealed his glory in a unique way in the Old Testament through the shekinah glory. This was a physical manifestation of the divine glory of God that appeared to the Israelites of Moses' day as a pillar of light by night and a pillar of cloud by day. This visual expression of the divine presence of God was a perpetual reminder of God's commitment and care for them, even as they wandered for forty years in the desert because of their disobedience.

But evidently the shekinah glory was not the full extent to which God intended to put his glory on display. The prophet Isaiah said, "The glory of the LORD will be revealed, and all people will see it together" (40:5). Isaiah pointed to a greater disclosure, a fuller revelation of God's glory.

Luke tells us about that fuller revelation, put on display when Jesus was born and the glory of the Lord shone around the shepherds (Luke 2:9). Hebrews 1:3 says, "The Son radiates God's own glory." The fullness of God was seen as it had never been seen before in Jesus Christ—especially when he hung on the cross (John 13:31). But surely this promise of revealed glory will find its full consummation when Jesus comes a second time. Revelation says that in the new city we dwell in with him, there will be "no need of sun or moon, for the glory of God illuminates the city, and the Lamb is its light" (Revelation 21:23). The glory of God in Jesus Christ will shine bright!

We have a confident hope, spoken to us ages ago by the prophet Isaiah, that though this world is dark and difficult, the glory of the Lord will be revealed to us. Even better, Paul tells us that the glory of the Lord is being revealed *in* us as the Holy Spirit transforms us into the image of Christ: "The Lord—who is the Spirit—makes us more and more like him as we are changed into his glorious image" (2 Corinthians 3:18).

† *Radiant Glory, while I long to see your glory revealed in this world, even greater is my longing for your glory to be revealed in my life. By faith I believe you are making me more like you, so that I will reflect your glory more brightly. I don't want to just grow older. I want to become glorious.*

THE NAME ABOVE EVERY NAME

Throughout the Old Testament, we read about God's passion for his name to be honored, and that his name is the singular source for salvation.

> Let all the world look to me for salvation!
>> For I am God; there is no other.
> I have sworn by my own name;
>> I have spoken the truth,
>> and I will never go back on my word:
> Every knee will bend to me,
>> and every tongue will confess allegiance to me. (Isaiah 45:22-23)

Jesus' claim that he had taken the mantle of God by coming in his Father's name was a source of great tension between him and the religious leaders. When he said he came in his Father's name, he not only meant that he was there to represent him, but that he shared the holy name of Yahweh. Praying to his Father for his disciples before his crucifixion, Jesus said, "Holy Father, you have given me your name" (John 17:11).

Though Christ has been given the divine name of Yahweh, he will be worshiped throughout eternity by his human name, Jesus, because it was in his deity with his humanity that he accomplished the work of salvation on the Cross. So Isaiah 45:23 will be fulfilled as every knee bows to Jesus:

> When he appeared in human form,
>> he humbled himself in obedience to God
>> and died a criminal's death on a cross.
> Therefore, God elevated him to the place of highest honor
>> and gave him the name above all other names,
> that at the name of Jesus every knee should bow,
>> in heaven and on earth and under the earth,
> and every tongue confess that Jesus Christ is Lord,
>> to the glory of God the Father. (Philippians 2:7-11)

✝ *Jesus, I know that now, every knee does not bow, every will does not bend, every heart does not burn for you. But I also know that the day is coming when every knee will bow and see that you are God and the sole source of salvation. You will receive the glory you deserve for endless ages.*

LOOK AT MY HANDS

The Israelites were suffering in exile under the Babylonians. They felt hopeless and were tempted to believe that God no longer cared about them. Then God told them through his prophet Isaiah:

> Jerusalem says, "The LORD has deserted us;
>   the Lord has forgotten us."
> "Never! Can a mother forget her nursing child?
>   Can she feel no love for the child she has borne?
> But even if that were possible,
>   I would not forget you!
> See, I have written your name on the palms of my hands.
>   Always in my mind is a picture of Jerusalem's walls in ruins."
>   (Isaiah 49:14-16)

Of course, the real issue was not that God had forgotten his people but that God's people too often forgot their God. They forgot the goodness of his abundant provision and the gladness of walking in his ways. It was not God who had deserted them, but they who had deserted God.

Jesus had the same heart toward God's faithless people as his Father in heaven. "O Jerusalem, Jerusalem, the city that kills the prophets and stones God's messengers! How often I have wanted to gather your children together as a hen protects her chicks beneath her wings, but you wouldn't let me," he said (Matthew 23:37).

To express the committed and affectionate love God has for his fear-filled and faithless people, the prophet Isaiah pictured God opening up his hands to reveal their names written there. Jesus also showed his hands to reveal the lengths his love had gone for those who were fearful and faithless:

> Eight days later the disciples were together again, and this time Thomas was with them. The doors were locked; but suddenly, as before, Jesus was standing among them. "Peace be with you," he said. Then he said to Thomas, "Put your finger here, and look at my hands. Put your hand into the wound in my side. Don't be faithless any longer. Believe!"
> (John 20:26-27)

† *Nail-scarred Savior, forgive me for ever doubting your mother-like care and concern for me. When I begin to wonder, I need only look in the palm of your hand where I see the marks of your love.*

THE SERVANT

Isaiah and other prophets frequently portrayed the character of the Messiah as that of a servant:

> Look at my servant, whom I strengthen.
>> He is my chosen one, who pleases me. (Isaiah 42:1)

> See, my servant will prosper;
>> he will be highly exalted. (52:13)

> My righteous servant will make it possible
> for many to be counted righteous,
>> for he will bear all their sins. (53:11)

This Servant who would suffer for his people came into full view in Jesus Christ, who, "though he was God, he did not think of equality with God as something to cling to. Instead, he gave up his divine privileges; he took the humble position of a slave" (Philippians 2:6-7).

In the supreme act of condescension of all time, the one who should be served became a servant. He carried out ordinary tasks—carrying water from the well for his mother, feeding the animals, cleaning up in the carpenter's shop. As his ministry began, he served the sick, the outcast, the hungry, the heartbroken.

But the supreme Servant was perhaps never so strikingly in view as he was the night before he was crucified. "He got up from the table, took off his robe, wrapped a towel around his waist, and poured water into a basin. Then he began to wash the disciples' feet, drying them with the towel he had around him" (John 13:4-5).

When the disciples entered the room that night, none of them wanted to pick up the bowl and the towel, which was the task of the slave or servant. But they all had dirty feet that needed to be washed, so Jesus, bearing the heaviness of what was ahead, got down on the floor and went to work. Certainly he was filled with anguish over what lay ahead, and still he "took the humble position of a slave," serving others when he deserved to be served.

† *Servant Jesus, you have given me an example to follow. As I fix my eyes on you, I find the grace I need to forsake my prideful perch and lower myself to serve my brothers and sisters.*

HE DID NOT HIDE HIS FACE

Isaiah wrote about a servant who was perfectly faithful and suffered on behalf of others. The Servant spoke with a profound sense of the cost of his mission:

> I offered my back to those who beat me
>> and my cheeks to those who pulled out my beard.
> I did not hide my face
>> from mockery and spitting.
> Because the Sovereign LORD helps me,
>> I will not be disgraced.
> Therefore, I have set my face like a stone,
>> determined to do his will. (Isaiah 50:6-7)

Isaiah identified Israel with this servant. But one Israelite in particular fulfilled the role of the righteous servant.

What must it have been like for Jesus to read this in the Isaiah scrolls, recognizing that these words would become his reality? Clearly he recognized he was the Servant that Isaiah wrote about.

> Taking the twelve disciples aside, Jesus said, "Listen, we're going up to Jerusalem, where all the predictions of the prophets concerning the Son of Man will come true. He will be handed over to the Romans, and he will be mocked, treated shamefully, and spit upon. They will flog him with a whip and kill him, but on the third day he will rise again." (Luke 18:31-33)

Jesus "set [his] face like a stone," determined to do God's will. This was the same face that looked with compassion on those who jeered him, the same face that was striped with tears as he wept over the city of Jerusalem that rejected him. He did not hide his face from the mockery or the slaps or the spit. He didn't seek to escape the beating and brutality. Instead, he entrusted himself to God, confident that God would vindicate him in the end.

† *I bow before such grace and goodness in the face of such evil. I wonder what kind of people could look Love in the face and spit at it? And I'm saddened to realize the answer is, "My kind of people . . . me." The day is coming when I will see you face-to-face, Jesus. How I long for that day when I can look you in the eyes and say, "I love you . . . for who you are and for what you endured for me."*

OCTOBER 1
DESPISED AND REJECTED

When Philip went to look for Nathanael, he told him, "We have found the very person Moses and the prophets wrote about! His name is Jesus, the son of Joseph from Nazareth."

"Nazareth!" exclaimed Nathanael. "Can anything good come from Nazareth?" (John 1:45-46).

It just didn't make sense to Nathanael that the Messiah would come from a place like Nazareth—a small town of no reputation. Certainly not a fitting birthplace for a coming King and Ruler of Israel. But, in fact, this is what the prophets had always said about the Messiah. Isaiah prophesied:

> The LORD, the Redeemer
>   and Holy One of Israel,
> says to the one who is despised and rejected by
>   the nations,
>   to the one who is the servant of rulers:
> "Kings will stand at attention when you pass by.
>   Princes will also bow low
> because of the LORD, the faithful one,
>   the Holy One of Israel, who has chosen you." (Isaiah 49:7)

The Messiah would come to his people as a servant who would be despised and rejected. But ultimately the kings and princes of the earth would honor him.

Perhaps Matthew was thinking about this prophecy when he wrote of Mary and Joseph taking their son to live in Nazareth, "This fulfilled what the prophets had said: 'He will be called a Nazarene'" (Matthew 2:23). Nowhere in the Old Testament is there a specific prophecy that speaks of Messiah being called a Nazarene. However, Matthew was making the point that the basic message of all the prophets was that the Messiah would be marginalized and looked down upon, just as the people of Nazareth were—hence Nathanael's comment. The Messiah would be mocked and sneered at (Psalm 22:7). He would be despised and rejected (Isaiah 53:3).

And so it was with Jesus. Born in Bethlehem, raised in Nazareth. Rejected by the scribes and the Pharisees, he had no clout, no earthly power, no outward glory. Yet he is the One before whom all will bow low.

† *Nazarene Savior, despised and rejected by men, I gladly share your reproach, knowing that I will also share in your glory.*

OCTOBER 2

HE DRANK THE CUP
OF THE LORD'S ANGER

Jerusalem was a city with a hangover from her sin, and Isaiah was trying to shake her from her drunken slumber. "Wake up, wake up, O Jerusalem! You have drunk the cup of the LORD's fury. You have drunk the cup of terror, tipping out its last drops" (Isaiah 51:17). The city was drunk, not with wine but with the wrath of God. They were incapable of waking themselves up, incapable of saving themselves from God's judgment. But then Isaiah offered hope.

> But now listen to this, you afflicted ones
>   who sit in a drunken stupor,
>   though not from drinking wine.
> This is what the Sovereign LORD,
>   your God and Defender, says:
> "See, I have taken the terrible cup from your hands.
>   You will drink no more of my fury." (51:21-22)

How could this be? Why did God have this change of heart? To understand these words, we have to see something even Isaiah could not fully see. God would take the cup of wrath away from those who have sinned, and he would place that awful cup into the hands of his only Son.

Jesus knew how bitter that cup would be. This was not just a cup that would cause disorientation; it was a cup that would bring death. And he didn't want to drink it. He prayed, "My Father! If it is possible, let this cup of suffering be taken away from me." But it was not possible. That was what he had come to do, what only he could do. So he said to his Father, "Yet I want your will to be done, not mine" (Matthew 26:39). Christ drank the full measure of God's wrath down to the last drop. When he cried out, "It is finished!" the bitter cup of God's wrath was finally empty.

Jesus drank the cup of God's wrath so that he could hand to us another cup to drink, the cup of salvation provided for us when Christ drained the bitter cup of judgment.

† *You drank the cup of wrath and judgment so that I can drink from the cup of forgiveness and salvation. So let me never refuse to drink my fill from this fountain of goodness and mercy. And let me never forget that cup you drank in my place.*

OCTOBER 3

THE ARM OF THE LORD

In numerous places throughout his book, Isaiah described the powerful "arm of the Lord," which is the power of God in action:

> Yes, the Sovereign LORD is coming in power.
>> He will rule with a powerful arm. (40:10)

> His arm will be against the Babylonians [meaning
>> against the enemies of God's people]. (48:14, NIV)

> My strong arm will bring justice to the nations. (51:5)

> Wake up, wake up, O LORD! Clothe yourself with strength!
>> Flex your mighty right arm! (51:9)

The people of Jesus' day knew the promises. They anticipated that the Messiah would reveal his power and glory, and with a mighty arm would bring justice on the world, obliterate evil, and sweep away the unrighteous. He would crush their enemies so that they would be vindicated in the eyes of the whole world.

But when the arm of the Lord was finally revealed in Jesus Christ, it was not powerful; it was weak. Instead of being impressive, it was unremarkable. The Lord himself came in all his power and authority—as nobody special. He wasn't handsome or imposing—there was no sense of majesty about him at all. He was just . . . *ordinary.*

Instead of using his power to crush the unrighteous, he reached out in love to win them back. Rather than defeating his enemies with his power, he surrendered to them, offering himself up for them.

Jesus stretched out his arm again and again in his three years of ministry to bring healing and wholeness and blessing. Yet John reports, "Despite all the miraculous signs Jesus had done, most of the people still did not believe in him. This is exactly what Isaiah the prophet had predicted: 'LORD, who has believed our message? To whom has the LORD revealed his powerful arm?'" (John 12:37-38).

† *Arm of the Lord, how grateful I am that you have opened my eyes, softened my heart, and revealed to me your powerful arm of salvation. I see you and I am saved by your mighty arm.*

OCTOBER 4
NOTHING BEAUTIFUL ABOUT HIS APPEARANCE

People like their leaders to be physically attractive and personally charismatic. But the Servant Messiah about whom Isaiah prophesied was neither. The Messiah would not be handsome or well built; he would have "nothing beautiful or majestic about his appearance, nothing to attract us to him" (Isaiah 53:2).

The Messiah would not be physically striking as was Eliab, King David's older brother. When Samuel went to Bethlehem to anoint one of Jesse's sons as the next king of Israel, he "took one look at Eliab and thought, 'Surely this is the LORD's anointed!'" (1 Samuel 16:6). Eliab was tall, handsome, powerful, and charismatic. He had to be the chosen of the Lord! But God rebuked Samuel, saying, "Don't judge by his appearance or height, for I have rejected him. The LORD doesn't see things the way you see them. People judge by outward appearance, but the LORD looks at the heart" (16:7). When people saw the Messiah, they would see no beauty, no majesty, no charisma. They would look at the Messiah and despise him.

The Messiah would not be handsome like King Saul, who "was the most handsome man in Israel—head and shoulders taller than anyone else in the land" (1 Samuel 9:2). Neither would he be physically flawless as was Absalom, King David's son. "Absalom was praised as the most handsome man in all Israel. He was flawless from head to foot" (2 Samuel 14:25).

Paul put it this way: "When he appeared in human form, he humbled himself in obedience to God and died a criminal's death on a cross" (Philippians 2:7-8).

When Jesus took on flesh, he chose to pour himself into the humblest of human forms. Just as Jesus chose poverty instead of wealth and servanthood instead of power, he chose to be ordinary instead of attractive. He chose the ugliness of the Cross so that we could become beautiful. The apostle John was given a preview of the day when we will finally exhibit all the beauty made possible by Christ: "I saw the holy city, the new Jerusalem, coming down from God out of heaven like a bride beautifully dressed for her husband" (Revelation 21:2).

† *Beautiful Jesus risen in glory, your scars will be forever beautiful to me. You became ugly so that I might become your beautiful bride. People couldn't even look at you, but you have turned toward me, so that I might enjoy your beauty forever.*

OCTOBER 5

MAN OF SORROWS

The prophet Isaiah described the Messiah as "a man of sorrows, acquainted with deepest grief" (Isaiah 53:3). And in numerous places in the Gospels, we are touched to see tears on the face of God in the person of Christ.

Jesus cried at the death of his friend Lazarus, personally pained at the hurt that death caused to people he loved. Jesus wept over the city of Jerusalem, seeing beyond their welcoming words into the hardness in their hearts toward God.

But it is in the very words of Jesus, spoken in the garden of Gethsemane the night before his crucifixion, that we see most clearly his fulfillment of Isaiah's moniker of "man of sorrows, acquainted with deepest grief." Matthew describes Jesus as "anguished and distressed," seen clearly in his words to Peter, James, and John: "My soul is overwhelmed with sorrow to the point of death" (Matthew 26:37-38, NIV).

The writer to the Hebrews shows us another facet of our agonized Savior as he wept in the garden that night:

> While Jesus was here on earth, he offered prayers and pleadings, with a loud cry and tears, to the one who could rescue him from death. And God heard his prayers because of his deep reverence for God. Even though Jesus was God's Son, he learned obedience from the things he suffered. (5:7-8)

The sorrow of Jesus had more to do with the sin he was about to bear than it did with physical suffering or even physical death. It is sin and its devastating effects on people he loves that made Jesus a Man of Sorrows.

But the day is coming when we will no longer have to cry over sin. Isaiah also prophesied of this day when "the Sovereign LORD will wipe away all tears" (25:8). Revelation 21:4 tells us that not only will Jesus wipe away all tears on that day, he also will remove all of the sorrow that caused the tears in the first place. God's plan for the future is to destroy forever the evil that has caused so many tears—for him and for us. Then, he will live forever with us in a place he has lovingly prepared—a place where there will be no more tears.

† *Man of Sorrows, knowing that you understand deep sorrow enables me to draw close to you in my sorrow. I thank you for showing me what is worthy of my tears and for your promise that you will wipe my tears away.*

OCTOBER 6
HE REMOVED OUR DISEASES

In his Gospel, Matthew tells his readers that the physical healings Jesus performed fulfilled Isaiah's prophecy found in Isaiah 53:4:

> When Jesus arrived at Peter's house, Peter's mother-in-law was sick in bed with a high fever. But when Jesus touched her hand, the fever left her. Then she got up and prepared a meal for him.
>
> That evening many demon-possessed people were brought to Jesus. He cast out the evil spirits with a simple command, and he healed all the sick. This fulfilled the word of the Lord through the prophet Isaiah, who said,
>
> "He took our sicknesses
>   and removed our diseases." (Matthew 8:14-17)

Matthew clearly saw the connection between Isaiah's prophecies of what the Messiah would do and what Matthew saw Jesus doing. To all who had eyes to see, Jesus' ministry of healing was a sign of his deity, his authority, and a call to believe in him.

Yet while Jesus healed many who came to him, he didn't heal everyone, and everyone he did heal still died at some point. So were the healing works of Christ during the three years of his ministry the essence of what Isaiah saw? Is this the sum of what Isaiah was describing when he said that Jesus "was whipped so we could be healed" (53:5)?

In reality, Isaiah saw something beyond the three years of Jesus' ministry of physical healing. He saw into his eternal ministry of healing both body and soul. Throughout his earthly ministry, Jesus demonstrated the character of the redemption he came to purchase on the Cross by forgiving sin and healing bodies. The physical healings Jesus performed give us a foretaste of what we can expect in the age to come when the curse of sin is finally eradicated.

Many readers of Isaiah's prophecy attempt to force into this age what God has reserved for the next—the age when there is no more sickness or death. In his first coming Christ gave us a foretaste of what it will be like in his second coming when his healing will be pervasive and permanent, given to all freely.

† *Lord, I pray for your healing power to be at work in my life. But if you should see fit for me to experience physical pain and impairment in this life, I know you will also give me the grace I need to endure faithfully—waiting in hope for the redemption of my body to everlasting life.*

OCTOBER 7
Our Substitute

Seven hundred years before Jesus came into the world, God opened the eyes of his prophet Isaiah to see into the very heart of Christ's saving work—the miracle and mystery of substitution. The Messiah would be pierced and crushed in our place. The righteous in the place of the unrighteous. The loving Shepherd in the place of the lost sheep. The exalted King in the place of his rebel subjects.

> Yet it was our weaknesses he carried;
> > it was our sorrows that weighed him down.
> And we thought his troubles were a punishment
> > from God,
> > a punishment for his own sins!
> But he was pierced for our rebellion,
> > crushed for our sins.
> He was beaten so we could be whole.
> > He was whipped so we could be healed.
> All of us, like sheep, have strayed away.
> > We have left God's paths to follow our own.
> Yet the LORD laid on him
> > the sins of us all. (Isaiah 53:4-6)

Isaiah reveals a stunning truth to us in his prophecy—a truth that we might easily reject were it not so clearly presented. God inspired Isaiah not only to write about the suffering of the Messiah, but also to identify the true source of that suffering. The Messiah will suffer, not for his own failures and rebellion, but for ours. And though God will use human instruments to nail Jesus to the cross, it is God himself who will lay upon his beloved Son the sin of humanity as well as the punishment for that sin. Jesus will not be a helpless victim, but our willing substitute.

Isaiah wrote the story of our salvation in detail 700 years before it happened. God sent Christ into the world not to be a teacher, although he taught. He did not send him to be a healer, although he healed. God sent his Son to become our substitute—the One who would bear our punishment in our place.

✝ *If you, Lord, have laid my sin on Jesus, then I do not have to bear it. It cannot be on my back and also on his. He cannot have taken it upon himself and yet left it on me. So I am free! I am clean!*

HE CAME TO SEEK AND TO SAVE

In the midst of his description of the Suffering Servant, Isaiah aptly described both the reason the Servant would come and those for whom he would suffer. "All of us, like sheep, have strayed away. We have left God's paths to follow our own" (Isaiah 53:6).

God created all people for his glory, to walk in his ways. But humanity—individually and corporately—said to God through our sin, *I will go my own way! And my way is away from you!*

> The LORD looks down from heaven
>   on the entire human race;
> he looks to see if anyone is truly wise,
>   if anyone seeks God.
> But no, all have turned away;
>   all have become corrupt.
> No one does good,
>   not a single one! (Psalm 14:2-3)

What hope is there for those who have left God's paths, those who don't even seek after God? Our hope is not in finding our own way back. Left on our own, we not only cannot find our way back, we have no desire to come back. Left on our own we would sink deeper and deeper into our sin, incur greater guilt, and be lost forever. Our only hope is that the Shepherd comes to find us, plucks us out of danger, and carries us on his shoulders into the safety of his fold.

This is exactly what Jesus came to do. He came "to seek and save those who are lost" (Luke 19:10). He came on a seeking and saving mission, to bring back to God all of those living in rebellion and unbelief—people going their own way. And when he finds one of his lost sheep, he places that sheep on his strong shoulders and carries it home (Luke 15:4-7).

Jesus brings his sheep into the fold of God, not to confine or limit our lives, but to give us "a rich and satisfying life" (John 10:10). And he provides this life for us at the cost of his own life. "I am the good shepherd," he said. "The good shepherd sacrifices his life for the sheep" (John 10:11).

† *Once I was like a sheep that wandered away. But now I have turned to you, my Shepherd, the Guardian of my soul. You sought me and brought me into the safety and abundance of your fold.*

HE DID NOT OPEN HIS MOUTH

Even as he wrote these prophetic words, Isaiah must have struggled to understand the violent abuse of the Servant and his response to it (or lack of response). "He was oppressed and treated harshly, yet he never said a word. He was led like a lamb to the slaughter. And as a sheep is silent before the shearers, he did not open his mouth" (Isaiah 53:7). The Servant simply does not respond in an ordinary way. He is being unjustly blamed for wrongdoing, yet he does not speak up to proclaim his innocence.

But this is exactly what Jesus did. After Jesus was accused by false witnesses, the high priest Caiaphas said to him, "'Well, aren't you going to answer these charges? What do you have to say for yourself?' But Jesus remained silent" (Matthew 26:62-63).

After Jesus was found guilty by the Jewish leaders, they sent him to Pilate, the Roman governor. "Pilate asked him, 'Aren't you going to answer them? What about all these charges they are bringing against you?' But Jesus said nothing, much to Pilate's surprise" (Mark 15:4-5).

Pilate sent Jesus to Herod, and Luke tells us that Herod "asked Jesus question after question, but Jesus refused to answer" (Luke 23:9).

While the death of Jesus was certainly a miscarriage of human justice, it was clearly Jesus' choice. He wasn't caught in a web of events beyond his control; he willingly laid down his life. Jesus wasn't overpowered; he simply chose not to fight back.

Jesus knew Isaiah's prophecy. He knew his calling. He was the Servant of the Lord, the Messiah, the Lamb of God who takes away the sin of the world. Therefore, "he did not retaliate when he was insulted, nor threaten revenge when he suffered. He left his case in the hands of God, who always judges fairly" (1 Peter 2:23). If Jesus had taken up his own defense with the intention of refuting his accusers and proving his innocence, he would have won! But we would have lost, and we would be lost for all eternity.

† *Silent Lamb, your refusal to defend yourself shows me that I don't always have to work so hard to defend myself—even when I am accused unfairly or lied about. I can be content, knowing that you are pleased with me when I do what is right and patiently endure unfair treatment.*

IT WAS THE LORD'S GOOD PLAN TO CRUSH HIM

Hundreds of years before it happened, the prophet Isaiah revealed that Jesus' death was not the result of God's plan gone out of control, but the result of God's good and pleasing plan being fulfilled.

> It was the LORD's good plan to crush him
> and cause him grief. (Isaiah 53:10)

It was God's good plan to what? To *crush* him and to cause him *grief*. Though it seems shocking, that's exactly what happened. "My soul is crushed with grief to the point of death," Jesus said (Matthew 26:38).

Here we find the mysterious intersection of God's sovereignty and human responsibility. We know that it was the religious leaders of Jesus' day, the angry mob, and the Roman soldiers who killed Jesus. Luke wrote that Jesus "taught daily in the Temple, but the leading priests, the teachers of religious law, and the other leaders of the people began planning how to kill him" (Luke 19:47). Matthew wrote that Pilate "ordered Jesus flogged with a lead-tipped whip, then turned him over to the Roman soldiers to be crucified" (Matthew 27:26). They did not know that they acted according to the divine purpose of God.

After Jesus' death, his disciples were distraught and disillusioned. The plan of God to establish his Kingdom through his Son, as they understood it, seemed to have failed. Jesus had died, and their hopes had died with him. But then Jesus appeared to two of his followers on the road to Emmaus. And "beginning with Moses and all the Prophets, he explained to them what was said in all the Scriptures concerning himself" (Luke 24:27, NIV). Perhaps Jesus quoted Isaiah 53, helping them to see that his death was not God's plan gone wrong but God's good plan all along. Then Jesus appeared to his disciples in Jerusalem and evidently they understood so well that Peter was able to preach in Jerusalem at Pentecost, "God knew what would happen, and his prearranged plan was carried out when Jesus was betrayed. With the help of lawless Gentiles, you nailed him to a cross and killed him. But God released him from the horrors of death and raised him back to life, for death could not keep him in its grip" (Acts 2:23-24).

† *Lord, you don't do things the way we expect you to. Rather than using your power to crush the unrighteous, you reach out in love to win them back. Rather than crushing your enemies, you surrendered yourself to be crushed, so that I can know freedom and joy.*

IT PLEASED THE
LORD TO BRUISE HIM

The King James Version of Isaiah 53:10 speaks of God's involvement in the suffering of Christ in a way that seems shocking to us: "It pleased the LORD to bruise him; he hath put him to grief: when thou shalt make his soul an offering for sin, he shall see his seed, he shall prolong his days, and the pleasure of the LORD shall prosper in his hand."

It *pleased* the Father to bruise the Son? How can that be?

The verse ends with the hope that "the pleasure of the LORD shall prosper in his hand." So God's pleasure was not in the suffering of the Son, but in the great success of what the Son would accomplish through his suffering. The Son would be an acceptable sacrifice for sin, putting an end to the sacrificial system. He would have spiritual offspring and would live beyond the grave along with his spiritual offspring. The sacrifice of Jesus gave God pleasure in a way none of the ancient sacrifices ever could. His sacrifice accomplished what the others only typified. The reason for God's pleasure in the Son's death becomes even clearer in the next verse: "He shall see of the travail of his soul, and shall be satisfied: by his knowledge shall my righteous servant justify many; for he shall bear their iniquities" (53:11, KJV).

This is the pleasure of God that prospers in the hand of the Son—the justification of sinners accomplished by the Son bearing their sin. This is why the Father is pleased to bruise the Son.

The writer to the Hebrews helps us to see that it was not only the Father who was pleased with the death of Christ; there was a sense of pleasure in it for Jesus, too. "Because of the joy awaiting him, he endured the cross, disregarding its shame. Now he is seated in the place of honor beside God's throne" (12:2). Jesus understood the extent of the blessing that would come from his bruising. He could see the joy beyond the pain. He anticipated with pleasure the redemption for sinners as well as his own return to his Father's presence where he will rule forever.

✝ *Loving Father, it is only because of your love for sinners that you could find any pleasure in the bruising of your Son. And because you did not spare even your own Son from being bruised, I know that there is nothing you will withhold from me, that it will be your joy throughout the ages to come to lavish your love on all those you call your own.*

OCTOBER 12

THE HOLY ONE

Isaiah is the prophet of divine holiness. His own prophetic call came in a profound revelation and experience of the holiness of God. He saw the Lord and heard the alternating chant of the fiery seraphim singing their triumphal hymn, "Holy, holy, holy is the LORD Almighty" (6:3, NIV).

And Isaiah was never the same again. Throughout Isaiah's prophecies in the rest of the book that bears his name, God is repeatedly called "the Holy One of Israel."

"He is your Redeemer, the Holy One of Israel, the God of all the earth" (54:5). This title placed the sins of Isaiah's society in stark contrast to God's moral perfection and his absolute separation from evil. In his holiness, God exists above and apart from the world he has made. How amazing, then, that God came down to the world he made—that the Holy One would become ordinary flesh, living in a world and among people so sullied by sin.

John wrote in his Gospel that Isaiah "saw the future and spoke of the Messiah's glory" (John 12:41). Jesus is the Holy One of Israel. And if it was not immediately obvious to the Jews, it was to the demons who were threatened by his power and purity. Luke wrote:

> In the synagogue there was a man possessed by a demon, an evil spirit. He cried out at the top of his voice, "Ha! What do you want with us, Jesus of Nazareth? Have you come to destroy us? I know who you are—the Holy One of God!"
>
> "Be quiet!" Jesus said sternly. "Come out of him!" Then the demon threw the man down before them all and came out without injuring him. (Luke 4:33-35, NIV)

Perhaps the more significant recognition of Jesus as the Holy One, the Messiah, came from Simon Peter, who spoke for the rest of the disciples even as many followers of Jesus turned away: "We believe, and we know you are the Holy One of God" (John 6:69). We *believe;* we *know.* In Jesus, God invites us to know him in his holiness, and even share in his holiness.

✝ *I believe and know you are the Holy One of God. Make me holy as you are holy. Set me apart by your Spirit. Discipline me so that I might share in your holiness.*

OCTOBER 13

WATER OF LIFE

God covenanted with David, "Your house and your kingdom will continue before me for all time, and your throne will be secure forever" (2 Samuel 7:16). God's covenant with David is also an invitation to us from God himself. The God who assured David of an eternal Kingdom also assures us of his eternal kindness to us as a part of that Kingdom. Isaiah saw this Kingdom and described it this way:

> Is anyone thirsty?
>> Come and drink—
>> even if you have no money!
> Come, take your choice of wine or milk—
>> it's all free! . . .
> Come to me with your ears wide open.
>> Listen, and you will find life.
> I will make an everlasting covenant with you.
>> I will give you all the unfailing love I promised
>>> to David. (Isaiah 55:1, 3)

God is saying that if we will come to him empty-handed, hungry, and thirsty, willing to receive what he gives, then he will bind himself with an oath to treat us forever with the same mercy and faithfulness that he demonstrated in his covenant with David.

The Jewish people undoubtedly had this promise from this passage from Isaiah in their minds when they came to the final day of the Festival of Shelters. On that day, jars of water were poured over the altar so that water streamed onto the pavement and down the steps. Jesus chose this dramatic moment to stand up and shout to the gathered crowd, "Anyone who is thirsty may come to me! Anyone who believes in me may come and drink!" (John 7:37-38). His invitation is repeated in Revelation 22:17, "Let anyone who is thirsty come. Let anyone who desires drink freely from the water of life." Jesus is the source of the living water that is offered freely to everyone.

✝ *Water of life, I am thirsty and I have no money, nothing of value to offer you to purchase what only you can provide. What a relief and a joy to know that you offer yourself generously and freely to anyone who believes in you. I believe in you. I'm coming to you to slake my thirst.*

HE COMFORTS
THOSE WHO MOURN

Isaiah portrayed a God who is determined to overcome and overrule the stubborn rebellion of the people he loves:

> "I was angry,
>   so I punished these greedy people.
> I withdrew from them,
>   but they kept going on their own stubborn way.
> I have seen what they do,
>   but I will heal them anyway!
>   I will lead them.
> I will comfort those who mourn,
>   bringing words of praise to their lips.
> May they have abundant peace, both near and far,"
>   says the LORD, who heals them. (57:17-19)

The people who read this prophecy must have longed for the day when God would settle their chaos with peace, restore their health with healing, and soothe their mourning with the comfort that only he can provide.

When Jesus came, he didn't seem quick to eliminate all mourning. He said, in fact, "God blesses those who mourn" (Matthew 5:4). Jesus wasn't denying the comfort God had promised; in fact he wanted to fulfill that very promise. But Jesus knew that lasting comfort for the sadness in this life begins with deep sadness over sin.

This blessed mourning begins when we stop blaming others and own up to what we are and what we've done. Only this redemptive anguish can make us happy forever because only it can lead us to the Cross.

This is the comfort Isaiah spoke of, the comfort God provides in the person and work of Jesus. Just when we are convinced that we are hopelessly lost in our sin, we open our eyes to see Jesus. He alone is our hope. He has removed our offense. He comforts us with the assurance that he has taken care of our guilt.

✝ *My Comforter, my heart has been broken in the best way as your Spirit has shown me my sinfulness and assured me of the sufficiency of your sacrifice. I'm comforted in knowing that my sin will not have the last word in my future. Your grace will have the final word when you wipe away my tears forever.*

OCTOBER 15

THE ONE ISAIAH WAS TALKING ABOUT

When the people of Isaiah's day read his prophecies about the One who would come to save his people, they wondered who this person would be. Even centuries after Isaiah wrote his prophecy, people read Isaiah's words and wondered. The apostle Philip was sent by an angel to an Ethiopian eunuch "reading aloud from the book of the prophet Isaiah" (Acts 8:28). He urged Philip to explain to him who Isaiah was writing about.

> He was led like a sheep to the slaughter.
> And as a lamb is silent before the shearers,
> he did not open his mouth.
> He was humiliated and received no justice.
> Who can speak of his descendants?
> For his life was taken from the earth. (8:32-33)

Philip worked his way through Isaiah, helping the eunuch to see that Jesus was the One Isaiah wrote about. Perhaps the eunuch found hope in the promise of "that day" when God would bring back the remnant of his people from Ethiopia (11:11). And he must have seen that Jesus was the hope he had been looking for when he got to Isaiah 56 and read about the Lord's promise to bless eunuchs:

> And don't let the eunuchs say,
> "I'm a dried-up tree with no children and no future."
> For this is what the LORD says:
> I will bless those eunuchs
> who keep my Sabbath days holy
> and who choose to do what pleases me
> and commit their lives to me.
> I will give them—within the walls of my house—
> a memorial and a name
> far greater than sons and daughters could give. (56:3-5)

In a culture in which descendants meant everything, this eunuch, who had no hope of a son who would carry on his name, understood that Jesus died without descendants so that he might give those who come to him by faith an everlasting heritage.

† *Jesus, you are the Hope of all who have experienced loss in this life. You will restore us, and you will provide for us beyond what this life has taken from us.*

OCTOBER 16
THE JUSTICE HE DEMANDS

Speaking for God, Isaiah took the people of Israel to task for their religious piety that was completely lacking in social justice and practical mercy. They fasted and went through the motions of penance, but it was all a cover for unjust gain.

> This is the kind of fasting I want:
> Free those who are wrongly imprisoned;
>   lighten the burden of those who work for you.
> Let the oppressed go free,
>   and remove the chains that bind people.
> Share your food with the hungry,
>   and give shelter to the homeless.
> Give clothes to those who need them,
>   and do not hide from relatives who need your help. (58:6-7)

But how would they do it? How would they break free of their enslavement to their own comfort and greed? Isaiah, writing just before 700 BC, knew that the Redeemer had not yet come, but that he would come. That Redeemer would bear the sins of injustice, and he would bring the very justice God demands.

> Then your salvation will come like the dawn,
>   and your wounds will quickly heal.
> Your godliness will lead you forward,
>   and the glory of the LORD will protect you
>   from behind.
> Then when you call, the LORD will answer.
>   "Yes, I am here," he will quickly reply. (58:8-9)

In other words, all the justice and righteousness and mercy that Isaiah demanded of God's people, Christ brought into the world in his own person. What they could not do, he did. What they could not be, he was. By his coming, a new power for justice and mercy arrived.

† *You, just and righteous One, are not merely an example for me in doing justice; you are the power I need in order to change. Give me your heart for the oppressed, your compassion for those who hurt, your generosity for those in need.*

OCTOBER 17

HE BRINGS GOOD NEWS TO THE POOR

Jesus had been speaking in the synagogues and people were drawn to his teaching. Then he did something stunning and perplexing. He stood up in the synagogue in Nazareth, the town where he had grown up, to read a passage from the scroll of the prophet Isaiah: "The Spirit of the Sovereign LORD is on me, because the LORD has anointed me to preach good news to the poor" (61:1, NIV). Then he sat down and said, "Today this scripture is fulfilled in your hearing" (Luke 4:21, NIV).

Jesus was saying that he—the son of Joseph, who had grown up in their backyard—was the Anointed One God had promised to send so long ago to "preach good news to the poor." *What message could this son of a carpenter who has no wealth or power of his own possibly have that would be considered good news?* they must have wondered.

They were hoping the Messiah would bring them into material wealth and freedom from oppression. They longed for the promised King who would end their struggle under the heavy taxation of the Romans. But that is not at all the message Jesus brought. Instead, Jesus began perhaps his most significant sermon, the Sermon on the Mount, with these words: "God blesses those who are poor and realize their need for him, for the Kingdom of Heaven is theirs" (Matthew 5:3). Jesus wanted them to see that to be poor in spirit—to be keenly aware that they are powerless and bankrupt and have nothing to offer to God to get in his good graces—is what would prepare them to receive God's riches.

The "good news" Jesus announced was his own coming—offering himself to them and for them. Paul wrote about Jesus: "Though he was rich, yet for your sakes he became poor, so that you through his poverty might become rich" (2 Corinthians 8:9, NIV).

Jesus' good news for the poor was that he had come to make them rich—not financially or materially or temporarily, but spiritually and eternally. The good news for the poor was that he would pay the debt for sin they owed to God, the debt they had no resources to pay on their own.

† *I hear and believe that God will meet all of my needs according to his glorious riches in Christ Jesus. Now I see that you, Jesus, are the Good News for someone like me who is destitute and empty and needy. I come to you with my poverty, and in you I am rich.*

OCTOBER 18

WE LIVE IN THE DAY OF HIS FAVOR

Oftentimes prophecies in the Old Testament are like faraway mountain peaks. From a distance, they appear almost beside one another; up close, however, we see that there are many miles between them. As the prophets wrote their prophecies under the inspiration of the Spirit, they recorded events that, while they might appear "next to" each other in a given prophecy, would actually come about many years or even centuries apart.

That's the case in Isaiah 61, where the Messiah speaks about the purpose and message God has given to him:

> The Spirit of the Sovereign LORD is on me,
>   because the LORD has anointed me
>   to preach good news to the poor.
> He has sent me to bind up the brokenhearted,
>   to proclaim freedom for the captives
>   and release from darkness for the prisoners,
> to proclaim the year of the LORD's favor
>   and the day of vengeance of our God,
> to comfort all who mourn. (Isaiah 61:1-2, NIV)

Jesus identified with this passage so closely that he launched his ministry by standing up and reading it in a synagogue service at Nazareth (Luke 4:16-21). After he read these verses, he looked around and stunned his hearers who knew him as Joseph's son by saying, "Today this scripture is fulfilled in your hearing" (4:21, NIV).

But when Jesus read this passage, he stopped short of reading all of verse 2. He left off the reference to "the day of vengeance of our God, to comfort all who mourn." Why? Because there is a gap between the two phrases in that verse—a gap not unlike that between mountain peaks in the distance. That gap represents many centuries between the first and second comings of Jesus.

At his first coming, Jesus preached good news to the poor, bound up the brokenhearted, proclaimed freedom and the year of the Lord's favor. At his second coming, he'll bring in the day of the vengeance of our God as he judges evil and concludes history as we know it.

† *Proclaimer of freedom, release, and favor, I hear and receive your glorious message even as I wait for you to come again.*

ROBE OF RIGHTEOUSNESS

In Isaiah 61, the Messiah is speaking, and he is celebrating: "I will greatly rejoice in the LORD; my soul shall exult in my God, for he has clothed me with the garments of salvation; he has covered me with the robe of righteousness" (61:10, ESV).

Back in Isaiah 59:17, we read that God clothed *himself* with righteousness and salvation. So the Messiah is celebrating that God has asserted himself and put his plan for saving sinners into action through him—the Anointed One, the Messiah. How will the Messiah provide salvation? He will offer his own robe of perfect righteousness to all those who recognize that, "We are all infected and impure with sin. When we display our righteous deeds, they are nothing but filthy rags" (64:6).

Jesus' greatest joy is sharing his robe of righteousness with those who have only filthy rags. But some people resist, insisting on wearing their own clothes. They are boldly foolish enough to think that their own goodness will be acceptable in the presence of a holy God.

Jesus told a parable about just such a person. In the parable, a king held a wedding feast and discovered that one of the guests was not wearing the proper clothes for a wedding. It was common in the ancient world for the king to offer appropriate wedding garments to his guests. But evidently this man had refused the king's offer of a wedding garment. "'Friend,' he asked, 'how is it that you are here without wedding clothes?' But the man had no reply" (Matthew 22:12). Evidently he thought his own clothes were fine. He didn't realize that they were nothing but filthy rags.

When we come to Revelation, we see the persistent generosity of Jesus in offering his robe of righteousness to those who recognize their need for covering. In his letter to the church in Laodicea, dictated to John, Jesus says, "You say, 'I am rich. I have everything I want. I don't need a thing!' And you don't realize that you are wretched and miserable and poor and blind and naked. So I advise you to . . . buy white garments from me so you will not be shamed by your nakedness" (Revelation 3:17-18).

✝ *My Covering in righteousness, I am naked and in need of a robe for the great feast I will one day share with you, not as a guest, but as your bride. Cover me in your garment of salvation, your robe of righteousness, and I will confidently come into your presence.*

YOUR SAVIOR IS COMING

Isaiah loved God's people. "Because my heart yearns for Jerusalem, I cannot remain silent," he said, speaking not just his personal thoughts, but the very words of God (Isaiah 62:1). God answered:

> "Tell the people of Israel,
> 'Look, your Savior is coming.
>   See, he brings his reward with him as he comes.'"
> They will be called "The Holy People"
>   and "The People Redeemed by the LORD."
> And Jerusalem will be known as "The Desirable Place"
>   and "The City No Longer Forsaken." (62:11-12)

What does Isaiah want those reading his prophecy to see? An ancient city, formerly forsaken but now revived, populated with redeemed people. Isaiah drew a picture of the future, when God's people will finally and forever be at home.

But it would not be accomplished at the Messiah's first coming. When Jesus looked over the city of Jerusalem, he wept, saying,

> O Jerusalem, Jerusalem, the city that kills the prophets and stones God's messengers! How often I have wanted to gather your children together as a hen protects her chicks beneath her wings, but you wouldn't let me. And now, look, your house is abandoned and desolate. (Matthew 23:37-38)

Yet Jerusalem, the city that rejected Jesus, will not be desolate and forsaken forever. Isaiah's prophecy will be fulfilled when Jesus comes again. John describes it in Revelation 21:2-3:

> I saw the holy city, the new Jerusalem, coming down from God out of heaven like a bride beautifully dressed for her husband. I heard a loud shout from the throne, saying, "Look, God's home is now among his people! He will live with them, and they will be his people. God himself will be with them."

No longer forsaken; finally at home with God.

† *My Savior, come and write these words across my life—"Holy," "Redeemed," "Desired," "Not Forsaken." I want to live forever with you in the new Jerusalem.*

BLOOD-SPATTERED WARRIOR

In Isaiah 63, the prophet wondered at the identity of a blood-spattered warrior: "Who is this who comes from Edom . . . with his clothing stained red? Who is this in royal robes, marching in his great strength? . . . Why are your clothes so red, as if you have been treading out grapes?" (63:1-2).

And the warrior answered:

It is I, the LORD, announcing your salvation!
It is I, the LORD, who has the power to save! . . .
I have been treading the winepress alone;
no one was there to help me.
In my anger I have trampled my enemies
as if they were grapes.
In my fury I have trampled my foes.
Their blood has stained my clothes. (63:1, 3)

Edom was a long-standing enemy of Israel going all the way back to the personal rivalry between Jacob and Esau—the nation of Edom having descended from Esau. Edom hated Israel so bitterly that it became the epitome of malice toward God and his people. Isaiah wondered who this was coming from Edom. Why was his clothing spattered with red? Then it became clear. He was blood-spattered with the gore of the enemies he had slaughtered. He had been taking vengeance on his enemies, and he had done it alone, not with a great army, but all by himself.

Isaiah was being given a vision of Jesus Christ at the end of history. The apostle John was given a similar vision of Jesus at the final judgment:

He wore a robe dipped in blood, and his title was the Word of God. . . .
He will release the fierce wrath of God, the Almighty, like juice flowing from a winepress. (Revelation 19:13, 15)

The blood on his garments here is not the blood of his work on the cross for the redemption of his elect; it's the blood of his work of judgment against his enemies. His victory is now complete, and through him, so is ours.

✝ *Righteous Warrior, I find myself full of desires for vengeance that churn inside me. How good it is to know that you will accomplish perfect justice in your righteous wrath. I can leave my anger to you to take care of. I can rest in the righteous wrath of the Lamb.*

OCTOBER 22

HE IS CREATING A
NEW HEAVEN AND EARTH

To a people who were alienated from their homeland and from their God, weary of the hardships and heartaches of life in this world, Isaiah brought a promise:

> Look! I am creating new heavens and a new earth,
>> and no one will even think about the old
>>> ones anymore.
> Be glad; rejoice forever in my creation!
>> And look! I will create Jerusalem as a place
>>> of happiness.
>> Her people will be a source of joy.
> I will rejoice over Jerusalem
>> and delight in my people.
> And the sound of weeping and crying
>> will be heard in it no more. (65:17-19)

Obviously God was speaking about something far more significant and pervasive than the Israelites simply returning to their homeland from captivity. That could never have satisfied this lofty description. Indeed, this new reality will not be ushered in until the coming of Christ—yet not in his first coming, but in his second. The apostle John spoke of the same event still to come: "Then I saw a new heaven and a new earth, for the old heaven and the old earth had disappeared. . . . And the one sitting on the throne said, 'Look, I am making everything new!'" (Revelation 21:1, 5).

When we read that God says, "I am making everything new!" we tend to think of new in terms of a replacement for the old. But this does not say that God is making new things; it says that he is making everything new—new in terms of quality, freshness, brightness, and strength.

We're living in a time when we regularly experience the reality that everything is breaking down and becoming old. And yet God is in the process of transforming this world so that everything will become new.

† *Lord, one day you will resurrect and glorify my earthly body to live with you, not in the clouds, but right here in the world you created, a world totally remade and renewed. Never let me settle my heart on anything less than the new heavens and a new earth you are creating.*

OCTOBER 23

THE TRUE TEMPLE

Defending early Christian teaching against charges of blasphemy toward the Temple, Stephen gave a speech that surveyed the Old Testament and showed that God's living presence among his people has always been God's intention (Acts 7). The Temple was merely a pattern, pointing people to the true Temple to come—Jesus Christ.

Stephen explained that the Tabernacle was given to symbolize both the presence of God among the people and the separation between a holy God and a sinful people. Solomon's Temple then became a fixed symbol of God's dwelling with his people. But even when the Temple was built according to God's promise, it was dedicated with the confession that God could not be contained in it. Solomon said, "But will God really live on earth? Why, even the highest heavens cannot contain you. How much less this Temple I have built!" (1 Kings 8:27).

It was an offense to the people of Stephen's day to hear him say that the true Temple was not being built by human hands but by the sacrificial work of Christ. "The Most High doesn't live in temples made by human hands," Stephen said (Acts 7:48). Then he quoted the prophet Isaiah:

"Heaven is my throne,
　　and the earth is my footstool.
Could you build me a temple as good as that?"
　　asks the LORD.
"Could you build me such a resting place?
　　Didn't my hands make both heaven and earth?"
　　　　(Acts 7:49-50, quoting Isaiah 66:1-2)

God's Temple was established when Christ emerged from the grave as the living Temple of God. No earthly temple made with human hands can ever again become the place of God's dwelling, for in Jesus Christ "lives all the fullness of God in a human body" (Colossians 2:9). No one can lay another foundation: Jesus Christ is the true, the final, the real Temple. Therefore, those who are joined to Christ are raised from the dead with him, and are made with him into the new and true temple of God.

✝ *Christ, you are the High Priest of good things to come. You have opened a new and living way. You will be the Temple in the new Jerusalem in the new heaven and new earth.*

OCTOBER 24
PRECIOUS PEARL

In the first message that Jeremiah preached, he challenged the people's foolish exchange of a nourishing, intimate love relationship with God for an enslaving, diminishing love relationship with idols: "This is what the LORD says: 'What did your ancestors find wrong with me that led them to stray so far from me? They worshiped worthless idols, only to become worthless themselves'" (Jeremiah 2:5).

Throughout the book of Jeremiah, whenever he mentioned idols, he usually described them as "worthless." Why would he do that? Perhaps because his audience saw their foreign gods as valuable, something worth giving themselves to. So Jeremiah sought to set them straight. "Idols are worthless; they are ridiculous lies! On the day of reckoning they will all be destroyed. But the God of Israel is no idol!" (10:15-16).

The people of Jesus' day still struggled with seeing the true worth of things. God stood in their midst, yet they didn't recognize him or value him. Jesus told them a parable to open their eyes to his worth. "The kingdom of heaven is like a merchant looking for fine pearls. When he found one of great value, he went away and sold everything he had and bought it" (Matthew 13:45-46, NIV).

The fact that Jesus used a pearl to express value is interesting because the Hebrews did not see pearls as precious or valuable. Yet the merchant in his story found the pearl so magnificent, so valuable, that it was worth selling everything he owned so that he could buy it.

Most people of Jesus' day never came to see his inestimable worth. But some did. Paul discovered that "everything else is worthless when compared with the infinite value of knowing Christ Jesus my Lord. For his sake I have discarded everything else, counting it all as garbage, so that I could gain Christ and become one with him" (Philippians 3:8-9). And one day everyone will see his marvelous worth. Revelation 5:12 describes that day when all will sing in a mighty chorus: "Worthy is the Lamb who was slaughtered—to receive power and riches and wisdom and strength and honor and glory and blessing."

† *Pearl of great value, you are beautiful and worthy of whatever it may cost me to have you as the center of my life. Give me eyes to see the true worth of things so that I can see the worthlessness of idols in my life and treasure only you into eternity.*

OCTOBER 25
BALM IN GILEAD

God's people were in exile, "battered from head to foot—covered with bruises, welts, and infected wounds—without any soothing ointments or bandages" (Isaiah 1:6). The prophet Jeremiah cataloged the sin that had done the damage—lying, adultery, greed, religious hypocrisy, twisting and rejecting God's Word. The people knew they were guilty, and they had lost all hope of recovery. "For the LORD our God has decreed our destruction and has given us a cup of poison to drink because we've sinned against the LORD," they lamented. "We hoped for a time of healing, but found only terror" (Jeremiah 8:14-15).

Jeremiah did not want to accept that there was no available cure for the sin-sickness of God's people. The hopeless state of his people broke the prophet's heart:

> I hurt with the hurt of my people.
>> I mourn and am overcome with grief.
> Is there no medicine in Gilead?
>> Is there no physician there?
> Why is there no healing
>> for the wounds of my people? (8:21-22)

Gilead was a country beyond the Jordan River where a tree grew that produced a resin known for its healing properties. The resin was made into a balm that cleansed, soothed, and cured. Because the tree grew only in Gilead, the balm produced from it was costly and precious.

When Jeremiah asked, "Is there no balm in Gilead?" (NIV), he meant it as a rhetorical question because he was confident of this balm's availability and effectiveness and therefore God's provision for healing. Of course there is more than enough supply of healing! There is more power in the balm to heal than there is power in guilt to wound. There is more power in grace to save than there is in sin to destroy."

Jeremiah saw the provision of healing that God would provide in Christ. Indeed the Balm of Gilead that brings healing to those wounded and infected with sin is nothing less than the costly and precious blood of Christ. "He personally carried our sins in his body on the cross so that we can be dead to sin and live for what is right. By his wounds you are healed" (1 Peter 2:24).

† *Balm of Gilead, you soften my heart, melt away my pride, and cure me of my bent toward the sin that sickens my soul. Heal me with your precious blood.*

OCTOBER 26
WHERE LOVE AND JUSTICE MEET

In chapter after chapter of the book of Jeremiah, the prophet teaches the same lesson: God is a holy God who does not overlook sin but brings sinners to judgment.

> Those who wish to boast
> should boast in this alone:
> that they truly know me and understand that I am the LORD
> who demonstrates unfailing love
> and who brings justice and righteousness to the earth,
> and that I delight in these things.
> I, the LORD, have spoken! (9:24)

The prophet says that to truly know and understand the Lord is to know and experience his unfailing love as well as his righteous judgment. And yet, how can he truly and fully demonstrate both? How can a loving God punish sin? But then, how can a just God simply overlook or excuse sin?

It is in Christ alone that God's unfailing love and his righteous justice embrace. Through Christ and his substitutionary death on the cross, God demonstrated his love for sinners as well as his just judgment against sin. Paul explained how God's love and justice come together in Christ:

> God, with undeserved kindness, declares that we are righteous. He did this through Christ Jesus when he freed us from the penalty for our sins. For God presented Jesus as the sacrifice for sin. . . . God did this to demonstrate his righteousness, for he himself is fair and just, and he declares sinners to be right in his sight when they believe in Jesus. (Romans 3:24-26)

Jeremiah and his contemporaries did not know how God would demonstrate both unfailing love and righteous judgment on sin. They simply trusted without seeing it clearly. But on this side of the Cross, we see what God intended all along—to demonstrate both his love and his justice through the death of Christ.

† *I was made to boast, Lord. But too often I have boasted in the wrong things. Now I see that there is one thing worthy of boasting about—who you are and what you've done for guilty sinners! I will boast of your unfailing love and your righteous judgment.*

OCTOBER 27

THE LORD OUR RIGHTEOUSNESS

The people of Jeremiah's day had a king—Zedekiah—who was foolish, capricious, and wicked, and they longed for a leader who would be wise, just, and righteous. So Jeremiah's prophecy was music to their ears:

> "The days are coming," declares the LORD,
> "when I will raise up to David a righteous Branch,
> a King who will reign wisely
> and do what is just and right in the land.
> In his days Judah will be saved
> and Israel will live in safety.
> This is the name by which he will be called:
> The LORD Our Righteousness." (23:5-6, NIV)

While Zedekiah's name meant "The LORD is Righteous," Jeremiah explained that this coming King would be called "The LORD Is Our Righteousness." He will be the opposite of leaders like Zedekiah. He will do what is just and right. He will bring restitution to the victims of theft, and he will protect the alien, the fatherless, and the widow. He will not shed innocent blood.

The people needed a righteous king not only because their king was unrighteous but because they, too, were unrighteous. And this wise King will be righteous for his people in a way that was, perhaps, beyond Jeremiah's comprehension. The goodness, integrity, and moral perfection of this Righteous Branch will belong to God's people. His righteousness will become their righteousness.

Jesus Christ is righteous for his people. His righteousness belongs to them. All his righteous deeds fulfill the law his people could never keep. His righteous sufferings satisfy the atonement they could never pay. "We are made right with God by placing our faith in Jesus Christ. And this is true for everyone who believes, no matter who we are" (Romans 3:22). The only way God can accept unacceptable sinners is when we, in faith, say, "The Lord Our Righteousness will be *my* righteousness."

† *You are "The Lord Our Righteousness" and you are my righteousness. And I know that tomorrow's sins will not erase this reality, nor will tomorrow's good works improve on your righteousness. I stand in your righteousness, not my own.*

THEY WILL BE MY PEOPLE

From the first chapter of Jeremiah, the prophet pronounced judgment on God's people for their disobedience. Jerusalem would become a city under siege, he said. But the ruin that came would not be God's final word. God also promised through Jeremiah that he would restore and rebuild: "This is what the LORD says: 'When I bring Israel home again from captivity and restore their fortunes, Jerusalem will be rebuilt on its ruins'" (30:18).

Jeremiah described the Messiah raising up a new city out of the ruins of the old. Its buildings will be rebuilt. There will be joy and music and dancing. The city will be populated yet spacious. It will be productive and fruitful. And it will be safe.

Jeremiah's prophecy was partly fulfilled in the life and ministry of Nehemiah. Under his leadership, God's people returned after the exile and rebuilt a new city on the ruins of the old. They were protected from their enemies, grew in number, and worshiped God. But God's people did not remain faithful, and so the time of blessing and protection did not last. The fulfillment of God's promises through Jeremiah would wait for the Messiah.

Yet Jesus came and went, and Jerusalem was once again left in ruins when the Romans destroyed it in AD 70. So when will this prophecy become blessed reality for Jerusalem? Even now, Jesus is building his city—not an earthly city, but a spiritual city, being built wherever he is adding to his church. Jesus is building this city to fulfill the one great purpose revealed through Jeremiah and others: "'In that day,' says the LORD, 'I will be the God of all the families of Israel, and they will be my people'" (31:1).

God made the promise to Abraham: "I will always be your God and the God of your descendants after you" (Genesis 17:7); expressed it to his people under Moses: "I will claim you as my own people, and I will be your God" (Exodus 6:7); and repeated it to the prophets. So when will it come to pass? The apostle John was given a vision of this great day. He saw the heavenly city, the new Jerusalem, and heard a loud voice saying, "Look, God's home is now among his people! He will live with them, and they will be his people. God himself will be with them" (Revelation 21:3).

† *Great Restorer and Rebuilder, you really are making all things new—even the city that scorned you and crucified you—so that one day we will dwell in that city with you in joy and safety.*

RACHEL'S COMFORT

In the middle of the beautiful Christmas story is a brutal and almost unbearable reality. Matthew recorded, "Herod was furious when he realized that the wise men had outwitted him. He sent soldiers to kill all the boys in and around Bethlehem who were two years old and under, based on the wise men's report of the star's first appearance" (2:16).

For Matthew, this tragedy brought to mind Jeremiah's prophecy: "A cry is heard in Ramah—deep anguish and bitter weeping. Rachel weeps for her children, refusing to be comforted, for her children are gone" (Jeremiah 31:15).

Rachel was the wife of Jacob. While she was traveling from Bethel to Bethlehem, she stopped near Ramah, ready to give birth to a second son.

> After a very hard delivery, the midwife finally exclaimed, "Don't be afraid—you have another son!" Rachel was about to die, but with her last breath she named the baby Ben-oni (which means "son of my sorrow"). The baby's father, however, called him Benjamin (which means "son of my right hand"). (Genesis 35:17-18)

For Jeremiah, Rachel represented every grieving mother in Israel who lost a child in the invasion of the Babylonians. Hundreds of years later, when Herod sought to kill the Messiah by killing all of the baby boys in the vicinity of Bethlehem, it reminded Matthew of Rachel, who went weeping to her grave at Ramah, not far from Bethlehem.

In his prophecy, Jeremiah searched for comfort for the agonized Rachel, and he found it in the promise of God. A few verses after the lament of Rachel, he pointed to the ultimate comfort to come, saying, "The LORD will create a new thing on earth—a woman will surround a man" (31:22, NIV). But this man will not be merely a man. He will be God himself, enclosed in a virgin's womb. This man will be the comfort every inconsolable Rachel craves. Matthew quoted Jeremiah to say that the Messiah has come to bring all the comfort and joy Jeremiah promised. Because of Jesus, her mourning will be turned into dancing. And one day he will wipe her tears away.

† *Even when I refuse to be comforted, you are my comfort. Even when I think death has claimed the ones I love, I find comfort in knowing that because of you, those who trust in you are not lost forever but are cared for lovingly by you.*

OCTOBER 30

NEW COVENANT

The people of Israel had the law; they knew what God wanted from them and for them. But they didn't have the power or strength to obey. They knew what to do, but they didn't have the "want-to" to live as God commanded and to love him as he desired. God's commands in the covenant of the law were just a list of external rules.

But the law was not God's last word, nor his best. Through his prophets Jeremiah and Ezekiel he spoke of a new covenant to come:

> "The day is coming," says the LORD, "when I will make a new covenant with the people of Israel and Judah. This covenant will not be like the one I made with their ancestors when I took them by the hand and brought them out of the land of Egypt. They broke that covenant, though I loved them as a husband loves his wife," says the LORD. "But this is the new covenant I will make with the people of Israel on that day," says the LORD. "I will put my instructions deep within them, and I will write them on their hearts. I will be their God, and they will be my people." (Jeremiah 31:31-33)

> I will give you a new heart, and I will put a new spirit in you. I will take out your stony, stubborn heart and give you a tender, responsive heart. And I will put my Spirit in you so that you will follow my decrees and be careful to obey my regulations. (Ezekiel 36:26-27)

In the new covenant, God's law would be written on the hearts of his people rather than on stone tablets. He would put his Spirit inside his people. In this way, he would give them a love for his will and his ways, and a hatred of sin. His people would finally be able to love his will and walk in his ways because they would *want* to.

Whereas the old covenant basically said, "Do this, and I will bless you; fail to do it, and I will curse you" (Deuteronomy 27–28), the new covenant says, "You've broken my law beyond your capacity to fix it, so I've done everything for you through Christ. Enter into him and live in eternal security." Everything God demands of us he also provides for us, freely and forever, through the finished work of Christ on the cross.

† *Lord, you have taken away my stony heart. Your Spirit has implanted within me a distaste for sin and a longing to please you. Write your instructions deep within my heart of flesh.*

OCTOBER 31
NOT "IF . . . THEN," BUT "I WILL"

God made a covenant with Israel in the days of Moses. It was founded on grace: "I am the LORD your God, who rescued you from the land of Egypt, the place of your slavery" (Exodus 20:2). But there was a weak point: "*If you will obey me and keep my covenant, you will be my own special treasure from among all the peoples on earth; for all the earth belongs to me*" (Exodus 19:5, emphasis added).

God set the terms of this covenant: "If you obey me, I'll bless you. If you disobey me, I'll curse you." But they did not obey. The problem wasn't God's law, but the human heart. Paul wrote, "The law of Moses was unable to save us because of the weakness of our sinful nature" (Romans 8:3).

But God didn't give up on his people. He made a new promise through the prophet Jeremiah: "I will put my instructions deep within them, and I will write them on their hearts" (31:33). Jesus replaced the "If . . . then" nature of our relationship with God to "I will." The old covenant of legal threats was replaced by the new covenant of full provision in the person of Christ. And while this new covenant doesn't do away with the law, it internalizes the law in our hearts. It changes us from people who pursue holiness through behavior modification efforts into people who long for a genuine inner holiness that emerges from hearts filled with the Holy Spirit.

It's when the Holy Spirit awakens us to the beauty of Christ that we can finally see that this is where the law was meant to lead us all along—not to better behavior, but to Christ. Paul put it this way in Galatians 3:24: "The law was our guardian until Christ came; it protected us until we could be made right with God through faith." And in Romans 10:4 he wrote, "For Christ has already accomplished the purpose for which the law was given. As a result, all who believe in him are made right with God."

So instead of trying harder to live up to a standard outside of ourselves, the new covenant empowers us from the inside out to live holy lives. No longer do we live in fear of the "If . . . then." Now we live in the freedom of Jesus' "It is finished!"

† *My Mediator of a better covenant, how I want to please you with my life! You have written your law on my heart, giving me the want-to I need in order to obey you—not out of imposed duty but because I love you and long to please you.*

NOVEMBER 1
GOD'S GOOD GIFT TO US

Jerusalem was under siege from the Babylonian army and the Lord told Jeremiah that he was about to hand over the city to Babylon. Surely it seemed to God's people that he had turned against them for good. But the Lord had more to say about the future of his people:

> This is what the LORD, the God of Israel, says: I will certainly bring my people back again from all the countries where I will scatter them in my fury. . . . I will make an everlasting covenant with them: I will never stop doing good for them. I will put a desire in their hearts to worship me, and they will never leave me. I will find joy doing good for them. (Jeremiah 32:36-37, 40-41)

"I will never stop doing good for them," God said. In fact, he said that he finds joy in doing good for them.

Jesus also spoke of God as a father who enjoys doing good for his children:

> Which of you fathers, if your son asks for a fish, will give him a snake instead? Or if he asks for an egg, will give him a scorpion? If you then, though you are evil, know how to give good gifts to your children, how much more will your Father in heaven give the Holy Spirit to those who ask him! (Luke 11:11-13, NIV)

Here Jesus gets specific about the "good gift" God wants to give his children that will bring them so much satisfaction and bring him so much joy—the Holy Spirit. And what does the Holy Spirit do? Jesus said, "When the Spirit of truth comes, he will guide you into all truth. . . . He will bring me glory by telling you whatever he receives from me" (John 16:13-14).

God finds joy in doing good for us. And his greatest gift to us is Jesus. He has given us the Holy Spirit to help us to understand and embrace Jesus. This good gift is a sign that he will never withhold anything good from us. "Since he did not spare even his own Son but gave him up for us all, won't he also give us everything else?" (Romans 8:32).

† *Gracious God, could it really be true that you find joy in doing good for me? The enemy wants to tell me that I cannot expect the goodness I desire from you. But then I look at Christ. The Holy Spirit speaks to me of Christ. And my heart is captured by your overflowing goodness.*

NOVEMBER 2
BETWEEN "IT IS FINISHED" AND "IT IS DONE"

Throughout the Old Testament, God obligated himself with promises of what he will do—*I will bless you . . . I will give you descendants . . . I will protect you . . . I will come to live with you . . . I will give you a new heart.* While God fulfilled some of what he promised to do for his people during the Old Testament period, much was left unfulfilled. However this was not a failure of God's promise or plan, but God's plan being enacted.

> The day will come, says the LORD, when I will do for Israel and Judah all the good things I have promised them.
>
> In those days and at that time
> I will raise up a righteous descendant from King David's line.
> He will do what is just and right throughout the land.
> (Jeremiah 33:14-15)

God had planned that his "I wills" would be fulfilled when David's "righteous descendant" would come and complete his work on the cross, saying, "It is finished!" (John 19:30).

But even on this side of the Cross we recognize that we still have not received all that God promised. Christ's work as Redeemer is finished, but his work as Restorer remains unfinished until all who are his are perfected. Christ's work as Savior at the Cross is finished, but his work as Sustainer is unfinished. His work as Atoner is finished, but his work as Advocate is unfinished. Christ's work as Sanctifier is both finished and unfinished. Those who are in Christ are positionally sanctified at regeneration, progressively sanctified as the Spirit provides the power to walk in increasing holiness, and will be fully sanctified in the holy presence of Jesus Christ. Christ's work of putting away sin "from" the believer is finished, but his work of putting away sin from "within" the believer is unfinished. Christ's dying to destroy sin's penalty for his own is finished, but his living to destroy sin's power over his own is unfinished.

So we now stand between Christ's statement of "It is finished!" that he spoke at the Cross, and his declaration of "It is done," which will come at the consummation of his Kingdom when all things are made new (Revelation 21:6, NIV). On that day we will begin enjoying the ages to come, secure in all the fulfilled promises of God.

† *I am certain that God, who began the good work within me, will continue his work until it is finally finished on the day when Christ returns.*

NOVEMBER 3
WEEPING OVER JERUSALEM

Jeremiah, known as the Weeping Prophet, lamented the sorrow Judah had brought upon herself through her rebellion against God:

> I have cried until the tears no longer come;
>> my heart is broken.
> My spirit is poured out in agony
>> as I see the desperate plight of my people. . . .
>> Who has ever seen such sorrow?
> O daughter of Jerusalem,
>> to what can I compare your anguish?
> O virgin daughter of Zion,
>> how can I comfort you?
> For your wound is as deep as the sea.
>> Who can heal you? (Lamentations 2:11, 13)

God did, in fact, send someone to heal the wounds of his people, a prophet greater than Jeremiah. This prophet would not only weep over judgment, but would also take upon himself the judgment his people deserved so that they would weep no longer. As Jesus arrived in Jerusalem to accomplish this saving work, he wept because he knew that so many would reject this free offer of his grace. "As he came closer to Jerusalem and saw the city ahead, he began to weep. 'How I wish today that you of all people would understand the way to peace. But now it is too late, and peace is hidden from your eyes'" (Luke 19:41-42).

Jesus knew that even though the people who loved his miracles were welcoming him with palm branches and praise, their hearts were fickle. Soon they would demand his crucifixion. And within a generation the city would be obliterated. Judgment was surely coming upon Jerusalem.

Though Jeremiah wept, he also expressed relief that "now the anger of the LORD is satisfied. His fierce anger has been poured out" (Lamentations 4:11). God had poured out his wrath on Judah. Yet this was just a taste of the wrath to come, the wrath that was poured out on Christ at the Cross. And we know that there is more wrath to be poured out in the last days. And so we also weep for those who continue to reject the goodness of God in Christ.

† *Weeping Prophet, give me your tears—deep-hearted sorrow over the judgment to come upon those who have rebelled against you, rejected you, ignored you. Break my heart over the very things that break your heart.*

NOVEMBER 4

WHEN I MAKE
ATONEMENT FOR YOU

Ezekiel 16, the Bible's longest allegory, reveals how God chose Israel.

> On the day you were born, you were unwanted, dumped in a field and
> left to die. But I came by and saw you there, helplessly kicking about
> in your own blood. As you lay there, I said, "Live!" And I helped you
> to thrive like a plant in the field. You grew up and became a beautiful
> jewel. . . . I wrapped my cloak around you to cover your nakedness
> and declared my marriage vows. I made a covenant with you, says the
> Sovereign LORD, and you became mine. (16:5-8)

This is how Israel began. God set his love on her, declaring binding marriage vows to her. But she was grossly unfaithful to him—chasing after other
gods and worshiping idols. "You gave yourself as a prostitute to every man
who came along. Your beauty was theirs for the asking. You used the lovely
things I gave you to make shrines for idols, where you played the prostitute"
(16:15-16).

Because of her unfaithfulness, God brought judgment upon his beloved:
"I will give you to these many nations who are your lovers, and they will
destroy you" (16:39).

Judgment fell. The nation was conquered and the people sent into exile.
At that point, it may seem that God was finished with his once-cherished
bride. But judgment was not his last word. He intended to do something
new. He will not only take her back, but he also will pay for all her sin.

> I will establish an everlasting covenant with you. . . . When I make
> atonement for you for all you have done, you will remember and be
> ashamed and never again open your mouth because of your humilia-
> tion, declares the Sovereign LORD. (16:60, 63, NIV)

How will God love his people in this new covenant way? Paul helps us
to see that Ezekiel's vision finds its fulfillment when Christ, the Son of God,
makes atonement for sin. "God is so rich in mercy, and he loved us so much,
that even though we were dead because of our sins, he gave us life when he
raised Christ from the dead" (Ephesians 2:4-5).

† *What love! You found me dead in sin, and you gave your Son to die for me
to make me alive. And now you will keep me close to you forever. Your grace
will provide the faithfulness I can never accomplish on my own.*

NOVEMBER 5

WICKED PEOPLE
CHANGED BY CHRIST'S POWER

Ezekiel had been given the role of Israel's watchman. He was to warn the people of the destruction ahead for those who did not repent. He was looking for a deep-seated repentance that would be reflected in a new way of living.

> Son of man, give your people this message: The righteous behavior of righteous people will not save them if they turn to sin, nor will the wicked behavior of wicked people destroy them if they repent and turn from their sins. When I tell righteous people that they will live, but then they sin, expecting their past righteousness to save them, then none of their righteous acts will be remembered. I will destroy them for their sins. And suppose I tell some wicked people that they will surely die, but then they turn from their sins and do what is just and right. . . . If they do this, then they will surely live and not die. (33:12-15)

Ezekiel described God's dealings with two kinds of people. There are "righteous" people who indulge their delusion that they are right with God because of their good behavior. These are people who trust in their own merit before God rather than the mercies of God. The "righteousness" of these people doesn't last. Though they profess a commitment to God, they do not persevere in grace.

The second kind of people are those who trust in the grace of God, a faith that issues from a regenerate heart. Though they once lived disgracefully, they repented and their lives changed. They began to practice justice and righteousness.

We become righteous before God when we trust in Christ's righteousness. Christ's own perfectly righteous life is reckoned to us as if it were our life. But we are also righteous before God because we live righteously. We are changed from bad to good when we are joined to Christ and made alive, and this change bears itself out as we live in Christ's power.

Paul preached this same message of genuine repentance that Ezekiel preached, saying, that "all must repent of their sins and turn to God—and prove they have changed by the good things they do" (Acts 26:20). The good news of the gospel is that a person is not bound by his or her past, but neither is he or she saved by it.

† *Thank you, God of grace, for giving me a heart of true repentance and the grace to persevere as you transform me into a person who lives righteously.*

ONE SHEPHERD, ONE FLOCK

Jerusalem had fallen and most of God's people were in exile in Babylon. But Ezekiel brought a message of hope and restoration from the Lord to his people who might have thought their God had abandoned them:

> I will rescue my flock, and they will no longer be abused. I will judge between one animal of the flock and another. And I will set over them one shepherd, my servant David. He will feed them and be a shepherd to them. And I, the LORD, will be their God, and my servant David will be a prince among my people. I, the LORD, have spoken! (34:22-24)

A "shepherd" in the ancient Near East was not only a term for one who tended sheep, it was also a common metaphor for a king. Good kings who led their people with strength and wisdom resembled good shepherds who endured the elements, protected their flocks against wild beasts, and tenderly led their sheep to good pastures. So when Ezekiel announced God's plan to send his royal Shepherd to tend his flock, it meant that God would put in place a Shepherd who would bring everyone back out of captivity and into his fold where he would rule with tenderness, not with brute power.

One flock, one Shepherd. No doubt it was this prophecy that was in Jesus' mind and in the minds of those who knew the Scriptures when he said:

> I am the good shepherd. The good shepherd sacrifices his life for the sheep. . . . I have other sheep, too, that are not in this sheepfold. I must bring them also. They will listen to my voice, and there will be one flock with one shepherd. (John 10:11, 16)

Jesus was the fulfillment of God's promise of a Shepherd. But obviously not all of Ezekiel's prophecy was fulfilled in Christ's first coming. Ezekiel said that God's people will "no longer be prey for other nations," will "live in safety" (34:28), and will "never again suffer from famines" (34:29). That day is still to come, and will surely come when the Great Shepherd returns. Finally all Israel will be able to lie down in green pastures and have her soul restored to her by the one Shepherd, God's Son, Jesus.

† *My strong Shepherd, I have heard your voice and I am yours. How I long for that day when you return and I can finally live in perfect safety.*

HE WILL SEPARATE THE SHEEP FROM THE GOATS

According to Ezekiel's prophecy, the Shepherd who will come in the last day will do more than simply tend the sheep. He will come to judge, separating the sheep from the goats: "As for you, my flock, this is what the Sovereign LORD says to his people: I will judge between one animal of the flock and another, separating the sheep from the goats" (Ezekiel 34:17).

When Jesus spoke about his return in glory at the end of time, he made it clear that he was the Shepherd about whom Ezekiel was prophesying:

> When the Son of Man comes in his glory, and all the angels with him, then he will sit upon his glorious throne. All the nations will be gathered in his presence, and he will separate the people as a shepherd separates the sheep from the goats. He will place the sheep at his right hand and the goats at his left. (Matthew 25:31-33)

Then Jesus told a parable about a King who will say to those on his right, "Come, you who are blessed by my Father, inherit the Kingdom prepared for you from the creation of the world" (25:34). To those on the left, the King will say, "Away with you, you cursed ones, into the eternal fire prepared for the devil and his demons" (25:41).

In Jewish parables, the King was always God, but in this passage, the King was clearly the Lord Jesus Christ. The King in the parable said, "Come, you who are blessed by *my Father*." Once again, Jesus was making clear claims to deity; shortly, he would be killed for such claims.

Jesus was describing a coming day when he will return, not as humble sufferer, but as a righteous judge. For believers, that day will provide the ultimate consolation. The judgment will be stacked. The judge will be their Savior, and he will welcome them into his Kingdom.

But for unbelievers and false believers, that day will be the ultimate terror. The judge will be the One they claimed to love but did not truly love. He will be the One whom they mocked or merely dismissed as unnecessary or unworthy. Those who wanted nothing to do with him during their lives will spend eternity separated from his life-giving presence.

† *Judging Shepherd, coming King, may the way I treat my brothers and sisters in need evidence my true love for you.*

THE LORD WHO MAKES YOU HOLY

Revealing his nature and name as well as his intentions toward his people, God repeatedly said to the Israelites: "I am the LORD, who makes you holy" (Exodus 31:13; Leviticus 20:8; 22:32).

The holy God intended to have a holy people. But they were not holy. Even on the rare occasions when they obeyed him, their hearts were far from him. So how, exactly, will the Lord make sinners holy?

Through the prophet Ezekiel, God gave a preview of how he would accomplish his sanctifying work. "I will put my Spirit in you so that you will follow my decrees and be careful to obey my regulations" (Ezekiel 36:27). So the Spirit will come to live inside God's people, empowering them for holiness.

At his Last Supper with his disciples, Jesus revealed when the Spirit would come in the way Ezekiel prophesied:

> It is best for you that I go away, because if I don't, the Advocate won't come. If I do go away, then I will send him to you. And when he comes, he will convict the world of its sin, and of God's righteousness, and of the coming judgment. The world's sin is that it refuses to believe in me. Righteousness is available because I go to the Father. (John 16:7-10)

The holiness God demands God also provides. It can only come when "the Lord who makes you holy" dwells within a person. "I give myself as a holy sacrifice for them so they can be made holy by your truth," Jesus said (John 17:19). Becoming holy—being set apart to God—is a position we are given by God. At the same time, it is an ongoing process by which the Holy Spirit uses the truth of God's Word to remove what is displeasing and create what is pleasing in us. The Spirit reshapes us so that we conform to the image of the Holy One of Israel, Jesus Christ.

† *Holy One, I know it is not what I do or don't do that makes me holy. I have been made holy because you determined to set me apart as your own. But because I am yours, I long to please you by closing the gap between what you've declared me to be and the reality of who I am and what I do. So Spirit, impress on me the truth of the Word. Increase my hunger for holiness. Make me truly holy through and through.*

NOVEMBER 9
I WILL OPEN YOUR GRAVES

Ezekiel was himself a captive, living among the exiles of Judah in Babylon. He prophesied to a community that had been forced from its homeland, a people who had broken faith with their God. Despairing, they said, "We have become old, dry bones—all hope is gone. Our nation is finished" (Ezekiel 37:11).

Into this deadness, dryness, and despair, Ezekiel spoke hope. Though their exile was due to their faithlessness toward God, this would not be the end of their story. By the work of the Spirit, God's people, though seemingly dead and without hope, would live again.

God gave Ezekiel a vision of a valley filled with dried bones. God instructed his prophet to speak to the bones, saying,

> This is what the Sovereign LORD says: Look! I am going to put breath into you and make you live again! I will put flesh and muscles on you and cover you with skin. I will put breath into you, and you will come to life. Then you will know that I am the LORD. (37:5-6)

Then Ezekiel spoke to the people of Israel, represented by the dry bones: "This is what the Sovereign LORD says: O my people, I will open your graves of exile and cause you to rise again. Then I will bring you back to the land of Israel" (37:12).

Ezekiel's vision of new life through the Spirit had a partial fulfillment in the return of the people of Israel to new life in their homeland. But its most significant fulfillment will come on the day Jesus spoke of, when he will call out to all those in their graves. "Indeed, the time is coming when all the dead in their graves will hear the voice of God's Son," Jesus said, "and they will rise again" (John 5:28-29).

Paul wrote of the same hope that Ezekiel saw in his vision. "The Spirit of God, who raised Jesus from the dead, lives in you. And just as God raised Christ Jesus from the dead, he will give life to your mortal bodies by this same Spirit living within you" (Romans 8:11).

† *Resurrection and Life, because of who you are, I know that my destiny is not the grave, but glory; not eternal death, but eternal life. One day you will come down from heaven with a commanding shout and all who have died will rise from their graves. And we will be with you forever!*

OUR SANCTUARY

From the moment of the dedication of Solomon's Temple, there began a long process of disobedience, apostasy, and judgment on the part of God's people that resulted in the destruction of their land and their Temple. But in the face of this catastrophe, the meaning of God's presence was revealed in a clearer way, because he never intended to dwell with his people only in a Temple separated by a curtain.

Ezekiel proclaimed that the exiles, although far from the ruins of Zion, were not without a sanctuary, for God said, "Although I have scattered you in the countries of the world, I will be a sanctuary to you during your time in exile" (Ezekiel 11:16). God himself has always been a sanctuary for his people. He was not consumed in the flames of the destroyed Temple, nor did his promises perish with the destruction of the city. Instead, they were reaffirmed as God spoke through his prophet about what he will do in the future: "I will give them their land and increase their numbers, and I will put my Temple among them forever. I will make my home among them. I will be their God, and they will be my people" (37:26-27).

Ezekiel's vision of a new Temple is part of a restoration so total that he can't be talking about a physical Temple of stone built in Jerusalem. In his vision, Ezekiel saw a stream flowing from the Temple that watered fruit trees. "The fruit will be for food and the leaves for healing" (47:12). John had the same vision, recorded in Revelation 22:1-2, in which he saw "a river with the water of life, clear as crystal, flowing from the throne of God and of the Lamb. It flowed down the center of the main street. On each side of the river grew a tree of life, bearing twelve crops of fruit, with a fresh crop each month. The leaves were used for medicine to heal the nations."

John could see the temple more clearly than Ezekiel because John had seen Christ. He recognized that when God's restoration is complete, the Temple will not be a building, but a person. "I saw no temple in the city," John wrote, "for the Lord God Almighty and the Lamb are its temple" (Revelation 21:22). God with us. From Christ alone flows a stream of healing and fruitfulness and refreshment. In him, we find sanctuary from anything and everything that would keep us from being at home with God.

† *My Sanctuary, you are my safe harbor, my place of rest, my eternal home. In you I enjoy abundance and healing.*

THE GREAT FEAST AND THE GRUESOME FEAST

Ezekiel foretold of a coming judgment of Israel's enemies in which birds of prey will feed upon the flesh of those defeated by Israel's God:

> This is what the Sovereign LORD says: Call all the birds and wild animals. Say to them: Gather together for my great sacrificial feast. Come from far and near to the mountains of Israel, and there eat flesh and drink blood! Eat the flesh of mighty men and drink the blood of princes as though they were rams, lambs, goats, and bulls—all fattened animals from Bashan! . . . Feast at my banquet table—feast on horses and charioteers, on mighty men and all kinds of valiant warriors, says the Sovereign LORD. (39:17-18, 20)

It is a gruesome scene. The apostle John saw it too, as recorded in the book of Revelation. At that time, the scene was connected not to Israel's defeat of enemy nations, but to God's judgment of those who reject Jesus.

> Then I saw an angel standing in the sun, shouting to the vultures flying high in the sky: "Come! Gather together for the great banquet God has prepared. Come and eat the flesh of kings, generals, and strong warriors; of horses and their riders; and of all humanity, both free and slave, small and great." (Revelation 19:17-18)

Earlier in this chapter John described another feast—the marriage supper of the Lamb (19:7). This is a joyous feast because those who belong to Christ are invited, not as mere guests, but as Christ's own bride. But then John revealed this other feast that will be no celebration. This will be a feast for the wild animals after the judgment of those who rebel against God.

God himself also issues the invitation to this banquet, but it goes out to all the birds of prey. All those who reject the mercies of Jesus Christ will be invited to this feast along with the birds. But they will not be invited as guests; they will be the main course!

† *My Bridegroom, Jesus, you have invited me to your marriage supper as your beautiful bride, and I am humbled and grateful. But my heart breaks for those who persist in their rejection of you, because they will not enjoy that feast with you and should rightly live in fear.*

NOVEMBER 12
THE LORD IS THERE

It had been twenty-five years from the start of the exile, and almost twenty years since Ezekiel's first life-changing vision of the glory of God. Early in those years Ezekiel had experienced the lowest point of his ministry—when he saw the glory of Yahweh departing from the Temple (10:18), and the Temple itself and the entire city of Jerusalem being consigned to destruction in the fire of God's judgment (11:9-12). God was no longer dwelling with his people. Israel had ignored the holiness of God and, as a result, God removed his presence from them.

But at this point, many years later, God gave Ezekiel a vision of everything brought back and made better than ever before: The Holy Land restored in the same basic dimensions defined to them before Israel entered the Promised Land. Brotherhood reigning again, all the tribes in unity with one another. The worship of God in a perfect Temple being supported by all the people. A prince to lead them. But best of all, this prophetic promise: "And from that day the name of the city will be 'The LORD Is There'" (48:35).

God's progressive self-revelation through his divine names came to a climax as Ezekiel described God's future Kingdom city named for its most distinctive inhabitant, Yahweh Shammah: The LORD Is There.

What Ezekiel heard as a promise, John saw as a reality. Yet the revelation John recorded far exceeded anything in Ezekiel's vision. John "saw the holy city, the new Jerusalem, coming down from God out of heaven" (Revelation 21:2). This will be far more than a rebuilt historical city of Jerusalem; it will be the new Jerusalem, the city of God. And sure enough, the Lord is there! John "heard a loud shout from the throne, saying, 'Look, God's home is now among his people! He will live with them, and they will be his people. God himself will be with them'" (21:3).

Finally, God himself will live with his people as he once did in the Garden of Eden, but this will be even better. This will be an eternal city, where the bride of Christ will make her home with her bridegroom, the Lamb. This new Jerusalem will not need a temple like the old Jerusalem because "the Lord God Almighty and the Lamb are its temple" (21:22).

† *Yahweh Shammah, "The LORD Is There," you came and walked the streets of Jerusalem but your people did not recognize you. They rejected you. They killed you. But when you come again, you will come to live forever with those who love you. The joy of living in your forever city is that you will be there.*

NOVEMBER 13

THE ROCK CUT
FROM THE MOUNTAIN

Nebuchadnezzar, king of the Babylonian empire, was desperate to discover the meaning of his troubling dream, but none of his astrologers could come up with an explanation. So Daniel went to God, who revealed to him not only the dream, but also its secret meaning. The dream, he told the king, foretold the rise and fall of the kingdoms to come after Nebuchadnezzar's kingdom came to an end. The dream also revealed that God would set up another kingdom of a completely different kind—a Kingdom that will last forever:

> The God of heaven will set up a kingdom that will never be destroyed or conquered. It will crush all these kingdoms into nothingness, and it will stand forever. That is the meaning of the rock cut from the mountain, though not by human hands, that crushed to pieces the statue of iron, bronze, clay, silver, and gold. (Daniel 2:44-45)

In his dream, Nebuchadnezzar had seen a rock "cut from a mountain, but not by human hands" (2:34). This rock crushed the other kingdoms and "became a great mountain that covered the whole earth" (2:35). The Israelites saw themselves as this stone of God that would one day crush all other kingdoms. In particular, they saw their Temple as having the authority that would one day rule the world.

So they didn't like it when Jesus came teaching in the Temple, claiming "the Kingdom of God is already among you" and exercising his own authority (Luke 17:21). In one confrontation in the Temple, Jesus looked at the religious leaders and, alluding to the crushing rock of Daniel 2, claimed to be that rock that will crush to pieces those who stand against him. But first, he would offer himself up to be crushed. He would be broken so that those who welcome his authority can themselves become "living stones" that God is using to build his spiritual house (1 Peter 2:5). Jesus is the Rock cut from the mountain, and we either trust in him and find life, or we will be crushed by him and experience eternal death.

† *Rock cut from the mountain, you were crushed so that I will not be. And because you live, so will I! How grateful I am that I do not have to live in fear of being on the wrong side of this stone. In mercy you have called me to yourself, and have made me a part of your eternal Kingdom.*

NOVEMBER 14
HE TAKES OUR
PLACE IN THE FURNACE

Imagine the sight—thousands of people are gathered on a desert plain in front of a nine-story golden statue. At the moment that musicians begin to play, all the people fall to their knees, bowing before the statue. But look! In the middle of the sea of bowing humanity you spot three figures who have not bowed. Three young Hebrew men—Shadrach, Meshach, and Abednego—are still standing. Out of loyalty to almighty God, they are unwilling to bow to the idol, and are therefore subject to the consequences: "Anyone who refuses to obey will immediately be thrown into a blazing furnace" (Daniel 3:6). King Nebuchadnezzar was informed of their refusal to bow and he gave them one more chance. But they still refused.

> O Nebuchadnezzar, we do not need to defend ourselves before you. If we are thrown into the blazing furnace, the God whom we serve is able to save us. He will rescue us from your power, Your Majesty. But even if he doesn't, . . . we will never serve your gods or worship the gold statue you have set up. (3:16-18)

So the soldiers tied up Shadrach, Meshach, and Abednego and threw them into the flames (and the soldiers themselves died because the fire was so hot). But suddenly, Nebuchadnezzar was rubbing his eyes and shouting, "Didn't we tie up three men and throw them into the furnace? . . . I see four men, unbound, walking around in the fire unharmed! And the fourth looks like a god!" (Daniel 3:24-25). What did he see? Perhaps this was the pre-incarnate Son of God walking with them in the flames, or perhaps it was an angel sent by God to protect them and to be a tangible reminder of his presence with them. In any case, it was enough to cause Nebuchadnezzar to call the men out of the furnace—and to praise their God.

While Shadrach, Meshach, and Abednego prayed and were delivered *from* the furnace, when Jesus prayed, he was delivered *into* the furnace of hell's fire and fury. When Nebuchadnezzar responded in amazement, saying, "There is no other god who can rescue like this!" (3:29), he didn't know the half of it. No other god saves in the way our God saves. No other god meets us in the midst of our fiery trials. No other god walks into the fire of God's wrath in our place.

✝ *Fourth Man in the flames, I believe that when I pass through the fires of adversity or suffering, I will look up and see you there. And because you faced the fires of hell in my place, I will never have to face that furnace.*

NOVEMBER 15
SUSTAINED BY PRAYER

Although in exile from his homeland, Daniel served God well even in the employ of pagan emperors—first under Nebuchadnezzar of Babylon and then under Darius of Medo-Persia. Daniel had a successful future ahead of him—all the influence and prestige and wealth he could have asked for as a provincial ruler serving in the Persian court. But this also made him a target for envy. Other officials in the court began looking for a vulnerability in his life that they could exploit to their advantage.

They found it—or so they thought—in Daniel's commitment to prayer. Daniel's habit of prayer to his God was so consistent that his enemies knew he would not compromise or fold under pressure. So they persuaded Darius to make a law that said anyone who prayed to any god or man during the next thirty days, except to King Darius, would be thrown into the lions' den.

So what did Daniel do? He did what he always had done, what he could not live without doing. "When Daniel learned that the decree had been published, he went home to his upstairs room where the windows opened toward Jerusalem. Three times a day he got down on his knees and prayed, giving thanks to his God, just as he had done before" (Daniel 6:10, NIV). Not praying was a worse prospect to Daniel than being eaten by lions. Prayer is what sustained and steadied Daniel as he lived in a kingdom and culture so far away from home.

Daniel's dependence on God through prayer prefigured the greater Daniel's dependence on and daily habit of prayer. Luke writes that "Jesus often withdrew to the wilderness for prayer" (Luke 5:16). Jesus didn't pray out of ritual or by rote. Jesus prayed in radical dependence on his Father. "I can do nothing on my own," he said (John 5:30).

Jesus, far away from his home in heaven with his Father, regularly turned to his Father to give thanks and ask for his help. Prayer was the secret of his power, the law of his life, the inspiration of his toil, and the source of his joy, communion, and strength.

✝ *Lord, I want to be courageous and consistent in prayer, but it is not news to you that I struggle with this. My commitment to prayer is not my vulnerability; it is my lack of commitment to prayer that makes me vulnerable to the influence of the pagan world I live in. If you were dependent on your Father, how much more dependent am I? If you needed to withdraw to a place of quiet to pray, how much more do I?*

In the Den of Death

Darius found himself in a predicament. He had been fooled into signing an unjust law that anyone who prayed to a god other than him would be thrown into a den of lions. He never expected that the one caught in the trap of the law would be his most trusted and capable administrator, Daniel. But Darius could not revoke the law—it was "an official law of the Medes and the Persians that cannot be revoked" (Daniel 6:8). So Daniel was thrown into the den of lions. A stone was put over the mouth of the den and the king sealed it with his signet ring. Full of anxiety and regret, Darius said to Daniel, "May your God, whom you serve so faithfully, rescue you" (6:16).

And God did rescue Daniel. The next morning when Darius opened the den, Daniel told him, "My God sent his angel to shut the lions' mouths so that they would not hurt me, for I have been found innocent in his sight" (6:22).

Centuries later, there was another victim of an unjust law. Those who hated him could find nothing to charge him with and so accused him of blasphemy. And just as the law could not be set aside for Daniel, neither could it be changed for this victim. So he was cast into the ultimate den of death and placed in a sealed tomb. He, too, entrusted himself to his God.

But one detail makes all the difference. No angel came to rescue Jesus from death. "Do you think I cannot call on my Father, and he will at once put at my disposal more than twelve legions of angels?" Jesus said to Peter when he tried to defend Jesus from those who came to arrest him. "But how then would the Scriptures be fulfilled that say it must happen in this way?" (Matthew 26:53-54, NIV).

Why does Jesus say it "must" happen? Because of God's perfect justice, punishment must be carried out. "The LORD roars from Zion and thunders from Jerusalem" (Amos 1:2, NIV). The lion of God's justice must roar against sin. And so that we can be rescued from the jaws of the justice we deserve, Jesus endured the violence of the Lion's wrath.

† *Innocent One who was shut in the den of death in my place, you have shown me what it looks like to entrust myself to God. While I might be delivered, like Daniel, I might face physical death like so many of your martyrs. But because you were sealed in the den of death in my place and emerged from that tomb triumphant, so will I! That is my sure hope and future!*

NOVEMBER 17
He Will Open the Books

As Daniel and his fellow exiled countrymen remained in captivity—first under the Babylonians and then under the Persians—they must have longed for the Judge of the earth to take up their case and return them to their land. In the midst of their exile and persecution, Daniel received a vision of the day when God will judge the world: "I watched as thrones were put in place and the Ancient One sat down to judge. . . . Then the court began its session, and the books were opened" (Daniel 7:9-10).

A few verses later Daniel says that "the Ancient One—the Most High—came and judged in favor of his holy people" (7:22). And we can't help but wonder, *How can he do that? On what basis can he rightly judge in the favor of his people? And how can he see them as holy?*

God can judge in favor of his people only because of the favor imputed to them by Christ. It is *his* holiness, *his* record of righteousness that will enable those who hide themselves in him to stand when the Judge opens the books. The apostle John saw this same scene and explained what is written in the books: "I saw a great white throne and the one sitting on it. . . . And the books were opened, including the Book of Life. And the dead were judged according to what they had done, as recorded in the books" (Revelation 20:11-12).

In this scene, John saw two kinds of books—"the books" with our deeds written in them and "the Book of Life," a record of the names of all who are in Christ. "The books" are a record of all that we've done and failed to do. No one wants to be judged solely on the basis of what is recorded in those books. As Paul wrote, "None is righteous, no, not one" (Romans 3:10, esv). No record of our actions can ever list enough good things to save us. Fortunately, we will instead be judged on the basis of whether or not our name is in the Book of Life—the book listing all those God calls his own. "God decided in advance to adopt us into his own family by bringing us to himself through Jesus Christ" (Ephesians 1:5). For those whose names are in the Book of Life, what is listed in "the books" will not bring condemnation, but confirmation that the believer is connected to Christ in a saving, transforming way.

† *Ancient One, by faith I believe that what you will find when you open the books will not bring condemnation but will be confirmation that I am yours. It will not be a record of my own feeble, fleshly works, but of the righteousness of Christ, both imputed to my account by grace and imparted to me through the grace of the Spirit's sanctifying power.*

NOVEMBER 18
SOMEONE LIKE A SON OF MAN

The Jews of Jesus' day were watching and waiting for a magnificient "son of man." They had their picture of the Son of Man shaped by the description given by the prophet Daniel:

> As my vision continued that night, I saw someone like a son of man coming with the clouds of heaven. He approached the Ancient One and was led into his presence. He was given authority, honor, and sovereignty over all the nations of the world, so that people of every race and nation and language would obey him. His rule is eternal—it will never end. His kingdom will never be destroyed. (7:13-14)

Daniel saw a commanding, redeeming, glorious figure he called the "son of man." This prophecy, along with many others like it, shaped the Jewish people's expectations for what the Messiah would be like.

This is why the people of Jesus' day struggled to accept that a man from a small town, a man who ate with prostitutes, walked the streets with dusty feet, and had no place to sleep at night, was really the "Son of Man" they had been waiting for. How could this man with a ragtag group of followers be the Son of Man that Daniel described?

They didn't realize that Jesus had willingly laid aside some of the glories of deity to take on flesh. They didn't realize that Daniel was able to see into the heart of ultimate reality where the exalted and glorified Jesus is on the throne. It was this same Jesus that John saw in the vision given to him on the island of Patmos: "I saw," John wrote, "someone 'like a son of man'" (Revelation 1:12-13, NIV).

In other words, John saw and recognized his glorious Lord, but the first thing that struck him was the humanness of the exalted Savior. Jesus was still in human form, with recognizable human features, and yet it wasn't the same humanness John knew from his years spent with Jesus during his earthly ministry. It was the same Christ, and this Christ was still human but is now exalted and glorified—forever the exalted Son of Man.

† *Glorious, exalted Jesus, your purity and power take my breath away! Your fiery eyes penetrate into my soul. Your voice thunders into the core of my being and leaves me speechless. Forgive me for how I reduce you in my mind to something less than the Son of Man who reigns in glory.*

NOVEMBER 19
SEATED AT GOD'S RIGHT HAND

Daniel had a dream vision of the time when the Kingdom of God comes to its full fruition.

> I saw someone like a son of man coming with the clouds of heaven. He approached the Ancient One and was led into his presence. He was given authority, honor, and sovereignty over all the nations of the world, so that people of every race and nation and language would obey him. His rule is eternal—it will never end. His kingdom will never be destroyed. (7:13-14)

In Daniel's dream vision, he sees "the Ancient One" (God the Father) take his seat on a throne flaming with fire (7:9). It is an awesome sight. The God of the universe moves to render worldwide judgment, even as he receives the praise of millions of the redeemed who have been awaiting this climactic event of history.

But the most significant person who comes before him is "someone like a son of man." He is a man, and yet he comes "with the clouds of heaven," implying deity as well as humanity. One need only observe what the Ancient One hands to him to know who he is: "He was given authority, honor, and sovereignty over all the nations of the world, so that people of every race and nation and language would obey him." This can only be Jesus.

At Jesus' trial, the high priest Caiaphas questioned his prisoner, "I demand in the name of the living God—tell us if you are the Messiah, the Son of God." In reply, Jesus applied the prophetic words of Daniel to himself: "You have said it. And in the future you will see the Son of Man seated in the place of power at God's right hand and coming on the clouds of heaven" (Matthew 26:63-64).

"I'm the one Daniel was describing," he said, in essence, to those who were bent on killing him for what they heard as blasphemy. They thought Jesus was their prisoner—that they had authority over him, that they could put an end to him. But they were wrong. One day the whole universe will see the Son of Man on his throne, and his rule will never end.

✝ *Son of Man, the Ancient One has given you authority, honor, and sovereignty over all the world, and yet I, like a fool, rebel and dishonor you, seeking to wrest control of my life from you. How I long for the day when that battle in my life will be over. You will have won, and the joy of it will never end.*

NOVEMBER 20

MESSIAH

Only a handful of Old Testament texts specifically predict a future "messiah" with that title. The title messiah (*mashia* in Hebrew) found in Daniel is translated as "Anointed One":

> A period of seventy sets of seven has been decreed for your people and your holy city to finish their rebellion, to put an end to their sin, to atone for their guilt, to bring in everlasting righteousness, to confirm the prophetic vision, and to anoint the Most Holy Place. . . . [After a time] a ruler—the Anointed One—comes. Jerusalem will be rebuilt with streets and strong defenses, despite the perilous times. . . . [After a time] the Anointed One will be killed, appearing to have accomplished nothing. (9:24-26)

Jesus claimed from his earliest preaching to be anointed by the Spirit of God. So why did he repeatedly urge people not to spread the word around that he was the Messiah?

Between the time of the prophets and the coming of Jesus, the term "messiah" became loaded with the hopes of a national, political, and even military Jewish restoration. It became even more acute in the days of servitude to the Roman empire. If Jesus had claimed openly to be the Messiah the people had been looking for, they would have placed a load of expectations on him that were never part of his mission. Jesus had no intention of fulfilling the people's expectations of a king who would conquer using military or political might. Certainly he was a King and was building a Kingdom, but it was of a very different sort, and would come about in a very different way.

Jesus, Messiah, intended to do just what Daniel had prophesied he would do—put an end to their sin, atone for their guilt, and bring in everlasting righteousness—but he would do it through the humility of suffering on the cross, not through the hubris of taking control. And just as Daniel foresaw, though it would appear he accomplished nothing through his humiliating death, in fact, he would accomplish the greatest feat of all time—the saving of all those who would put their faith in him.

† *Messiah, you have come into my life to put an end to my sin, to atone for my guilt, to make me righteous forever. I welcome you to do your holy work in my heart. I receive the sanctification that comes by your Spirit, the justification that comes by your atonement, and the righteousness that comes through your perfect life, credited to me.*

MESSENGER FROM HEAVEN

As a sign of his identification with the trials of his brothers and sisters in Judah, Daniel gave up many of the things that made his life comfortable. Then, in the midst of his mourning, he saw something spectacular:

> I looked up and saw a man dressed in linen clothing, with a belt of pure gold around his waist. His body looked like a precious gem. His face flashed like lightning, and his eyes flamed like torches. His arms and feet shone like polished bronze, and his voice roared like a vast multitude of people. (Daniel 10:5-6)

This man told Daniel that he needed the archangel Michael to help him battle with spiritual forces, so this heavenly messenger was most likely not the pre-incarnate Christ. More likely he was one of the angelic attendants of God who reflects his Master's glory.

John saw a similar vision of a man, but he saw not reflected glory, but glory that radiated from the Son of Man himself.

> He was wearing a long robe with a gold sash across his chest. His head and his hair were white like wool, as white as snow. And his eyes were like flames of fire. His feet were like polished bronze refined in a furnace, and his voice thundered like mighty ocean waves. He held seven stars in his right hand, and a sharp two-edged sword came from his mouth. And his face was like the sun in all its brilliance. (Revelation 1:13-16)

John saw the glorified Jesus wearing the robe of a perfect priest and the sash of a reigning king. His hair, "white like wool," revealed his eternal wisdom and purity. His eyes, "like flames of fire," burned with anger against his enemies. His feet, "like polished bronze refined in a furnace," revealed power that had been tested by fire. His commanding, unavoidable voice "thundered like mighty ocean waves." His face radiated the glory of God in all its brilliance.

† *Messenger from heaven, seeing you in your glorified humanity stuns and silences me. Hearing your voice challenges and convicts me. When you look at me with your flaming eyes, see me through your Cross, so I will not be consumed.*

They Prophesied but Did Not Understand

Before his study of the prophet Jeremiah, Daniel was clueless concerning the time frame of his nation's captivity. "I, Daniel, learned from reading the word of the LORD, as revealed to Jeremiah the prophet, that Jerusalem must lie desolate for seventy years" (9:2). So even though prophets revealed aspects of what is to come, they did not grasp the full picture.

Even the revelations Daniel himself personally received, he did not always understand: "I, Daniel, was troubled by all I had seen, and my visions terrified me. So I approached one of those standing beside the throne and asked him what it all meant" (7:15-16).

Peter tells us that the Old Testament prophets searched intently "trying to find out the time and circumstances to which the Spirit of Christ in them was pointing when he predicted the sufferings of Christ and the glories that would follow" (1 Peter 1:11, NIV). They wanted to know the timing and circumstances of the coming Messiah. Daniel asked, "How will all this finally end, my lord?" to which he was told by God's messenger, "Go now, Daniel, for what I have said is kept secret and sealed until the time of the end" (Daniel 12:8-9).

The coming of Christ was not for the prophets to completely comprehend in their day. Peter said that "it was revealed to them that they were not serving themselves but you, when they spoke of the things that have now been told you by those who have preached the gospel to you by the Holy Spirit sent from heaven" (1 Peter 1:12, NIV). Peter was telling the people of his day that they were the ones who were getting to see the fulfillment of the prophecies. Those who received and recorded the prophecies longed to see and know what the people of Jesus' day finally saw and understood.

The prophets weren't philosophers or mystics propounding principles gathered by their own reflections. They saw, in various ways and to various degrees, the saving work of the coming One. And what they knew fed their hunger to know more.

† *Glorious Fulfillment of the prophecies, how blessed I am to live on this side of the Cross, to have available your Word that makes your plan for salvation so clear and so compelling. Yet there is so much more to know of you and your Second Coming. Like the prophets of old, I want to know the timing and the circumstances. How I long for that day!*

MINOR
PROPHETS

HE BOUGHT US BACK

God told his prophet Hosea to do something shocking. "Go and marry a prostitute, so that some of her children will be conceived in prostitution. This will illustrate how Israel has acted like a prostitute by turning against the LORD and worshiping other gods" (Hosea 1:2). God wanted Hosea's brokenhearted relationship with an unfaithful wife to be a living illustration of his own divine brokenness over Israel's chasing after other lovers—the Canaanite gods.

Hosea married Gomer and sure enough, she was repeatedly unfaithful to him. But the affairs she had with other men all turned sour. She sank lower and lower in the social scale until at last she was being sold as a slave. But God was not done illustrating how he treats sinners, so he told Hosea: "Go and love your wife again, even though she commits adultery with another lover. This will illustrate that the LORD still loves Israel, even though the people have turned to other gods and love to worship them" (3:1).

Hosea had to go to the slave market in Samaria, where Gomer was put up for sale on the auction block. Hosea reported, "I bought her back for fifteen pieces of silver and five bushels of barley and a measure of wine" (3:2). He bought his own wife back for a meager price, indicating that she had little value. Now, as the legal owner of his wife, he could do with her as he pleased. He could sell her again, or put her to work, or even put her to death. But once again, Hosea illustrated God's love for his unfaithful people. Instead of seeking revenge, Hosea clothed Gomer and took her home. He showed her his goodness and began wooing her heart to love him again.

Just as Hosea purchased Gomer for himself, so Christ came to the marketplace where we were slaves to sin. We had little value. Although we belonged to him already, he bought us back for himself. "The ransom he paid was not mere gold or silver. It was the precious blood of Christ, the sinless, spotless Lamb of God" (1 Peter 1:18-19). He took us and covered our nakedness with the garments of salvation and the robe of his righteousness. He has taken away our shame and has cleansed us. One day we will live with him in his home forever.

† *My Redeemer, I see that I have broken your heart as I have sold myself to many other lovers in this world. Yet you have paid the greatest price to buy me back. You are wooing me to love you from the heart. Envelop me in your faithful, redeeming love as you heal me of my idolatry and faithlessness.*

NOVEMBER 24
GATEWAY OF HOPE

In Hosea 2, God spoke through his prophet Hosea to his unfaithful wife, Israel. God's people had shamelessly forsaken him. They forgot that every good thing they had came from him. Instead of worshiping God, they burned incense to the false god Baal, and they gave all the good gifts God had given them to this false god.

God began to list all of the things he was going to take away from Israel and how he would punish her. But then his message turned from his plan to punish to his further plan to restore the love and closeness they once shared. "I will return her vineyards to her and transform the Valley of Trouble into a gateway of hope. She will give herself to me there, as she did long ago when she was young, when I freed her from her captivity in Egypt" (2:15).

Why is the Valley of Trouble mentioned here? Because that valley had a tremendous symbolic meaning for Israel. That was the valley where Achan (whose name means "trouble") was stoned to death after he went against the decree of God and hid spoils from the battle with Jericho in his tent. Achan's sin brought trouble on the entire nation of Israel so that they lost the next battle at Ai (Joshua 7).

So through Hosea, God was promising that the Valley of Trouble, the place of swift judgment for sin, was going to be transformed into a gateway of hope for troubled people. Rather than a dark pit in which people had to die, this valley would become a place where God's people would know victory and enjoy peace.

But how can God do this? How can the Valley of Trouble, the place of judgment, become a gateway of hope?

Only through Christ, because he took our troubles upon himself. Remember what he said in the hours before the Cross: "Now my heart is troubled, and what shall I say? 'Father, save me from this hour'? No, it was for this very reason I came to this hour" (John 12:27, NIV). Why was Jesus troubled? Because the weight of our sins—our troubles—was pressing in on him.

Jesus took our troubles upon himself so he could say to us, "Do not let your hearts be troubled. Trust in God; trust also in me" (John 14:1, NIV).

† *Jesus, you have borne all of the trouble birthed from my sin and have opened wide the doorway of hope for me. I can walk through without fear and with full confidence in your mercy.*

MY PEOPLE

"I will be your God, and you will be my people." In this refrain, repeated throughout the Old Testament, we hear the heartbeat of God. It was his covenant promise to Abraham and to Israel through Moses. He says it again and again through his prophets Jeremiah and Ezekiel. When we come to the prophet Hosea, we find that God intends for "my people," to include more than the physical descendants of Abraham:

> I will show love
> to those I called "Not loved."
> And to those I called "Not my people,"
> I will say, "Now you are my people."
> And they will reply, "You are our God!" (Hosea 2:23)

Hosea prophesied that the day would come when those whom God called "not my people" would become "my people." In Romans 9:25, Paul quoted this prophecy of Hosea, saying it was "concerning the Gentiles." It became clear that enjoying the covenant promises of God is not related to national heritage; it is solely through faith in the Mediator of the new covenant. "There is no longer Jew or Gentile," Paul wrote. "For you are all one in Christ Jesus. And now that you belong to Christ, you are the true children of Abraham. You are his heirs, and God's promise to Abraham belongs to you" (Galatians 3:28-29).

Therefore, in the New Testament, all of the Old Testament imagery that describes Israel—branches of a vine, a flock led by a shepherd, the elect, the priesthood, the remnant, the true circumcision, Abraham's seed—is applied to the church. The church doesn't replace Israel, nor is it simply identical to Israel. But a new historical and redemptive development—the incarnation, crucifixion, and resurrection of Jesus—forever transformed and redefined the people of God, so that Peter saw Hosea's prophecies (1:6, 9-10; 2:23) as fulfilled in the church:

> You are a chosen people. You are royal priests, a holy nation, God's very own possession. . . .
>
> Once you had no identity as a people;
> now you are God's people. (1 Peter 2:9-10)

† *My God, I deserve to be on the outside, far away from you and barred from your good graces and gifts. But you have chosen me and called me and made me your own.*

NOVEMBER 26
I Desire Mercy, Not Sacrifice

The people in Hosea's day had not abandoned offering sacrifices. They were very religious, in fact, but they had lost a true sense of worship. They had come to believe that by offering sacrifices and performing rituals they could ingratiate themselves to God and get him to do good things for them. And, of course, they believed they could live however they pleased. But God was not amused by their empty religiosity.

> "O Israel and Judah,
> what should I do with you?" asks the LORD. . . .
> "I want you to show love,
> not offer sacrifices.
> I want you to know me
> more than I want burnt offerings." (Hosea 6:4, 6)

God's people just didn't seem to get it. Their offering of sacrifices devolved into religious hypocrisy. Similar to the Israelites of Hosea's day, the Pharisees of Jesus' day also thought they could please God with their outward rituals and religious formalities while they cared little about loving God or loving others.

> Matthew invited Jesus and his disciples to his home as dinner guests, along with many tax collectors and other disreputable sinners. But when the Pharisees saw this, they asked his disciples, "Why does your teacher eat with such scum?"
>
> When Jesus heard this, he said, "Healthy people don't need a doctor—sick people do." Then he added, "Now go and learn the meaning of this Scripture: 'I want you to show mercy, not offer sacrifices.' For I have come to call not those who think they are righteous, but those who know they are sinners." (Matthew 9:10-13)

Jesus came to transform religious hypocrites into lovers of mercy, promising that "God blesses those who are merciful, for they will be shown mercy" (Matthew 5:7).

✝ *Great Physician, I am sick with hypocrisy and religiosity like the Pharisees, and with greed and worldliness like those who sat at the table with you. How I need your healing touch! Show me your tender mercy and melt my heart so that I can extend your mercy to those around me.*

NOVEMBER 27

THE TRUE VINE

In Hosea 10, God compared Israel to a vine:

> How prosperous Israel is—
> a luxuriant vine loaded with fruit.
> But the richer the people get,
> the more pagan altars they build.
> The more bountiful their harvests,
> the more beautiful their sacred pillars. (10:1)

When Hosea described Israel as a vine, it was a familiar image to the chosen nation. Numerous prophets described Israel as a vine—a vine that God himself planted, a vine that had survived and grown large and strong, producing a good crop of fruit. So what was the problem?

The fruit Israel was producing, according to Hosea's prophecy, was merely outward religion. They built altars, obelisks, and other sacred objects by the hundreds, but not to honor the Lord. It was all a show of religiosity. God told them that the only way they, as the vine of God, could produce good fruit was to turn their hearts back to him, fellowship with him, draw their life from him. "I am like a tree that is always green; all your fruit comes from me" (14:8).

Jesus picked up on this familiar picture of the vine when he said, "I am the true vine" (John 15:1, NIV), inviting us to draw our life from him. Into the empty religion and fruitless ritual of his day, Jesus offered a way to bear genuine, abundant fruitfulness for God. The only way to get in on the fruit-bearing life of the vine, he said, is to abide in him. Jesus was establishing himself as the true and only way God's people can have a fruitful relationship with God. "No branch can bear fruit by itself; it must remain in the vine. Neither can you bear fruit unless you remain in me" (John 15:4, NIV).

We have something the people of Hosea's day didn't have—the indwelling Holy Spirit who empowers us to bear fruit that gives evidence that we are abiding in the true Vine. "The fruit of the Spirit is love, joy, peace, patience, kindness, goodness, faithfulness, gentleness and self-control" (Galatians 5:22-23, NIV).

✝ *True Vine that gives me life and makes me fruitful, I know that if I am left to my own resources apart from you, I will produce only empty effort and religious activity. I choose to abide in you and draw my life from yours.*

TRUE ISRAEL

The prophet Hosea described God's relationship with Israel as that of a loving father with a son: "When Israel was a child, I loved him, and I called my son out of Egypt" (Hosea 11:1).

Israel was God's beloved son, yet this son was disobedient and disloyal. For Israel to experience all of the Father's covenantal blessings would require that another Son, the true Israel, walk in perfect obedience before him in Israel's stead.

Throughout his Gospel, Matthew sought to show that Jesus did exactly that. Early in his Gospel, Matthew applied this statement from Hosea to Jesus: "Joseph left for Egypt with the child and Mary, his mother, and they stayed there until Herod's death. This fulfilled what the Lord had spoken through the prophet: 'I called my Son out of Egypt'" (Matthew 2:14-15).

Matthew wanted his readers to see that Jesus is the true Israel, succeeding where Israel failed in its mission, obeying the law where they disobeyed, and submitting to his Father's will where they rebelled. Matthew told the story of Jesus in such a way that we see a reenactment of significant events in Israel's history, beginning with Hosea's reference to the Exodus from Egypt. Just as Israel crossed the Red Sea, so after his baptism, "Jesus came up out of the water" and a voice from heaven said, "This is my dearly loved Son, who brings me great joy" (3:16-17). Just as God had promised through his prophets to "pour out my Spirit on your descendants" (Isaiah 44:3), Matthew wrote that Jesus "saw the Spirit of God descending like a dove and settling on him" (3:16). Just as Israel faced temptations in the desert and failed, "Jesus was led by the Spirit into the wilderness to be tempted there" (Matthew 4:1), and he overcame the temptation. Whereas Israel came to Mount Sinai to receive the law, Jesus "went up on the mountainside and sat down. His disciples gathered around him, and he began to teach them" (Matthew 5:1-2).

Jesus was not just the Savior of Israel. In fact, he was the embodiment of all that Israel was meant to be.

✝ *True Israel, obedient Son, you succeeded where I have failed, you obeyed where I have disobeyed, you submitted where I have rebelled. Yet because you have called me to yourself, your obedience has become mine. You have become my salvation.*

NOVEMBER 29
TEACHER OF RIGHTEOUSNESS

At first, Joel 2:23 appears to say nothing about the Messiah:

> Be glad, O people of Zion,
> rejoice in the LORD your God,
> for he has given you
> the autumn rains in righteousness.
> He sends you abundant showers,
> both autumn and spring rains, as before.

Most translations footnote an alternate meaning of the word *moreh,* which, instead of being translated "autumn rain" or "former rain," can also be "teacher." So the promise becomes that of a teacher of righteousness. It promises teaching on how to live rightly that will be poured out like rain from heaven, a shower of words that will refresh and nourish the soul.

God would show himself faithful to his covenant and would once again refresh the lands. And this refreshment and restoration will come from a teacher of righteousness, who will speak with grace and truth.

When Jesus opened the scrolls to teach in the Temple or stood out on the hillside and spoke, many recognized that he was the teacher of righteousness God had promised. He spoke of living a lifestyle of integrity and authenticity before God that was nothing like the legalism, ritual, and religiosity taught by their Jewish teachers.

> What sorrow awaits you teachers of religious law and you Pharisees. Hypocrites! For you are like whitewashed tombs—beautiful on the outside but filled on the inside with dead people's bones and all sorts of impurity. Outwardly you look like righteous people, but inwardly your hearts are filled with hypocrisy and lawlessness. (Matthew 23:27-28)

The "autumn rain" or teaching of the Old Testament fell in the form of the law and the prophets. Jesus then brought showers of truth as the Teacher of Righteousness. And he left us with the Counselor, the Holy Spirit, who impresses his teaching into our hearts and lives.

✝ *Teacher of Righteousness, I am your student and I long to learn from you. I want to learn from what you said and how you lived and how you loved. I want to learn from how you served and how you suffered.*

THE LORD WHO SAVES

Joel prophesied to the people of Judah and Jerusalem about a century before they were taken into captivity to Babylon. The nation was facing a catastrophe that threatened their very existence. A massive locust plague had struck the land. The insects consumed every green plant, which, of course, resulted in famine. The starving people began to ask, "Has God sent the locust plague to punish us for our failure to live in right relationship to him? Do we have a future?"

God responded to their questions through his prophet Joel, promising to take pity on the people and restore their material lives following the locust plague. But then he spoke of a more distant future when he would restore their spiritual lives. He promised to pour out his Spirit before the "great and terrible day of the LORD" arrives, which will be a day of judgment. "But," Joel reassured, "everyone who calls on the name of the LORD will be saved" (Joel 2:31-32).

In Acts 2:17-21, on the Day of Pentecost, Peter declared that Joel's prophecy was being fulfilled, signaling that "the last days" had arrived. God poured out his Holy Spirit on the people and they began to speak in other languages. "Let everyone in Israel know for certain that God has made this Jesus, whom you crucified, to be both Lord and Messiah!" (Acts 2:36), Peter declared, making it clear that to call on the name of the Lord as Joel prophesied is to call on Jesus.

Later, in Acts 4:12, Peter went even further: "There is salvation in no one else, for there is no other name under heaven given among men by which we must be saved" (ESV).

We know our own failures too well to assume that we deserve anything better than to experience the consequences of our rebellion toward God. But on that great and terrible Day of the Lord, we know where to find safety and salvation! We call on the only One who has the power and the will to save us. We call on Jesus, the Lord who saves.

† *Yeshua, "the Lord Who Saves," I call out to you to save me! I have no intention of waiting until the last moment to call upon you in desperation as judgment begins to fall all around me. I call on you now and for the rest of my days to save me from myself and from the sin that entangles and entices me. Save me from the judgment I deserve!*

DECEMBER 1
THE DAY OF THE LORD

Amos was one of many prophets to write about a coming "day of the LORD": "What sorrow awaits you who say, 'If only the day of the LORD were here!'" (Amos 5:18).

Zephaniah spoke of the "day of the LORD," which was to be a day of the wrath of God visited upon those who have broken his covenant (Zephaniah 1:7-18). Isaiah wrote about the wrath of the day of the Lord as a day of vengeance (Isaiah 13:9), and Joel described the darkness of the day and called it "dreadful" (Joel 2:11, 31, NIV). However, Joel's prophecy was not only concerned with the wrath of that day, but also with the blessing and salvation of that day. Joel wrote that the Spirit of God will be poured out on the people, and that every person who calls on the name of the Lord will be saved (2:28-29, 32).

The day of the Lord, then, will be the day of God's wrath and judgment against his enemies, but it will also be the day of salvation for his people. Although throughout the Old Testament era God sometimes judged the enemies of Israel and saved his people from destruction when they turned to him, clearly this had not happened in the complete and pervasive way the prophets had predicted.

At the coming of the Holy Spirit on Jesus' followers at Pentecost, Peter said, "What you see was predicted long ago by the prophet Joel" (Acts 2:16). And throughout the rest of the New Testament, the apostles proclaimed the death and resurrection of Jesus as the day of the Lord. The day of the Lord came as the wrath of God was poured out upon our Substitute on the cross and salvation was purchased for us. The day of the Lord came as the people of God rose from the grave in the person of our Substitute and ascended to sit with him at the right hand of God.

But this prophecy still awaits full consummation. Scripture promises that one day all of God's chosen people will embrace Jesus as the Messiah; and then the prophecy will have its final fulfillment. That final day of the Lord will be irrefutable and undeniable. It will be a day of both judgment on God's enemies and salvation for his children.

✝ *Your day has come and is coming, Lord, and because of what you have accomplished in my stead, I don't have to fear or dread your coming day. Instead, my heart awaits that day with joy in your salvation and rest in your promises.*

DECEMBER 2
THE ONLY HOPE
FOR RELIGIOUS HYPOCRITES

Amos prophesied to the northern kingdom of Israel in days of outward prosperity but spiritual famine. He was sent right to the center of corruption, namely, the cult city of Bethel, where their first king, Jeroboam, had built high places of idol worship and set up his own priesthood and new holy days (1 Kings 12:25-33).

The Israelites were very religious—they sacrificed daily, tithed every three days, and gave thank offerings. But it was all a sham. They were using the name of God for their own religious purposes, while their hearts were far from him, made obvious by their oppression of the poor and needy.

Amos spoke for God into the emptiness of their religious hypocrisy:

I hate all your show and pretense—
the hypocrisy of your religious festivals and solemn assemblies.
I will not accept your burnt offerings and grain offerings.
I won't even notice all your choice peace offerings.
Away with your noisy hymns of praise!
I will not listen to the music of your harps.
Instead, I want to see a mighty flood of justice,
an endless river of righteous living. (Amos 5:21-24)

Many years after Amos, Jesus confronted this kind of hypocrisy in the Pharisees, who were also full of religious show and pretense, saying:

They crush people with unbearable religious demands and never lift a finger to ease the burden. Everything they do is for show. . . . You are careful to tithe even the tiniest income from your herb gardens, but you ignore the more important aspects of the law—justice, mercy, and faith. . . . Outwardly you look like righteous people, but inwardly your hearts are filled with hypocrisy and lawlessness. (Matthew 23:4-5, 23, 28)

Jesus is the only hope for religious hypocrites. Only he can give us the courage to face the truth about ourselves and the grace we need to trust him under the weight of that truth. Only he can work an internal transformation so that we can walk in humility and integrity.

† *Jesus, you see right through my façade of spirituality into the apathy of my heart. Yet you don't reject me for this hypocrisy; you welcome me into authentic relationship.*

DECEMBER 3
THE PLUMB LINE

A plumb line is a string with a weight fastened to the end that helps a builder keep the walls of the structure straight (or "plumb"). It works like a level, revealing if the walls are becoming crooked, and thus vulnerable to collapse.

The prophet Amos used this familiar imagery to help the people of the northern kingdom see that God had a standard that he would use to judge their "straightness": "I saw the Lord standing beside a wall that had been built using a plumb line. He was using a plumb line to see if it was still straight. . . . The Lord replied, 'I will test my people with this plumb line. I will no longer ignore all their sins'" (Amos 7:7-8).

Compared to the "plumb line" of God's perfect law delivered at Sinai—the standard he expected of his people—the nation of Israel was completely crooked and destined for collapse. Fulfilling God's promise to destroy the wall that did not measure true to his plumb line, within just a few years the Assyrians defeated the northern kingdom and sent the people into exile.

A plumb line is an unrelenting standard, as is God's law. And God's standard has not become lax. "Everyone has sinned; we all fall short of God's glorious standard" (Romans 3:23). God holds up a plumb line to our lives and asks, "How do you measure up? Are you built straight? I cannot just ignore your sin." And we have to answer, "We do not measure up. We are hopelessly crooked."

Into the harsh reality of our catastrophic crookedness, Jesus comes to show us a plumb line—not weighted by the law but by grace. Jesus comes to us and says, "So you don't measure up? I do. I lived up to God's standard perfectly. And by grace through faith, I will give you my own perfect record so that when God tests you with his plumb line, instead of condemning you for your crookedness, he'll bless you for my holiness."

In the gracious plan of God, the Cross of Jesus has become the plumb line by which our lives are judged. Through the Cross of Christ, we receive mercy instead of condemnation, pardon instead of punishment.

† *Plumb Line of God's righteous standard, your Cross has become the only plumb line that I will be judged by. In your Cross you took the condemnation for my crookedness and I find grace that conforms me to your holiness.*

DECEMBER 4

HE WILL JUDGE THOSE WHO HARM HIS PEOPLE

The Edomites, who were the descendants of Jacob's brother Esau, should have assisted their brothers when the southern kingdom of Judah was under siege by Babylon. But as the invaders carried the people into captivity, the Edomites sided with the foreign invaders and even took advantage of Judah's misfortune. By making themselves an enemy to God's chosen people, the Edomites made themselves enemies of God.

> The day is near when I, the LORD,
>   will judge all godless nations!
> As you have done to Israel,
>   so it will be done to you.
> All your evil deeds
>   will fall back on your own heads. (Obadiah 1:15)

But while Obadiah prophesied doom for Edom, he also prophesied restoration for God's people: "The people of Israel will come back to reclaim their inheritance. The people of Israel will be a raging fire, and Edom a field of dry stubble" (1:17-18).

Obadiah encouraged God's people that God will punish those who oppose, persecute, and unjustly treat his people. He will save and restore his own.

This was good news not only to God's people in Obadiah's day, but also to the persecuted believers in the first century. As John was imprisoned on the isle of Patmos, he was allowed to see the day when the judgment of Israel's enemies will become an eternal reality for all those who have set themselves against Christ and his bride. John quoted an angel who celebrates this just judgment of God: "You are just, O Holy One, who is and who always was, because you have sent these judgments. Since they shed the blood of your holy people and your prophets, you have given them blood to drink. It is their just reward" (Revelation 16:5-6).

At the same time that the Holy One judges those who have persecuted his people, he will also restore his people in his eternal land forever. And as Obadiah told the people in his prophecy, "The LORD himself will be king!" (Obadiah 1:21).

† *Just Avenger, though I have never known the suffering of intense persecution, it gives me courage and confidence to know that you will bring justice to all those who suffer for your name in this life.*

THE SIGN OF JONAH

Matthew wrote that unbelieving and scoffing Jewish leaders came to Jesus asking for a special sign to prove that he really was the long-awaited Messiah. They were not satisfied with Jesus' many miracles of healing the sick and casting out demons. But Jesus knew that evidence was not the issue.

> Only an evil, adulterous generation would demand a miraculous sign; but the only sign I will give them is the sign of the prophet Jonah. For as Jonah was in the belly of the great fish for three days and three nights, so will the Son of Man be in the heart of the earth for three days and three nights. (Matthew 12:39-40)

Certainly the Jews who heard his answer were perplexed. They knew the story of Jonah—the prophet who ran from God, was thrown into a raging sea, was swallowed by a great fish, and was spit out onto the shore three days later. *What could that possibly have to do with seeing a miracle?* they must have wondered. Even when Jesus told his disciples clearly that "he would be killed, but three days later he would rise from the dead" (Mark 8:31), they simply couldn't understand or anticipate what Jesus meant.

Using the familiar story of Jonah, Jesus was drawing his listeners a picture that would show them exactly what he came to do—in fact, the greatest work he would do. Just as Jonah was delivered from certain death, so would Jesus be delivered from the throes of death. Just as the fish could not contain Jonah and coughed him up, so the grave would not contain Jesus. Death's claim on Jesus would have a limit of three days.

But unlike Jonah, who ran from God's mission for him, Jesus willingly came to accomplish his mission. And unlike Jonah, who languished in the belly of the fish, powerless to save his own life, Jesus had the authority to lay his life down and the authority to take it up again (John 10:18). Jesus gave us this sign of Jonah, the sign of miraculous, unstoppable life and of authority over death, so that we will believe, and that by believing we will have life in his name (John 20:31).

† *Risen Jesus, I have seen the sign of Jonah in your death and in your resurrected life. Thank you for giving me eyes to see the sign, and the faith to believe that your resurrection life is but a preview of the life you are giving to me as I place my faith in you.*

LOVER OF HIS ENEMIES

The word of the Lord came to the prophet Jonah, and it was not at all what he wanted to hear. "Get up and go to the great city of Nineveh. Announce my judgment against it because I have seen how wicked its people are" (Jonah 1:2). The next verse shows how Jonah felt about the very idea of being used by God to bring the people of Nineveh to repentance. "But Jonah got up and went in the opposite direction."

Jonah didn't want to go to Nineveh because he knew God. He knew about God's heart of mercy toward wicked Gentiles and his longing that they repent and be saved from judgment. Jonah knew that God would have mercy and bring his enemies to repentance. And Jonah didn't want them to repent; he wanted them to be destroyed. He selfishly wanted the Israelites to keep salvation to themselves.

What a contrast to the One who was greater than Jonah! While Jonah was selfish, resentful, and unmerciful toward his nation's enemies, Jesus moved toward his enemies, coming into this sin-filled world with compassion, love, and mercy. This is especially good news for us because we were once God's enemies. In his mercy, Jesus broke through our rebellion to bring us to himself. Paul wrote, "Our friendship with God was restored by the death of his Son while we were still his enemies" (Romans 5:10).

And Jesus wants us to treat our enemies with the same kind of mercy he lavished on us. "But to you who are willing to listen, I say, love your enemies! Do good to those who hate you," he said (Luke 6:27).

As Jonah came to his senses inside the big fish, he said, "My salvation comes from the LORD alone" (Jonah 2:9). Jonah knew that salvation is the Lord's to give to whomever he pleases. God would rather save than destroy. He shows mercy to whomever he chooses. And we who have received God's mercy are to be the conduits of God's mercy to others—even to our enemies.

† *Merciful Savior, I was once a rebel against you and you were merciful to me. I know you intend for me to share the mercy you have lavished on me with those around me—even those I have seen as my enemies. That is what I want to do. That is who I want to be—one who has been so changed by the mercy extended to me in Christ that I can't help but extend your mercy to everyone around me.*

ONE MAN OFFERS HIS LIFE TO SAVE OTHERS

The book of Jonah begins with "The LORD gave this message to Jonah . . ." But then Jonah ran from obeying God's mission for him and stole away on a ship heading in the direction opposite of Nineveh. Then "the LORD hurled a powerful wind over the sea, causing a violent storm that threatened to break the ship apart" (1:4).

Jonah knew that God had sent the storm that threatened the lives of everyone on the ship. He also knew that he was the real object of God's displeasure. So he calmly offered himself up, saying to his shipmates, "Throw me into the sea, . . . and it will become calm again" (1:12).

In Jonah's offering of himself up to die so that others might live, we see a picture of Jesus offering himself up to die so that we might live. Yet a glaring contrast reveals why Jesus is "greater than Jonah" (Matthew 12:41). Jonah had to offer himself because he had been disobedient in refusing to submit to God's will. Jesus, the obedient prophet, did what Jonah had been unwilling to do. Jesus didn't run from preaching repentance and announcing judgment. He didn't refuse to invite people outside the boundaries of Israel into God's Kingdom. He welcomed them. Jesus didn't avoid God's will; his greatest joy was in accomplishing God's will, saying to God, "I want your will to be done, not mine" (Matthew 26:39).

When the sailors picked Jonah up and threw him into the raging sea, the storm stopped at once. The Lord had arranged for a great fish to swallow Jonah. And Jonah was inside the fish for three days and three nights.

Likewise, when Jesus gave up his spirit and died, the storm of God's judgment for sin was stilled. God's justice was satisfied with Christ's substitutionary death on our behalf. And Jesus was inside the earth for three days and three nights.

What does this mean for us? It means that even though we run from God, refuse to give out God's Word to others, and like Jonah, are filled with bigotry, self-centeredness, and self-pity, God is satisfied with us—not because of who we are or what we've done, but because of who Christ is and what he has done. "Christ died for sins once for all, the righteous for the unrighteous, to bring you to God" (1 Peter 3:18, NIV).

† *One who died so I might live, you offered yourself to die in my place. You, the righteous One, for me, the unrighteous one. I don't understand this mysterious and glorious exchange, but I accept it and receive it by faith.*

DECEMBER 8
SALVATION IS OF THE LORD

We might not expect that someone sitting in the stomach of a fish would be the source of the most significant truth in the universe. But as Jonah pieced together various psalms into a prayer, he expressed just such a profound truth. "My salvation comes from the LORD alone" (Jonah 2:9).

Jonah wasn't talking about the temporary deliverance of not being digested by the fish. He was talking about the great work of the salvation of his soul for all eternity that God would accomplish for him—whether or not the fish spit him out. Jonah understood that he was helpless in terms of saving himself; it was completely up to God.

No created intelligence assisted God in planning salvation. Even before he made the world, God devised a way whereby he might save humanity, which he knew would fall into sin. And just as no one helped God plan for salvation, neither did any person help him provide salvation. God did it all himself. And he still does not need our help; it has been accomplished at the Cross.

Salvation is of the Lord—it begins with him, it is sustained by him, and it finds fulfillment in him.

> God saved you by his grace when you believed. And you can't take credit for this; it is a gift from God. Salvation is not a reward for the good things we have done, so none of us can boast about it. For we are God's masterpiece. He has created us anew in Christ Jesus, so we can do the good things he planned for us long ago. (Ephesians 2:8-10)

When we talk about salvation, it only makes sense to ask ourselves, "What or who do we need to be saved from?" And here is the answer that seems scandalous to some: we need to be saved from God—namely the wrath of God. The glory of the gospel is that the One from whom we need to be saved is the very One who saves us. In saving us through the work of Christ, God saves us from himself. "This is a trustworthy saying, and everyone should accept it: 'Christ Jesus came into the world to save sinners'" (1 Timothy 1:15).

✝ *My salvation comes from you alone. I like to think I was somehow smart enough or spiritual enough to choose you, but I know better. It was you who chose me and drew me to yourself. And it is you who keeps me saved and safe.*

DECEMBER 9

SOMEONE GREATER THAN JONAH

We tend to think mostly of Jonah's failure to obey when God sent him to Nineveh. Yet when Jonah was given a second chance at obedience, he went to the evil city of Nineveh, shouting, "Forty days from now Nineveh will be destroyed!" (Jonah 3:4). The people believed Jonah's message and God didn't carry out the threatened destruction.

Jonah had an amazing response to his preaching in this Gentile city. They believed God and repented in sincerity. In contrast, when Jesus preached to the covenant people of Israel, the majority of them remained hardened and would not repent. Jesus said to them, "The people of Nineveh will stand up against this generation on judgment day and condemn it, for they repented of their sins at the preaching of Jonah. Now someone greater than Jonah is here—but you refuse to repent" (Matthew 12:41).

So how was Jesus "greater than Jonah"? We see his superiority in many ways. While Jonah ran away from his calling to preach the gospel of repentance to those far away from God, Jesus embraced that calling, beginning his ministry by calling people to "Repent, for the kingdom of heaven is near." And while it was Jonah's disobedience that put him in the belly of the fish, it was Jesus' obedience that put him in the grave. Jesus was "obedient to death—even death on a cross!" (Philippians 2:8, NIV).

Jonah wept because the people of Nineveh repented, but Jesus wept over the city of Jerusalem because they would not repent.

Jonah desired to die rather than embrace God's will because his heart was so hard and his hatred for the Assyrians was so strong. Jesus submitted to God's will, saying, "I want your will to be done, not mine" (Matthew 26:39), not because he wanted to die, but because his love for sinners was so great.

But perhaps most significantly, while a guilty Jonah was thrown off the ship into the raging sea by sailors who were saying, "O LORD, . . . don't make us die for this man's sin" (Jonah 1:14), an innocent Jesus cast himself into the storm of God's judgment to die for the sins of guilty people. He died so we don't have to.

† *Sinless Savior, my disobedience deserves nothing less than being tossed into the stormy seas of your judgment. But instead, you have absorbed that judgment and granted me mercy. Your obedience covers my disobedience.*

DECEMBER 10
HIS ORIGINS ARE
FROM THE DISTANT PAST

Micah, like most of the prophets, was burdened with questions about Israel's future. He knew that the Messiah was Israel's ultimate hope. He even knew where the Messiah would be born; he just didn't know when. He saw the outlines of the One who was coming to save his people, but he could not see him clearly.

> But you, O Bethlehem Ephrathah,
> > are only a small village among all the people of Judah.
> Yet a ruler of Israel will come from you,
> > one whose origins are from the distant past.
> The people of Israel will be abandoned to their enemies
> > until the woman in labor gives birth. . . .
> He will stand to lead his flock with the LORD's strength. . . .
> > He will be the source of peace. (Micah 5:2-5)

The religious leaders in Jesus' day knew that Micah 5 was a reference to the Messiah. That's why they told King Herod to send the wise men to Bethlehem to look for the baby king (Matthew 2:1-6). And because the people were confident that the Messiah would come from Bethlehem, they were confused by the fact that Jesus was raised in Nazareth (John 7:41-43).

But Jesus' birth in Bethlehem may not be the most striking thing about this prophecy. Micah wrote that the child born to a woman in Bethlehem will be "one whose origins are from the distant past." Though the Messiah would be born in Bethlehem, that was not the beginning of his life. He would be a ruler whose life would stretch from the distant past into a glorious future, describing the Messiah as eternal—not just a man, but God himself.

And that is exactly what Jesus said about himself when he told the religious leaders, "I tell you the truth, before Abraham was even born, I AM!" (John 8:58). Jesus stands before and beyond the limits of a human lifetime, leading his flock, bringing us into the peace of his fold.

✝ *Eternal Word who was with God in the beginning and who is God, you have existed uncreated into eternity past and you will rule and reign into eternity future. Gazing on your glorious eternal nature brings me peace.*

THE MESSENGER WITH GOOD NEWS!

The long shadow of Assyrian supremacy cast a cloud over God's people. Israel, Judah's sister kingdom to the north, had already fallen to the Assyrians, and now Judah faced the same imperial enemy.

Into this gloom and doom, God sent his prophet, Nahum, whose name means "comfort." And that is exactly what Nahum's prophecy brought to Judah—the message that her Assyrian oppressors would face utter destruction. Nahum's oracle after oracle of certain and irrevocable judgment on Assyria comforted the people of Judah, assuring them that even though it may have seemed slow in coming, God was enacting his righteous judgment on their enemies.

Nahum's prophecy proved true when Nineveh was destroyed in 612 BC, marking the end of the great empire. The great Assyrian city of Nineveh was never rebuilt and the Assyrians disappeared from history. This fulfillment of God's promise gives us confidence that the day is coming when all of God's enemies will be destroyed, never again to persecute the people of God.

In the middle of Nahum's menacing pronouncement of woes is the Good News of the gospel: "Look! A messenger is coming over the mountains with good news! He is bringing a message of peace" (1:15).

Who is the messenger and what is his message? In the New Testament book of Acts, Peter was very specific about this messenger and his good news:

> This is the message of Good News for the people of Israel—that there is peace with God through Jesus Christ, who is Lord of all. . . . Jesus is the one appointed by God to be the judge of all—the living and the dead. He is the one all the prophets testified about, saying that everyone who believes in him will have their sins forgiven through his name. (Acts 10:36, 42-43)

Nahum's "good news" was that the God who brings judgment also provides an escape from judgment. The One who executes judgment on the enemies of God is also an emissary for peace with God.

† *Messenger of peace with God, I know that judgment is what I deserve. Yet I have heard your message and it is such good news to me! I don't have to fear the judgment I deserve because you, God's Messenger, have taken God's wrath upon yourself. This news comforts me and brings me peace.*

DECEMBER 12

The One Who Makes Us Right with God

Unlike some of the other prophets, Habakkuk didn't call people to repentance. When he began to prophesy, it was too late for that. Instead, he predicted the destruction of Judah. But even though destruction was surely coming for the nation, Habakkuk held out hope for those who would hold fast their confidence in God.

"Look at the proud! They trust in themselves, and their lives are crooked," Habakkuk said, before drawing a contrast with the righteous people, "but the righteous will live by their faithfulness to God" (Habakkuk 2:4). The prophet was saying that no matter what happened, the righteous would put all of their hope in God—and he would save them.

Habakkuk didn't clarify how righteousness and faith are related or how sinful, faithless people will become righteous, faithful people. But Habakkuk's words do become clear when Paul speaks in the New Testament about justification by faith. In his letters to the Romans and Galatians, Paul made it clear that the righteousness God requires is the perfect righteousness of Christ, which he gives to us as a gift. We could never work up this righteousness on our own. But where we are faithless, he is faithful. He imputes his own perfect righteousness to us when we recognize our need for it and turn toward him to receive it.

Habakkuk couldn't see exactly how God was going to make sinful men and women righteous. He couldn't see how God would preserve his holy hatred for sin and yet offer his merciful forgiveness to sinners. God didn't reveal that much to Habakkuk, but he did reveal it to Paul who wrote,

> God, with undeserved kindness, declares that we are righteous. He did this through Christ Jesus when he freed us from the penalty for our sins. For God presented Jesus as the sacrifice for sin. People are made right with God when they believe that Jesus sacrificed his life, shedding his blood. This sacrifice shows that God was being fair when he held back and did not punish those who sinned in times past, for he was looking ahead and including them in what he would do in this present time. (Romans 3:24-26)

† *Provider of my righteousness, how could I ever hope to stand before a holy God and expect anything less than judgment? It's only because of what you've done and what you've given to me—your own perfect righteousness. I simply can't work it up on my own, so I gladly and gratefully receive it from you.*

DECEMBER 13
OUR SINGING SAVIOR

The prophet Zephaniah delivered the word of the Lord during the reign of Josiah, king of Judah, when the people turned toward God in repentance. Zephaniah prophesied that God was going to purge and purify his people Israel. This will bring God so much joy that he will break out into singing. Zephaniah prophesied:

> On that day the announcement to Jerusalem will be,
>> "Cheer up, Zion! Don't be afraid!
> For the LORD your God is living among you.
>> He is a mighty savior.
> He will take delight in you with gladness.
>> With his love, he will calm all your fears.
>> He will rejoice over you with joyful songs." (Zephaniah 3:16-17)

Zephaniah helped God's people look forward to "that day" when the Lord their God will not only dwell in the Temple but will live among them. John described it this way, "The Word became human and made his home among us" (John 1:14). When Jesus lived among his people, there was cause for cheer and not for fear, just as Zephaniah said. "God sent his Son into the world not to judge the world, but to save the world through him" (John 3:17). He is a mighty Savior. With his love, he calms our fears about the wrath of God we know we deserve. And perhaps most surprisingly, he rejoices over us.

When do we see Jesus rejoicing? He helps us to see his rejoicing heart by telling stories. In Luke 15, Jesus told the parable of the shepherd who finds his lost sheep and says, "Rejoice with me" (15:6). He told the parable of the woman who loses a valuable coin and when she finds it, she calls her friends and neighbors, saying, "Rejoice with me" (15:9). Perhaps best known of all is the story of the father of the Prodigal Son who returns home. The joyful father says, "We must celebrate with a feast, for this son of mine was dead and has now returned to life" (15:23-24). Jesus was picturing for us how his heart bursts into joyful song when the lost are found. And not Jesus only, but all of heaven, for Jesus also said that "there is joy in the presence of God's angels when even one sinner repents" (Luke 15:10).

✝ *My mighty Savior who delights in me, loves me, calms me, and rejoices over me, drown out the voice of the evil one who condemns me. Help me to hear your song of joy, forgiveness, and acceptance.*

DECEMBER 14
FILLED WITH HIS GLORY

The book of Haggai contains a series of messages from the Lord delivered to his people after the Exile. Many of them returned to Jerusalem. They planned to rebuild their destroyed Temple, but they got sidetracked fixing up their own homes. Through his prophet Haggai, God encouraged a change in priorities: "Why are you living in luxurious houses while my house lies in ruins?" (1:4). So the people began to restore God's Temple, but they soon realized with great sadness that it would never be as glorious as Solomon's Temple had been. So God sent another message, assuring them that he would once again fill his Temple with his glory:

> This is what the LORD of Heaven's Armies says: In just a little while I will again shake the heavens and the earth, the oceans and the dry land. I will shake all the nations, and the treasures of all the nations will be brought to this Temple. I will fill this place with glory, says the LORD of Heaven's Armies. (2:6-7)

How was this prophecy fulfilled? When did or will this shaking come? Like so many of the Old Testament prophecies, it is being fulfilled in stages, with a partial fulfillment in the coming of Jesus and a final fulfillment yet to come.

By the time Jesus began his ministry, Herod had rebuilt the Temple in Jerusalem. And the Lord did indeed fill his Temple with his glory just by Jesus stepping into it and beginning to teach.

But this was not the end of the shaking or the ultimate filling with glory that God had in mind. Jesus predicted another shaking of the Temple that would come when he was crucified. Jesus said, "'Destroy this temple, and in three days I will raise it up.' . . . When Jesus said 'this temple,' he meant his own body" (John 2:19, 21).

And we know there is more shaking and more filling with glory to come. That glory will be the reality we live in for all eternity in heaven. John described his vision of heaven, saying, "I saw no temple in the city, for the Lord God Almighty and the Lamb are its temple" (Revelation 21:22).

✝ *O Shaker of the heavens and the earth, shake me from my complacency so I will strengthen my grip on you for the final shaking. I thank you and I worship you with holy fear and awe, for you have given me the undeserved gift of a place in your unshakable Kingdom.*

DECEMBER 15
MY KING IN ZION

Throughout the Old Testament we read about Zion, the city of God. But what is Zion? And where is it?

Zion is first mentioned in 2 Samuel 5:7, where we read that "David captured the fortress of Zion, which is now called the City of David." David brought the Ark of the Covenant into this fortress and so it became the center of worship and of God's presence. The more than 150 times Zion is mentioned in the Old Testament, it refers to the city of Jerusalem. But Zion is not just an alternate name for the city of Jerusalem; it also expressed that this was the place where God was present and near to his people. From Zion, God provided blessing, deliverance, and help to his people. For example, David asked rhetorically, "Who will come from Mount Zion to rescue Israel?" (Psalms 14:7; 53:6).

But Zion—the City of David, the earthly Jerusalem—was not the ideal city. Enemies invaded and decimated it in the form of conquering armies as well as pagan idols. God's people began to see that the Zion they loved had to be pointing to a future Zion, a perfected Zion, where God's King would rule in perfection and peace. Joel prophesied, "Then you will know that I, the LORD your God, live in Zion, my holy mountain. Jerusalem will be holy forever, and foreign armies will never conquer her again" (Joel 3:17).

David wrote about God's reign in another psalm, "I have installed my King on Zion, my holy hill" (Psalm 2:6, NIV). And Zechariah prophesied the arrival of this King:

Rejoice, O people of Zion!
Shout in triumph, O people of Jerusalem!
Look, your king is coming to you. (Zechariah 9:9)

Jesus is the King of Zion. And when we turn to Christ, we enter into Zion: "You have not come to a physical mountain. . . . You have come to Mount Zion, to the city of the living God, the heavenly Jerusalem. . . . You have come to Jesus" (Hebrews 12:18, 22, 24).

† *King of Zion, I have come to you, and in you I find the peace and safety your people have always longed for. You are on your throne in Zion, and one day you will welcome me into your heavenly city.*

DECEMBER 16
LOWLY AND RIDING ON A DONKEY

In order to present themselves in all their power and splendor, ancient kings would ride into the cities they ruled over astride a stout, white stallion. But according to Zechariah, this is not how Israel's coming Messiah-King will enter Jerusalem:

> Look, your king is coming to you.
> He is righteous and victorious,
> yet he is humble, riding on a donkey—
> riding on a donkey's colt. (9:9)

Zechariah's prophecy revealed unexpected qualities about the Messiah. He will not be a tyrant from another empire, but a people's king, coming for their benefit. He will not arrive on a warrior steed to conquer or enslave them, but to free them and bring peace to them.

But still Israel looked for a great conquering military leader to come into Jerusalem with his armies to expunge the filthy Gentile Romans from the land. Even though they had the prophecy from Zechariah, they didn't recognize—or perhaps did not want to recognize—what Jesus was saying about himself when he entered Jerusalem riding on a young borrowed donkey (Matthew 21:2-5; John 12:14-15).

Why did Jesus choose to ride into Jerusalem in this way? Matthew explained, "This took place to fulfill what was spoken through the prophet" (Matthew 21:4, NIV), quoting Zechariah's prophecy. Jesus was emerging from obscurity to make clear his claims as Messiah-King and as Savior. By arriving on a donkey instead of a warhorse, Jesus was saying, "I am not coming to slay you, but to serve you; not with sword but with salvation."

The day is still to come when Jesus will enter Jerusalem on the most valiant white horse the world has ever seen (Revelation 19:11). His heart will not be burdened with the weight of offering himself as a sacrificial Lamb for lost sinners. That victory is forever won! At that time, he will come as a conquering King! The victorious processional parade into Jerusalem will find Jesus Christ riding atop a white horse, victorious in battle and riding with the full regalia of a mighty King's majesty into the city of God.

† *You have come gently, my King, announcing the day of salvation, and still you hold the door open. But one day that door will close, and you will come swiftly to judge all those who have refused to bow.*

DECEMBER 17
SOLD FOR THIRTY PIECES OF SILVER

The prophet Zechariah described a shepherd rejected by the flock. The shepherd requested pay for services rendered:

> I said to them, "If you like, give me my wages, whatever I am worth; but only if you want to." So they counted out for my wages thirty pieces of silver.
>
> And the LORD said to me, "Throw it to the potter"—this magnificent sum at which they valued me! So I took the thirty coins and threw them to the potter in the Temple of the LORD. (Zechariah 11:12-13)

Matthew practically quoted Zechariah when he recorded events of Jesus' final week. "Judas . . . went to the leading priests and asked, 'How much will you pay me to betray Jesus to you?' And they gave him thirty pieces of silver" (26:14-15). It was an insulting sum—the price of a slave. He had no value as far as they were concerned, no more value than a slave in the marketplace. The chief priests used the thirty pieces of silver Judas eventually threw back at them to buy the potter's field as a cemetery for foreigners that came to be known as the Field of Blood (27:3-8).

Then Matthew wrote: "This fulfilled the prophecy of Jeremiah that says, 'They took the thirty pieces of silver—the price at which he was valued by the people of Israel, and purchased the potter's field, as the LORD directed'" (27:9-10). Since there is no exact quotation in Jeremiah for this, we recognize that Matthew was doing something common in his day—creating a composite quotation of more than one Scripture but referring to only one of its sources by name. He was combining themes and phrases from both Jeremiah 32, where the prophet bought a field near Jerusalem, and Zechariah 11.

Matthew was not suggesting here that what has happened is the fulfillment of actual predictive prophecy, and he was not inventing history to match prophecy. But he was making the point to his Jewish readers that God was at work, even in the tragic events of Jesus' betrayal and Judas's death, just as he had been at work in the highly symbolic ministries of the prophets Zechariah and Jeremiah. Matthew was convinced that the key events in salvation history all happened under the guiding hand of God's providence.

† *Precious Jesus, how valuable you are, and yet you were betrayed for such a paltry sum. If you could entrust yourself to the justice of God when betrayed and belittled so unjustly, you can empower me to do likewise.*

DECEMBER 18
THE ONE THEY PIERCED

Zechariah 12 describes a coming day when God will begin to destroy all of the nations who have attacked Jerusalem.

> Then I will pour out a spirit of grace and prayer on the family of David and on the people of Jerusalem. They will look on me whom they have pierced and mourn for him as for an only son. They will grieve bitterly for him as for a firstborn son who has died. (12:10)

The apostle John pointed to Jesus' crucifixion as a fulfillment of Zechariah's prophecy:

> When [the soldiers] came to Jesus, they saw that he was already dead, so they didn't break his legs. One of the soldiers, however, pierced his side with a spear, and immediately blood and water flowed out. . . . These things happened in fulfillment of the Scriptures that say, "Not one of his bones will be broken," and "They will look on the one they pierced." (John 19:33-34, 36-37)

But the mourning over the One who was pierced does not seem to take place at the Crucifixion. While a few mourned his death, most cheered it. And the victory described here didn't happen at that time either. Soon Jerusalem would be trampled and destroyed, not her enemies. So this aspect of Zechariah's prophecy must still be in the future.

Just as John saw a partial fulfillment of this prophecy in the death of Jesus, so was he given a vision of the prophecy's final fulfillment, which he recorded in Revelation:

> Look! He comes with the clouds of heaven.
>> And everyone will see him—
>> even those who pierced him.
> And all the nations of the world
>> will mourn for him.
> Yes! Amen! (Revelation 1:7)

✝ *Son who was pierced, Lamb who was slain, I look to you now and I see your pierced side. I mourn—for my sin that required such a sacrifice, my cold rejection of you, and my apathy toward you. Thank you for the spirit of grace poured out on me that has caused me to see you and mourn so redemptively.*

DECEMBER 19
FOUNTAIN OF CLEANSING

Throughout the book of Zechariah, God says over and over and in a variety of ways that he is going to do something good for Jerusalem. In chapter 13, he made what is, perhaps, the most important promise of all: "On that day a fountain will be opened for the dynasty of David and for the people of Jerusalem, a fountain to cleanse them from all their sins and impurity" (13:1).

The prophet Zechariah promised that at some future time, a fountain would be opened that would take away their sin and guilt. In other words, Zechariah was telling them that while the animal sacrifices expressed faith in God's promise to provide cleansing from sin, the day was coming when that fountain of cleansing would flow freely and abundantly, and the animal sacrifices would no longer be needed.

The writer to the Hebrews explained this fountain and our need for it:

> The sacrifices under that system were repeated again and again, year after year, but they were never able to provide perfect cleansing for those who came to worship. If they could have provided perfect cleansing, the sacrifices would have stopped, for the worshipers would have been purified once for all time, and their feelings of guilt would have disappeared.
>
> But instead, those sacrifices actually reminded them of their sins year after year. For it is not possible for the blood of bulls and goats to take away sins. . . . Our guilty consciences have been sprinkled with Christ's blood to make us clean, and our bodies have been washed with pure water. (Hebrews 10:1-4, 22)

For anyone to be saved from sin, a fountain of cleansing would have to be opened up. This fountain would not be the neck of a spotless lamb, but the pierced side of the Son of God. Some people resist and refuse this fountain, but it is the only way to be cleansed from the sin that stains our thoughts and motives and deeds.

† *O Fountain of cleansing, how I need to be washed by you, to be cleansed from the contamination and condemnation of my sin. I see the cost of this fountain that flows from your wounded side, and I worship you.*

DECEMBER 20

MY SHEPHERD, MY PARTNER

Zechariah 13 depicts a scene in which the people of Israel have rejected their Good Shepherd, the Messiah. Yet it is not the people that God sets his sword against:

> "Awake, O sword, against my shepherd,
>   the man who is my partner,"
>   says the LORD of Heaven's Armies.
> "Strike down the shepherd,
>   and the sheep will be scattered,
>   and I will turn against the lambs." (13:7)

Who is this shepherd? Obviously he is no ordinary herder of sheep and goats, because the Lord calls him "my shepherd." He is human—"the man"— yet divine—"my partner." Surely this is a revelation of Christ in both his divine and human nature. The man, the smitten Shepherd, is spoken of by God as his partner, sharing an equality with him and yet distinct from him.

Zechariah included something shocking here—that Yahweh himself will use the sword against his Shepherd. It is an echo of Isaiah's words about the Messiah, that "it was the LORD's good plan to crush him" (53:10).

Jesus drew on this prophecy of Zechariah, identifying himself as this Shepherd who will be struck by the sword of God. The night before his death, he said to his disciples: "Tonight all of you will desert me. For the Scriptures say, 'God will strike the Shepherd, and the sheep of the flock will be scattered'" (Matthew 26:31).

When the soldiers arrested Jesus, the disciples fled in all directions. Just as Zechariah prophesied, his sheep were scattered. After his death, they barricaded themselves behind locked doors in fear of the Jewish religious leaders. A few years later the flock of Israel was dispersed as refugees when Roman soldiers tore down the walls of Jerusalem and destroyed the Temple in AD 70. By rejecting the Shepherd, the nation brought judgment upon itself. Even so, a remnant will be saved. "They will call on my name, and I will answer them. I will say, 'These are my people,' and they will say, 'The LORD is our God'" (Zechariah 13:9).

✝ *Shepherd, stricken by God for me so that I might live, how grateful I am to have been brought into your fold, to be a part of the remnant that you have saved and brought to yourself.*

DECEMBER 21
THE KING COMES

We first see the Kingdom of God in the Garden of Eden where Adam and Eve lived in willing obedience to God's word and rule. But the Kingdom was destroyed by their sin, and the rest of the Bible is the story of God restoring a people to be the willing subjects of his perfect rule.

When God promised Abraham that his descendants would possess the Promised Land and be the people of God under his authority, he was describing his Kingdom. When he rescued Israel out of captivity in Egypt, it was so that he could bring them into the place where the Kingdom would be established. Then, while Israel's kings revealed many aspects of the nature of the Kingdom of God, these human kings—Saul, David, Solomon, and those who followed—inevitably failed to measure up. Human kings and kingdoms always fall short of the glory of God's true Kingdom. So in the face of the judgment on Israel's sin, the prophets restated the promise of the Kingdom as something that would be fulfilled in the future, and the Israelites, living in exile, longed for that day.

But return from exile failed to produce the Kingdom foretold by prophets such as Isaiah, Jeremiah, and Ezekiel. Haggai, Zechariah, and Malachi, prophesying after the Exile, continued to direct the eyes of Israel to a great future day when the perfect and everlasting Kingdom of God would be revealed. The Old Testament ends on that note of promise and expectation: "And the LORD will be king over all the earth. On that day there will be one LORD—his name alone will be worshiped" (Zechariah 14:9). But there was no fulfillment in sight as the Jews endured nearly four hundred years of prophetic silence.

Then, into this silence, Jesus appeared, saying, "The time promised by God has come at last! . . . The Kingdom of God is near! Repent of your sins and believe the Good News!" (Mark 1:15).

The Kingdom was "near" because Jesus had come. Jesus is the fulfillment of the promises, but still, the fact that God's Kingdom will triumph could only be received by faith. The consummation of the Kingdom is still to come. "When Christ, who is your life, is revealed to the whole world, you will share in all his glory" (Colossians 3:4).

† *My King, you have come! You have plunged your flag into this earth by your Cross, and the consummation of your Kingdom is sure. Come quickly, Lord Jesus, and take your throne. We long to be your glad subjects.*

DECEMBER 22
OUR PERFECT PRIEST

None of Israel's high priests ever lived up to what God intended for those he set apart to serve him in his Temple. Aaron sinned by leading the people in false worship. His sons sinned by offering unholy fire on God's altar. Eli sinned by failing to discipline his sons who were such wicked priests that God struck them both down on the same day. Eventually the priesthood broke down altogether, so that the Old Testament ends with this warning:

> "The words of a priest's lips should preserve knowledge of God, and people should go to him for instruction, for the priest is the messenger of the LORD of Heaven's Armies. But you priests have left God's paths. Your instructions have caused many to stumble into sin. You have corrupted the covenant I made with the Levites," says the LORD of Heaven's Armies. (Malachi 2:7-8)

While the priesthood was responsible for its sinful failure, it was never meant to last forever, but rather to prepare God's people for the perfect Priest God would send. Jesus came, not to fit into the earthly system of priestly ministry, but to fulfill and put an end to that human priesthood, and to orient our attention to his ministry on our behalf in heaven.

As our perfect High Priest, Jesus ministers in a superior place—not in the Temple, but in heaven itself. "For Christ did not enter into a holy place made with human hands, which was only a copy of the true one in heaven. He entered into heaven itself to appear now before God on our behalf" (Hebrews 9:24). Jesus ministers to us with superior righteousness—not external, like a holy set of clothes, but intrinsic to his own holy person. "He is holy and blameless, unstained by sin" (7:26). Jesus ministers to us with superior sympathy—he "understands our weaknesses, for he faced all of the same testings we do, yet he did not sin" (4:15). Jesus ministers to us with superior longevity—"There were many priests under the old system, for death prevented them from remaining in office. But because Jesus lives forever, his priesthood lasts forever" (7:23-24). And Jesus ministers to us, offering a superior sacrifice—not by the repeated sacrifices of animals, but with the once-for-all sacrifice of himself. "With his own blood—not the blood of goats and calves—he entered the Most Holy Place once for all time and secured our redemption forever" (9:12).

† *Jesus, my merciful and faithful High Priest, you are the kind of priest I need because you are holy and blameless, unstained by sin.*

THE LORD COMES TO HIS TEMPLE

The people in the prophet Malachi's day had grievances with God who seemed, in their estimation, to be slow in dealing with the wicked people all around them. "Where is the God of justice?" they asked indignantly (Malachi 2:17).

And through his prophet, God answered, saying, "Suddenly the Lord you are seeking will come to his temple" (3:1, NIV).

These complainers were seeking their promised Messiah, the One they anticipated would enact justice in a world where it seemed there was none. But perhaps they were surprised to hear where Messiah would begin setting things right in the world. He "will come to his temple." The Lord would begin setting things right—not in the godless world around them, but in his very own house.

Just as God promised, the Lord came to his Temple. Shortly after his birth, Jesus' parents took him to the Temple where they offered a purification offering. Later, when he was twelve years old, his parents searched for him for three days only to find him in the Temple, sitting among the religious teachers, listening to them and asking questions. During his ministry Jesus taught in the Temple and healed people there.

He also dealt with the wickedness he found in the Temple and in its leaders. Luke wrote, "Jesus entered the Temple and began to drive out the people selling animals for sacrifices. He said to them, 'The Scriptures declare, "My Temple will be a house of prayer," but you have turned it into a den of thieves'" (Luke 19:45-46). The Messiah came to set things right in his Temple, but it didn't sit well at all with the religious leaders. "After that, he taught daily in the Temple, but the leading priests, the teachers of religious law, and the other leaders of the people began planning how to kill him" (Luke 19:47).

Our God of justice will never let evil go unpunished, even when—and especially when—he finds it in his own house. As Peter wrote, "For the time has come for judgment, and it must begin with God's household" (1 Peter 4:17).

† *God of justice, how grateful I am that when you poured out your wrath on wickedness, it fell on Jesus and not on me. I long for you to come and set things right in the place you make your home now—in my body. Come to this temple and drive out what is displeasing to you.*

DECEMBER 24
REFINING FIRE

The prophet Malachi spoke of Jesus when he said:

> The Lord you are seeking will suddenly come to his Temple. The messenger of the covenant, whom you look for so eagerly, is surely coming. . . . He will be like a blazing fire that refines metal, or like a strong soap that bleaches clothes. He will sit like a refiner of silver, burning away the dross. (Malachi 3:1-3)

What does it mean that Jesus will "sit like a refiner of silver, burning away the dross"? In ancient times, a workman would take a piece of ore hewn from the earth, crush it into pieces, and place it in a piece of pottery that he would then thrust into a fire. The refiner carefully tended the fire, knowing just how intense the flame needed to be to soften the ore and cause the impurities to rise to the top so they could be skimmed off, leaving a bubbling treasure of molten metal. The refiner was patient, knowing just how long the metal should stay in the fire so that more and more dull impurities would rise to the surface. Finally, he would look into the liquid silver and see what he had been working for and waiting for—his own reflection.

Jesus came into this world and into our lives like a refiner's fire. Of course, we have good reason to fear fire. Fires destroy and consume. But a refiner's fire is different. A refiner's fire purifies. When the fires of affliction burn in our lives, our Refiner is at work burning away the impurities of our pride and apathy and unbelief. He is removing what is unfit and impure, transforming the ordinary ore of our lives into a shining treasure that reflects his image.

The day will come when we'll be glad we allowed the Refiner to do his work in us. "These trials will show that your faith is genuine," Peter wrote in 1 Peter 1:7. "It is being tested as fire tests and purifies gold—though your faith is far more precious than mere gold. So when your faith remains strong through many trials, it will bring you much praise and glory and honor on the day when Jesus Christ is revealed to the whole world."

† *Blazing Fire, how foolishly I resist the fire of your refinement. I forget that you know exactly how intense the flame needs to be and how long I need to stay in the fire. Plunge me into the fire if you must, to make me reflect your image.*

DECEMBER 25

WHO CAN STAND?

A question is repeated several times in the Old Testament, and though it receives no direct answer, it is a worthy question to consider.

Those carrying the Ark of the Lord, fearful of death after God killed seventy men because they looked into the Ark, cried out, "Who is able to stand in the presence of the LORD, this holy God?" (1 Samuel 6:20). David asked, "Who may climb the mountain of the LORD? Who may stand in his holy place?" (Psalm 24:3). Malachi asked the same question this way, "Who will be able to endure it when he comes? Who will be able to stand and face him when he appears?" (Malachi 3:2).

The Old Testament writers rightly asked the question, "Who can stand before a holy God?" Finally there is an answer to the question. Jesus made it possible for sinners to stand before God. In fact, Jesus' sacrifice not only makes it possible for us to stand before God when we are united with him, but because of what Jesus has done for us, nothing and no one can effectively stand against us.

Paul asked the question, "If God is for us, who can ever be against us?" (Romans 8:31). In giving us Jesus, God showed us that he is not against us; he is for us! Paul continued,

> Who dares accuse us whom God has chosen for his own? No one—for God himself has given us right standing with himself. Who then will condemn us? No one—for Christ Jesus died for us and was raised to life for us, and he is sitting in the place of honor at God's right hand, pleading for us. (Romans 8:33-34)

On our own, we could never dare to stand before the withering judgment of the holy God. But Jesus has satisfied God's justice, and now he advocates for us so that we need not fear.

So when we hear Malachi ask the question, "Who will be able to stand and face him when he appears?" we can answer, "I will be able to stand and face him. But not because of anything I am or anything I've done. Only because Jesus is mine and I am his."

† *Jesus, you have brought me into this place of undeserved privilege where I can stand, not cowering in fear of judgment, but confident and joyful in anticipation of sharing God's glory.*

DECEMBER 26
SUN OF RIGHTEOUSNESS

The prophet Malachi spoke of Jesus when he delivered a message from God, saying, "But for you who fear my name, the Sun of Righteousness will rise with healing in his wings. And you will go free, leaping with joy like calves let out to pasture" (Malachi 4:2).

Malachi had just issued a warning that those who proudly resist God will be consumed by fire on the day of judgment. But he had a completely different message for those who humbly fear God, assuring his hearers of a completely different reality. For those who fear God, when Jesus comes, he will bring light where there was darkness, security where there was danger, health where there was sickness, freedom where there was bondage, and joy where there was gloom. Jesus will come into a world of chaos and injustice and set things right with beams of his glorious righteousness.

Surely this Sun of Righteousness, Jesus, flooded the world with healing. Matthew recorded that "people soon began bringing to [Jesus] all who were sick. And whatever their sickness or disease, or if they were demon possessed or epileptic or paralyzed—he healed them all" (Matthew 4:24). As Jesus healed the paralytics and those with fever and hemorrhaging and leprosy, he was showing that he has power not only to heal our bodies, but also to heal our souls from our sin-sickness.

And Jesus brought freedom. To everyone who was trapped by empty religiosity and life-depleting sin, Jesus offers a yoke that is easy and a burden that is light. This freedom is not temporary or merely a mirage. "If the Son sets you free, you are truly free" (John 8:36).

When the sun begins to shine with more intensity after a cold and wet winter, we turn our faces toward it, close our eyes, and welcome the rays of warmth that penetrate us to the core. How much more do we need the Sun of Righteousness to rise over us, shining his rays of healing and wholeness and joy, penetrating us to the core with the warmth of his presence!

✝ *Sun of Righteousness, how I need your light and warmth to penetrate the dark and cold places in my heart. I need your power to heal the broken places in my life. I need release from the bondage of searching for joy apart from you. Rise over me and in me. Set me free.*

DECEMBER 27
PREPARED BY REPENTANCE

The Jewish people remembered the prophecy found in Malachi 4:5: "Look, I am sending you the prophet Elijah before the great and dreadful day of the LORD arrives." They were on the lookout for this One who would be like the prophet Elijah.

Zechariah, the father of John the Baptist, remembered Malachi's prophecy, especially when the angel of the Lord said to him about his son,

> He will turn many Israelites to the Lord their God. He will be a man with the spirit and power of Elijah. He will prepare the people for the coming of the Lord. He will turn the hearts of the fathers to their children, and he will cause those who are rebellious to accept the wisdom of the godly. (Luke 1:16-17)

Did you catch what John the Baptist would do? He would prepare people for the coming of the Lord Jesus. And how would he prepare them? He would "turn" them. He would turn them away from rigorous law-keeping and empty ritual toward their God.

But shouldn't God's people naturally have their hearts turned toward God? Yes, we should. But we don't. The old hymn captures it perfectly: "Prone to wander, Lord, I feel it. Prone to leave the God I love." We have hearts that, left on their own, turn away from God.

But God has not left us on our own. Not only has he come to us in the person of Jesus, he sent ahead of Jesus one who would help to prepare our hearts to receive him, one who would call us to repentance. God has extended mercy that frees us from the fear of judgment.

Just as John prepared the people for the coming of Jesus, so also we prepare for the coming of Jesus in our lives when we embrace John's message of repentance. Repentance means turning the direction of our lives and the affections of our hearts so that we become oriented to God and love the things he loves. Repentance is altering what we rely on in life, what we hope in, what we are counting on for salvation.

God has turned his heart toward us in Jesus Christ, and he's inviting us to turn our hearts toward him in repentance.

† *I hear the voice calling, "Prepare the way for the Lord," and that's what I want to do. Show me where my heart is hard toward you or turned away from you so I can welcome you gladly into my life.*

DECEMBER 28
THE GRACE THAT WAS TO COME

We tend to think of the Old Testament in terms of law and the New Testament in terms of grace. But in reality, God has always dealt with his people in grace. In the Old Testament, it is the Hebrew word *khen*, which is most often translated "grace" or "favor." Grace is the good pleasure of God that inclines him to freely bestow blessing on undeserving people.

We see God's grace in the Old Testament when, rather than destroying Adam and Eve for their sin, the judgment of the curse came with a promise of grace. We see it in the saving of Noah and the continuation of a godly line. We see it when Lot was spared from the judgment falling on Sodom. God, who is perfect in justice, was able to pour out his grace on undeserving sinners in the Old Testament in anticipation of what Christ would do. Grace is, and has always been, more than a sentiment or an attitude on God's part. God's grace has always centered on and flowed out of Jesus Christ.

Sinners have always been saved the same way—by grace through faith. The people and prophets of Old Testament times looked *forward* in faith to the coming of the Messiah and his work of grace on their behalf. Our faith looks *back* to the Messiah and his work of grace on our behalf. While the Old Testament prophets had only the *prophetic* record to examine to understand the saving work of Christ, we have the advantage of the *historical* record concerning the coming of Christ and his death on our behalf at Calvary.

Peter told the people of his day that the Old Testament prophets spoke of salvation in terms of "the grace that was to come to you" (1 Peter 1:10, NIV). The people in Peter's day had personally seen and experienced the grace that finally came in the person of Jesus. Though they had been slow to understand, it was exactly what Jesus had told them when he said,

> Blessed are your eyes, because they see; and your ears, because they hear. I tell you the truth, many prophets and righteous people longed to see what you see, but they didn't see it. And they longed to hear what you hear, but they didn't hear it. (Matthew 13:16-17)

Jesus personified the grace that generations had longed for. He is the grace who has come to us.

† *Great Grace that was to come, you finally came! And you were better than the prophets and people of the Old Testament even imagined you would be. How blessed I am to see your work of salvation in the clear light of the Cross.*

DECEMBER 29
OUR HOPE IN FAILURE

In many ways, the Old Testament is a record of repeated human failure; it contains very few real "success" stories. Only three chapters into the book of Genesis, Adam and Eve sin, perhaps the most impactful human failure of all time. A couple of chapters later, the human race has become so wicked that God decides to destroy everyone. From Noah's drunken exposure, to Abraham's lying and giving Sarah to a king, to Jacob and his sons' deceit, human failures far outnumber the successes.

In Exodus, we find the covenant God made with Moses broken "before the ink has dried" (so to speak). In Leviticus, just as the priesthood God established with Aaron and his sons begins its service in the Tabernacle, Aaron's sons are consumed by fire because of their irreverent abuse of their holy calling. In the book of Numbers, the Israelites failed to go into the land for fear of the "giants" who possessed it. In Numbers, even Moses, the greatest leader the nation had yet known, failed in such a way that he was barred from entering Canaan.

What do these repeated failures reveal? Paul tells us in his first letter to the Corinthians: "These things happened to them as examples for us. They were written down to warn us who live at the end of the age. If you think you are standing strong, be careful not to fall" (10:11-12). And he says this in his letter to the Romans: "Such things were written in the Scriptures long ago to teach us. And the Scriptures give us hope and encouragement as we wait patiently for God's promises to be fulfilled" (15:4). But how can these stories caution us about our propensity to fall and give us hope at the same time?

It is only in coming to terms with human hopelessness that we can embrace biblical hope. And biblical hope is not hope for perfection or even improvement in human terms. Biblical hope is centered in Jesus Christ. Jesus is the only hope for humans who have failed.

In fact, there is only one human failure that can bar a person from sharing in the victory of God. That is the failure to grab hold of Christ, the failure to receive his grace and mercy that covers all human failure. "Look after each other so that none of you fails to receive the grace of God" (Hebrews 12:15).

† *It's as if you've been waiting for me to come to the end of myself and turn to you, Jesus. And I'm turning to you. Out of my shameful failure and loss, Jesus, I come. I come to you with only failed human effort to offer. Yet, in your grace and mercy you receive me.*

DECEMBER 30
The Day He Returns

Many of the Old Testament prophets wrote about the "Day of the Lord." We find the "day of the LORD's revenge" in Isaiah 34:8, and the "day of his fierce anger" in 13:13. Many prophets record the Lord speaking of this coming day in the first person: "the very day I punish Israel for its sins" (Amos 3:14); "the day I take away their stronghold" (Ezekiel 24:25); "the day I come for them" (Jeremiah 27:22, NIV); "the day of reckoning" (Jeremiah 10:15); "the day when I act in judgment" (Malachi 3:17); the day "I will stand and accuse" (Zephaniah 3:8). Over and over again the emphasis falls on the Lord's personal coming to intervene and bring this world to its conclusion. It is the Lord's personal intervention that makes this coming day so cataclysmic and so definitive in its outcome.

In the Old Testament prophecies about the Day of the Lord, we find the near and the distant future brought together in a single vision of things to come. The prophets saw the temporal days of the Lord—his days of judgment in their own lifetimes or shortly thereafter—as precursors of and the pattern for one final *dies irae*, the day of the divine wrath.

When the Day of the Lord is discussed in the New Testament, it exclusively refers to the second coming of Christ. We read of "the day of the Lord's return" (1 Thessalonians 5:2), "the day when our Lord Jesus Christ returns" (1 Corinthians 1:8), "the day when Christ Jesus returns" (Philippians 1:6), and "the day of Christ's return" (2:16). All these phrases refer to the same day and to the same event: the time of Christ's final and decisive visitation of this world in judgment and salvation. Paul provides insight into the agony and the glory of that day:

> He will come with his mighty angels, in flaming fire, bringing judgment on those who don't know God and on those who refuse to obey the Good News of our Lord Jesus. They will be punished with eternal destruction, forever separated from the Lord and from his glorious power. When he comes on that day, he will receive glory from his holy people—praise from all who believe. (2 Thessalonians 1:7-10)

† *Because I belong to you, Lord Jesus, the day of your return is not a day to dread; it is a day to anticipate, celebrate, and prepare for. And what a day it will be, when you return in all of your glory to do what is right and good. Place in my heart a holy fear and longing for that day.*

DECEMBER 31
THEY POINT TO ME

The Old Testament is an uncompleted story—not just because it prophesies events that have not yet happened, but also because its problems are not resolved; its longings are not satisfied.

From before the creation of humanity, God knew that people would sin. He put into place a plan to bring sinners back into an unfettered relationship with him. His plan was always centered in Christ, but to prepare his people to receive Christ and understand the significance of his work, God took his people through a number of good, but insufficient, remedies.

God gave his people the law that would show them how to live, but they couldn't live up to it. The law only condemned. God gave his people priests who would mediate for them, but the priests were corrupt and defiled God's Temple. God gave his people judges to rescue them from attackers, but they didn't listen to the judges and prostituted themselves by worshiping other gods. God gave his people kings to rule over them, but the kings oppressed the people and worshiped idols. God gave his people prophets to speak his word to them, but the people would not listen.

What was needed was a perfect law-keeper, an all-powerful judge, a gracious king, an eternal priest, and a prophet who perfectly speaks the words of God. Throughout the Old Testament, it is as if God said, "Not this . . . not this . . . not this . . ." and then, in the coming of Christ, God said, "This is it! This is the One the law, the judges, the prophets, the priests, and the kings were all pointing to."

Jesus said to the hard-hearted Jewish leaders of his day, "You search the Scriptures because you think they give you eternal life. But the Scriptures point to me!" (John 5:39). Jesus was not merely speaking of the prophecies that spoke of his coming, but of the whole of Scripture. Long before his coming, God had established the offices of prophet, priest, and king, and it had always been God's plan to save his people through prophecy, priesthood, and kingship. Jesus is the One in whom all these offices combine in perfect fulfillment.

✝ *You are the Alpha and Omega, my all in all. You write your law on my heart, you rule over me with grace, you speak to me the Word of life, and you represent me before the Father. You are everything I need to make my home at peace with God, now and forever.*

SOURCES AND ACKNOWLEDGMENTS

Writing this book has been a journey of discovery for me as I have "gone to school" on numerous biblical scholars and pastors who have shown me the beauty of Christ throughout the Old Testament through their commentaries, articles, sermons, and books. I am very grateful to Dr. Stephen Estock, Minister of Christian Education at Kirk of the Hills Presbyterian Church and Adjunct Professor of Homiletics at Covenant Theological Seminary, for his gracious theological guidance as well as his generous encouragement. Here are the sources I have relied on most heavily, all of which I commend to you for further study.

Christ in All the Scriptures by A. M. Hodgkin, originally published in 1909. Reprinted and © 1989 by Barbour and Company, Inc., Westwood, NJ

Christ in the Old Testament or *Footsteps of the Redeemer as Revealed in Type, in Prophecy, in Sacrifice, and in Personal Manifestation from the Creation to His Birth* by Rev. Henry Linton, published by Samuel Bagster and Sons, London, 1873

Christ Is All: The Gospel of the Old Testament, Genesis by Venerable Henry Law, Archdeacon of Wells, published by Weetheim and Macintosh; Hamilton, Adams, and Company, 1855

Exodus: Saved for God's Glory © 2005 by Philip Graham Ryken, published by Crossway Books, Wheaton, IL

Far As the Curse Is Found: The Covenant Story of Redemption © 2005 by Michael D. Williams, published by P & R Publishing, Phillipsburg, NJ

Genesis: Beginning and Blessing © 2004 by R. Kent Hughes, published by Crossway Books, Wheaton, IL

Gleanings in Genesis; Gleanings in Joshua; The Life of David, Volumes I & II, from Arthur Walkington Pink's Archive, 1886–1952, available online at www.pbministries.org

Gospel & Kingdom © 1981 by Graeme Goldsworthy, published by Paternoster, an imprint of Authentic Media, a division of IBS-STL UK

Isaiah: God Saves Sinners © 2005 by Raymond C. Ortlund Jr., published by Crossway Books, Wheaton, IL

Knowing Jesus Through the Old Testament © 1992 by Christopher J. H. Wright, published by InterVarsity Press, Downers Grove, IL

Leviticus: Holy God, Holy People © 2009 by Kenneth A. Mathews, published by Crossway Books, Wheaton, IL

Numbers: God's Presence in the Wilderness © 2006 by Iain M. Duguid, published by Crossway Books, Wheaton, IL

The ESV Study Bible © 2008 by Crossway Bibles, a ministry of Good News Publishers, Wheaton, IL

The Gospel According to Job © 1994 by Mike Mason, published by Crossway Books, Wheaton, IL

The Messiah in the Old Testament © 1995 by Walter C. Kaiser Jr., published by Zondervan Publishing House, Grand Rapids, MI

The NLT Study Bible © 2008 by Tyndale House Publishers, Carol Stream, IL

The Unfolding Mystery: Discovering Christ in the Old Testament © 1988 by Edmund P. Clowney, published by P & R Publishing, Phillipsburg, NJ

Recorded audio of the "Preaching Christ in a Postmodern World" seminar taught by Dr. Edmund P. Clowney and Dr. Timothy J. Keller at Reformed Theological Seminary

In addition, I gained tremendous insights from reading and listening to countless Christ-centered Old Testament sermons by Bill Baldwin, Bryan Chapell, Edmund Clowney, Sinclair Ferguson, David Helm, Tim Keller, Ray Ortlund Jr., John Piper, Wil Pounds, Kim Riddlebarger, Charles Haddon Spurgeon, and Ray Stedman.

SCRIPTURE INDEX

Genesis 1:1	January 1, 2
Genesis 1:2-3	January 3
Genesis 1:3-5	January 4
Genesis 1:16	January 4
Genesis 1:26	January 2, 5
Genesis 1:26-28	January 6
Genesis 1:31	January 26
Genesis 1:31, 2:3	January 7
Genesis 2:15-17	January 10
Genesis 2:16-17	January 11, 14
Genesis 2:18, 21-24	January 12
Genesis 2:25	January 13
Genesis 3:1, 4	January 14
Genesis 3:3	January 11
Genesis 3:6-7	January 13
Genesis 3:15	January 15, 16; February 7
Genesis 3:17	January 20
Genesis 3:17-18	January 21
Genesis 3:20	January 17
Genesis 3:22-24	January 18
Genesis 3:23	May 20
Genesis 3:24	February 2
Genesis 4:1	January 22
Genesis 4:9-11	January 23
Genesis 4:16	February 2
Genesis 4:16-17	January 24
Genesis 4:25-26	January 24
Genesis 5:3	January 25
Genesis 5:29	January 31
Genesis 6:5	August 8
Genesis 6:5-6	January 26
Genesis 6:5-9	January 27
Genesis 6:9	February 10
Genesis 6:14	January 29
Genesis 6:18	February 18
Genesis 7:23	January 29
Genesis 9:1	February 3
Genesis 9:13-15	January 30
Genesis 11:2, 6-8	February 2
Genesis 11:4-7	February 3
Genesis 11:4-5, 8	February 1
Genesis 12:1	February 4
Genesis 12:2-3	February 5, 6
Genesis 14	February 8
Genesis 15:1	February 9
Genesis 15:6	February 10, 11
Genesis 15:8	February 12
Genesis 15:13	February 13; March 6
Genesis 15:16	June 13
Genesis 15:18	February 14
Genesis 16:13	February 15
Genesis 17:1	February 16, 17, 18
Genesis 17:7	February 18; May 26; October 28
Genesis 17:8	February 14
Genesis 17:10, 13	February 17
Genesis 17:17, 21	February 19
Genesis 18:10	February 20
Genesis 18:12	February 19
Genesis 18:13-14	February 20
Genesis 18:25	February 21
Genesis 21:6	February 19
Genesis 22:1-3	February 22
Genesis 22:3	February 23
Genesis 22:6, 8	February 23
Genesis 22:7-8	February 24
Genesis 22:12	February 22
Genesis 22:13-14	February 24
Genesis 22:16-18	February 25
Genesis 22:17	February 15; June 23
Genesis 24:15-16	February 26
Genesis 25:23	February 27
Genesis 27:13	February 27
Genesis 27:19	February 27
Genesis 28:12	February 28
Genesis 28:15	February 28
Genesis 29:17	March 1
Genesis 29:30-32, 35	March 1
Genesis 32:25-26	March 2
Genesis 32:30	March 2
Genesis 35:17-18	October 29
Genesis 37:3	March 3
Genesis 37:4	March 3
Genesis 37:18	March 3, 4
Genesis 38:1-2	February 7
Genesis 40:13, 19	March 5
Genesis 41:48-49	March 7
Genesis 41:51-52	March 6
Genesis 41:55-56	March 7
Genesis 41:56-57	March 8
Genesis 43:9	March 9
Genesis 44:16	March 10
Genesis 44:32-33	March 9

Genesis 45:4-5, 7-8	March 10
Genesis 48:15-16	March 11
Genesis 49:9-10	March 12
Genesis 50:20	March 14
Exodus 2:23	March 17
Exodus 3:2-3, 5	March 16
Exodus 3:4	February 15
Exodus 3:5	February 15
Exodus 3:7-8	March 17
Exodus 3:8	March 18
Exodus 3:13-15	March 19
Exodus 3:14	March 20
Exodus 4:2-5	March 21
Exodus 4:22-23	March 22
Exodus 6:7	October 28
Exodus 9:16	April 7
Exodus 11:5	March 24
Exodus 12:3, 5-6, 8, 46	March 26
Exodus 12:6-7, 12-13	March 25
Exodus 12:6-7, 23	March 24
Exodus 12:8, 10	March 27
Exodus 12:12	March 23
Exodus 12:14, 25-27	March 29
Exodus 12:17, 19-20	March 28
Exodus 13:21-22	March 30
Exodus 14:11	April 1
Exodus 14:13-14	April 1
Exodus 14:13-14, 21-22	March 31
Exodus 15:1-2	April 1
Exodus 15:3-5, 16-18	April 2
Exodus 15:22-23, 25	April 3
Exodus 15:26	April 4
Exodus 16:3-4	April 5
Exodus 17:5-7	April 6
Exodus 19:5	April 29; October 31
Exodus 19:18	April 9
Exodus 19:18-19	April 8
Exodus 20:2	October 31
Exodus 20:6	April 29; May 25
Exodus 20:24	April 12
Exodus 23:29-30	June 9
Exodus 24:8	February 18
Exodus 25:8	April 12
Exodus 25:8-9	April 13
Exodus 25:10-11, 16-18	April 14
Exodus 25:14	July 1
Exodus 25:31-32, 37, 40	April 16
Exodus 26:31-33	April 15
Exodus 28	April 17
Exodus 28:1	April 18
Exodus 28:2, 4, 9-21, 36-38	April 19
Exodus 31:13	November 8
Exodus 31:18	April 20
Exodus 32:11-14	April 21
Exodus 32:32	July 19
Exodus 33:13	April 25
Exodus 33:14	April 22
Exodus 33:18-19, 21-23	April 23
Exodus 34	April 27
Exodus 34:5	March 18
Exodus 34:6	April 24
Exodus 34:6-7	April 25; July 6
Exodus 34:34	April 28
Exodus 40:12	April 18
Exodus 40:13-15	April 26
Leviticus 1:4-5	May 1
Leviticus 1:9	May 2
Leviticus 2	May 4
Leviticus 3	May 5
Leviticus 4:5-7	May 6
Leviticus 5:16	May 7
Leviticus 8:4-6	May 8
Leviticus 11	May 9
Leviticus 13:45-46	May 10
Leviticus 14:2-7	May 11
Leviticus 16	April 14
Leviticus 16:15, 21-22	May 12
Leviticus 16:29-30	May 13
Leviticus 16:32-33	May 14
Leviticus 20:8	November 8
Leviticus 22:32	November 8
Leviticus 23:3	May 15
Leviticus 23:10	May 16
Leviticus 23:16-17	May 17
Leviticus 23:24-25	May 18
Leviticus 23:42-43	May 19
Leviticus 25:8-55	May 20
Leviticus 25:10	May 20
Leviticus 26:12-13	February 13
Leviticus 26:13	March 17
Numbers 11:29	June 4
Numbers 12:3	May 21
Numbers 13:16	June 7
Numbers 14:34	May 25
Numbers 20:9-12	May 21
Numbers 21:6, 8-9	May 22
Numbers 23:19-20	May 23
Numbers 24:17-19	May 24
Numbers 35:10-11	June 14
Deuteronomy 3:21-22	June 8
Deuteronomy 4:24	March 16
Deuteronomy 6:4-5	May 25
Deuteronomy 7:7-8	May 26
Deuteronomy 8:2-3	May 27
Deuteronomy 10:16	February 17
Deuteronomy 11:26-28	May 28
Deuteronomy 17:14-15	May 29
Deuteronomy 18:15	May 21, 30
Deuteronomy 18:16-18	May 31
Deuteronomy 21:22-23	June 2

Deuteronomy 27–28	October 30	2 Samuel 7:16	June 23; July 4; October 13
Deuteronomy 28:12	July 15		
Deuteronomy 28:23	July 15	2 Samuel 9:1, 3, 7	July 5
Deuteronomy 28:29, 48, 65-66	May 28	2 Samuel 11:27	July 6
Deuteronomy 29:4, 29	June 3	2 Samuel 12:11	July 7
Deuteronomy 30:6	June 4	2 Samuel 14:25	October 4
Deuteronomy 31:26-27	June 5	2 Samuel 15:23	July 7
Deuteronomy 34:9	June 7	2 Samuel 23:16-17	July 8
Joshua 1:3	June 9	1 Kings 4:29	July 9
Joshua 1:3, 5	June 8	1 Kings 6:11-13	July 10
Joshua 1:3, 6, 11	June 7	1 Kings 8:27	October 23
Joshua 2:9-12	June 10	1 Kings 8:28-30	July 11
Joshua 3:3, 5, 14-16	June 11	1 Kings 12:25-33	December 2
Joshua 5:13-15	June 12	1 Kings 18:24, 38	July 12
Joshua 7	November 24	2 Kings 1–2	July 12
Joshua 8:29	June 2	2 Kings 4	July 13
Joshua 10:20	June 13	2 Kings 4:32-34	July 14
Joshua 10:26-27	June 2	2 Kings 4:38-39, 40-41	July 15
Joshua 20	June 14	2 Kings 4:42-44	July 13
Joshua 21:43-44	June 15	2 Kings 5	July 13
Joshua 21:44	April 22	2 Kings 5:10, 13	July 16
Joshua 24:2	February 4	2 Kings 6:1-7, 17	July 13
Judges 2:12, 16, 18	June 16	2 Kings 9:13	August 7
Judges 6:1, 12, 14-15	June 17	2 Kings 19:30-31	July 17
Judges 13:3, 5	June 18	2 Kings 25:8-9	July 10
Judges 13:22	February 15	2 Kings 25:10-11	July 18
Judges 16:29-30	June 19	1 Chronicles 10:13	July 23
Ruth 3:1-4, 8-9	June 20	1 Chronicles 14:2	February 18
1 Samuel 1:11	June 21	1 Chronicles 21:1, 16-17	July 19
1 Samuel 2:6	June 21	1 Chronicles 22:6-10	July 20
1 Samuel 2:10	June 22	1 Chronicles 29:9, 17-19	July 21
1 Samuel 2:14, 22, 35	June 23	2 Chronicles 7:3	March 18
1 Samuel 6:20	December 25	2 Chronicles 9:1-4	July 9
1 Samuel 7:1	July 1	2 Chronicles 34:14, 19	July 22
1 Samuel 7:10	June 22	2 Chronicles 35:7-9, 11	July 22
1 Samuel 8:5	May 29; June 24	2 Chronicles 36:14	July 23
1 Samuel 8:7	May 29	Ezra 7:10	July 24
1 Samuel 9:2	October 4	Nehemiah 1:3	July 25
1 Samuel 12:22	April 7	Nehemiah 1:8-9	July 27
1 Samuel 15:12, 17-19	June 25	Nehemiah 4:2	July 25
1 Samuel 16:6, 7	October 4	Nehemiah 5:19	July 27
1 Samuel 16:12-13	June 26	Nehemiah 6:3, 9	July 26
1 Samuel 17:4	June 27	Nehemiah 6:14	July 27
1 Samuel 18:1, 3-4	June 28	Nehemiah 13:13-14, 22, 29	July 27
1 Samuel 20:14-15	July 5	Esther 4:14-16	July 28
1 Samuel 22:1-2	June 29	Job 1:1	July 29
2 Samuel 2:4	June 26	Job 1:12	July 30
2 Samuel 5:3	June 26	Job 2:6	July 30
2 Samuel 5:6-7	June 30	Job 9:8-10, 12	July 31
2 Samuel 5:7	December 15	Job 9:32-35	August 1
2 Samuel 6:6-7	July 1	Job 10:1	July 29
2 Samuel 6:17	July 11	Job 13:15	July 29; August 2
2 Samuel 7:11-13	July 3	Job 14:14	August 3
2 Samuel 7:12-13, 16	July 2	Job 19:25-26	August 3
2 Samuel 7:12-13, 19	August 22	Job 19:26	July 29

Job 27:5	July 29
Psalm 2	August 4
Psalm 2:6	August 5; December 15
Psalm 2:6-8	August 6
Psalm 7:11-13	January 30
Psalm 8:1-2	August 7
Psalm 8:5-6	January 6
Psalm 14:2-3	August 8; October 8
Psalm 14:7	December 15
Psalm 16:9-10	August 9
Psalm 16:10-11	August 13
Psalm 18:2	August 10
Psalm 18:30	May 23; August 11
Psalm 19:1	August 12
Psalm 22:1	August 13; September 12
Psalm 22:7	October 1
Psalm 22:7-8	August 14
Psalm 22:14-15	August 15
Psalm 22:22	August 16
Psalm 23	March 11
Psalm 23:1	August 29
Psalm 24:3	December 25
Psalm 27:1	April 16
Psalm 32:1-2	August 17; September 5
Psalm 40:6-7	May 2
Psalm 41:9	August 18
Psalm 51:1-2	July 6
Psalm 51:1-2, 7	August 19
Psalm 51:10	May 9
Psalm 51:16-17	August 20
Psalm 53:6	December 15
Psalm 61:2-3	August 21
Psalm 61:6-8	August 22
Psalm 69:9	August 23
Psalm 69:21	August 15
Psalm 72:10-11	August 24
Psalm 78:1-3	August 25
Psalm 78:21-22, 38, 58-59	August 26
Psalm 78:67-68	March 12
Psalm 80:1	August 29
Psalm 81:10	August 27
Psalm 84:10	August 30
Psalm 89:20	June 26
Psalm 92:9-10	August 10
Psalm 98:1-3	August 28
Psalm 100:3	August 29
Psalm 103:8-10	August 26
Psalm 103:12	May 12
Psalm 103:13	April 24
Psalm 105:18	March 4
Psalm 106:20	August 30
Psalm 110:1	September 1
Psalm 110:1-2, 4	August 31
Psalm 110:4	February 8
Psalm 118:15-16	August 7
Psalm 118:19-20, 22	September 2
Psalm 118:22	September 23
Psalm 119:99-100	September 3
Psalm 130:1-2, 7-8	September 4
Psalm 130:3-4	September 5
Psalm 132:17	August 10
Psalm 133:2	April 26
Proverbs 1:30-31	September 7
Proverbs 2:8, 13, 15	September 6
Proverbs 14:12	September 6
Ecclesiastes 1:2	September 8
Ecclesiastes 1:14	September 9
Ecclesiastes 2:16	September 8
Ecclesiastes 7:1	September 9
Ecclesiastes 12:13	September 9
Song of Songs 2:16	September 10
Song of Songs 4:7, 9-10	September 11
Song of Songs 6:3	September 10
Song of Songs 7:10	September 10
Isaiah 1:6	October 25
Isaiah 6:1-3	September 13
Isaiah 6:3	October 12
Isaiah 6:5, 7	September 14
Isaiah 7:14-16	September 15
Isaiah 8:14	September 23
Isaiah 9:1-2	September 16
Isaiah 9:2	April 16
Isaiah 9:6	February 16; September 17
Isaiah 9:6-7	July 2; September 18
Isaiah 10:27	March 17
Isaiah 11:1	September 19
Isaiah 11:1-9	January 20
Isaiah 11:6	September 12
Isaiah 11:11	October 15
Isaiah 13:9	December 1
Isaiah 13:13	December 30
Isaiah 25:6	September 20
Isaiah 25:7-8	September 21
Isaiah 25:8	October 5
Isaiah 25:9	September 22
Isaiah 26:19	September 21
Isaiah 27:13	May 18
Isaiah 28:16	September 23
Isaiah 34:8	December 30
Isaiah 35:1-10	January 20
Isaiah 35:4	September 24
Isaiah 40:3-4	September 25
Isaiah 40:5	September 26
Isaiah 40:10	September 12; October 3
Isaiah 42:1	September 29
Isaiah 44:3	November 28
Isaiah 45:22-23	April 7
Isaiah 45:23	September 27
Isaiah 48:14	October 3

Isaiah 49:7	October 1
Isaiah 49:14-16	September 28
Isaiah 50:4-5	September 3
Isaiah 50:6	September 12
Isaiah 50:6-7	September 30
Isaiah 51:5	October 3
Isaiah 51:9	October 3
Isaiah 51:17, 21-22	October 2
Isaiah 52:13	September 29
Isaiah 53:2	April 13; October 4
Isaiah 53:3	October 1, 5
Isaiah 53:3, 5	September 12
Isaiah 53:4-5	October 6
Isaiah 53:4-6	October 7
Isaiah 53:5	September 18
Isaiah 53:6	May 12; August 29; October 8
Isaiah 53:7	October 9
Isaiah 53:10	March 14; October 10; December 20
Isaiah 53:10-11	October 11
Isaiah 53:11	September 29
Isaiah 53:12	March 5
Isaiah 54:5	October 12
Isaiah 55:1, 3	October 13
Isaiah 56:3-5	October 15
Isaiah 57:17-19	October 14
Isaiah 58:6-9	October 16
Isaiah 59:17	October 19
Isaiah 60:3	August 24
Isaiah 60:19	September 12
Isaiah 61:1	September 24; October 17
Isaiah 61:1-2	October 18
Isaiah 61:10	October 19
Isaiah 62:1, 11-12	October 20
Isaiah 63:1-3	October 21
Isaiah 64:6	October 19
Isaiah 65:17-19	October 22
Isaiah 65:17-25	January 20
Isaiah 66:1-2	October 23
Jeremiah 2:5	October 24
Jeremiah 8:14-15, 21-22	October 25
Jeremiah 9:24	October 26
Jeremiah 10:15	December 30
Jeremiah 10:15-16	October 24
Jeremiah 13:11	May 26
Jeremiah 17:9	August 8
Jeremiah 23:5-6	October 27
Jeremiah 27:22	December 30
Jeremiah 30:18	October 28
Jeremiah 31:1	October 28
Jeremiah 31:15, 22	October 29
Jeremiah 31:31-33	October 30
Jeremiah 31:33	June 4; October 31
Jeremiah 32	December 17
Jeremiah 32:36-37, 40-41	November 1
Jeremiah 33:14-15	November 2
Jeremiah 50:20	July 17
Lamentations 2:11, 13	November 3
Lamentations 4:11	November 3
Ezekiel 1:26-28	September 13
Ezekiel 10:18	November 12
Ezekiel 11:9-12	November 12
Ezekiel 11:16	November 10
Ezekiel 16	November 4
Ezekiel 16:8	June 20
Ezekiel 18:4	July 28
Ezekiel 24:25	December 30
Ezekiel 33:12-15	November 5
Ezekiel 34:17	November 7
Ezekiel 34:22-24, 28-29	November 6
Ezekiel 36:25-27	May 9
Ezekiel 36:26-27	October 30
Ezekiel 36:27	June 4; November 8
Ezekiel 36:33-36	January 20
Ezekiel 37:5-6, 11-12	November 9
Ezekiel 37:26-27	November 10
Ezekiel 39:17-18, 20	November 11
Ezekiel 47:12	November 10
Ezekiel 48:35	November 12
Daniel 2:34-35, 44-45	November 13
Daniel 3:6, 16-18, 24-25, 29	November 14
Daniel 6:8, 16, 22	November 16
Daniel 6:10	November 15
Daniel 7:9	September 13
Daniel 7:9-10, 22	November 17
Daniel 7:9, 13-14	November 19
Daniel 7:13	August 31
Daniel 7:13-14	November 18
Daniel 7:15-16	November 22
Daniel 9:2	November 22
Daniel 9:24-26	November 20
Daniel 10:5-6	November 21
Daniel 12:8-9	November 22
Hosea 1:2	November 23
Hosea 1:6, 9-10; 2:23	November 25
Hosea 2:15	November 24
Hosea 2:23	November 25
Hosea 3:1-2	November 23
Hosea 6:4, 6	November 26
Hosea 10:1	November 27
Hosea 11:1	March 22; November 28
Hosea 13:14	September 21
Hosea 14:8	November 27
Joel 2:11, 28-29, 31-32	December 1
Joel 2:23	November 29
Joel 2:31-32	November 30
Joel 3:17	December 15
Amos 1:2	November 16

Amos 3:14	December 30
Amos 5:18	December 1
Amos 5:21-24	December 2
Amos 7:7-8	December 3
Obadiah	December 4
Jonah	December 5
Jonah 1:2	December 6
Jonah 1:4, 12	December 7
Jonah 1:14	December 9
Jonah 2:9	December 6, 8
Jonah 3:4	December 9
Micah 5:2-5	December 10
Nahum 1:15	December 11
Habakkuk 2:4	December 12
Zephaniah 1:7-18	December 1
Zephaniah 3:8	December 30
Zephaniah 3:9	February 3
Zephaniah 3:16-17	December 13
Haggai 1:4	December 14
Haggai 2:6-7	December 14
Zechariah 9:9	December 15, 16
Zechariah 11	December 17
Zechariah 12:10	December 18
Zechariah 13:1	December 19
Zechariah 13:7	December 20
Zechariah 13:9	December 20
Zechariah 14:9	December 21
Malachi 2:7-8	December 22
Malachi 2:17	December 23
Malachi 3:1	December 23
Malachi 3:1-3	December 24
Malachi 3:2	December 25
Malachi 3:17	December 30
Malachi 4:2	December 26
Malachi 4:5	December 27
Matthew 1:2-3	March 12
Matthew 1:5	June 10
Matthew 1:18, 22-23	September 15
Matthew 1:21	June 7
Matthew 2:1-2, 9, 11	August 24
Matthew 2:1-6	December 10
Matthew 2:14-15	November 28
Matthew 2:15	March 15
Matthew 2:16	October 29
Matthew 2:23	October 1
Matthew 3:10-12	July 12
Matthew 3:16-17	April 26; November 28
Matthew 3:17	February 22; March 3; September 17
Matthew 4:1	January 14; April 13; November 28
Matthew 4:3-4	May 27
Matthew 4:8-10	January 24
Matthew 4:12-14	September 16
Matthew 4:17	July 4
Matthew 4:24	December 26
Matthew 5:1-2	November 28
Matthew 5:3	October 17
Matthew 5:4	October 14
Matthew 5:7	November 26
Matthew 5:17	June 1; July 24
Matthew 5:19	July 4
Matthew 6:10	July 4
Matthew 7:13-14	July 17; September 6
Matthew 7:22-23	July 16
Matthew 8:14-17	October 6
Matthew 8:20	June 29
Matthew 9:2	April 4
Matthew 9:6	July 11
Matthew 9:10-13	November 26
Matthew 9:18-25	July 13
Matthew 9:20-22	July 1
Matthew 9:36	April 24
Matthew 10:2-4	March 13
Matthew 11:2-6	September 24
Matthew 11:12-13	January 16
Matthew 11:28-29	May 21
Matthew 11:28-30	April 22
Matthew 12	May 15
Matthew 12:39-40	December 5
Matthew 12:41	December 7, 9
Matthew 12:42	July 2, 9; September 9
Matthew 13:16-17	May 30; December 28
Matthew 13:34-35	August 25
Matthew 13:44-46	August 30
Matthew 13:45-46	October 24
Matthew 14:13-21	July 13
Matthew 14:25	July 31
Matthew 16:18	July 25
Matthew 16:24-25	February 4
Matthew 16:24-26	September 9
Matthew 17:1-2	April 27
Matthew 17:2-3	April 23
Matthew 17:5	March 3
Matthew 18:27	September 5
Matthew 19:28	March 13
Matthew 19:28-29	February 4
Matthew 21:2-5	December 16
Matthew 21:9	August 7
Matthew 21:15-16	August 7
Matthew 21:33-46	September 2
Matthew 21:43-44	September 23
Matthew 22:12	October 19
Matthew 22:37-38	May 25
Matthew 23:4-5, 23, 28	December 2
Matthew 23:27-28	November 29
Matthew 23:37	September 28
Matthew 23:37-38	October 20
Matthew 24:9	February 4
Matthew 24:29	January 4

Matthew 24:30 — August 12
Matthew 24:30-31 — May 18
Matthew 24:37-39 — January 28
Matthew 25:21 — July 23
Matthew 25:31-34, 41 — November 7
Matthew 26:2 — March 26
Matthew 26:14-15 — December 17
Matthew 26:26 — January 10; August 20
Matthew 26:29 — September 20
Matthew 26:31 — December 20
Matthew 26:37-38 — October 5
Matthew 26:38 — October 10
Matthew 26:39 — January 14; October 2; December 7, 9

Matthew 26:50 — August 18
Matthew 26:53-54 — August 14; November 16
Matthew 26:62-63 — October 9
Matthew 26:63-64 — November 19
Matthew 26:64 — August 31
Matthew 27:3-10 — December 17
Matthew 27:11 — June 24
Matthew 27:12 — July 29
Matthew 27:26 — October 10
Matthew 27:35 — March 3
Matthew 27:39-43 — August 14
Matthew 27:46 — August 13
Matthew 27:50-51 — April 9, 15
Matthew 28:18-20 — June 8
Mark 1:9 — June 7
Mark 1:11 — August 4
Mark 1:15 — January 22; December 21

Mark 1:22 — July 9
Mark 1:40-41 — May 10
Mark 2:17 — September 4
Mark 3:6 — March 3
Mark 3:11 — August 4
Mark 4:41 — August 4
Mark 5:19 — April 4
Mark 5:34 — April 4
Mark 7:15 — May 9
Mark 7:34 — April 4
Mark 8:31 — December 5
Mark 9:7 — August 4
Mark 10:23-27 — February 20
Mark 10:52 — April 4
Mark 12:34 — July 31
Mark 12:35-37 — September 19
Mark 13:26-27 — February 1
Mark 14:24 — February 18; July 8
Mark 14:61-62 — April 17; August 4
Mark 15:2 — June 24
Mark 15:4-5 — October 9
Mark 15:29-32 — July 26
Mark 15:39 — August 4

Mark 16:19 — September 1
Luke 1:16-17 — December 27
Luke 1:17 — July 12
Luke 1:32-33 — July 2, 4
Luke 1:34 — February 20
Luke 1:35 — January 3; June 26
Luke 1:37 — February 20
Luke 1:53 — August 27
Luke 1:55 — February 5, 18
Luke 1:68, 72-73 — February 5
Luke 1:68-72, 74-75 — August 10
Luke 1:69-70, 72-73 — February 18
Luke 2:7 — May 14
Luke 2:9 — September 26
Luke 2:11 — August 28
Luke 2:13-14 — September 18
Luke 2:29-30 — September 22
Luke 2:32 — February 6
Luke 2:46-47 — July 24; September 3
Luke 2:47, 52 — September 7
Luke 2:49 — March 22; September 17
Luke 2:52 — September 3
Luke 3:21-22 — June 26
Luke 3:23 — March 25
Luke 3:23-38 — January 25
Luke 4:16-21 — October 18
Luke 4:18 — April 26
Luke 4:21 — October 17
Luke 4:33-35 — October 12
Luke 5:6 — August 27
Luke 5:16 — November 15
Luke 6:27 — December 6
Luke 6:36 — April 24
Luke 6:40 — July 24
Luke 7:13-16 — July 14
Luke 8:32 — July 30
Luke 9:22 — July 29
Luke 9:28-31 — April 30
Luke 10 — February 1
Luke 11:11-13 — November 1
Luke 14:16-24 — September 20
Luke 15:4-7 — October 8
Luke 15:6, 9-10, 23-24 — December 13
Luke 15:23-24 — May 5
Luke 16:24 — August 15
Luke 17:21 — November 13
Luke 18:31-33 — September 30
Luke 19:8-9 — May 7
Luke 19:10 — October 8
Luke 19:41-42 — June 16; November 3
Luke 19:45-47 — December 23
Luke 19:47 — October 10
Luke 22:14-15, 19-20 — March 29
Luke 22:19 — March 28
Luke 22:31-32 — July 30

Luke 22:37 — March 5
Luke 23:3 — June 24
Luke 23:9 — October 9
Luke 23:34 — March 10
Luke 23:39 — March 5
Luke 23:39-43 — January 9
Luke 23:40-43 — March 5
Luke 23:46 — July 27; August 13
Luke 24:21 — August 14
Luke 24:27 — August 9; October 10
John 1:1-3 — January 2
John 1:1-5 — January 4
John 1:4 — April 16
John 1:9 — January 4; April 16
John 1:11 — March 3
John 1:12 — March 23
John 1:14 — April 13; May 19; June 23; December 13
John 1:14, 18 — April 23
John 1:16 — March 7
John 1:16-18 — August 27
John 1:17 — June 6
John 1:23 — September 25
John 1:29 — February 24; March 25
John 1:45-46 — October 1
John 1:47 — February 28
John 1:51 — February 28
John 2 — August 27
John 2:14-17 — August 23
John 2:18-22 — July 10
John 2:19, 21 — December 14
John 3:13 — March 18
John 3:14-15 — May 22
John 3:16 — February 22
John 3:16-17 — January 28; September 17
John 3:16-18 — March 23
John 3:17 — June 16; July 15; December 13
John 3:31-34 — May 31
John 4:1-29 — February 26
John 4:10-11, 13-14 — April 3
John 4:32, 34 — May 4
John 4:34 — September 17
John 5:24-25 — January 17
John 5:25, 28-29 — September 21
John 5:28-29 — November 9
John 5:30 — November 15
John 5:39 — August 9; December 31
John 6:13 — August 27
John 6:14 — May 30
John 6:32-35 — April 5
John 6:41 — March 18
John 6:45 — July 24
John 6:51 — March 20

John 6:53 — January 10
John 6:53-56 — March 27
John 6:57-58 — July 15
John 6:69 — October 12
John 7:5 — March 3
John 7:37-38 — October 13
John 7:41-43 — December 10
John 8:4-7 — April 20
John 8:7 — April 10
John 8:12 — March 20, 30; September 16
John 8:24 — March 20
John 8:29 — March 4
John 8:34-36 — March 17
John 8:36 — December 26
John 8:42 — May 25
John 8:56 — February 11, 19
John 8:58 — March 19; December 10
John 10:9 — March 20
John 10:10 — January 15; October 8
John 10:11 — March 11, 20; August 29; October 8
John 10:11, 16 — November 6
John 10:18 — February 23; December 5
John 10:28 — September 10
John 10:38 — July 31
John 11 — April 4
John 11:25 — March 20; September 21
John 12:14-15 — December 16
John 12:23-24 — May 16
John 12:23, 27 — July 28
John 12:24 — August 20
John 12:27 — November 24
John 12:27-31 — June 22
John 12:28 — March 3
John 12:32 — April 13
John 12:37 — March 23
John 12:37-38 — October 3
John 12:41 — September 13; October 12
John 12:47 — March 23
John 12:48 — September 7
John 12:49-50 — May 31
John 13:1 — June 28
John 13:2, 10-11, 18-19 — August 18
John 13:4-5 — May 14; September 29
John 13:7-8 — May 14
John 13:31 — September 26
John 14 — January 3
John 14:1 — November 24
John 14:6 — March 20; April 13; September 6
John 14:17 — March 30
John 15:1 — March 20

John 15:1, 4 — November 27
John 15:3 — May 8
John 15:13-15 — June 28
John 15:16 — May 26
John 16:7-10 — November 8
John 16:13 — March 30
John 16:13-14 — November 1
John 17:6 — July 17
John 17:11 — September 27
John 17:19 — June 26; November 8
John 18:1 — July 7
John 18:33-34 — June 24
John 19:1-3 — January 21
John 19:17 — February 23
John 19:28-29 — August 15
John 19:30 — May 1; November 2
John 19:33 — March 25
John 19:33-34, 36-37 — December 18
John 19:40 — May 14
John 20:26-27 — September 28
John 20:28 — April 13
John 20:31 — December 5
Acts 1:8 — January 3
Acts 2:4 — February 3
Acts 2:5, 37-38, 41 — May 17
Acts 2:16 — December 1
Acts 2:17-21, 36 — November 30
Acts 2:23 — August 1
Acts 2:23-24 — October 10
Acts 2:27 — March 28
Acts 2:29-31 — August 9
Acts 2:32-33, 36 — August 6
Acts 3:22, 24 — May 30
Acts 3:25-26 — February 5
Acts 4:12 — March 7; November 30
Acts 4:24-28 — August 5
Acts 7 — October 23
Acts 7:48-50 — October 23
Acts 8:28, 32-33 — October 15
Acts 10:36, 42-43 — December 11
Acts 13:33 — August 4
Acts 15:11 — January 27
Acts 26:20 — November 5
Romans 1:18, 20 — August 12
Romans 2:29 — February 17
Romans 3:10 — November 17
Romans 3:20 — June 6
Romans 3:22 — October 27
Romans 3:23 — December 3
Romans 3:23-25 — April 14
Romans 3:24-26 — October 26; December 12
Romans 3:25-26 — February 21; May 3
Romans 4:7-8 — September 5
Romans 5:1-2 — July 20

Romans 5:6, 9 — August 8
Romans 5:10 — September 18; December 6
Romans 5:14 — January 8
Romans 5:14, 17 — January 25
Romans 5:17 — January 8, 11; March 8
Romans 5:20 — June 5
Romans 8:3 — June 6; October 31
Romans 8:3-4 — June 5
Romans 8:11 — November 9
Romans 8:20 — September 8
Romans 8:20-21 — January 31
Romans 8:20-22 — January 20
Romans 8:28 — March 14
Romans 8:29 — January 5; March 22
Romans 8:31, 33-34 — December 25
Romans 8:32 — February 18; November 1
Romans 8:34 — April 21
Romans 8:37 — June 27
Romans 8:38-39 — August 2
Romans 9:25 — November 25
Romans 9:33 — September 23
Romans 10:4 — October 31
Romans 11:5-6 — July 17
Romans 11:11 — March 8
Romans 11:26 — March 8
Romans 12:1 — May 2
Romans 15:4 — December 29
Romans 15:8 — May 23
Romans 16:20 — January 16
1 Corinthians 1:8 — December 30
1 Corinthians 1:24-25 — February 16
1 Corinthians 1:30 — July 9; September 7
1 Corinthians 2:2, 7 — March 14
1 Corinthians 3:11-14 — September 8
1 Corinthians 5:7 — March 25, 26
1 Corinthians 6:11 — May 9
1 Corinthians 10:1, 4 — April 6
1 Corinthians 10:11-12 — December 29
1 Corinthians 10:13 — January 14
1 Corinthians 15:3 — March 15
1 Corinthians 15:20, 23 — May 16
1 Corinthians 15:23, 42-44 — August 20
1 Corinthians 15:42, 57 — August 3
1 Corinthians 15:45 — January 8
1 Corinthians 15:54-57 — September 21
1 Corinthians 15:57 — April 1; June 27
1 Corinthians 15:58 — September 8
2 Corinthians 1:20 — February 10; August 11
2 Corinthians 1:21-22 — April 26
2 Corinthians 3:13 — April 27
2 Corinthians 3:14, 16-17 — April 28
2 Corinthians 3:18 — April 28; September 26
2 Corinthians 4:4 — April 28

2 Corinthians 4:6 — March 2; April 27
2 Corinthians 5:21 — January 7; July 29
2 Corinthians 8:9 — October 17
2 Corinthians 12:9 — June 17
2 Corinthians 13:4 — February 16
Galatians 1:4 — August 14
Galatians 3:8, 14 — February 6
Galatians 3:10-13 — March 21
Galatians 3:13 — January 21; May 28; June 2
Galatians 3:13-14 — February 12
Galatians 3:16 — February 7
Galatians 3:19 — June 5
Galatians 3:24 — October 31
Galatians 3:26 — March 22
Galatians 3:28-29 — November 25
Galatians 4:4 — January 22; February 17
Galatians 4:5 — February 13
Galatians 5:22 — July 23
Galatians 5:22-23 — November 27
Ephesians 1:3 — February 14; March 2; May 23
Ephesians 1:4-5 — January 1; May 26
Ephesians 1:5 — November 17
Ephesians 1:9-13 — June 3
Ephesians 1:11 — January 19
Ephesians 1:22-23 — August 27
Ephesians 1:23 — January 12
Ephesians 2:4-5 — November 4
Ephesians 2:6 — January 19; July 14
Ephesians 2:7 — January 19; July 5
Ephesians 2:8-10 — January 27; December 8
Ephesians 2:10 — January 5
Ephesians 2:13-14 — May 5
Ephesians 2:19-20 — July 3
Ephesians 4:10 — August 27
Ephesians 5:2 — May 2
Ephesians 5:25-27 — September 11
Ephesians 5:30 — January 19
Ephesians 5:31-32 — January 12
Ephesians 6:24 — September 10
Philippians 1:6 — November 6; December 30
Philippians 1:21 — September 8
Philippians 2:5-7 — June 25
Philippians 2:6-7 — September 29
Philippians 2:7 — March 4; September 3
Philippians 2:7-8 — May 21; October 4
Philippians 2:7-11 — September 27
Philippians 2:8 — March 16, 18; December 9
Philippians 2:9 — March 4
Philippians 2:9-11 — April 7
Philippians 2:16 — December 30
Philippians 3:3 — February 17

Philippians 3:5, 7-9 — April 11
Philippians 3:8-9 — August 30; October 24
Philippians 3:9 — January 19; July 29
Philippians 3:12-14 — June 9
Philippians 4:13 — February 16
Philippians 4:19 — February 9
Colossians 1:15 — January 5; February 27
Colossians 1:15-16 — January 2
Colossians 1:22 — March 16
Colossians 1:27 — February 9; June 3
Colossians 2:2 — June 3
Colossians 2:3 — September 7
Colossians 2:9 — October 23
Colossians 2:14 — September 5
Colossians 2:15 — January 15
Colossians 3:3 — January 29
Colossians 3:4 — April 23; December 21
1 Thessalonians 1:10 — January 29; August 14, 28
1 Thessalonians 4:16 — March 18; May 18; August 3
1 Thessalonians 5:2 — December 30
1 Thessalonians 5:9 — August 26, 28
1 Thessalonians 5:24 — July 23
2 Thessalonians 1:7-8 — June 16
2 Thessalonians 1:7-9 — May 1
2 Thessalonians 1:7-10 — December 30
1 Timothy 1:15 — December 8
1 Timothy 2:5 — August 1
2 Timothy 1:9 — January 1
2 Timothy 2:13 — July 23
2 Timothy 4:7 — June 9
Titus 3:3-7 — January 26
Titus 3:4-6 — July 6
Hebrews 1:1 — February 28
Hebrews 1:1-2 — March 19
Hebrews 1:2 — April 8
Hebrews 1:3 — January 5; September 26
Hebrews 1:8-9 — June 26
Hebrews 2:8-9 — January 6
Hebrews 2:10 — June 29
Hebrews 2:10-12 — August 16
Hebrews 2:11 — January 19
Hebrews 2:14 — January 15
Hebrews 3:3 — March 15
Hebrews 3:6 — June 23
Hebrews 4:1 — April 22
Hebrews 4:8-9 — June 15
Hebrews 4:10 — January 7
Hebrews 4:14-16 — April 17
Hebrews 4:15 — December 22
Hebrews 5:1 — April 17
Hebrews 5:7-8 — October 5
Hebrews 5:8 — February 28
Hebrews 5:8-9 — March 6

Hebrews 5:9	April 29
Hebrews 5:10	February 8
Hebrews 6:17	February 18
Hebrews 6:18	January 29; June 14
Hebrews 6:18-20	February 25
Hebrews 7:3	February 8
Hebrews 7:16	March 16
Hebrews 7:19	August 21
Hebrews 7:22	March 9
Hebrews 7:23-24	December 22
Hebrews 7:23-25	April 21
Hebrews 7:25	July 11
Hebrews 7:26	December 22
Hebrews 7:26, 28	May 13
Hebrews 9:12	December 22
Hebrews 9:13-14	May 6; July 22
Hebrews 9:22	January 13
Hebrews 9:24	June 11; December 22
Hebrews 10:1	June 14
Hebrews 10:1-4, 22	December 19
Hebrews 10:4	May 11
Hebrews 10:10	May 3
Hebrews 10:12	April 13
Hebrews 10:12-13	September 1
Hebrews 10:17	June 14
Hebrews 10:19-20	April 15
Hebrews 10:22	April 18; August 19
Hebrews 10:27	May 1
Hebrews 11:4	February 10
Hebrews 11:6	February 10
Hebrews 11:7	January 28; February 10
Hebrews 11:8	February 4
Hebrews 11:9-10, 13, 16	February 14
Hebrews 11:11-12	January 3
Hebrews 11:13	January 22; February 10
Hebrews 11:16	January 20; July 18
Hebrews 11:19	February 19
Hebrews 11:31	June 10
Hebrews 12:2	January 13; July 11; October 11
Hebrews 12:15	December 29
Hebrews 12:18-19, 22, 24	April 8
Hebrews 12:18, 22, 24	December 15
Hebrews 12:23	February 27
Hebrews 12:24	January 23
Hebrews 12:25	April 8
Hebrews 12:26	April 9
Hebrews 13:5	August 13
Hebrews 13:20	August 29
Hebrews 13:20-21	March 11
1 Peter 1:7	December 24
1 Peter 1:10	September 22; December 28
1 Peter 1:10-11	June 1
1 Peter 1:11	January 22; September 12; November 22
1 Peter 1:12	November 22
1 Peter 1:18-19	August 17; November 23
1 Peter 1:19	March 25, 26
1 Peter 1:20	January 1
1 Peter 2:5	July 3; November 13
1 Peter 2:9-10	November 25
1 Peter 2:23	October 9
1 Peter 2:24	October 25
1 Peter 2:25	August 29
1 Peter 3:18	March 22; December 7
1 Peter 4:17	December 23
1 Peter 5:4	March 11; August 29
2 Peter 1:4	January 19
2 Peter 1:20-21	September 12
2 Peter 3:9-10	June 13
1 John 1:1	July 1, 31
1 John 1:7	August 19
1 John 3:2	January 5
1 John 3:8	January 15
1 John 4:9	February 22
1 John 4:15-16, 18-19	September 10
Jude 1:5	April 30
Jude 1:24-25	March 15
Revelation 1:7	December 18
Revelation 1:12-13	November 18
Revelation 1:13-16	November 21
Revelation 1:16	April 27
Revelation 1:17-18	June 21
Revelation 1:18	August 2
Revelation 2:27	March 21
Revelation 3:17-18	January 13; October 19
Revelation 3:21	September 13
Revelation 4:2	July 2
Revelation 4:11	January 21
Revelation 5:5	March 12; July 2
Revelation 5:6	March 12
Revelation 5:6; 7:15-17	March 11
Revelation 5:9	March 8, 25
Revelation 5:12	October 24
Revelation 6:12, 15-17	April 9
Revelation 7:9	February 6
Revelation 7:9-10	February 3
Revelation 7:16-17	August 29
Revelation 13:8	February 24
Revelation 15:1	August 12
Revelation 16:5-6	December 4
Revelation 18:2	January 24
Revelation 18:21	February 2
Revelation 19:3	January 24
Revelation 19:7, 17-18	November 11
Revelation 19:11	July 23; December 16
Revelation 19:13, 15	October 21
Revelation 19:14-15	June 12

Scripture Index

Revelation 19:16   June 24
Revelation 20:10   January 16
Revelation 20:11-12   November 17
Revelation 21   March 13
Revelation 21:1   January 20
Revelation 21:1, 5   October 22
Revelation 21:2   January 24; March 1;
                        September 11; October 4
Revelation 21:2-3   October 20
Revelation 21:2-3, 22   November 12
Revelation 21:3   May 19; October 28
Revelation 21:4   October 5
Revelation 21:5   January 31
Revelation 21:6   November 2

Revelation 21:10, 27   June 30
Revelation 21:18-19, 27 July 18
Revelation 21:22   November 10;
                        December 14
Revelation 21:23   January 4; April 16;
                        September 26
Revelation 21:24   August 24
Revelation 22:1-2   November 10
Revelation 22:2   January 18
Revelation 22:3   January 21
Revelation 22:16   May 24; September 19
Revelation 22:17   October 13

Books by Nancy Guthrie

Holding On to Hope
978-1-4143-1296-5

Hearing Jesus Speak
into Your Sorrow
978-1-4143-2548-4

Hoping for Something Better
978-1-4143-1307-8

When Your Family's
Lost a Loved One
978-1-58997-480-7

The One Year Book of Hope
978-1-4143-0133-4 (softcover)
978-1-4143-3671-8 (leatherlike)

One Year of Dinner Table
Devotions and Discussion
Starters
978-1-4143-1895-0

Let Every Heart Prepare
Him Room
978-1-4143-3909-2

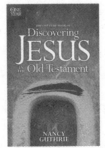

The One Year Book of
Discovering Jesus in the
Old Testament
978-1-4143-3590-2

Abundant Life in Jesus
978-1-4964-0948-5

For more information on these titles, visit www.tyndale.com or www.nancyguthrie.com.
For information about David and Nancy Guthrie's Respite Retreats for couples who have
faced the loss of a child, go to www.nancyguthrie.com/respite-retreat.   CP0066